Company Law Textbook

7th edition

Edited by Chris Shepherd
LLB, MA, Cert Ed, Barrister
Senior Lecturer in Law at South Bank University

HLT Publications

HLT PUBLICATIONS
200 Greyhound Road, London W14 9RY

First published 1989
7th edition 1995

© The HLT Group Ltd 1995

ISBN 0 7510 0540 1

British Library Cataloguing-in-Publication.
A CIP Catalogue record for this book is
available from the British Library.

Acknowledgement

The publishers and author would like to
thank the Incorporated Council of Law
Reporting for England and Wales for kind
permission to reproduce extracts from the
Weekly Law Reports.

Extracts from British Company Cases
(BCC) are reproduced with kind
permission of CCH Editions Limited.

Extracts from Butterworths Company Law
Cases (BCLC) are reproduced with kind
permission of Butterworths.

Printed and bound in Great Britain

Contents

Preface

HLT Textbooks are written specifically for students. Whatever their course, they will find our books clear and concise, providing comprehensive and up-to-date coverage. Written by specialists in their field, our textbooks are reviewed and updated on an annual basis.

In addition to the usual updating that we undertake each year for this book, we have added a new chapter called 'Recent Cases'. This chapter includes the most significant cases that have occurred in the last year. In order to assist the student extracts from the judgments and commentary, where appropriate, have been included. In many instances these cases highlight new interpretations of particular facets of existing law.

Knowledge of recent cases is extemely important for those studying their examinations. It demonstrates not only an active interest in the law as it develops, but also the dynamic nature of the law which is constantly adapting to changing social and economic trends.

The courts have once again been very busy this year in the area of company law. The House of Lords, in *Seaboard Offshore Ltd* v *Secretary of State for Transport* [1994] 1 WLR 541, has ruled on the extent to which a company can be vicariously liable for crimes committed by all or any of its employees. It has also considered the use of transcripts of oral examinations of directors conducted by liquidators under s236 of the Insolvency Act 1986 in later criminal proceedings. See *Re Arrows Ltd (No 4)* [1994] BCC 641. The Court of Appeal's important judgement in *Secretary of State for Trade and Industry* v *Gray and Another* (1994) The Times 24 November, a directors disqualification case, is also considered.

There have also been potentially far-reaching first instance decisions such as that in *Re Sherborne Associates Ltd* [1995] BCC 40, dealing with the wrongful trading provisions in s214 Insolvency Act 1986, and *Re Macro (Ipswich) Ltd & Anor* [1994] BCC 781, on whether mismanagement can amount unfairly prejudicial conduct.

The opportunity has been taken to include appropriate references to the Cadbury Code of Best Practice in Chapter 9 on Directors. The section in Chapter 6 on Capital, dealing with the prohibition against a company giving financial assistance in connection with the purchase or acquisition of its own shares, has also been expanded. These additions have been made to reflect the increasing academic and practical interest being shown towards corporate governance and the financial assistance rules. This growing interest is often exhibited by the appearance of examination questions on these topics.

New developments and cases reported up to 1 April 1995 have been included.

Table of Cases

Table of Statutes

Abbreviations

Word/phrase	Meaning
articles	articles of association
CA	Companies Act [date]
CDDA	Company Directors Disqualification Act 1986
Cork Report	Insolvency Law and Practice – Report of the Review Committee 1982 (Cmnd 8558)
DTI	Department of Trade and Industry (including statutory references to the Secretary of State)
FSA	Financial Services Act 1986
IA	Insolvency Act 1986
Jenkins Report	Report of the Company Law Committee 1962 (Cmnd 1749)
memorandum	the memorandum of association
registrar	the Registrar of Companies
registry	Companies Registration Office ('the Companies Registry')
Table A	Table A of the Companies (Table A to F) Regulations SI 1985/805

Citations of sections of the Companies Act 1985 are given without a prefix, eg 's125'. Sections of other Acts are cited with the abbreviation of the Act as a prefix, eg 'IA s212'.

References to 'Table A' denote the 1985 model articles. Earlier versions are distinguished by a prefix, eg '1948 Table A'.

Commencement dates of the Companies Act 1989

PART I COMPANY ACCOUNTS

Sections 1 (part), 2–6,	)	1 April 1990, subject
7 (part), 8–10, 11 (part), 13–22,	)	to certain transitional
23 (Schedule 10 – excluding	)	provisions.
para 19)	)	
Section 23 (in respect of		1 August 1990, subject
Schedule 10 para 19)		to certain transitional provisions

Paving provision in ss1 and 15 to enable regulations to be made	1 March 1990
Regulations with respect to summary financial statements (s15)	1 April 1990
Signing of defective accounts (s7 new s233(5) of 1985 Act)	7 January 1991, subject to transitional arrangements
New civil procedure for defective accounts (s12)	7 January 1991, subject to transitional arrangements
Civil penalties for late filing of accounts (s11 new s242A of 1985 Act)	1 July 1992

PART II ELIGIBILITY FOR APPOINTMENT AS AUDITOR

Sections (all or part in force)) 24, 30–33, 37–40,) 41(1), (3)–(6), 42–45,) 47(1), 48(1) and (2), 49–54) Schedules 11, 12, 14)	1 March 1990
Register of auditors regulations) with commencement) of s35 and s36)	26 June 1991
Recognition of supervisory) bodies and fully commence) Part II)	1 October 1991

PART III INVESTIGATION AND POWERS TO OBTAIN INFORMATION

Section 75(2), (3) and (7)	25 January 1990
All other aspects (except in relation to Parts of Act not yet in force)	21 February 1990

PART IV REGISTRATION OF COMPANY CHARGES

All aspects	To be decided

A consultation exercise on the registration of charges is due to take place in the summer of 1994.

PART V OTHER AMENDMENTS OF COMPANY LAW

Sections:		
	108–112 Ultra vires	4 February 1991
	113–117 Elective regime	1 April 1990
	118–124 Auditors	1 April 1990

125 and 127(1), (2), (4) Company records	7 January 1991
126 and 127(3) Company records	1 July 1991
128 Partnership company (Table G)	To be decided
129 Membership of holding company	1 November 1990
130 Company seals	
130(1), (2), (4) and (7)	31 July 1990
130(5)	31 July 1990
130(6)	31 July 1990
131 Members' rights to damages	1 April 1990
132 Financial assistance employees' share schemes	1 April 1990
133 Issue of redeemable shares	Not to be commenced
134 Disclosure of interests in shares	134(1), (2), (3), (5) and (6) 31 May 1990 134(4) 1 November 1991
(Regulations under s134(5) and (6) 18 September 1993)	
135 Restrictions on shares	7 January 1991
136 Company's registered office	1 April 1990
137 Insurance for directors etc	1 April 1990
138 Directors' loans	31 July 1990
139 Annual returns	1 October 1990
141 Dissolution of company void	In force on Royal Assent
142 Deemed notice	To be decided (with Part IV)
143 Rights of inspection	1 November 1991
144 Definition of subsidiary	1 November 1990
145 Minor amendments	
Paras 1, 8, 9, 12 19 and 21 of Schedule 19	1 March 1990
Paras 2–7, and 14	1 October 1990

Para 10	7 January 1991
Para 11	4 February 1991
Para 13	To be decided
Paras 15–18	1 April 1990
Para 20	1 July 1992

PART VI MERGERS AND RELATED MATTERS

Sections: 146 Prior notice   1 April 1990
147–150:
    – Undertakings as   )
    alternative to   )   In force
    merger reference   )   on Royal Assent
)
    – Enforcement of   )
    undertakings   )
)   In force on
    – Temporary   )   Royal Assent
    restrictions on   )
    share dealings   )
)
    – Obtaining   )
    control by   )
    stages   )

151 False or misleading information	1 April 1990
152 Fees	1 March 1990
153 Other amendments	1 April 1990

PART VII FINANCIAL MARKETS AND INSOLVENCY

Order making powers	25 March 1991
All remaining sections (except ss169(4), 170–172, 176, 178, 181, still to be decided)	25 April 1991

PART VIII AMENDMENTS OF THE FINANCIAL SERVICES ACT 1986

Sections:
192 (insofar as it inserts s47A into the FS Act)	15 March 1990
Remainder of s192	To be decided
193 (insofar as it is necessary to make regulations under s62A and Sch 11 to the FS Act)	15 March 1990
Remainder of s193	1 April 1991 see also [K]
194–200	15 March 1990

201   25 April 1991
202   In force on
                                             Royal Assent
                                             (16 Nov 1989)

PART IX TRANSFER OF SECURITIES

Section 207   1 November 1990
(Commencement of order
making power CREST)   To be decided

PART X MISCELLANEOUS

Sections: 209 Insider dealing   21 February 1990
             210 Premium income   1 April 1990
             211 Building societies   211(1) 1 October 1991,
                                             211(2), (3) 31 July 1990
             212 Repeals   With relevant
                                             section of 1989 Act

             215 Commencement and
                 transitional provisions   As appropriate
             216 Short title   25 January 1990

1

Introduction and Corporate Personality

1.1 The scope of the law

1.2 Corporate personality

1.3 Lifting the veil of incorporation by the courts

1.4 Statutory lifting of the veil of incorporation

1.5 Types of company

1.1 The scope of the law

There are many different ways in which persons may associate for purposes of business. The more important ones are referred to below. This textbook deals with one, important type, the registered company with liability limited by shares. Its immediate history has been comparatively short, not much more than a century or so, but those have been busy years, and the story is by no means finished.

Much of modern company law is to be found in judicial decisions, despite the enormous volume of statutory rules. The leading cases should be read and thoroughly understood, and the arguments for and against difficult points should be rehearsed carefully. Company law is very much a case law subject.

The cases are complemented by a number of statutes, which contain a mass of detailed rules. The student should read through the sections to which he is referred. This does not mean that he needs to know all the details by rote – very often a short statement encompasses the salient features. But it is as important to grasp the working of the Acts as it is to grasp the reasoning of the judges.

In 1985 statute law on companies was consolidated in the Companies Act 1985, which is the principal statute. It was supplemented by the Business Names Act 1985 and by the Company Securities (Insider Dealing) Act 1985, which deal with special topics relating to companies. The latter Act has since been repealed by Part V of the Criminal Justice Act 1993.

In 1985 there was also a major reform of the law on corporate as well as individual insolvency. The Insolvency Act 1986 which consolidates the law in this

1

field includes the whole statutory code on company receivership and liquidation, which had previously been found in the latter part of the Companies Act 1985. In the course of these consolidation measures of 1986 the statute law on disqualification of directors and other company officers was separately re-enacted in the Company Directors Disqualification Act 1986.

There are also a considerable number of regulations made by statutory instrument. Among these are the Companies (Tables A to F) Regulations 1985, which include the latest statutory model set of articles (Table A) for companies limited by shares, and the Insolvency Rules 1986 which contain the procedural details of company liquidation.

The Financial Services Act 1986 repeals Part III of the Companies Act 1985 on company prospectuses and replaces it with a new system applicable to listed and unlisted securities. In particular the information to be given by way of 'listing particulars' is prescribed by Stock Exchange regulations, published in what is colloquially known as 'The Yellow Book'.

The Companies Act 1989 received Royal Assent on 16 November 1989 but its provisions are being brought into effect by stages. Commencement dates, specified and estimated, and the dates of regulations, actual and estimated, have been summarised by the Department of Trade and Industry (as at 3 May 1994).

Much of the 1989 Act is in the form of revised sections incorporated into CA 1985. These are cited below as sections of the 1985 Act. For example, s108 of the Companies Act 1989 substitutes a new s35 into the Companies Act 1985 on ultra vires.

This textbook expresses the law as at 1 April 1995 including all provisions of CA 1989.

Extra-legal rules and sanctions may be as important in practice as legal rules, emanating for example from the Stock Exchange and the Council on the Securities Industry: see, eg, *Re Chez Nico (Restaurants) Ltd* [1991] BCC 736. However, this textbook is in general restricted to those rules that are legally binding.

1.2 Corporate personality

Separate legal personality

In this textbook the word 'company' is used to mean a company formed by registration under the Companies Act 1985 or an earlier Companies Act.

A company is one type of 'corporate body' or 'corporation', which has the essential characteristic, in contrast to partnerships and other unincorporated associations such as clubs or societies, that it is a legal person or entity distinct from its members. With minor exceptions company law does not apply to any type of corporate body other than companies.

It is worth noting, however, that corporate bodies may also be formed by royal charter or by special Act of Parliament. In this category are found many types of corporate body, such as an eminent learned society or a local authority, which are not 'companies' in any ordinary sense of the word. However, commercial enterprises may also be formed in this way though it is not common. For example, in the nineteenth century canal and later railway companies were formed by special Act of Parliament, partly because they could thereby be given statutory power to acquire land etc, which would not be given to companies formed under the Companies Acts.

Since a company is a separate legal entity it has rights and obligations of its own. Company property belongs to the company. It may employ people to work in its business, enter into contracts and incur debts. The members of a company own and control it but they are not parties to its legal transactions nor are they agents of the company.

Salomon's *case*

The distinction between a company and its members is called the 'veil of incorporation'. The expression is not really appropriate since the identity of the members of a company is not veiled from public view but is ascertainable from a register of members which is open to public inspection. However, it is well understood in its common usage.

The principle of the veil of incorporation was tested and finally established by the decision of the House of Lords in *Salomon* v *Salomon & Co* [1897] AC 22. In the study of company law it is essential to understand the essential facts and issues of this case, which is the most fundamental decision of the courts in this field. Many subsidiary rules are derived from it.

S had for many years carried on a successful business as a leather merchant and wholesale boot manufacturer. He decided to reorganise his business by transferring it to a new company which he formed for the purpose. At that time company law required every company to have a minimum of seven members. So S took one share and arranged for his wife, four sons and a daughter to have one share as his nominees. In this way he became the sole beneficial owner of the company.

S sold his business to the company at a rather optimistic price but this did not matter since he was the sole owner of the company. The price was satisfied partly by the allotment to S of 20,000 £1 shares issued as fully paid and partly by the issue to him of a £10,000 debenture, which was secured by a charge on the company's property. The company later lost valuable supply contracts and ran into financial difficulties. To raise money S sold his debenture to an outsider (B) but the latter could only have such rights as the debenture, when issued, had conferred on S.

When the company failed its remaining assets were worth less than £10,000 and it also had debts to unsecured trade creditors. The question which arose was whether the holder of the debenture or the other creditors had better claim to the assets. In the High Court and then in the Court of Appeal the decision went against the debentureholder. It was said that some principle of agency or of trust law should apply to identify S with the company, so that he could not, under the debenture, have the rights of a creditor against it as his debtor. It was also argued that any company must have at least seven independent members with the result that the relatives of S could not be regarded as proper members, so that the company had not been validly incorporated.

The House of Lords, in overruling the conclusions of the lower courts on these various points said (per Lord MacNaughten) that 'the company is at law a different person altogether from the subscribers to the memorandum … the company is not in law the agent of the subscribers or trustee for them.'

The effect of the veil of incorporation

The principle established in *Salomon*'s case has been applied in a variety of other situations.

Ownership of property. In *Macaura* v *Northern Assurance Co Ltd* [1925] AC 619 M had transferred to a company, of which he was sole owner, valuable timber then lying on M's land. He insured the timber in his own name. The timber was later destroyed by fire in rather suspect circumstances. M claimed under the insurance policy but it was held to be invalid since M lacked any 'insurable interest' in the timber. He no longer owned it and his undoubted interest in the company as shareholder did not suffice. This case was decided on its particular facts, though the principle is clear enough. It has been held in another case (*Wilson* v *Jones* (1867) LR 2 Ex 139) that shareholders have a sufficient interest in the success or failure of a business venture of the company to validate an insurance policy, against loss, taken out in their names.

Employment. In *Lee* v *Lee's Air Farming* [1961] AC 12, L had been the sole owner of a company whose business was aerial crop spraying in New Zealand. L managed the business and acted as chief pilot. He was killed in an air crash while working for the company. If the company was liable to L's widow, as his executor, for compensation it could recover the payment from the statutory workman's compensation fund. The New Zealand courts rejected the widow's claim but the Privy Council reversed their decision, holding that L could be and was an employee of the company with normal rights against it.

Landlord and tenant. There have been a number of cases in which the issue has been whether a member of a company, who is its sole owner, can claim the rights of a landlord or of a tenant of property which is vested in the company in that capacity. If the member is an individual, such claims are usually unsuccessful. That was the result, for example, in *Tunstall* v *Steigmann* [1962] 2 QB 593, where S as a member of S Ltd asserted a landlord's right, in priority over the tenant, to resume possession of the premises on the expiry of the lease, so that S might use the premises for her own business. The claim failed since S had transferred the premises to S Ltd and no longer qualified as landlord under the Landlord and Tenant Act 1954.

However, paragraph 1.3 *Agency* cites cases where a group of companies is treated as a single entity even though one owns business premises as landlord and the other occupies them as tenant. This is not the issue which arose in *Steigmann*'s case.

Fiduciary duties. The fiduciary duty which a director owes to the company is not, in ordinary circumstances, owed to its members. The members, even where they exercise practical control over the directors whom they have appointed to office, owe no duty to the company: *Multinational Gas and Petrochemical Co* v *Multinational Gas and Petrochemical Services Ltd* [1983] Ch 258.

The recognised exceptions to the principle of the veil of incorporation, ie cases where the company and its members or directors are identified as if they were the same person, are considered in paragraph 1.3, since they cover a wide field.

Essential features of a company

This is a preliminary statement of a number of aspects of company structure which are described in greater detail elsewhere in the manual in the appropriate context.

Limited liability

The members of a company are never directly liable for its debts, since those are debts owed by the company. But members will be liable to contribute to the company's assets whatever is required to enable it to pay its debts unless their liability is expressly restricted by a statement in the memorandum that 'the liability of members is limited'. What this means is that the members liability for the company's debts is limited to the amount which is unpaid on their shares. If the shares are fully paid up then there will be no further liability. The company's liability for its debts is, of course, unlimited. With the exception of one type of private company the fact of members' limited liability is also disclosed by the company's name, which ends with the word 'limited' (for a private company) or 'public limited company' or the appropriate abbreviation. There may of course be companies with unlimited liability of members, which do not have the word 'limited' etc in their names.

There are special circumstances in which members, or directors, may become liable to contribute towards the debts of a limited company. This is generally a sanction against irregularity or default by the persons concerned and is explained later in the appropriate places.

Unless the memorandum has additional particulars (for a company limited by guarantee) the liability of members of a limited company is to pay to the company the amount due on their shares, if anything is still outstanding.

It is of course open to persons who deal with a limited company to demand from its members or directors their personal guarantees of the company's liabilities to them. Banks sometimes require such guarantees as a condition of making advances to a limited company which has only small resources. But that kind of guarantee is a contract between creditor and guarantor and does not arise under rules of company law.

Management

As an abstract person a company cannot manage itself. It is therefore required to have at least one director, if it is a private company, and at least two if it is a public company: s282. The articles may fix a higher minimum and it is unusual for a private company to have only one director.

The Act does not define the powers or functions of the directors. This is found in the articles (eg Table A art 70) since different companies have different requirements. It is normal practice to give very wide general powers to the directors though the Act (and possibly the articles) reserves to a general meeting some important decisions. For example, Table A art 32 requires the general meeting to pass an ordinary resolution before the share capital of a company can be increased. The directors need not manage the company personally but may merely supervise the company's full-time staff.

A member of a company as such has no inherent right to participate in the management and he is not an agent of the company in dealings with third parties. This is one of the most important practical differences between a company and a partnership.

A member may of course be appointed a director and/or become an employee of the company by agreement. It is common, in the case of private companies, for the directors and members to be the same persons. The articles may provide that a member is also to be a director.

Shareholdings

Unless the company has no share capital (in the case of a company limited by guarantee) membership is combined with being the registered holder of one or more shares. In that capacity a member is also a 'shareholder'.

Shares are units of ownership of the company (and of liability to pay for shares). Many statutory rights given to shareholders are related to the size of their shareholdings (see paragraph 11.2 *Specific statutory rights*).

The articles define the shareholders' entitlement (if any) by virtue of their shares to receive dividends out of profits, return of capital and to vote at general meetings.

Shares are personal property and, other than shares in uncertificated form, are transferable by the proper procedure but subject to any restrictions on transfer contained in the articles: s182.

A change of membership does not affect the continuing existence of the company which in that respect is said to have 'perpetual succession'. Even if all the members of the company were to die the company would, as a separate legal entity, continue to exist.

Written constitution

The constitution of a company consists of two documents which must be in writing. They are the memorandum and the articles of association. The memorandum is the company's external constitution, in that it gives outsiders essential information about the company such as the name clause of the company, which is important for the purposes of litigation, and the objects for which the company is formed. The articles of association are the internal constitution of the company, dealing with such matters as the calling of meetings and the appointment of directors. These documents are discussed at length later on in the book.

Capital

The memorandum of a company defines its 'authorised capital' (unless it has no share capital). This fixes the maximum amount of share capital which it may issue. If it needs more it must increase the limit by the correct procedure (see paragraph 6.3 *Increase of share capital*).

The total capital is divided into shares of specified nominal (or 'par') value: s2. When shares are issued the company fixes an issue price, which may be the same ('issue at par') or more ('issue at a premium') than the nominal value, but may not be less ('issue at a discount'). Unless the whole issue price is paid at the time of issue, liability to pay the amount outstanding passes with ownership of the shares.

The capital subscribed by members for their shares is retained by the company and may not be distributed as dividend nor returned to members (unless the company is unlimited) except under strict rules of procedure. This principle is applied to protect the interests of creditors of limited companies who have a first call on its assets for payment of their debts. It also underlies the rules on profits distributable as dividends (see paragraph 6.5).

Litigation

As a general principle (the rule in *Foss* v *Harbottle*) no one other than the company may sue or be sued to enforce its rights or obligations. In those legal proceedings where knowledge is an issue, as it may often be in a criminal case, the knowledge of living persons who are officers, employees or agents of the company may be attributed to it (see paragraphs 2.4 and 2.5).

In the absence of exceptional circumstances, the Rules of the Supreme Court [see: RSC O.5 r.6(2) & O.12 r.1(2)] make it clear that a company cannot litigate except through legal advisors. In *Radford* v *Samuel & Anor* [1993] BCC 870, C was a sole director and 99 per cent shareholder of the company who appealed against a judge's order that the company should not be allowed to appear without legal representation. C wanted to appear on behalf of the company himself. He argued that the company did not have the means to instruct lawyers, that the company had a good defence to the action, that by not being heard the company would lose the case by default, and that as a result of this his personal and business reputation would be damaged. The Court of Appeal took the view that none of these arguments amounted to exceptional circumstances. Sir Thomas Bingham MR, explained the justification for the rule by emphasising that limited liability is a privilege in that those who are owed money by the company cannot look to the assets of the directors and shareholders.

> 'That is an enormous benefit to a limited company but it is a benefit bought at a price. Part of the price is ... that a corporation cannot act without legal advisors.'

Other types of business organisation

Before considering the pros and cons of carrying on business through a company as a separate entity it may be useful to consider the alternatives:

Sole trader

An individual may carry on business, on his own as a sole trader. He will, subject to contractual restrictions, incur unlimited personal liability for his acts and will be subject to taxation in a personal capacity. Modern business, on more than a very modest scale, will necessitate his setting up or joining a form of business association.

Partnership

Partnership is the relation which subsists between persons carrying on a business in common with a view of profit (s1 Partnership Act 1890). This tells us little, although the 1890 Act excludes companies from the definition and s716 generally prohibits partnerships of more than 20 members, requiring them to register as a company. Partnerships are suitable for small businesses involving a relationship of mutual trust and confidence. The partners are agents for each other. Thus, they are normally jointly and severally liable for the acts of each other and the liability of each partner to third parties is unlimited, although they are liable to contribute to each other's liability and entitled to claim an indemnity from the partner at fault.

Limited partnership

A limited partnership may be registered under the Limited Partnership Act of 1907. The disadvantage of this type of business organisation is that not all of the partners are allowed to have limited liability. Section 4(2) of the Act provides:

> 'A limited partnership shall not consist of more than twenty persons, and must consist of one or more persons called general partners, who shall be liable for all debts and obligations of the firm, and one or more persons to be called limited partners, who shall at the time of entering into such partnership contribute thereto a sum or sums as capital or property valued at a stated amount, and who shall not be liable for the debts or obligations of the firm beyond the amount so contributed.'

Further drawbacks to a limited partnership are that the limited partner may not withdraw his contribution during the continuance of the partnership, and he is prohibited from taking part in the management of the partnership business or from binding the firm. See ss4(3) and 6(1).

As with ordinary partnerships, a limited partnership does not enjoy a separate legal personality. This was recently illustrated in *Mephistopheles Debt Collection Service (A Firm)* v *Lotay* (1994) The Times 17 May. An individual was subject to a civil proceedings order under s42 of the Supreme Court Act 1981, under which he was judged to be a vexatious litigant. As such, he was prohibited from commencing civil proceedings without leave of the court. The individual then assigned his debt to a limited partnership which he had formed and commenced proceedings in the name of the firm. The Court of Appeal held that he was acting in breach of the order. Nourse LJ said that it was important to remember that the plaintiffs were the three individual partners. Their entitlement, under the Rules of the Supreme Court to sue in the name of the firm, was procedural only. It does not confer corporate status on a partnership. His Lordship also held that it was not possible for the application to be made by two of the partners, without the third as well. See Chapter 15, paragraph 15.1, for further details.

These disadvantages which flow from registering as a limited partnership mean that they are comparatively rare, and the registration of a limited company is to be preferred. Some professions do not allow their members to carry on business through the medium of a limited company. Here, a limited partnership, as opposed to an ordinary partnership, might be used where one of the partners is not prepared to have full liability, or where the other partners do not want him to take part in its management. Once again, it must be stressed that such circumstances are rare, but it might cover the situation where a senior partner is retiring and is kept on as a consultant.

At the end of March 1994, 1,947 limited partnerships were registered in England and Wales (see also paragraph 1.5 *Numbers of companies*).

Unincorporated association

A group of individuals can combine as members of an unincorporated association, which may be recognised as a legal entity in itself (see *Bonsor* v *Musicians Union* [1956] AC 194; *Willis* v *Association of Universities of the British Commonwealth* [1965] 1 QB 140). But the liability of members is unlimited and their number must be limited to 20 if they carry on business for gain: s716. They are not suitable forms for trading.

Advantages and disadvantages of incorporation

The previous section on the characteristics of a company has incidentally indicated some of the important advantages of incorporating a company as an organisation through which to carry on a business or other activity. The alternatives are generally to trade as a sole trader or as a partnership.

Among the considerations already described the most important are the protection of limited liability and the relative freedom of members to transfer their shares.

The separation of management (directors) from ownership (shareholders) makes it possible for proprietors to employ competent professional managers and to limit the managing body to a workable number. There is of course no assurance that satisfactory management will be secured. The freedom of directors in the day-to-day management of the company makes them less readily accountable to members. This is the price of delegation.

A company finds it easier to raise loan capital since it is permitted to give security in the form of a floating charge on its assets. A floating charge hovers over the assets described in the charge and is particularly useful where the company does not have any fixed assets such as land. A good example of property which can be the subject of a floating charge is the company's stock in trade. The company is free to deal with the assets which are subject to a floating charge.

In strict legal theory, it is possible for sole traders and partnerships to create a floating charge but in practice they do not do so. This is because it would come within the provisions of the Bills of Sales Acts of 1878 and 1882. As such, it would need to be registered in the Bills of Sale Registry and a schedule is also required specifying the chattels which are the subject of the charge. This is wholly impractical because by its very nature, floating charge assets are fluctuating. Many commentators have pleaded for the Bills of Sale Acts, which do not apply to companies, to be repealed.

One of the main drawbacks of a company as a business organisation is that it is strictly regulated by law. For example, it is required to produce annual accounts in a set form and to have them audited (see paragraph 14.1). For this reason the routine administration of a company is often more cumbersome and expensive than that of a partnership.

The other feature of a company which is usually reckoned to be a disadvantage is that it must disclose, eg through its accounts and its annual return, a great deal of information; which other businesses may keep in confidence. The public has the right to inspect company documents at the Companies Registry and at the registered office of a company (see paragraph 3.2).

The basis of taxation of companies, and of shareholders on company dividends, is quite different from that applicable to partners or to sole traders. The tax burden is therefore often one of the deciding factors.

Sometimes there is effectively no choice. In many professions it is not permissible to carry on the practice through a company and so there is no alternative to a partnership (or a one-man practice). In recognition of this fact professional firms are exempt from the general rule which prohibits partnerships or more than 20 partners: s716.

The above point also incidentally indicates that if capital for a business is to be raised from a considerable number of persons it is hardly possible to do otherwise than form a company. In theory it is possible for capital to be provided as a loan. But there is a risk that the lenders will be found to have constituted themselves partners. Moreover, it is much more difficult to keep track of what goes on in a large partnership. As already stated 20 is the legal maximum number of partners permitted in a non-professional business. Above that limit it must be a company.

For the small enterprise, in which there really may be a choice of type of organisation, the protection of limited liability 'separate legal personality,' and the impact of tax are usually the deciding factors in making the choice.

1.3 Lifting the veil of incorporation by the courts

Introduction

Notwithstanding the principle of *Salomon* v *Salomon*, there are certain situations where the courts have shown themselves willing to 'lift the veil of incorporation', ie to set aside the separate legal personality of the company and proceed against the individual members (or directors). This has not only been done in cases where the principal question before the court is one of company law, but also where the principle of separate legal personality has worked hardship and injustice.

—There is not one single guiding principle which the courts apply as a basis for their decisions nor are all the decisions entirely consistent with each other (compare *Trebanog Working Men's Club* v *Macdonald* [1940] 1 KB 576 and *Wurzel* v *Houghton Main Home Service Ltd* [1937] 1 KB 380). Where the court has disregarded the company's corporate personality and paid attention to the real control and ownership of the company, it has relied on public policy or the principle that devices used to evade obligations or devices of fraud, are a nullity. The courts have also relied on a presumption of agency and trusteeship.

—The main heads, under which judicial intervention to lift the corporate veil has occurred, are set out below. Students should note that there is a wealth of literature on lifting the veil. See further C.M. Schmitthoff, 'Salomon in the Shadow' [1976] JBL 305, and S Ottolenghi, 'From peeping behind the corporate veil, to ignoring it completely' (1990) 53 MLR 338. Paragraph 1.4 summarises the important statutory exceptions to the veil of incorporation.

Company identity used to evade obligations

The court will intervene to prevent the misuse of the separate identity of a company to enable members to evade legal or contractual obligations or restrictions binding on them personally.

In *Re Bugle Press Ltd* [1961] Ch 270 a shareholder objected to the compulsory acquisition of his shares following a takeover bid under ss428–430. Under these provisions, which are fully explained later (see paragraph 12.4), if Company A made an offer for the shares of Company B and within four months secured acceptances from holders of at least 90 per cent of the shares of Company B, Company A was entitled to acquire compulsorily on the same terms the shares for which no acceptance of the offer had been received. In this particular case X and Y, who held 90 per cent of the shares of Bugle Press Ltd, wished to acquire compulsorily the 10 per cent shareholding of Z in the same company. To bring their plan within the ambit of s428 X and Y formed another company, of which they were sole shareholders, and caused that company to make an offer for the shares of Bugle Press Ltd. X and Y accepted the offer in respect of their shares, thereby creating the necessary 90 per cent acceptance, and their company invoked s428 to acquire the 10 per cent shareholding of Z. Z, however, applied to the court to set aside the notice served on him to acquire his shares. Technically the resort to s428 was justified. However, the court refused to sanction the acquisition of Z's shares, since the company formed by X and Y was simply a device to make use of powers not available to them as individuals. The distinction between them and their company was ignored.

In *Jones* v *Lipman* [1962] 1 WLR 832 the veil of incorporation was lifted where the defendant tried to use corporate personality as a means to evade legal obligations. The defendant contracted to sell his house but he sought to avoid his legal obligation to complete by conveying the property to a company in which he and his nominee were the sole shareholders and directors. Russell J in granting specific performance, described the company as 'a device, a sham, and a mask'. Here, the veil was lifted, otherwise the defendant could have made a mockery of his contractual obligations.

In *Gilford Motor Co* v *Horne* [1933] Ch 935 Horne had contracted with the appellant company not to solicit its customers when he left their employment. On ceasing employment Horne formed a company to carry on a competing business and solicited the appellant company's customers. The court granted the appellant company an injunction to enforce the covenant not to solicit against Horne. The veil was lifted to stop an attempt to avoid a restrictive covenant.

In order to do justice, the 'eye of equity' (per Russell J in *Jones* v *Lipman* [1962] 1 WLR 832, 836) may look behind the corporate veil in order to see that one company is the ultimate parent of another: *Atlas Maritime Co SA* v *Avalon Maritime Ltd, The Coral Rose (No 1)* [1991] 4 All ER 769 where the doing of justice required the granting of a Mareva injunction. In *Atlas Maritime Co SA* v *Avalon Maritime Ltd, The Coral Rose (No 2)* [1991] 4 All ER 781, the Court of Appeal decided that leave to appeal from an order granting or refusing an application for the variation of a Mareva injunction is not required under s18(1) of the Supreme Court Act 1981. In *Atlas Maritime Co SA* v *Avalon Maritime Ltd, The Coral Rose (No 3)* [1991] 4 All ER 783 the Court of Appeal concluded that, in the light of the relationship between a parent and its subsidiary and in the absence of any denial by the parent, that funds would continue to be made available to meet the subsidiary's legal costs, it would not be 'right and just' to vary the injunction to enable the subsidiary to draw on the frozen funds for that purpose.

Where a company with a contingent liability to the plaintiff (here, by way of an award of damages for wrongful dismissal) transfers its assets to another company which continues its business under the same trade name, the court will lift the veil of incorporation in order to allow the plaintiff to proceed against the second company: *Creasey* v *Breachwood Motors Ltd* [1992] BCC 625.

Agency and groups

In *Salomon* v *Salomon* Lord MacNaughten said, 'the company is not in law the agent for its subscribers or trustees for them'. Nevertheless the courts have tended to overlook this part of the judgment where convenient and have made an inroad on the principle of separate legal personality by implying in some cases that the company was acting as an agent for its shareholders and have held that a company can be an agent for another which held all the shares.

In some cases the courts have found on the particular evidence before them that a holding company was in fact carrying on a business through the agency of its subsidiary company. It is important to note, however, that the mere fact that one company is the subsidiary of another is not by itself sufficient to make the subsidiary an agent of the holding company.

The activities of the subsidiary must be so closely controlled and directed by the parent company that the former can be regarded as merely an agent conducting the business of the parent company.

In *Smith, Stone & Knight Ltd* v *Birmingham Corporation* [1939] 4 All ER 116 Atkinson J held that a holding company was in occupation of the subsidiary's premises and was consequently entitled to compensation for the disturbance of its business on the compulsory purchase of the premises by a local authority, even though the business was carried on at the premises in the name of the subsidiary. Six points were deemed relevant for the court to consider when determining whether a subsidiary is carrying on its business as an agent of the holding company:

1. Were the profits treated as the profits of the parent company?
2. Were the persons conducting the business appointed by the parent company?
3. Was the parent company the head and brain of the trading adventure?
4. Did the parent company govern the adventure?
5. Did the parent company make the profits by its skill and direction?
6. Was the parent company in effectual and constant control?

These six points are really one point relevant to the question, 'Who is really carrying on the business?' and are merely facets of control.

In this case the subsidiary had been formed simply in order to formally separate the business carried on in its name from another business carried on by the holding company. The freehold in the premises and the assets of the business were never transferred by the holding company to the subsidiary. All the subsidiary's shares were held in trust for the holding company and the subsidiary's directors were all directors of the holding company. The accounts of the subsidiary were kept as part of the holding company's accounts and its profits were dealt with as if earned by the holding company. It is difficult to imagine a more complete identification of a holding company with its subsidiary.

In the earlier case of *Cory* v *Dorman Long* [1936] 2 All ER 386 the court refused to treat the subsidiary as the holding company's agent so that the holding company might be deemed the owner of the subsidiary's property, although in a business sense the identification of the holding company with its subsidiary was equally as close as in *Smith, Stone & Knight Ltd* v *Birmingham Corporation*. A possible explanation for this would be that the property in question, a barge, was vested in the subsidiary so that impeded the court from holding that the true owner of it was the holding company.

Atkinson J's decision in *Smith, Stone & Knight* v *Birmingham Corporation* represents the modern tendency of the courts.

Atkinson J in *Smith, Stone & Knight* v *Birmingham Corporation* described the subsidiary company as 'the agent, employee, or tool or simulacrum' of the holding company. The description of the subsidiary as the holding company's agent or trustee often appears to be merely an epithet to indicate the subsidiary's subjection to the holding company and not to describe their legal relationship at all.

In *DHN* v *Tower Hamlets LBC* [1976] 3 All ER 462 the facts were similar to *Smith, Stone & Knight* v *Birmingham Corporation*, except that the freehold of the premises where the holding company carried on its business was vested in its wholly owned subsidiary. The Court of Appeal held that a group of companies should be treated as such so that the major holding company could be treated as the owner of land nominally held by the subsidiary which had been its licensee and could claim damages for disturbance of its business when forced to close by the Council's compulsory purchase order.

This decision is hard to reconcile with *Cory* v *Dorman Long* and shows that the courts recognise economic realities. The degree of dominance of the subsidiary by the holding company in *DHN* v *Tower Hamlets LBC* is nowhere stated with precision. It is, therefore, difficult to predict with any certainty when separate legal personality of the companies within a group will be set aside by the courts. Note that a public policy consideration also emerges as criterion in lifting the veil; if the rule in *Salomon*'s case had been strictly applied, the council would have been able to possess land without having to pay compensation!

It may be that the *DHN* case is best regarded as being limited to its own facts. It is important to recognise that it has not established a general principle of lifting the veil between groups of companies in all situations. *DHN* was doubted and not followed in *Woolfson* v *Strathclyde Regional District Council* 1978 SLT 159, HL, although the House of Lords in *Woolfson* were able to distinguish the facts from *DHN*. One important consequence of treating companies in a group as having separate legal personalities is that a holding company will not normally be liable for the debts of its subsidiaries. The position is as stated by Temple LJ in *Re Southard* [1979] 1 WLR 1198 at 1208:

> 'If one of the subsidiary companies ... turns out to be the runt of the litter and decline into insolvency to the dismay of its creditors, the parent company and other subsidiary companies may prosper to the joy of the shareholders without any liability for the debts of the insolvent subsidiary.'

For a recent example see: *Kleinwort Benson Ltd* v *Malaysian Mining Corp Bhd* [1989] 1 WLR 379.

One additional criterion implicit in the fifth point of Atkinson J in *Smith, Stone & Knight* v *Birmingham Corporation* may well be whether the subsidiary is obviously undercapitalised for the carrying on of an independent existence. This could be regarded as another ground for lifting the veil. In *Re F G Films Ltd* [1953] 1 WLR 483 an American film company seeking to gain the advantages afforded to British films, incorporated a company in England. That company had no other place of business apart from a registered office and no staff except three directors, one of whom was the president of the American company. Its capital was £100, of which the president held £90. The film was produced nominally by the English company but all the finance was by the American company. It was held that the true maker of the film was the American company.

In *Littlewoods* v *IRC* [1969] 1 WLR 1241 (see below), the minimal capital of the subsidiary was considered significant by Karminski LJ. Sandborne J in *US* v *Milwaukee Refrigerator Transit Co* (1905) 142 Fed 247 names two broad grounds for lifting the veil: first, where the holding company dominates the subsidiary and, secondly, obvious undercapitalisation.

– Tax

This area is in reality a sub-section of the agency principle (above). It is in revenue cases that the court has shown the strongest inclination to treat subsidiaries as agents of their holding companies, so that the holding companies may be taxed in respect of their subsidiaries' profits. The courts lift the veil usually to the companies' disadvantage, rendering them liable to taxation.

In *Firestone Tyre Rubber Co* v *Llewellyn* [1957] 1 WLR 464 an American company formed a wholly owned subsidiary in England to manufacture and sell its tyres. Orders were sent direct to the subsidiary from distributors without consulting the American company. The subsidiary received payments and would forward the balance to the American company. All directors of the subsidiary were in England and were free from day-to-day control by the American company. The House of Lords held that the American company was carrying on a business through its English subsidiary acting as agent and consequently it was liable to pay United Kingdom tax.

In *Littlewood Stores* v *IRC* [1969] 1 WLR 1241 Lord Denning went further and lifted the veil on a subsidiary company which was nominally the holder of a piece of property purchased by the holding company and transferred to it for tax purposes.

The agency principle is applied for the benefit of companies, as in *Smith, Stone & Knight* v *Birmingham Corporation*. Here, however, it works to their disadvantage. Note that the six points enunciated by Atkinson J came from tax cases.

– Trust

The courts have used the concept of trusteeship to escape from the principle of separate legal personality.

In *Trebanog Working Men's Club* v *Macdonald* [1940] 1 KB 576 the committee managing the club purchased liquor in its name and sold it to the members. The club was prosecuted for selling liquor without a licence. The court acquitted the club, holding that there had been no sale because the members were in reality the owners of the liquor when it was purchased on their behalf by the committee.

Enemy dealings

In *Daimler Co Ltd* v *Continental Tyre and Rubber Co (GB) Ltd* [1916] 2 AC 307, the House of Lords was prepared to pierce the veil of incorporation where, although a company was incorporated in England, all of it directors and all of its shareholders bar one, were German residents. By looking at the true character of Continental, their Lordships decided that to allow it to obtain summary judgment against Daimler for the value of goods supplied and not paid for would amount to trading with the enemy and therefore contravene the Trading with the Enemy Act 1914.

Companies and criminal/civil responsibility

In certain cases the acts of a company's agents can render a company criminally liable. The crucial question is whether the person behind the company is in sufficient control of it as to make it liable for any criminal act. This principle of corporate liability is sometimes referred to as the alter ego doctrine. This allows the law to attribute the mental state of those who in fact control the company and manage the company, to the company as being its 'directing mind and will'.

In *Lennard's Carrying Co* v *Asiatic Petroleum* [1915] AC 705 the question was whether a company could take advantage of s502 Merchant Shipping Act 1894 where an owner of a vessel has a defence and can exempt himself from liability for any injury caused without 'his actual fault or privity'. It was held that the fault concept could be applied to a corporate body although in this case the appellants were exempt. Viscount Haldane LC said, 'the Corporation is an abstraction, it has no mind of its own. Its active and directing will must be sought in the person who is really the directing mind and will of the corporation.'

In *Bolton Engineering* v *Graham* [1956] Ch 577 Lord Denning explained what is known as the organic theory. He said that a company may be likened to a human body: it has a brain and nerve centre which controls what it does. He enforced the view that the state of mind of the managers is the state of mind of the company so that in cases where the law requires personal fault as a condition of liability, then the fault of the manager will be the fault of the company.

In *Tesco Supermarkets* v *Nattrass* [1972] AC 153 Tesco supermarkets was prosecuted under the Trade Descriptions Act 1968. Tesco raised the defence in the Act which provided that where the offence was due to the act of another person, the defendants would not be guilty. It was held that the act of the shop assistant in replacing special offer packs of washing powder with packs at the regular price were the acts of 'another person' within the Act. The branch manager, who failed to detect the shop assistant's fault, was not the directing mind of the company. (Note that this was a chain of supermarkets and that a shop manager of one shop, who is the major shareholder, may well be in control of the company.)

In *Attorney-General's Reference of 1984 (No 2 of 1983)* [1984] 2 QB 456 the question whether a person in total control of a limited company by reason of his shareholding and directorship was capable of stealing the company's property was referred to the Court of Appeal for its opinion. The defendants, who were both shareholders and directors, appropriated company funds for their own use by drawing cheques on the company's bank account. It was held that where all the shareholders and directors of a company acted illegally and dishonestly in relation to the company, their knowledge of consent to the illegal or dishonest act could not be imputed to the company. The essence of the defendants' defence was that, since they and the company were one and the same, their consent was the same as the company's consent to the appropriations. They could not, therefore, rely on the defence provided by s2(1)(b) Theft Act 1968, because it was not possible to regard the company as the 'other person' whose consent had been given.

These cases can be considered as not lifting the veil of incorporation in the true sense. Attributing conduct of directors, managers or members to the company does not really involve lifting the veil.

In proceedings arising out of the Zeebrugge ferry disaster, at the Central Criminal Court Turner J directed the jury to acquit all eight defendants, including P & O European Ferries, owner of the Herald of Free Enterprise. Writing in The Independent on 20 October 1990, Professor Michael Zander suggested that conclusions could be drawn from this decision as follows:

1. corporate manslaughter is legally admissible as a charge in an English court;
2. in order for such a charge to succeed, the prosecution must not simply prove recklessness – it must also show that the defendant was reckless in regard to an obvious and serious risk;
3. although the prosecution did not press the argument for 'aggregation' of alleged shortcomings on the part of the company's top employees, the judge inferred that he would not have accepted it;
4. corporate manslaughter looks harder than ever to prove and victims of future disasters will probably have to be content with civil remedies.

Where criminal responsibility of a company is based on vicarious liability, it appears that this may not always cover liability for all acts of all of the company's employees. As a result of the Sheen inquiry into the *Herald of Free Enterprise* disaster, a new offence, contained in s31 of the Marine Shipping Act 1988, was introduced requiring vessels to be operated in a safe manner. It provides that:

> 'It shall be the duty of the owner of a ship to which this section applies to take all reasonable steps to secure that the ship is operated in a safe manner.'

In *Seaboard Offshore Ltd* v *Secretary of State for Transport* [1994] 1 WLR 541 HL, Seaboard Offshore Ltd were the charterers and managers of the mv *Safe Carrier*, which set sail from the River Tyne bound for Aberdeen. The vessel broke down three times within a period of 24 hours, leaving her drifting at sea. The chief engineer, who was responsible for the mechanical running of the ship, boarded the vessel only 2 hours and 50 minutes before she put to sea. The minimum time needed to familiarise himself with the vessel was in fact three days. The company was charged under s31.

The House of Lords held that, construed properly, Parliament could not have intended that s31 made the owner of a ship always liable for the acts or omission of his subordinate employees, if he had himself taken all reasonable steps. In the case of a company, Lord Keith, applying *Tesco Supermarkets* v *Nattrass* [1971] 2 All ER 127, said:

> 'Where the owner, charterer or manager is a corporation which can act only through natural persons, the natural persons who are to be treated in law as being the corporation for the purposes of acts done in the course of its business are those who by virtue of its constitution or otherwise are entrusted with the exercise of the powers of the corporation.'

Seaboard's conviction was quashed. The justices had convicted the company by finding that it was the fault of an employee, the chief engineer, by not having sufficient time to familiarise himself with the vessel, rather than the senior management, and Lord Keith felt this was erroneous. It was further argued that there had been a personal failure by those entrusted with the duty under s31, in that there was no system for establishing that the ship did not go to sea before the chief engineer had an opportunity to familiarise himself with its machinery and equipment. This argument failed as the case was not originally presented to the justices in this way, so they could not have considered it, and therefore it could not be appealed against.

Finally on this case, it is worth noting that the Lords felt that it was unhelpful to categorise the offence as either being or not being one of strict liability. On this point Lord Keith said:

> 'It consists simply in failure to take steps which by an objective standard are held to be reasonable steps to take in the interests of the safe operation of the ship ...'

See Chapter 15, paragraph 15.1, for further details.

In *El Ajou* v *Dolar Land Holdings plc & Anor* [1994] BCC 143 the Court of Appeal held that a non-executive director who was also the company's chairman was the directing mind and will of the company. He had knowingly received money from persons who had obtained it by carrying out a massive share fraud. The money was then used by the company in a joint venture to carry out a property development in London. The plaintiff was a victim of the fraud and was claiming to be able to trace the proceeds of the fraud to the London development. To do this he had to establish that the company held the proceeds on the basis of the 'knowing receipt' head of constructive trust. The company itself had no knowledge of the fraud but the Court of Appeal held that the director's knowledge of the fraud could be treated as the knowledge of the company and the plaintiff's appeal succeeded. It made no difference that the director had since resigned, because he had the requisite knowledge at the time the joint venture was entered into.

Conclusion

It is not possible to present a single principle or a consistent policy applied by the courts in lifting the veil of incorporation. The development has been essentially haphazard and irrational. Although the result is usually that justice is done, the lack of policy produces inconsistency and uncertainty.

Despite some fairly recent evidence of a relaxation of a strict approach to lifting the veil, the important case of *Adams* v *Cape Industries plc* [1990] 2 WLR 657 marks a return to a rigid application of the Salomon principle. The Court of Appeal, in a most complex case, had to decide whether a parent company was 'present' in the United States through one of its subsidiaries. If it was, then the plaintiff could enforce an award of damages made against the subsidiary, against the parent Cape Industries plc, a company registered in England. The plaintiff argued:

1. that the companies in the group were a single economic unit;
2. that the corporate structure was a mere facade concealing the true facts; and
3. that the subsidiary in the United States was the parent's agent. All of these submissions failed.

Gower, *Principles of Modern Company Law* 5th ed at p133, believes that the end result is that the courts will only lift the veil when construing a contract, statute or document or, when a company is a 'mere facade' concealing the true facts or, if the company is an agent of another.

1.4 Statutory lifting of the veil of incorporation

There are a number of situations when the veil of incorporation will be effectively lifted by statute. The result is usually to make someone other than the company liable for its debts or, to make a person liable to contribute to the assets of the company in the event of liquidation. Some of the most important examples are identified below.

Liability by statute for fraudulent or wrongful trading

This is a brief introduction to a principle which is further explained in the chapter on company liquidation (see paragraph 13.6).

If a company is in liquidation and the court is satisfied that its business has been carried on with intent to defraud its creditors, or creditors of any other person, or for any fraudulent purpose, the court may on the application of the liquidator declare that any persons who were knowingly parties to carrying on the company business in this manner shall make such contribution (if any) to the company's assets as the court thinks proper: IA s213. In practice only the directors of an insolvent company in liquidation are exposed to this liability, since it rests with them to decide whether the company should cease trading and thus incurring debts which it cannot pay.

Fraudulent trading is also a criminal offence. There may be a criminal prosecution even if the company is not in liquidation: s458.

Because of its criminal implications the courts will not usually make directors civilly liable for fraudulent trading unless there is very clear evidence of dishonest intent on their part. Such evidence is not easy to find.

The 1985 reform of insolvency law therefore added a new civil (but not criminal) liability for 'wrongful trading': IA s214. All which the liquidator has to show to the court is that the directors knew or ought not have concluded that there was no reasonable prospect of avoiding the insolvent liquidation which has in fact ensued. The directors, who alone may be made liable under s214, may then seek to escape liability by satisfying the court that they took every reasonable step to minimise the loss to creditors (see also paragraph 13.6).

The effect of establishing fraudulent or wrongful trading is that the directors will be personally liable to contribute towards paying the company's debts. The distinction between them and the company as a separate person is disregarded.

Other statutory lifting of the veil of incorporation

The Companies Act 1985 creates further departures from the principle of separate legal personality. It is arguable that these are not strictly exceptions to the *Salomon* v *Salomon* principle since Parliament is not bound by a legal principle developed by the courts, but rather part of the terms on which the privilege of limited liability is granted.

Section 24 – members of companies other than private companies limited by shares or by guarantee may be personally liable for the company's debts where their number is not kept up to the specified amount, two in the case of public companies. A rare example of a member breaching this provision occurred recently in the Court of Appeal decision *Nisbet* v *Shepherd* [1994] BCC 91. Leggatt LJ, said that the case served as a useful reminder to small traders that, because of s24, they would not succeed in limiting their liability by setting up a company if they failed to ensure that no more than six months went by without the company having at least one member. Hoffmann LJ had 'considerable sympathy' with the sole member in the case who had fallen foul of an 'ancient and obsolete' rule of company law.

The case is not only rare but also almost certainly the last case to be decided under s24 involving a private company. This is because s24 was amended from 15 July 1992 by the Companies (Single Member Private Limited Companies) Regulations 1992 (SI 1992/1699), and now only applies to public limited companies.

Section 349(4) – any officer of the company or person acting on his behalf may incur personal liability if he uses or authorises the use of the company seal, cheques, receipts and the full name of the company is not shown on them. To incur liability under this section, the defect in the document must be misleading and obvious abbreviations will not suffice (see paragraph 2.2 *Display of company name*). Similarly if the mistake in the name of the company is trivial then there will be no personal liability. In *Jenice Ltd &*

Ors v *Dan* [1994] BCC 43, a company's cheque had the name 'Primkeen Limited' instead of its correct name 'Primekeen Ltd'. The omission of a letter in the middle of a word did not make the defendant director liable under s349(4).

Sections 216 and 217 Insolvency Act 1986 – under s216 a director or shadow director is prohibited from using the name or a similar name by which his company was known in the previous twelve months, if it has gone into insolvent liquidation. The name is prohibited, without leave of the court, for a period of five years commencing on the date it went into liquidation. This provision is designed to stop the practice of forming so called 'phoenix companies' whereby the directors would liquidate one company and then immediately form another company with the same name, thereby misleading the company's creditors. Moreover under s217, a director who breaches s216 may be personally liable for the company's debts. These sections were recently invoked in the case of *Thorne* v *Silverleaf* [1994] BCC 109 where a director of three companies, which had all become insolvent and had a similar name, was held liable to the plaintiff investor to the sum of £135,000 representing loans made to the company.

Section 117(8) – provides that the directors may be jointly and severally liable for the company's debts where a public limited company commences business without having obtained a certificate from the registrar that the company's allotted share capital is not less than the authorised minimum of £50,000 (see section 1.5 Types of company).

Section 15 Company Directors Disqualification Act 1986 – this provision makes directors personally liable for the debts of the company while they act in breach of a disqualification order.

Where it is found that a relationship of parent company and subsidiary exist (see s736 and paragraph 1.5 Holding and subsidiary companies) the separate legal personality is ignored for some purposes and the companies in the group are treated as one legal and economic unit. For example ss229–230 impose obligations to prepare and present group accounts to give a true and fair view of the state of affairs and profit or loss of the group as a whole (see paragraph 14.1 Duties with respect to accounts).

Conclusion

Given the courts traditional reluctance to lift the veil of incorporation, as illustrated by the Adams decision, it is likely that lifting of the veil is in the future more likely to occur by invoking the statutory provisions.

1.5 Types of company

Introduction

Companies are formed for many different purposes and yet the statutory requirements imposed on companies are elaborate and demanding.

To provide a reasonable degree of flexibility and freedom to choose what suits the user best the law permits the formation of different kinds of company, with features adapted to the circumstances of the case. It also provides for the conversion of an existing company so as to make it a company of a different type. This conversion is effected by making changes in the company's structure under the prescribed procedure and then applying to the registrar for validation of the change by the issue of a certificate of re-registration (at the registry) of the company in its new category.

This section describes the different types of company and how they may be re-registered in a new category.

Limited and unlimited liability

A previous section (paragraph 1.2 *Essential features of a company, Limited liability*) has explained that a member's liability is to the company but it may be a liability which is limited. Unless it is so limited he is liable, if the company becomes insolvent, to contribute whatever amount is required to enable it to pay its debts in full. That is the position of a member of an unlimited company.

A limited company is limited either by shares or by guarantee. The former is by far the more important and numerous of the two types.

It is always possible to discover whether a company is limited, and if so, by what means, by inspecting its memorandum.

A company limited by shares

The memorandum of a company limited by shares includes a clause which states merely that 'the liability of members is limited'. There is no express reference to limitation of liability by shares.

The effect is that a holder of shares is liable to contribute to the company's assets the amount of the issue price of the shares which is fixed at the time of issue. If that amount has been paid by him or by a previous holder, the liability attached to the shares has been discharged and they are 'fully paid'. The present holder of fully paid shares has no further liability to the company. The company may not without his consent increase the amount due on the shares: s16. If the company fails the shares will be worthless but that is the entire loss of the holder.

If a person ceases to be a holder of partly-paid shares and the holder of those shares at the time of liquidation is unable to pay the amount due on them, the previous holder is liable to pay on them, if he ceased to be a shareholder within the previous year and the company has debts incurred while he was a member and still owing: IA s74.

A company limited by guarantee

In this case the memorandum contains the same basic statement of limited liability but also has another clause, whereby every member agrees to contribute to the company's assets, if it is in liquidation and unable to pay its debts in full. The maximum amount which he is to contribute is stated, and it is not usually large. That is the limit of his liability in respect of his guarantee.

If present members are unable to satisfy their undertakings to the company any persons who ceased to be members within a year before the commencement of winding up are liable to contribute. But their liability is restricted to the amount of any debts of the company incurred while they were members and still outstanding (see paragraph 13.2 *Contributions*).

In the past it was possible, though unusual, to form companies limited by guarantee which also had a share capital. In those cases members (and past members) had a double liability in respect of shares and of guaranteed contributions. However, since 1980 it has not been possible to incorporate new companies of this hybrid type: s1(4).

A creditor of a company limited by guarantee has no right of direct recourse against its members as guarantors. If the company does not pay his debt, he should take action to get the company put into liquidation. It will then be the duty of the liquidator to call for payment under the members' guarantees and apply the money towards payment of the debts.

If the company charges its assets as security the charge does not apply to the members' obligation to the company since their guarantees are not an 'asset' in the technical sense.

Companies limited by guarantee are usually formed for non-commercial purposes, such as education, research, charity, or as a trade association. The company applies its current income, possibly fees earned by its services, to meet its recurrent outgoings. The members' guarantees are held in reserve to provide additional funds which may be needed in winding up the company.

Unlimited companies

There is no statement of limited liability in the memorandum and the members are liable to contribute, without limit, whatever is required for payment of the debts of the company, in liquidation. The position of creditors and of past members is as stated in paragraph 1.4 *A company limited by guarantee*.

An unlimited company usually has a share capital but it is not required to do so.

An unlimited company is not subject to the restrictions, applied to limited companies, on return of capital to members. It is not liable to pay the 1 per cent capital duty on consideration received for its shares.

The most important advantage of an unlimited company is that it need not usually deliver to the registry a copy of its annual accounts for filing. It may therefore keep secret its financial affairs. However, an unlimited company does not have this privilege if it has a subsidiary undertaking which is a limited company or if it is the subsidiary undertaking of a limited company or is controlled by two or more limited companies: s254.

An unlimited company is most suitable if its purpose is to hold property or to perform some activity which does not entail liabilities.

Re-registration of limited companies as unlimited and vice versa

In either case the re-registration procedure (ss49–52) requires that the company shall first alter its memorandum (including its name), and possibly its articles if they refer to its previous status, before making application with the relevant documents to the registrar.

For conversion from limited to unlimited status the written consent of every member is required since each will then have unlimited liability.

For conversion from unlimited to limited a special resolution of the company suffices. To prevent abuse, however, former members of the company, if it goes into insolvent liquidation within three years of re-registration, may be liable to contribute towards payment of outstanding debts incurred while they were members: IA s77.

Re-registration of this type is irreversible, ie the company may change once from limited to unlimited or the other way, but may not thereafter convert back.

Public and private companies

A public company is one which:

1. is limited by shares (including the rare case of a company limited by guarantee which also has a share capital);
2. includes in its memorandum a clause stating that it is a public company; and
3. has been registered at the registry as a public company. To obtain that registration the company must have an authorised share capital of at least £50,000 and adopt a name which ends with the words 'public limited company' or its abbreviation 'plc' (or the Welsh equivalent if it is a Welsh company): s1(3).

Any company which is not a public company is a private company. A company limited by guarantee, unless it also has a share capital, and an unlimited company must always be private companies since they do not satisfy requirement (1) above.

In various parts of this textbook mention is made of the more stringent rules applicable to public companies. On the other hand only a public company is permitted to raise capital in large amounts by the issue of securities on the Stock Exchange or other securities markets (as explained in paragraph 5.2) on flotation. Normally, therefore, it suits a private company best to preserve that status until, if ever, it is large enough to be 'floated' and has need to raise capital by that means.

A subsidiary of a public company may be either public or private.

A private company which has an authorised capital of £50,000 or more is not required to register as a public company. It is entirely optional.

For a public company the minimum membership is two, but one person may, for a lawful purpose, by subscribing his name to a memorandum of association and otherwise complying with the requirement of the 1985 Act in respect of registration, form an incorporated company being a private company limited by shares or by guarantee: s1(3A) of the 1985 Act, as inserted by the Companies (Single Member Private Limited Companies) Regulations 1992.

The name of a private limited company ends with 'Limited' or 'Ltd' unless it qualifies under s30 to omit it (as explained in paragraph 2.2 *Omission of the word 'Limited' from a company name*). This is the readiest means of distinguishing, in examination questions, whether the company is public or private.

Many private companies, especially if formed before 1981, when the basis of classification was altered, include in their articles a power to the directors to reject a share transfer (among other restrictions). These restrictions are no longer required by law but private companies often prefer to have the means of excluding from membership an unwelcome transferee of shares (see paragraph 6.7 *Refusal to register a transfer*).

Public company – commencement of business

The procedure for forming a new company is described in the next chapter. It is the same for a public as for a private company.

However, if a company is formed as public from the outset, it is required by s117 to obtain from the registrar an additional certificate which entitles it to commence business. For that purpose the company must have allotted shares of a nominal value of at least £50,000 and received the consideration to the extent of at least one quarter of the nominal value plus the whole of any premium.

A newly formed private company may commence business as soon as it has been incorporated. It is therefore more convenient and usual in practice, if a public company is required, to form it as a private company and then re-register it as a public company under the procedure described below.

Re-registration of a private company as public

A private company limited by shares may apply to the registrar for re-registration as a public company under s43.

In outline the procedure is that the company first holds a general meeting to pass a special resolution to apply for re-registration and to make alterations to its memorandum, and if appropriate to its articles. The essential alterations to the memorandum are (1) to adopt a name with the ending 'public limited company' or 'plc' and (2) to include a clause declaring that this is a public company.

With the application to the registrar are submitted accounts and an auditors report. Among other points the registrar must satisfy himself from the documents that the company has an authorised and issued share capital of at least £50,000.

The final and decisive stage is the issue of the registrar's certificate of re-registration as a public company.

Re-registration of a public company as private

If the authorised capital of a public company is reduced to less than £50,000 eg under an authorised reduction of capital, it must be re-registered as a private company.

There is also a procedure for voluntary re-registration under s53. The procedure requires a general meeting to pass a special resolution to make the necessary change of name and to omit the clause from the memorandum declaring that this is a public company.

The conversion of the company to a private company may prejudice the interests of members. It is therefore provided that members who hold at least 5 per cent of the issued share capital, or of a class of capital, or if the company is not limited by shares 5 per cent of the members, or 50 members may within 28 days of the passing of the resolution apply to the court for relief. Among other possibilities the court may order the company to purchase the shares of the objectors.

Holding and subsidiary companies

There are now two different definitions of the relationship which constitutes a 'group of companies'. For determining when consolidated group accounts are required (see paragraph 14.1 *Parent companies and subsidiary undertakings*) the defined terms are 'parent company' and 'subsidiary undertaking'. To prevent evasion these terms have been so defined that group accounts are required in some cases where the narrower relationship of 'holding company' and 'subsidiary company' does not exist.

For all other purposes company statute law uses the terms 'holding company' and 'subsidiary', as defined by the revised s736 which is explained below. For example a subsidiary may not usually acquire shares of its holding company (paragraph 6.4 *Prohibition against shareholdings*) and the directors of a holding company are subject to a general prohibition against obtaining loans from the holding company and its subsidiaries (paragraph 9.1 *Directors' transactions*): ss23 and 330.

By the revised definition one company (H) is a holding company and another company (S) is its subsidiary in any of the following circumstances:

1. H holds a majority of the voting rights in S;
2. H is a member of S and has the right to appoint or remove a majority of the board of directors of S;
3. H is a member of S and has sole control, pursuant to an agreement with other shareholders or members, of a majority of voting rights in S;
4. S is a subsidiary of X (a company) which in turn is a subsidiary of H.

S is the 'wholly-owned subsidiary' of H if it has no members other than (1) H itself (2) wholly-owned subsidiaries of H or (3) persons acting on behalf of H or its other wholly-owned subsidiaries.

Voting rights mean rights to vote at general meetings of S on all, or substantially all, matters.

H is treated as having the right to appoint a director or directors of S if (by the articles of S) directors of H are automatically directors of S or H itself is a director of S. If however H must obtain the consent of another person in exercising its power to appoint or remove directors of S, that is not a right which (2) above takes into account.

Among other statutory provisions (of s736A) the rights of a nominee (of H or another person) are in this context attributed to H or the other person, and rights of subsidiaries are attributed in their entirety to the holding company. If, for example, H is the registered holder of 10 per cent of the shares of S, but another 10 per cent is held by a nominee of H and 31 per cent by X Ltd, in which H has a 60 per cent shareholding, H is deemed to have 51 per cent of the shares of S and so has a majority of the voting rights for the purposes of case (1) above.

The general intention and effect of these definitions is to make S the subsidiary of H, if H has control of S. The current definition, unlike the previous one, does not apply an alternative criterion by which beneficial ownership of more than half the shares of S would count. In practice there is less difficulty over these complex rules than might appear at first sight, since most subsidiaries are wholly-owned.

In the past the term 'parent' or 'parent company' has been used colloquially as a synonym for 'holding company'. It is now incorrect usage since 'parent company' is itself a defined term with a different meaning.

Other types of company

The following categories require only brief mention:

1. '*body corporate*' or '*corporation*' are terms used occasionally in the Companies Act to apply a legal rule to companies incorporated outside as well as inside the UK. Thus, all such corporations, if members of the company, may send an authorised representative to its general meetings: s375 (paragraph 8.1 *Attendance at meetings*);
2. '*oversea company*' means a company incorporated outside Great Britain (which does not include Northern Ireland) which has established a place of business in Great Britain. Such companies are subject to selective and adapted rules of British company law;
3. '*Welsh company*' means (s21) a company which by its memorandum provides that its registered office shall always be situated in Wales. It may then make use of the Welsh language for certain purposes. Very few companies established in Wales, for which this is a possible arrangement, do in fact include such a stipulation in their memorandum;
4. '*listed company*' means a company whose securities are listed on the Stock Exchange (as explained later (see paragraph 5.2) in connection with 'flotation' of companies). Strictly it is the securities, ie shares or debentures, which are listed and not the company. The same company may, for example, have listed shares and unlisted debentures. 'Listed' is the correct expression, since it means that the securities have been admitted to the Official List for Stock Exchange dealings.

Formerly the same idea was expressed by the word 'quoted' and this is still sometimes used instead of 'listed'. A listed company must always be a public company: FSA s143(3). But not every public company is listed. An unlisted company, including all private companies, is one whose securities are not listed;

5. '*small*' or '*medium sized*' company, as defined by s247, as amended, is a private company which falls within certain limits (as explained later (see paragraph 14.1) in connection with accounts) and so qualifies for certain remissions in the contents of the copy of its accounts delivered to the registry for filing (see paragraph 14.1 *Exemptions from statutory requirements*).

Numbers of companies

The procedure to register a company at Companies House is described in paragraph 2.1 Registration. Under s729 the Secretary of State is required to lay before Parliament an annual report of matters within the Companies Acts. The report called, *Companies in 1993–94*, HMSO 1994, and prepared by the DTI, includes a wealth of statistical data on registered companies as well as some other types of business organisations. The report discloses that for the year ending March 1994 there were 902,500 companies registered in England and Wales. Of these just 1.2 per cent were public companies. There were 109,000 newly registered companies, while 147,200 were removed from the register. Over half of all registered companies have an issued share capital of less than £100.

2

Memorandum of Association

2.1 Registration

Documents

Certain documents must be filed with the registrar before the company can be registered.

The memorandum of association which inter alia specifies the objects and powers of the company, the company's name (usually indicating its status by the last word); whether it is a public limited company; whether the registered office is to be in England; the fact that members' liabilities are limited, if this is so; the amount of share capital with which it proposes to be registered (at least £50,000 for a public company) and its division of shares into fixed amount, each subscriber writing opposite his name the number of shares he takes (which must not be less than one). Each subscriber must sign the memorandum: s2.

The articles of association (the terms by which the members agree to regulate their association): s7. (The memorandum and the articles together are commonly referred to as the company's regulations, although the term may be confined to the contents of the articles.) Generally speaking, the articles will include the regulations set out in Table A (The Companies (Tables A–F) Regulations 1985). On the Table G model articles see paragraph 3.1 *Table A and other models*. Each subscriber must sign the articles: s7(3).

Form 12: statutory declaration by a solicitor or director or the secretary of the company of compliance with the statutory requirements must be produced to the registrar: s12(3).

Form 10: statement of first directors and secretary must accompany the memorandum (s288, s10) and they must each sign it to signify consent to the appointment.

The intended situation of a company's registered office must be specified in the statement of first directors and secretary.

Where the memorandum is delivered for registration the Registrar will not register the memorandum unless he is satisfied that all the requirements of the Companies Acts in respect of registration have been complied with: s12.

The documents must then be sent to the registrar, accompanied by the registration fee. The fee for registering a company at Companies House is now £20. This was reduced from £50 by the Companies (Fees) (Amendment) Regulations 1994 (SI 1994/2217) which came into force on 20 September 1994. The reduction has been made possible, partly by increased efficiency at Companies House, and partly by the Government's decision that fees charged should now reflect the actual cost of administering the registration procedure. Previously, Companies House funded, out of registration fees, activities carried out by the DTI, such as company investigations. The fees charged by Companies House had to take this external funding responsibility into account. As this is no longer the case, a reduction in the registration fee was made possible.

Shelf companies

If time is of the essence to the promoter and the company needs to be formed immediately, then it is possible to buy a company 'off the shelf', that is, a company which has already been created. These companies are formed by company formation agents who stock-pile ready-made companies which are available for purchase. Purchasing a company in this way saves the time involved in preparing the documentation and waiting for the registrar to issue the certificate of incorporation. On the other hand, the purchaser will need to ensure the company's objects clause is appropriate (see paragraph 2.3 The objects clause) and will often be disappointed with the bland name that has been allocated to the company. These are not difficult problems to overcome but everything comes at a price. The cost of a name change for example is £50.

Registration

If the documents are in order and the company's objects are lawful, the registrar is required, and may in case of need be ordered by mandanus, to register the company: *R* v *Registrar of Companies, ex parte Bowen* [1914] 3 KB 161. If the objects are unlawful, he may refuse, as in *R* v *Registrar of Companies, ex parte More* [1931] 2 KB1 197, where his decision was upheld in a refusal of registration of a company whose objects were to sell in this country tickets in the Irish Sweepstake.

On registering a new company the registrar issues a certificate of incorporation which states that the company has been registered, gives its name in the correct form (see paragraph 2.2 *Company names – formal requirements*) which it should always use, and states, if that is the case, that it is registered with limited liability.

The registrar's certificate is conclusive evidence that the company has been incorporated even if it later emerges that it should not have been: *Princess Bos* v *Reus* (1871) LR 5 HL 176. There is an obiter dictum (in *Bowman* v *Secular Society* [1917] AC 439) that the Attorney-General may apply to the court for judicial review of the issue of a certificate of incorporation. While in other contexts (see paragraph 7.3 *Registration procedure*) the courts have held that they cannot intervene where a statute states expressly that a certificate issued by the registrar is to be conclusive, in *R* v *Registrar of Companies, ex parte Attorney-General* [1991] BCLC 476 it was decided that if a company is registered with objects which involve it entering into contracts which are sexually immoral and hence illegal, the court will grant judicial review of the registration decision and strike the company off the register.

Another method of deregistration of a company whose objects are unlawful is to petition for its compulsory liquidation on the just and equitable ground under IA s122(1)(g). The DTI may take such action following the report of inspectors appointed to investigate the affairs of the company, if the report discloses that its objects are in fact illegal: ss432 and 440. The fact that a company with illegal objects is still on the register does not of course legalise its activities in pursuit of those objects.

On registering a new company the registrar allocates to it a serial number which must be inserted on all documents delivered to the registry: s705. It must also be shown on the company's business letters and order forms: s351 (see paragraph 2.2 *Company letterheads, etc*).

The registrar also opens a file at the registry and encloses in it the original documents delivered to him for the incorporation of the company (see paragraph 2.1 *Documents*), a copy of the certificate of registration, and of every formal certificate, eg of re-registration on change of name (see paragraph 2.2 *Change of company name*), which he may issue later. All documents delivered to the registrar for filing on behalf of the company are also enclosed in the file. These include the annual accounts (see paragraph 14.1 *Duties with respect to accounts*), special, extraordinary and elective resolutions (see paragraph 8.1 *Registration and publicity*) and the annual return (see paragraph 3.2 *Annual return*), and notices of such events as changes of directors (see paragraph 9.1 *Publicity about directors*), address of registered office (see paragraph 3.2 *Registered office*), the appointment of a receiver (see paragraph 7.4 *The appointment of a receiver*) and various documents relating to winding up (see paragraph 13.4 *Types of resolution required*). However, two types of company document of some importance are not found on the file:

1. a charge on the company's property, since only the prescribed particulars are delivered for registration (see paragraph 7.3 *Registration procedure*). But any person may inspect the copy of the complete charge which the company must hold at its registered office (see paragraph 7.3 *Company register of changes*);

2. an ordinary resolution unless it is one of the several types specified for registration (see paragraph 8.1 *Registration publicity*). The important decision in *Turquand's Case* (see paragraph 2.5 *The indoor management rule*) turns on the fact that the creditor had no opportunity to inspect the ordinary resolution (authorising the directors' borrowing) since it was not on file at the registry.

The principle of constructive notice does not now apply to the documents on a company's title at the registry, with one exception: s711A. This means that in the normal course a person dealing with a company is affected by what he actually knows of its constitution and affairs, so far as they are material. But what he does not know does not affect him, unless his ignorance is due to a failure to make enquiries which it was reasonable to make. It is expressly provided however that there is no duty as a matter of routine precaution to make a search at the registry: s35C. The one exception, where constructive notice continues to apply, is a registered charge on the company's property. Here the person concerned is affected by what he could have discovered even though he has not done so and is ignorant of it.

Section 711 contains a long list of documents of various kinds, on the issue or receipt of which, the registrar must publish a notice in the *London Gazette*. The notification merely states, with reference to the company, that a document of a particular kind has been issued or received. It does not give the contents.

Failure by the company to deliver a document to the registrar as required by law exposes the company and its officers to penalties, which in some cases increase at a daily rate until the default is remedied. In addition a company may not rely in dealings with another person on any documents of the following types, unless they have been delivered to the registry or the other person has notice of them:

1. the making of a winding up order or the appointment of a liquidator in a voluntary liquidation (see paragraphs 13.3 *Procedure* and 13.4 *Type of resolution required*);
2. an alteration of the memorandum or articles;
3. a change of directors;
4. a change of address of the registered office as regards due service of documents on the company (see paragraph 3.2): s42.

Commencement of business

On obtaining a certificate of incorporation a private company may forthwith commence business. It has officers since the director and secretary are automatically appointed to office by virtue of the certificate of incorporation: s13.

There are a number of other preliminary steps to be taken, such as appointing a chairman, adopting a common seal, opening a bank account and perhaps alloting shares to raise capital. For these purposes it is normal practice to hold a first meeting of the directors as soon as convenient.

A public company on the other hand must obtain the registrar's certificate under s117 before it may commence business by dealings with third parties. This has already been explained (see paragraph 1.4 *Public company – commencement of business*). In practice these formalities are by-passed by forming a private company and then re-registering it as public.

Re-registration

The company may change its status by re-registration:

1. it may re-register as public if it was originally private or vice-versa under ss43–48 and 53–55;
2. it may re-register as limited, if incorporated as unlimited, or as unlimited, if originally incorporated as limited, under ss49–52. But only one such change is permitted, so that it is irreversible.

The procedure has been described in paragraph 1.4.

2.2 Memorandum of association

Introduction

Every company is required to have a memorandum of association (hereafter 'the memorandum') as one of the documents presented to obtain incorporation of the company. It may under the appropriate procedure alter its memorandum (with the exception of the clause which states the country in which the registered office is to be situated since this determines its permanent domicile during its existence). In its original or altered form the memorandum must state (1) the name of the company (2) its country of domicile (see above) (3) its objects, and (4) its authorised capital (see paragraph 6.1 *Share capital – basic terms and principles*). If it is a limited company and/or a public company those facts must also be stated: s2.

There are model forms of memorandum for the various different types of company. Every company must have a memorandum in the prescribed form or 'as near to that form as circumstances admit': s3. The memorandum must be 'printed'. That requirement, which also applies to the articles, is explained in the next chapter (see paragraph 3.1 *Introduction*).

The memorandum may include additional clauses at the company's option. This is not usual but suitable clauses in the memorandum may define the rights of classes of shares, or 'entrench' provisions which are to be unalterable, or adopt restrictions which entitle the company to omit the word 'limited' from its name (see paragraph 2.2 *Omission of the word 'Limited' from a company name*). Generally, however, class rights are set out in the articles. There are limited powers to alter a clause of the memorandum which might have been in the articles: s17 (see paragraph 4.1 *Alteration of optional clauses of the memorandum*).

If there is conflict between the memorandum and the articles, the memorandum prevails: s9.

There are circumstances in which the court may order that an alteration be made to the memorandum, or that some existing part of the memorandum shall be unalterable. If such an order is made, eg in connection with an alteration of the objects clause under s5(6), the company cannot make an alteration thereafter to that part of its memorandum unless it first obtains leave of the court.

On the procedure for alteration of the memorandum see paragraph 4.1. Whenever the memorandum is altered the company must within 15 days deliver to the registry a copy of the memorandum in its altered form: s18. The same requirement applies to an alteration of the articles.

Every member is entitled, on request and payment of a small fee if demanded, to receive from the company a copy of the memorandum and articles (including all alterations made up to that time): ss19–20.

The memorandum and articles have effect, for certain purposes, as a contract under seal binding on the company and on its members: s14. That topic is considered in the next chapter in connection with the articles (see paragraph 3.1 *The articles and contracts with the company*).

Some elements of the memorandum, such as the limited liability of members, the authorised capital and the special features of the memorandum of a public company are dealt with in their context in paragraph 1.4. The remainder of this section deals with the name of the company and related subjects. The next section (paragraph 2.3) deals with the objects clause and the now limited effect of the ultra vires doctrine.

Company names – formal requirements

Part I Chapter 2 (ss25–34) of the Companies Act 1985 contains the statutory provisions relating to company names. A company which carries on business under a name other than its registered company name must also comply with the Business Names Act 1985 (see paragraph 2.2 *Business names*).

From the time of its incorporation a company has a name (and also a serial number – s705) by which it is identified in the register of companies at the registry and this name is shown in its memorandum and on its certificate of incorporation (or a certificate of re-registration following change of name). The name and number must appear on all documents delivered to the registry by or on behalf of the company and the company must display the name for certain purposes (see paragraph 2.2 *Display of company names*). It is one of the means by which persons dealing with the company can identify and distinguish it from other companies.

A company is generally required to include, as the final word or words of its name, an indication that the liability of its members is limited (see paragraph 1.2 *Limited liability*). Obviously this requirement does not apply to an unlimited company. One type of limited company may be exempt (see paragraph 2.2 *Omission of the word 'Limited' from a company name*) from the normal requirement.

The word(s) to be used (to disclose limited liability) are:

1. the name of a public company must end with the words 'public limited company' or its abbreviation 'plc';
2. the name of a private limited company must end with the word 'limited' or its abbreviation 'ltd', unless it is in the exempt category (see paragraph 2.2 *Omission of the word 'Limited' from a company name*).

A Welsh company (see paragraph 1.4 *Other types of company*) is permitted to use the Welsh equivalents: s25.

A company may not use these words elsewhere in its name than at the end. It is an offence for any person who is not a limited company to use 'Ltd', 'plc' etc, in his business name: ss33–34.

Similar names

The most significant restriction on choice of company names is the prohibition against the use of a name which is the same (disregarding minor differences such as 'and' and '&') as that of another company already on the register: s26(1).

There is also a procedure by which the registrar may require a company to change its name, within 12 months of registration of an original or altered name, if he finds it to be the same or 'too like' the name of another company: s28(2). In practice this power is generally exercised as a result of an appeal by the other company to the registrar following its discovery that confusion has or may arise between them. It is his practice then to invite both companies to submit to him a written statement of their case before he takes his decision. The time limit of 12 months safeguards a company from being required to alter a name which it has used without objection for more than a year.

Any person may sue a company in a common law 'passing off' action and it is no defence that the defendant company has been registered with the name which it uses and to which objection is now raised.

Misleading names

The DTI has statutory power to make regulations by which the inclusion of specified words in a company name requires special official approval: s29.

Until the present system was enacted in 1981 it was the registrar's practice to examine every proposed company name and to reject those which contravened certain criteria. This system was found unworkable and has been replaced by the selective control of the use of words which might mislead if used when not really appropriate to the company. Examples of words regulated under s29 are 'chamber of commerce', 'charitable', and 'post office'. These words, among many, have been listed and any company which wishes to include such a word or phrase in its name is required to apply for preliminary clearance. The same list of 'sensitive' words is used in the control of 'business names' (see paragraph 2.2 *Business names*).

No company may use a name which in the opinion of the DTI would constitute a criminal offence or be offensive: s26(1). It is said that a lady has been refused the company name of 'Prostitutes Ltd'.

In 1967 Parliament foisted on a reluctant DTI a statutory power by which it may require a company at any time to abandon a misleading name, if it is likely to cause harm to the public: s32. The company has a right of appeal to the court against such a direction. This power is hardly ever used since it is difficult to demonstrate that continued use of any name will cause harm to the public.

A rather different type of problem may arise when the directors of an insolvent company form a new company with almost the same name in order to take over the business of the insolvent company. This is colloquially called 'the phoenix syndrome' since the new company, like the mythical bird, arises from the ashes of the old. There are now statutory provisions to restrain this abuse: Insolvency Act 1986 s216 (see paragraph 13.4 *Creditors' voluntary winding up*).

The registrar has power to require an oversea company, ie a company incorporated outside Great Britain but with a place of business within it, to carry on business here under a different name: s694.

Change of company name

A company may by special resolution change its name: s28(1). However, the resolution does not of itself change the company's name. The company then applies to the registrar and, if he sees no objection, he issues a certificate of incorporation in the new name. The same general restrictions apply to the adoption of a new name by an existing company as to the name under which it may be incorporated (see paragraph 2.2 *Company names – formal requirements* to *Misleading names*).

The statutory powers to require a change of name on grounds of similarity and misleading the public have already been mentioned. There is a similar power, exercisable within five years, to require a company to change its name if it is later found that the company, in securing the registration of its name, gave false information or undertakings which it has failed to observe: s28(3). The cost of changing the name of a company is now £20. This was reduced from £50, by the Companies (Fees) (Amendment) Regulations 1994 (SI 1994/2217).

Omission of the word 'Limited' from a company name

These provisions apply to a company which satisfies all the following conditions:

1. it is a company limited by guarantee (or a private company limited by shares to which this exemption had been granted under the system in force up to 1982);

2. its objects are the promotion of any of the following: commerce, art, science, education, religion, charity or a profession, or matters conducive to any such object;
3. its memorandum or articles require its profits or other income to be applied to its objects (so that it cannot pay dividends) and require that in a winding up its assets, otherwise distributable to members, shall be transferred to a similar or charitable body, s30.

To obtain the exemption the company delivers to the registry a statutory declaration, usually by the directors, of its eligibility under the above conditions. There are safeguards which would entail withdrawal of the exemption in case of abuse.

A company which is a designated agency may also be exempt from using the word 'limited' as part of its name: see Financial Services Act 1986, s116, Schedule 9, para 2(1).

Display of company name

In brief a company is required to display its registered name in its correct form in the following places:

1. on its letterheads and other business stationery and forms;
2. on its cheques (see, eg, *Rafsanjan Pistachio Producers Co-operative* v *S Reiss* [1990] BCLC 352), promissory notes, bills of exchange, orders for goods or money: s349;
3. in a conspicuous position and in easily legible lettering outside every office and place of business: s348;
4. on its common seal: s350 (see paragraph 3.2 *The common seal and other seals*).

As to charitable companies, see 2.3 *Charitable Companies*, below.

The penalty for failure to comply is that the company officer in default is liable to a fine and, in respect of the documents in (2) above he is personally liable unless the company discharges the obligation arising from it. Most of the case law relates to those situations.

Nowadays banks issue cheque forms on which the name of a company customer is preprinted in the correct form. This practice greatly reduces the risk of error and consequent liability. The earlier case law establishes that a company officer who signs (for the company) any bill of exchange which does not include the correct company name, eg omitting the word 'limited', is personally liable: *Penrose* v *Martyr* (1858) EB & E 499. The requirement to display the company name still produces modern case law, for example in *Blum* v *OCP Repartition SA* (1988) 4 BCC 771 a director was held personally liable on seven cheques which omitted the word 'limited'. This was followed in the *Rafsanjan* case above in which a director was again held personally liable on a cheque contained in a temporary cheque book, which had an account number but no company name at all.

However, in recent times the courts have exonerated the company director who signed, as acceptor, a bill of exchange on which the drawer had inserted the company name in an incorrect form: *Durham Fancy Goods Ltd* v *Michael Jackson (Fancy Goods) Ltd* [1968] 2 All ER 987. However, in *Lindholst & Co A/S* v *Fowler & Anor* (1988) 4 BCC 776, Donaldson MR who was the trial judge in *Durham Fancy Goods*, held a director liable on four bills of exchange to the sum of £170,000 odd pounds, despite the fact that the bills, which did not have the word 'limited' on them, were prepared by the plaintiffs. The case was however distinguished on its facts.

Company letterheads, etc

Although the statutory requirements for particulars on company business stationery etc are not confined to the inclusion of the company name in its correct form, it is convenient to deal with these particulars as a whole at this point. These provisions are derived from a European Community Directive.

The following requirements relate to 'business letters and order forms of the company': s351. There is some doubt as to whether 'order forms' means orders issued by the company to its suppliers or by its customers to the company, eg coupons detached from advertisements published by the company in newspapers. It is safest, since the DTI inclines to the latter interpretation, to assume that both fall under the rule.

The particulars to be given are as follows:

1. the place of registration, ie whether in England and Wales or in Scotland. This is a guide to the address of the Companies Registration Office which holds the file relating to the company if a company search is required;
2. the serial number under which the company is registered at the registry;
3. the address of the registered office, which must be identified as such;
4. if the company is permitted to omit 'limited' from its name, the fact that it is a limited company;
5. if it is an investment company (to which special rules apply in determining its distributable profits (see paragraph 6.5 *Distributable profits of public companies*) or a charitable company (not identified as such by its name (see paragraph 2.3 *Charitable companies*) the fact that it is such a company.

Business names

The Business Names Act 1985 re-enacts provisions which originally appeared in the Companies Act 1981 but they are not confined in their operation to companies. Any person (company, sole trader or partnership) who carries on business under a name other than his own, ie other than the registered company name in the case of a company, must comply with these requirements. If say H P Smith (Provisions) Ltd trades as High Street Grocers it must:

1. state its registered company name (as well as its business name) on its business letters and other commercial stationery. It would have to do this in any event to comply with company law (see paragraph 2.2 *Display of company name*);
2. display its company name in a prominent position on all premises where the company business is carried on, if the public has access to those premises. This too is a company law requirement for every company (see paragraph 2.2 *Display of company name*).

In addition the company must in all those contexts give an address in Great Britain at which any document such as a legal notice may be effectually served on the company. This address would ordinarily be the registered office of the company, and this also has to be displayed (see paragraph 3.2 *Registered office*). There are some other minor contingent requirements.

The same list of 'sensitive' words applies to business as to company names (see paragraph 2.2 *Misleading names*). This is partly to prevent a company which has failed to secure the company name of its choice from getting round the prohibition by using a 'business name' in addition to, and with greater prominence than, its company name. If, for example, it wishes to call itself 'Royal' or 'International' (both are in the list) its necessary application for permission to adopt such a business name would fail if, as is likely, its attempt to register with a company name in this style had been rejected.

2.3 The objects clause

Contractual capacity

Every company is required in its memorandum to 'state the objects of the company': s2(1). If the company enters into a transaction which exceeds the limits, express or implied, set by its declared objects, the transaction may in some instances be void or voidable. This principle, known as the ultra vires doctrine, now has a very much reduced effect on the company's capacity to enter into binding contracts by reason of ss35–35B (enacted by s108 and some related provisions of CA 1989 on the basis of the Prentice Report). But a company is still required to have an objects clause in its memorandum, mainly for the purpose of defining the authority of the directors and other agents of the company to represent it in making contracts on its behalf. By its nature, as an artificial person, a company can never make its contracts in person.

An objects clause may now state merely that 'the object of the company is to carry on business as a general commercial company'. It then has power to carry on any trade or business whatsoever and to do anything incidental or conducive to carrying on any trade or business: s3A. In effect an objects clause in this form confers unlimited capacity on the company and unlimited authority on its agents to contract for it. It will often be a convenient short form of objects clause for a small private company whose shareholders are also its directors.

However many companies will continue to have objects clauses which define in detail their commercial activities and the transactions into which it is intended they should enter. Such a definition will no longer provide grounds for asserting that the company itself lacks capacity: s35(1). It will however continue to limit the powers of management delegated to the directors (see paragraph 8.2 *The directors' general powers of management*). When such issues arise, the first question for consideration is always what the objects clause means and implies.

As an example in *Rolled Steel Products (Holdings) Ltd* v *British Steel Corporation* [1985] 2 WLR 908 CA the Court of Appeal decided that a power to give guarantees of the debts of other persons 'as may seem expedient' limited the power to guarantees given to benefit the company.

Although a full length objects clause includes a series of express powers, eg to borrow money or to hold shares in other companies, there may be no express power applicable to a transaction and the question will arise whether such a power is to be implied as incidental to the declared objects. As an example an express object covering sale of by-products of a manufacturing process implies a power to purchase materials needed to prepare the by-products for sale: *Deuchar* v *Gas Light and Coal Co* [1925] AC 691.

A long objects clause begins with two or three paragraphs stating the main objects and then specifies some twenty or so additional standard powers (to enter into transactions) to avoid the uncertainty of mere implied powers. On general principles of construction it has been argued, in some of the older cases, that the main objects imply limits on any subsequent paragraphs. Thus a main object of operating a specified mine in India could imply a limitation that subsequent objects and powers related only to other mining activities in India and did not authorise mining outside India: *Stephens* v *Mysore Reefs (Kangundy) Mining Co Ltd* [1902] 1 Ch 745. However more recent decisions, such as *Re Kitson & Co* [1946] 1 All ER 435, adopted a less restrictive approach.

To avoid the risk of being restricted in this way draftsmen sometimes adopted the device of including in an objects clause a declaration that no object should be 'in any way limited by reference to or inference from the terms of any other paragraph'. The House of Lords recognised that in suitable cases such a statement of intent should be accepted in construing the objects clause: *Cotman* v *Brougham* [1918] AC 514. But this formula will not suffice to give independent status to a power which by its nature is subordinate. Thus a power to borrow money must be limited to borrowing for the commercial objects set out in the opening paragraphs of the clause, notwithstanding a *Cotman* v *Brougham* declaration: *Re Introductions Ltd* [1970] Ch 199.

Another useful, but entirely optional, drafting device is to state the first commercial object in sufficiently exact terms but to follow it with a power 'to carry on any other trade or business which can in the opinion of the directors, be advantageously carried on by the company in connection with or as ancillary to any of the above businesses or the general business of the company'. Thus a company which acquires valuable knowledge in its primary business may, under this formula, carry on the ancillary business activity of selling its knowledge to others: *Bell Houses Ltd* v *City Wall Properties Ltd* [1966] 2 QB 656. But there must of course be a primary business to which the ancillary business may be attached, however subjective a judgment of the directors it may be to connect them. The *Bell Houses* formula does not give as much flexibility as the object of being a 'general commercial company' under the new statutory provision mentioned above: s3A.

A company whose objects involve it in entering into contracts which are sexually immoral and therefore illegal and unenforceable will be struck off the register: *R* v *Register of Companies, ex parte Attorney-General* [1991] BCLC 476.

Validity of transactions

If it is established that the objects clause does not provide the required authority, that fact no longer affords grounds for asserting that the company itself lacks capacity to enter into the transaction: s35(1). Thus the company itself may benefit from this saving provision, if it wishes to enforce its rights under a transaction beyond the limits set by its objects clause. In the *Bell Houses* case the defendant company argued, though without success on the facts, that it would not be liable to pay an agreed fee if the transaction itself was *ultra vires* the plaintiff company. That defence is now effectually abolished by s35(1).

The other party to a transaction, which is now found to be beyond the limits set by the company's objects clause, is likewise not prejudiced by the company's mere lack of capacity. But, to enforce his claim, he has also to show that the directors, or other agent acting under their authority, could in the circumstances commit the company to a binding contract. To succeed in this he must have dealt with the company 'in good faith': s35A(1).

This test of 'good faith' was first introduced by s9(1) of the European Communities Act 1972 but there has been no judicial decision on its meaning. It is derived from the EC First Directive which refers to knowledge of the limitation of capacity as a bar to giving protection. However the 'good faith' test probably excludes the person who, without having actual notice, chooses to disregard circumstances of suspicion and does not make 'such enquiries as ought reasonably to be made' (see (4) below). It is probable that a person who has read the relevant part of the objects clause but has misunderstood its effect would be deemed to have acted in good faith; this was the situation in the *Introductions* case in paragraph 2.3 *Contractual capacity*.

The following specific provisions give additional safeguards to a person who seeks to rely on the basic protection given by s35A(1):

1. His good faith is presumed until the contract is proved: s35A(2)(c).
2. His mere knowledge that the directors are exceeding their powers is not by itself proof of bad faith: s35A(2)(b).

3. He is not bound to inspect the memorandum or articles to discover whether there are relevant limitations on the capacity of the company or the authority of the directors: s35B(1).

4. He is not affected by constructive notice of any such limitation merely because the memorandum and articles are available for inspection at the registry: s711A. But this provision does not absolve him from making 'such enquiries as ought reasonably to be made': ibid.

To sum up a state of honest ignorance of the relevant limitations of the company's constitution will not prevent the person concerned from enforcing his rights. But evidence of dishonesty of some sort will do so.

Section 35A(1) refers to 'the power of the directors to bind the company, or authorise others to do so'. This formula avoids the uncertainty, inherent in the original 1972 version, as to whether a person dealing with a single director or with some employee or agent of the company can rely on s35A(1). Thus if the directors leave the management of the company in the hands of one director that is an implied authorisation: *International Sales and Agencies Ltd* v *Marcus* [1982] 3 All ER 551.

Some articles, including the 1985 Table A model articles (paragraph 8.2 *The Directors' general powers of management*) empower the company in general meeting to issue 'directions' as to the exercise of powers of management delegated to the directors. If such directions have been issued, the position of a person dealing with the company and claiming that he did so 'in good faith' is the same as if the relevant limitation was found in the memorandum or articles: s35A(3).

Management of the company

It is the duty of the directors to observe any limitation of their powers which flows from the company's memorandum. But if they have taken action which but for s35(1) (see paragraph 2.3 *Contractual capacity*) would be beyond the company's capacity, the company in general meeting may by passing a special resolution ratify it: s35(3).

The directors are not exonerated by the ratification of their action, but the company may by a separate special resolution relieve the directors or any other person of liability arising from what they have done: ibid.

Any member may bring proceedings to restrain the doing of an act which, but for s35(1), would be beyond the company's capacity. However no such proceedings may be taken in respect of an act to be done in fulfilment of a legal obligation arising from a previous act of the company: s35(2). As an example, if the directors borrow money for a purpose which is within the company's capacity, a member may apply to the court to restrain them from using the money for an unauthorised purpose, but not to prevent them from repaying the loan, in accordance with the terms of the loan contract, if the money has already been misapplied.

Invalid transactions of directors

A director has a fiduciary duty to avoid placing himself in a situation in which there is a conflict of interest between himself and the company, but there are procedures by which he may be permitted to do so. The board of directors has a duty not to exceed its powers (see paragraph 9.2 *The directors' duties*). The general effect of the new s322A which deals with these duties in combination is explained later in connection with the duties of directors generally (see paragraphs 9.1 *Directors' transactions* and 9.3 *Conflict of interest*). It does safeguard the rights of a third party who is ignorant of a breach of these duties in a transaction in which he has acted in good faith and has given value.

The ultra vires principle and CA 1989

The changes summarised in paragraph 2.3 *Contractual capacity* to *Invalid transactions of directors* are a compromise between conflicting considerations. In 1875 the House of Lords held that the ultra vires doctrine applied to the powers of registered companies, so that a transaction which exceeded the express and implied limits of the objects clause was void and unenforceable: *Ashbury Railway Carriage and Iron Co Ltd* v *Riche* (1875) LR 7 HL 653.

Over the next century it became clear that more harm than good to all concerned followed from this principle. Creditors of the company could suffer loss; directors might incur personal liability for breach of duty; shareholders and the company itself were often in a most uncertain position. Yet all this could happen as a result of an innocent oversight or misunderstanding of the objects clause.

It would have been possible simply to abrogate the doctrine of limited powers in relation to registered companies (it does not apply to chartered companies) and confer on registered companies an unrestricted capacity to enter into contracts. But this would exacerbate other problems inherent in the necessary system of management of companies by directors.

The general purpose and effect of the changes which now appear in ss35–35B is:

1. to confer on the company itself an unrestricted contractual capacity, by which the company itself is enabled to enforce its rights under a transaction which would otherwise be beyond its capacity: s35(1);
2. to give to a person who deals with a company through its directors or other representatives acting under their authority enforceable rights in such a transaction, subject to the 'good faith' test. If however he is aware that the transaction exceeds the limits of the objects clause or that the directors etc are exceeding their authority he does not have a protection which he does not deserve: s35A(1);
3. to retain as part of the company's written constitution an objects clause which (taken with the articles – see paragraph 8.2 *The directors' general powers of management*) serves to define the directors' authority to make contracts for the

company and gives to members a power to restrain them, and if necessary to call them to account, if they propose, or have already exceeded, their authority: s35A(4).

A regulatory structure of this kind serves little purpose however if the members of the company are also its directors, or if the shareholders entirely approve of the directors' policy in exceeding the limits of the objects clause. The provisions for adopting the object of carrying on business as 'a general commercial company' and for ratification and exoneration where directors exceed their authority provide a simple solution if the members of the company find it convenient to resort to them.

Problems of a rather different nature may arise over disposal of the property of a company, either because its main object is charitable or because it makes gifts, relying on express or implied powers to do so. The next two paragraphs deal with these topics.

Charitable companies

The law on charities is part of the law of trusts, supplemented by the Charities Act 1960, the Charities Act 1992 (as and when it is brought into force) and other statutes. A charity may be administered by trustees without bringing it under the provisions of company law. However many large charities find it convenient to carry on their work through companies, which are usually limited by guarantees and have in their memorandum restrictions against distribution of income or return of capital to shareholders which entitle the company to dispense with the word 'limited' in their names (see paragraph 2.2 *Omission of the word 'Limited' from a company name*).

The Prentice Report (Chapter VIII) drew attention to the fact that a charitable company is not a trustee of its assets. However the courts had already held that if a charitable company alters its constitution so that it ceases to be charitable, its property including income accumulated up to that point, must be applied under the original constitution to charitable purposes: *Liverpool and District Hospital for Diseases of the Heart* v *Attorney-General* [1981] 1 All ER 994. A new s30A(1) of the Charities Act, enacted by s111 CA 1989, puts that ruling on a statutory basis.

As a further safeguard, any alteration of the objects clause in a charitable company's memorandum of association, or of any other provision in its memorandum of association, or any provision in its articles of association, which is a provision directing or restricting the manner in which property of the company may be used or applied, is ineffective without the prior written consent of the Charity Commissioners. Where such a company has made any such alteration and in connection with the alteration is required by virtue of s6(1) of the 1985 Act (delivery of documents following alteration of objects), or that provision as applied by s17(3) of that Act (alteration of condition in memorandum which could have been contained in articles), to deliver to the registrar of companies a printed copy of its memorandum, as altered, or is required by virtue of s380(1) of the Act (registration etc of resolutions and agreements) to forward to the registrar a printed or other copy of the special resolution effecting the alteration, the copy so delivered or forwarded by the company must be accompanied by a copy of the Commissioners' consent. Section 6(3) of the 1985 Act (offences) applies to any default by a company in complying with these requirements as it applies to any such default as is mentioned in that provision: s30A(2), (3) of the 1960 Act as substituted by s40 of the Charities Act 1992.

To claim the safeguards arising from ss35 and 35A (see paragraph 2.3 *Contractual capacity* to *Invalid transactions of directors*) a person dealing with a charitable company must show that:

1. he gave full consideration in money or money's worth; and
2. he did not know that the act of the company was beyond the limits set by the objects clause of the company or, as the case may be, beyond the delegated authority of the directors.

As an alternative to the above conditions he may rely on the fact that at the time he did not know that the company was charitable. As to dispositions of charity land, see ss32 and 33 of 1992 Act.

A special resolution to ratify a transaction or to relieve the directors of a charitable company of liability (see paragraph 2.3 *Management of the company*) is ineffective: s30B(4) Charities Act 1960. Section 41 of the 1992 Act adds s30BA to the 1960 Act, requiring the written consent of the Commissioners to certain acts, eg, a payment to a director in respect of loss of office or retirement under s312 of the Companies Act 1985.

A person to whom property acquired from the charitable company is later transferred has good title to it (in spite of any irregularities in the original transfer by the company) if he gives full consideration and has no notice of the irregularity.

Finally, a charitable company's name must appear on correspondence, etc (s30BB of the 1960 Act, as inserted by s42 of the 1992 Act) and, if its gross income in its last financial year exceeded £5,000, its status as a registered charity must appear on all of its official publications (including appeals, invoices and receipts): s3 of the 1992 Act (see paragraph 2.2 *Display of company name*).

Gifts by companies

The objects clause of any company may include an express power to make gifts, including the provision of benefits such as pensions or the acceptance of liabilities such as guarantees without receiving consideration for them.

Although the previous case law was somewhat confused, it has been established that the exercise of that power in a proper manner by the directors is valid: *Charterbridge Corporation Ltd* v *Lloyds Bank Ltd* [1969] 2 All ER 1185 and *Re Horsley & Weight Ltd* [1982] 3 WLR 431.

In the absence of a suitable express power it was more difficult to find authority, usually after the event, for making a gift. Such a power could only be implied if the gift could be said to be incidental and beneficial to the company's business: *Re Lee*

Behrens & Co Ltd [1932] 2 Ch 46) Thus to make a donation to research funds in the field of the company's business would satisfy the test: *Evans* v *Brunner Mond & Co Ltd* [1921] 1 Ch 359. The decision in the *Charterbridge* case was related to a guarantee given by company in respect of a debt of an associated company.

Much of the case law relates (as in the *Lee Behrens* and *Horsley & Weight* decisions) to the grant of a pension to a retired director or his widow, where it was difficult to show that the company could possibly benefit from this retrospective generosity. The *Roith* case (see paragraph 9.4 *Relief from liability*) provides an extreme example, where the arrangement was held invalid. On the other hand a gift to an employee on his retirement of an ex-gratia sum could be justified as part of a policy, from which the company might benefit in future, by sustaining the reputation of being an enlightened employer.

However no future benefit could be envisaged if the company, after selling or closing down its business, made payments to its now redundant employees: *Parke* v *Daily News* [1962] 2 All ER 929. To counter the unwelcome decision in *Parke*'s case as statutory power (s719) was given to all companies to make provision for employees or former employees, following the cessation or transfer of the company's business, even though the exercise of the power was not in the best interests of the company.

To sum up, either an express power in the objects clause, which can first be altered to create the power, or the statutory power (s719) will often provide the necessary sanction for a gift to or for the benefit of an employee, including a working director, or his dependants.

If the gift is for a purpose rather than for people (as in the *Brunner Mond* case) and it has some relevance, however general, to the company's business, there is an implied power to benefit the company's business in this way. But always pensions and other benefits for directors and their dependants approved by the board of directors will be more rigorously scrutinised, if it is not covered by an express power.

The Charity Commissioners, as well as the Attorney-General, may authorise the making of ex gratia payments by charity trustees in certain circumstances: see s23A of the Charities Act 1960, as inserted by s17 of the Charities Act 1992.

2.4 Torts and crimes

The company's liability

As a matter of principle, it is open to question whether a company can be liable for torts or crimes.

1. It is arguable that authority or power to commit torts or crimes cannot be included in the memorandum, therefore, since all torts and crimes will be ultra vires, the company cannot be liable for them. But obviously the law has not been prepared to grant companies immunity in these respects.

2. It has therefore been said that companies may incur tortious or criminal liability because the ultra vires rule only applies in cases of contract. Against this, it has been argued that an action in tort might be used in a case where an action for breach of contract on an ultra vires contract was not available. But such a possibility is not unknown in other areas of the law.

3. A suitable compromise is therefore to say that companies may be liable for crimes or torts committed during intra vires activities. But the issue is perhaps not so simple and depends not so much on the liability of the company in the abstract but on questions of vicarious liability and company agency – whether the acts of a servant are within the course of his employment or whether the acts of one of the company's organs or officers take effect as acts of the company itself.

Torts

So far as vicarious liability for torts is concerned, a company will be liable for a tort committed by a servant during an intra vires activity if the act comes within the scope of his employment, whether because it is expressly or impliedly authorised, or because it is incidental to the course of his employment. Similarly, the reasons underlying vicarious liability justify imposing liability on the company for authorising an ultra vires act of the servant: *Campbell* v *Paddington Corp* [1911] 1 KB 869. But a servant would not normally have implied authority to commit a tort during an ultra vires activity: *Poulton* v *LSWR Co* (1867) LR 2 QB 534.

Crimes

So far as criminal liability is concerned, three initial problems arise:

1. The scope of vicarious liability in criminal law is narrower than in the law of tort, since mens rea is a normal prerequisite to liability.

2. A central problem is usually in deciding not so much for whose acts the company is liable but whose acts take effect as acts of the company itself for which it is directly liable (albeit the actor may in turn be liable to his company for so making it liable) – the question to ask is, who is really the directing mind and will of the corporation: *Lennard's Carrying Co* v *Asiatic Petroleum Co Ltd* [1915] AC 705.

3. The imposition of liability may be a question not so much of company law but of statutory interpretation in giving effect to the policy underlying the offence.

In general the company will be directly liable for any offence committed by a person who has control over the management of the company's affairs. This may be because the actual perpetrator of the crime is an organ of the company in the sense described in paragraph 9.1 (eg the board of directors or the managing director). But it is perhaps more likely that the criminal is merely an agent of the company (eg a member of the board of directors). The important point is his status. A company is not to be fixed with the knowledge of any servant: *John Henshall (Quarries) Ltd* v

Harvey [1965] 2 QB 233; contrast the scope of a company's 'knowledge' in civil matters: *Stanfield Properties Ltd* v *National Westminster Bank plc* [1983] 1 WLR 568.

Following the lead in *Lennard's* case companies have been held guilty of intent to deceive: *DPP* v *Kent and Sussex Contractors Ltd* [1944] KB 146; *Moore* v *Bresler Ltd* [1944] 2 All ER 515; and of conspiracy to defraud *R* v *ICR Haulage Ltd* [1944] KB 551. The company having a separate legal personality, it can conspire with its responsible officers but Nield J decided in *R* v *MacDonnell* [1966] 1 QB 233 that it would be extending conspiracy too far to say that a company could conspire with its sole director, so that the two conspirators were one and the same. And a company has been said not to have conspired with its directors where the company was the victim of the conspiracy: *Belmont Finance Corporation Ltd* v *Williams Furniture Ltd* [1979] 1 All ER 118.

It follows, of course, from what has been said, that the company will not automatically be liable for acts of all its officers or employees. Thus, in *Tesco Supermarkets Ltd* v *Nattrass* [1972] AC 153, the House of Lords gave effect to an otherwise illusory defence where an assistant had placed on display articles for sale in contravention of the Trade Descriptions Act 1968, by holding that the 'commission of the offence was due to ... the act or default of another person'. It may be noted that the Act also expressly extended liability in certain cases to any director, manager, secretary or other similar offence where an offence committed by a body corporate had been committed with his consent or connivance. The prosecution against the company will fail if the actor did not control the management of the company affairs: *R* v *Andrews Weatherfoil Ltd* [1972] 1 WLR 118.

2.5 Liability for acts of officers and agents

Introduction

We have seen that there are certain circumstances in which a company may incur liability (ie for contracts, torts and crimes). This may be because the company itself has committed an act, through one of its organs, the constitutional position of which (see paragraph 9.1) means that its acts are the acts of the company (see *Lennard's* case above). More likely, an act will be done on behalf of the company not by an organ but by a servant or agent. Whether or not such an act will make the company liable depends on the power of the company to act in such a situation (the ultra vires rule and its exceptions) and on whether or not the person acting is capable of binding the company, which is the point we must consider now.

The issue is basically one of the law of agency so far as it is applicable in the context of company law. (A principal (here, the company) will be liable for the acts of his agent if the latter is acting within his express, implied, ostensible (apparent) or usual authority, or where his actions have been ratified by the principal) (see also paragraph 2.3 *Gifts by companies*).

The following case is an example of the law of agency being used in a company law context, although on the facts liability did not attach to the company or its directors. In *New Zealand Guardian Trust Co Ltd* v *Kenneth Stewart Brooks and Others* [1995] 1 WLR 96, the Privy Council held that a company was vicariously liable for the negligence of its directors in preparing 'reporting certificates' for a trustee representing lenders. The certificates had to state, inter alia, whether any matters had arisen which would affect the position of the lenders. Lord Keith said that in preparing the certificates the directors had been acting as the company's agents within the scope of their authority. The company and the directors were joint tortfeasors, so that when the trustee accepted less than the amount due in full satisfaction of the company's outstanding debt, this also released the directors from any further liability. As such, the Privy Council was satisfied that the directors had properly been struck out as third parties to the proceedings. See Chapter 15, paragraph 15.2, for further details.

Who is an agent?

It is for the company to decide whom it wishes to act on its behalf and whom it wishes to appoint as agents. Some persons, namely the directors, will be assumed to have authority because of their position. The liquidator is agent of a company in the course of winding up. Others must normally be expressly appointed. Until recently it was assumed that a company secretary only had ministerial or administrative functions, having a supportive rather than a managerial, controlling role. However, it has now been recognised that the modern company secretary is more than a servant and his extensive duties and responsibilities, having at the least ostensible authority to enter into contracts regarding the administrative side of company affairs: *Panorama Developments (Guilford) Ltd* v *Fidelis Furnishing Fabrics Ltd* [1971] 2 QB 711. Now the Act sets standards of qualification, knowledge and experience for the secretary of a public company: s286. Furthermore, paragraph 1.6 of the Cadbury Code of Best Practice (see paragraph 9.1 *The Cadbury Committee*) provides that:

> 'All directors should have access to the advice and services of the company secretary, who is responsible to the board for ensuring that board procedures are followed and that applicable rules and regulations are complied with. Any removal of the company secretary should be a matter for the board as a whole.'

In *First Energy (UK) Ltd* v *Hungarian International Bank Ltd* [1993] BCC 533, the Court of Appeal held that a senior manager of the defendant bank had ostensible authority to communicate head office approval of a loan facility to the plaintiffs.

The indoor management rule

This expression means that a person dealing with a company is deemed to know (by constructive notice) of any procedural requirements contained in the company's articles. However, he is also entitled to assume, unless he knows or has reason to suspect the contrary, that the company has correctly carried out any internal procedure which he has no means of investigating.

The rule is also associated with *Royal British Bank* v *Turquand* (1855) 5 E & B 248 and is known as 'the rule in *Turquand*'s case'. The case itself provides a good illustration of the effect of the rule. The articles provided that the directors might borrow whatever amounts the company in general meeting had authorised. A general meeting passed a resolution which authorised the directors to borrow but did not specify any amount. Accordingly it was quite ineffective. However, it was an ordinary resolution of a type which the company is not required to deliver to the registry for filing (see paragraph 2.1 *Registration* and paragraph 8.1 *Registration and publicity*). The bank had no means of discovering, by a search at the registry, what were the terms of the resolution. It did not make any direct enquiries of the company nor had it any obligation to do so. It lent the company £2,000. In the liquidation of the company, the liquidator (Turquand) repudiated the loan agreement as made without authority.

The court held that the bank must be presumed to know that the directors needed the authority but, in these circumstances, was entitled to assume without enquiry that the authority had been properly given. So the loan agreement was valid.

The same principle is applied to other irregularities of internal procedure. If a board decision is invalid because there was no quorum present, or because the directors had not been properly appointed (*Mahony*'s case in paragraph 2.5 *Holding out*), the other party may nonetheless hold the company bound. The importance of this rule has largely disappeared now that s35 has much the same effect.

One of the problem areas is where a single director, who might have been appointed a managing director or otherwise given authority, in fact lacks it. Section 35 probably does not apply. It has also been held that the presumption raised by the indoor management rule does not extend to assuming that a single director has been given authority, merely because it was possible for the board to do so: *Houghton & Co* v *Nothard, Lowe & Wills* [1927] 1 KB 246.

The other point to be kept in mind is the distinction of principle between the indoor management rule and liability by 'holding out' a person as agent (see paragraph 2.5 *Holding out*).

The indoor management rule, when it applies, does not require any form of 'holding out' by the company. It is simply a presumption that the company observes its own rules of procedure. Holding out does require some form of representation though it may be no more than passive acquiescence with knowledge of what is going on.

Holding out

If a person has been properly appointed as an agent of the company, the company will be liable for acts he does within the scope of his authority.

However, to be liable for the acts of someone not properly appointed, the company must by one of its organs or a properly authorised officer, have held out the agent as authorised to act so as to bind it. But the law has not been strict about the capacity of an organ or officer to hold out another as an agent. Thus, persons permitted to act as directors without formal appointment have bound their company: *Mahony* v *East Holyford Mining Co* (1875) LR 7 HL 869; s285 provides that the acts of a director of manager shall be valid notwithstanding any defect that may afterwards be discovered in his appointment or qualification and s382 provides that, until the contrary is proved, minuted meetings of the members or directors will be deemed to be duly held and appointments of directors and managers deemed to be valid. But these rules will not avail the third party where there is no appointment at all as opposed to an appointment which is defective: *Morris* v *Kanssen* [1946] AC 459. Furthermore, s285 only validates defects in the initial appointment of directors.

To entitle a contractor to rely on holding out in order to enforce against a company a contract entered into on its behalf by an agent who had no authority to do so, four conditions must be shown (*Freeman & Lockyer* v *Buckhurst Park Properties (Mangal) Ltd* [1964] 2 QB 480):

1. that a representation that the agent had authority to enter on behalf of the company into a contract of the kind sought to be enforced was made to the contractor;
2. that such a representation was made by a person or persons who had actual authority to manage the business of the company either generally or in respect of those matters to which the contract relates (the contractor cannot rely on the agent's own representation as to his actual authority);
3. that the contractor was induced by such representation to enter into the contract (ie he in fact relied on it); and
4. that under its regulations the company was not deprived of the capacity either to enter into a contract of the kind sought to be enforced or to delegate authority to enter into a contract of that kind to the agent (unless the contractor can take advantage of the provisions of s35 so that he is not affected by constructive notice of the regulations).

Knowledge of the other contracting party

Where a transaction is decided on by the directors, the third party who can otherwise satisfy the provisions of s35 will be able to enforce the contract despite limitations as to capacity and authority in the regulations.

The fourth of the above conditions was based on the common law doctrine of constructive notice of documents available for inspection on the company's file at the registry. That doctrine however no longer applies to the memorandum or articles (paragraph 2.1 *Registration* and paragraph 2.3 *Validity of trnsactions*).

There is more doubt over the position of a person who inspects the articles of the company and thereby discovers that, for purposes of the transaction, the directors require authority by special resolution and notes that no such resolution has been filed, as it should be in compliance with s380(4)(a). These were the facts in *Irvine* v *Union Bank of Australasia* (1877) 2 App Cas 366. This is a situation where arguably 'inquiries ought reasonably to be made': s711A(2). If that is so then the person who does not seek an explanation of the absence from the file of the special resolution, of which he has actual notice, either has constructive notice of the directors' want of authority or he is not acting in good faith. Either factor prevents him from holding the company bound.

False documents

Just as an agent cannot clothe himself with any authority, so a forged document which purports to be sealed by or signed on behalf of the company will not, without more, bind it: *Ruben* v *Great Fingall Consolidated* [1906] AC 439.

But if an agent of the company acting with authority (of whatever kind) represents it as a company document, the company will be bound by it: cf *Lloyd* v *Grace, Smith & Co* [1912] AC 716.

Finally, in favour of a purchaser of property a deed shall be deemed to have been duly executed by a corporation if its seal be affixed thereto in the presence of and attested to by its secretary and a member of the board of directors: s74(1) Law of Property Act 1925.

Agent's liability and ratification

An unauthorised agent who succeeds in making his company liable will be liable to indemnify it. If the third party cannot enforce the contract against the company, he may be able to proceed against the agent for breach of warranty of authority.

But in either case, the company may (subject to the ultra vires rule) ratify (ie validate ex post facto) the unauthorised acts.

3

Articles of Association

3.1 The articles of association

3.2 Registered office and statutory registers

3.1 The articles of association

Introduction

Every company must have articles of association ('the articles' hereafter). A company limited by shares has some choice in the matter. It may either adopt its own articles or adopt the statutory model articles (Table A) instead.

The articles must be printed and divided into numbered paragraphs. If the documents presented to form the company include its articles (instead of letting Table A take their place) those original articles must be signed by the subscribers to the memorandum, with similar formalities of witness and date. Any subsequent version of the articles in altered form derives its validity from a special resolution passed in general meeting and so it does not need to be signed for that purpose. The chairman of the meeting usually signs, at the top of the first page, the copy delivered to the registrar, for purposes of identification only.

The word 'printed' is flexibly interpreted to include copies reproduced by duplicator, photostat or electrostatic ('xerox') copying and some other like methods. However, the registrar will not accept a typed document as 'printed'.

The articles are regulations of the company on such matters as the issue of shares, the convening and conduct of general meetings, the appointment and powers of directors, the payment of dividends and the issue of notices to members. Obviously these matters are of interest to the members. They may also be of concern to outsiders; eg a lender to the company will wish to know whether any limit has been placed by the articles on the directors' borrowing powers.

An article which operates to fetter a statutory power of the company to alter its articles is invalid: *Russell* v *Northern Bank Development Corporation Ltd* [1992] 1 WLR 588. This case is discussed further in paragraph 4.2 *Alteration of the articles*.

Table A and other model articles

Every major Companies Act since 1862 has provided a model set of articles (Table A for a company limited by shares). The Companies Act 1985 differs from earlier Acts by providing its Table A in separate regulations and not as a schedule to the Act itself.

The date of formation of a company determines which version of Table A is applicable to it. For example, companies formed between 1929 and 1948 are subject to the Table A of the 1929 Act.

However, a company is free to exclude Table A altogether and adopt in its place 'special' articles adapted to its needs. Most public companies follow that procedure since Table A does not contain many of the additional clauses which are required by stock exchanges as a condition of permitting dealings in the securities of such companies.

Private companies, on the other hand, usually find it convenient to adopt Table A, with some exclusions and modifications. In these cases there are 'short articles' which state that a specified Table A will be the articles, subject only to the modifications set out below. This saves money on drafting and printing costs.

Even where a company has its own 'special', full-length articles, its text usually includes a great deal of Table A standard material, since it has been tested and interpreted in the courts and it is familiar, well understood legal language. For examination purposes it may be assumed that questions will usually be set on Table A articles. A sound knowledge of these articles is useful but it is not necessary to memorise them.

The majority of existing companies were formed before mid-1985 and so they will have articles on the model of the 1948 Table A, unless they have had occasion to up-date their articles by adopting the 1985 model instead. This distinction is important. The 1985 Table A resulted from a thorough revision, undertaken by the legal profession as advisers to the DTI. There are considerable differences between the 1985 and earlier versions.

The aim of the 1985 Table A is to provide only basic common-form provisions for general use. As almost all companies adopt their own articles, in short or full form, they can then add on whatever extra provisions they deem necessary. For example, the 1985 Table A does not contain an article limiting the borrowing powers of the directors. Many companies do require such a limit and they are free to retain the 1948 Table A art 79 (although it is rather badly worded) or to adopt some other formula of their choice.

Companies limited by guarantee, with and without share capital, and unlimited companies have statutory model articles, closely related to Table A, in Tables C, D and E, which they must follow by adopting articles 'as near to that form as circumstances admit': s8(4). But they must, on incorporation, be registered with their own articles, in whatever form.

Regulations may be made to add a new Table G containing model articles for a partnership company, ie a company limited by shares whose shares are intended to be held to a substantial extent by or for its employees: s8A.

The effect of the memorandum and articles

Section 14 provides:

> 'Subject to the provisions of this Act, the memorandum and articles shall, when registered, bind the company and the members thereof to the same extent as if they respectively had been signed and sealed by each member, and contained convenants on the part of each member to observe all the provisions of the memorandum and of the articles.'

The memorandum prevails over the articles where they are in conflict with each other: *Re Duncan Gilmour* [1952] 2 All ER 817.

The effect of s14 is to create a binding obligation on the members in their dealings with the company, between the members themselves and on the company in its dealings with the members. Those who are not members cannot enforce the provisions either against the company or for themselves and a member cannot enforce the provisions for his benefit in some other capacity than that of member.

Section 14 then, has contractual effect, however it is unlike an ordinary contract in that its terms may be altered without the agreement of all the parties. Section 9 allows the articles to be altered by the passing of a special resolution, which only requires a 75 per cent majority. Also the normal contractual remedies are not available. In particular the remedy of rectification is not allowed. The reason for this seems to be that the s14 contract is a statutory contract and the statute, the CA 1985, provides the only way to alter the articles, and that is under s9: *Scott v Frank F Scott (London) Ltd* [1940] Ch 794.

It is also not possible to imply a term into the articles in order to give them business efficacy, which of course is possible in a normal contract: *Bratten Seymour Service Co Ltd v Oxborough* [1992] BCC 476. It had been thought that damages too were not available for a breach of s14 on the basis of *Houldsworth v City of Glasgow Bank* (1880) 5 App Cas 317. This decision has now though been reversed by s111A so that damages may now well be recoverable. Practically, the two most sought after remedies in relation to the articles are declarations and injunctions.

Contract between the members inter se

Although s14 does not expressly impose an obligation on members in their dealings with each other, it is treated as a contract between them which is enforceable under normal principles of contract law. The leading case here is *Rayfield v Hands* [1960] Ch 1 where the articles required the directors (1) to hold at least one share (so that necessarily they were also members) and (2) to buy the shares of any member who might wish to sell them. The plaintiff was a shareholder who sought to enforce the directors' obligation to buy his shares. The court held that this obligation, as between members, was enforceable under s14. In practice this issue is usually avoided by providing in the articles that the company, whose position under s14 is clear, shall be the intermediary between members in share transactions (see paragraph 6.7 *Pre-emption rights over transfers*).

Contract between the company and third parties

A third party cannot enforce a provision in the articles to obtain a benefit in them intended for him, eg where the articles state that a person is to be appointed as company solicitor. In *Eley* v *Positive Assurance Co Ltd* (1876) 1 Ex D 88 the articles of the company provided that the plaintiff who was a shareholder should be appointed as solicitor for the company and to be removed only for misconduct. After a period of time the company began to employ other solicitors instead, although there was no suggestion of impropriety on the part of the plaintiff. The plaintiff sued for breach of contract of the articles. The court held that he could not enforce the contract because the contract was res inter alios acta.

Contract between the company and its members

The articles are only binding on the members in their capacity as members. Two situations arise here: first, where the shareholder is suing in his capacity as member to enforce rights held as a member and, secondly, where the shareholder is suing as a member to enforce rights not held as a member. In both these situations, the member is suing as member, ie wearing the hat of a shareholder. The two situations will be dealt with in more detail:

Suing as member to enforce rights held as member. The rights held as member are those which all the shareholders of a company have and is a right held by all the shareholders jointly. In *Pender* v *Lushington* (1877) 6 Ch D 70 the chairman of the company in general meeting refused to count the votes cast by the plaintiff in breach of the articles. Pender brought an action qua shareholder to enforce a right held qua shareholder. It was held that a member is entitled to enforce his right to have his vote counted at a general meeting as a contractual right.

Other typical enforceable members' rights are:

1. to properly declare a dividend payable in cash: *Wood* v *Odessa Waterworks Company* (1889) 42 Ch D 636; (see paragraph 6.5 *The right to dividends*);
2. to receive a share certificate: *Burdett* v *Standard Exploration* (1899) 16 TLR 112;
3. to transfer shares: *Re Swaledale Cleaners Ltd* [1968] 1 WLR 1710;
4. to sell shares: *Rayfield* v *Hands* above.

Suing as member to enforce rights not held as member. The traditional view is that a shareholder cannot bring an action to enforce rights not held as a member. This view was taken by Astbury J in *Hickman* v *Kent or Romney Marsh Sheepbreeders Association* [1915] 1 Ch 881 in his interpretation of what is now a s14 contract. Professor Wedderburn does not favour this view, however, and argues that 'outsider rights' are enforceable on the basis of *Quinn & Axten v Salmon* [1909] AC 442 in which the plaintiff, a majority shareholder and one of two managing directors, brought an action to restrain the company from acting on a resolution passed concerning the acquisition of land which was passed without both managing directors' agreement as required by the articles. The plaintiff was granted an injunction to restrain the company. The fact was that the plaintiff, who was a majority shareholder, was enforcing a right held as a member and any benefit to himself as managing director was purely incidental and therefore allowed.

Goldberg's view of outsider rights is that they are enforceable where it is necessary to ensure the correct organ of the company is making the decisions. This is inconsistent with the wording of s14 which refers to 'all the provisions of the memorandum and articles' whereas Goldberg is suggesting that only some are enforceable.

Gregory traces the difficulties of the s14 contract to the fact that the older case law was confused and concerned with whether or not s14 constituted a contract or not and not whether outsider rights are enforceable. He comes down in favour of Professor Wedderburn's view that outsider rights are enforceable and it is not for the courts to say which provision or which right is enforceable and which is not.

The articles and contracts with the company

As illustrated by *Eley*'s case and *Hickman*'s case above (see paragraph 3.1 *The effect of the memorandum and articles*) the effect of the articles as a contract in themselves is probably confined to cases where the rights claimed are those of a member as such. There are in addition a group of cases where a person has made a contract with the company by reference to the articles but not on membership matters. The most common case is where a director holds that office, or some executive office such as managing director, by reference to the relevant provisions of the articles. In these cases the articles are not the contract but the terms of the separate contract, eg the amount of directors' fees, are derived from the articles: *Re New British Iron Co, ex parte Beckwith* [1898] 1 Ch 324.

Two broad propositions then seem to emerge from the case law:

1. If the director merely gives his services on the basis of the articles, and no other agreed terms, he accepts that the company is free to terminate his appointment in accordance with the articles or to alter the articles to permit termination. In the latter situation he has no remedy for breach of contract since the articles are by statute inherently alterable.

2. If the appointment is made in accordance with the provisions of the articles but additional terms are agreed, he may seek a remedy in damages (but not by injunction) for breach of contract, if the company acting under the original articles or by alteration of the articles, breaches the agreed terms of his appointment.

The cases from which these conclusions have been extracted are set out below. The articles provided for the appointment of a managing director and for the termination of that appointment by resolution passed in general meeting. R was appointed managing director for an indefinite period at a weekly wage of £7. In these circumstances the company was free to terminate his appointment without notice, since although there was a contract of employment (not at this time subject to employment protection legislation) he was subject to instant dismissal: *Read* v *Astoria Garage (Streatham) Ltd* [1952] Ch 637.

The articles provided that named individuals, including S, should be 'permanent directors'. By failing to account to the company for its moneys in his hands, S caused prejudice to the interests of the company. The other director-shareholders carried a resolution to alter the articles to provide that any permanent director should vacate office if called upon to do so by the other directors. They then used this power to terminate S's position as permanent director. It was held that he had accepted that the articles might be altered (in good faith in the interests of the company) and had no claim for breach of contract or invalid alteration of the articles: *Shuttleworth* v *Cox Bros & Co (Maidenhead) Ltd* [1927] 2 KB 9.

We come now to the cases on which proposition (2) above is based. In one of these cases the articles contained the standard provision by which the directors might appoint a managing director 'for such period as they think fit' (1948 Table A art 107). N was appointed to hold office as managing director for so long as he continued to be a director. That express term, although agreed under the articles, constituted a separate arrangement. Its breach, by the removal of N from office while still a director, gave rise to a successful claim for damages: *Nelson* v *James Nelson & Sons Ltd* [1914] 2 KB 770.

The most important modern case, since it was a decision of the House of Lords, was *Southern Foundries (1926) Ltd* v *Shirlaw* [1940] AC 701. A shareholder who had recently acquired control of the company used his votes to alter the articles so that he had power to remove any director from office. He then removed S from the board and so terminated his appointment as managing director, under a service agreement which had not then expired. It was held that S could not restrain the company from altering its articles but he was entitled to damages for breach of the service agreement.

Class rights

There are two concepts to consider, ie (1) class rights and (2) variation of such rights.

There is no statutory requirement for particular rights to be attached to shares. It is left to the company to determine what its capital structure shall be. Accordingly there may be shares which carry different rights. In a typical case they are preference and ordinary shares (see paragraph 6.3 *Class rights – preference shares*). Unless all the shares carry uniform rights, they form 'classes' and the rights attached to them, including particular rights which are common to all classes, are 'class rights'.

The person(s) who hold(s) a class of shares form a class of members with vested rights arising from their shareholdings. In the normal case the company creates a class of shares and then issues it, thereby creating a class of shareholders. However, if the company alters its articles so as to confer on the holder of issued shares special rights, eg of pre-emption (see paragraph 6.7 *Pre-emption rights over transfers*), that constitutes a class: *Cumbrian Newspaper Group Ltd* v *Cumberland & Westmoreland Herald Newspaper & Printing Co Ltd* [1986] 2 All ER 816.

Normally class rights are defined in the articles (and that is why the subject is dealt with at this point in the textbook). If class rights are defined in the memorandum, the same special variation procedure (s125) applies though with some modifications, and the general power to alter the memorandum (see paragraph 4.1 *Alteration of optional clauses of the memorandum*) is not applicable to class rights.

It will usually be possible to discover whether a company has more than one class of shares, and what are the class rights, by searching the file at the registry, which will contain an up-to-date copy of the memorandum and articles (s18) and a copy of any special resolution which may have been passed to create a class of shares: s380. If, however, none of those documents give the information, the company must within one month of allotting shares or creating a class of members with special rights, give notice to the registry so that the information is provided and available to the public: ss128–9.

As explained below (see paragraph 3.1 *Variation of class rights – procedure*) statutory protection is given both to a class of shareholders and also (see paragraph 3.1 *Variation of class rights – statutory right of objection*) to a dissenting minority of the class in respect of any variation of class rights. However, judicial interpretation has narrowed the meaning given to 'variation', to which these safeguards apply. Variation of class rights means a change of capital structure which reduces (or increases) or directly alters the rights of an issued class of shares. In particular changes of the following kinds, although they may affect class rights or reduce their value, are not treated as variation in the sense of s125:

1. the creation of a class of preference shares by a company which until then has only ordinary shares is not a variation of the rights of the latter: *Andrews* v *Gas Meter Company Ltd* [1897] 1 Ch 361. A company has an inherent power to create different classes of shares;

2. if there is an existing class of shares the issue of additional shares of that class to persons not already members of the class is not a variation of the rights of the original members of the class: *White* v *Bristol Aeroplane Co* [1953] Ch 65;

3. the subdivision of shares of another class, with the result that their voting power in general meeting is increased because they hold more shares each carrying one vote, is not a variation of the class rights of other shares, although their proportionate voting power is reduced: *Greenhalgh* v *Arderne Cinemas* [1946] 1 All ER 512;

4. a repayment of preference shares in accordance with their priority rights, under an approved reduction of capital, which gives to the remaining ordinary shareholders the entire participation in the future profits and surplus assets of the

company (in which the preference shareholders had no rights) is not a variation of class rights: *Prudential Assurance Co Ltd* v *Chatterley-Whitfield Collieries Ltd* [1949] AC 512.

A variation of class rights was held to have occurred in *Re Northern Engineering Industries plc* [1994] BCC 618. The company was seeking the courts approval of a reduction of capital (see paragraph 6.3 Reduction of share capital), which involved paying off the preference shares and cancelling them. The reduction was opposed by a preference shareholder. The company's articles provided in Art 7(B) that, 'The rights attached to any shares shall be deemed to be varied by a reduction of the capital paid up on such shares...'. Art 6 required such a variation to be consented to by the preference shareholders or by an extraordinary resolution passed at a separate meeting of the preference shareholders. The preference shareholders argued that in the absence of consent or an extraordinary resolution, the court should not confirm the capital reduction. The company argued that Art 7(B) only applied where the reduction of capital paid up on particular shares was to a figure above zero. In other words 'reduction' means something different from 'cancellation' or 'extinction'. The Court of Appeal declined to confirm the reduction. It held that Art 7(B) had the effect that the proposed cancellation of the preference shares was a variation of the rights attached to the preference shares and a class meeting was therefore required by Art 6. As no such meeting had been held, the reduction had not been carried out in accordance with the articles. See Chapter 15, paragraph 15.3, for further details.

However, more recent developments in 'minority protection' (see paragraphs 4.3 and 11.2) may possibly be relevant if the purpose of such changes is to discriminate against a class of members: Lord Greene MR reserved this point in *Greenhalgh*'s case.

Finally, an alteration of the rights of unissued shares comes under a different, and much simpler, system (see paragraph 6.3 *Increase of share capital*). It will usually be necessary to alter the articles to insert or remove relevant material. But no consent of a class of shareholders is required since no member holds any of the shares thus affected.

Variation of class rights – procedure

The articles of a company which has more than one class of shares usually include provisions for obtaining the consent of the class before altering the articles (or less often the memorandum) to redefine the class rights. The standard procedure, which is found in Table A art 4 of the 1948 model articles provides for obtaining consent either by (1) holding a class meeting (with a quorum of members holding one third of the shares of the class) to pass an extraordinary resolution by a three quarters majority of votes cast or (2) obtaining the written consent of the holders of at least three quarters of the issued shares of the class. The second alternative is a more demanding requirement but it is convenient in cases where all the shares of the class are held by one person, so that there are difficulties in holding a class meeting for which the initial quorum is two (s370(2)).

However, not all companies have articles in this form and some have articles which contain no procedure for variation at all. To resolve difficulties which had arisen in exceptional cases there is now a statutory formulation of the standard procedure in s125. When the 1985 Table A was prepared it was decided that it was no longer necessary to include in standard articles a variation procedure since s125 provided it when required.

Section 125 is by its nature complicated since, in addition to the standard three quarters majority principle set out above, it deals with other less usual situations, including:

1. an alteration of the articles to introduce a variation procedure for the first time is itself a variation of existing class rights;
2. if, as is commonly the case, class rights are subject to a variation procedure of any kind set out in the memorandum or articles, that procedure will apply to the exclusion of the statutory procedure. But if it does not require a normal three quarters majority approval, that requirement must also be satisfied in certain circumstances;
3. if the class rights are set out in the memorandum and there is no variation procedure in the memorandum or articles, variation of the rights requires the consent of all members of the company.

There are two stages. First the consent of the class is obtained under the appropriate procedure. Then the company in general meeting resolves to make the changes. There is no objection to holding the two meetings in the same room in sequence provided that those members of the company, who are not also members of the class, do not take part in the preliminary class meeting: *Carruth* v *Imperial Chemical Industries Ltd* [1937] AC 707. A signed copy of the resolution, usually a special resolution, which effects the alteration, is delivered to the registry for filling: s380. A copy of the articles (or memorandum) as altered must also be delivered: s18.

Variation of class rights – statutory right of objection

Up to one quarter of the members of the class may oppose the variation without being able to prevent the consent of the class being given, since it requires only a three quarters majority, which is binding on the class.

However, holders of at least 15 per cent of the shares of the class who did not consent may within 21 days apply to the court to cancel the consent of the class on the grounds that it is 'unfairly prejudicial' to them: s127. It is rarely possible to persuade the court to cancel the consent given by the majority, unless it can be shown that the majority were acting in their own interests as members of another class and would obtain benefit from the change in that capacity. That aspect is further considered (see paragraph 4.3 *Discrimination against a minority*) in connection with minority protection (see also *Holder's Investment Trust* case in paragraph 6.3 *Reduction of share capital*).

3.2 Registered office and statutory registers

Introduction

As part of the system of regulation of companies it is a legal requirement that every company shall have an established legal address and shall maintain a number of registers open to public inspection, usually but not always at that address. If any of the registers are held elsewhere notice of the place where they are located must be given to the registry. Another source of information already described (see paragraph 2.1 *Registration*) is the file on each company maintained at the registry. In this section we will also deal with the annual return and with the significance and use of the company seal on documents.

Registered office

From the moment of its formation a company is required to have a registered office: s287. One of the clauses of the memorandum specifies the country in which the registered office will be situted (s2(1)) and another of the documents delivered to the registry to form the company states the precise address in that country at which the registered office will be located until further notice: s10(6).

Thereafter the directors, in the exercise of their general power of management may move the registered office to a different address, which must always be in the country specified in the memorandum. Whenever the address of the registered office is changed, notice of the new address must be given to the registry within 14 days. During the period of 14 days following the delivery of the notice to the registry a document may validly be served at the previous address: s287.

The address of the registered office, identified as such, must be shown on all business letters and order forms of the company: s351 (see paragraph 2.2 *Company letterheads, etc*). It is also one of the particulars given on the annual return (see paragraph 3.2 *Annual return*).

On receiving notice of a change of the address of the registered office the registrar gives notice in the *London Gazette* that he has received such a notice: s711(1)(n). If the directors fail to give notice to the registrar of the new address, and in consequence he gives no notice of it in the *Gazette*, a person who is unaware of the change may take legal action against the company at the previous address and the company is not permitted to object that its registered office is no longer there: s42(1). Any such default also exposes the company and its officers to liability to a fine: s287.

A document such as a notice, writ or summons may be served on the company by leaving it at or sending it by post to its registered office: s725. The standard litigation procedure is to make a search at the registry to find out the address of the registered office as shown on the file and then to serve legal process at the address. Evidence that this has been done is conclusive of due service for the reasons already given.

Apart from its importance as the address at which the company has its legal presence, the registered office is also the place at which the registers etc, which the company is required to maintain, may be and in some cases must be held (see paragraph 3.2 *Statutory registers, etc*).

The registered office may be one of the principal places of business of the company, but this is entirely optional. A small company which entrusts to its auditors the maintenance of its statutory books and accounts may arrange that their office, not its own, is the designated registered office. It is entirely a matter of convenience, provided always that the registered office must be within the country specified in the memorandum.

Statutory registers, etc

The following must always be held at the registered office:

1. register of directors and secretary (see paragraph 9.1 *Publicity about directors*): s288;
2. register of charges and related documents (see paragraph 7.3): s407;
3. minute book of general meetings (see paragraph 8.1 *Proceedings at meetings*): s383;
4. a copy of any contract for the purchase of the company's shares made within the previous ten years (see paragraph 6.4 *Purchase by a company of its own shares*): s169(4).

The following may be held at the registered office or at some alternative address in the country of incorporation, of which notice is given to the registrar:

5. register of members and where required the alphabetical index to it (see paragraph 6.6 *Register of members*): s353;
6. register of directors' interests in shares or debentures (see paragraph 9.1 *Publicity about directors*): s325;
7. register of substantial interests in shares of public companies (see paragraph 6.6 *Interests in shares*): s211;
8. register of debenture holders (see paragraph 7.1 *Ownership and transfer of debentures*): s190;
9. copies of any directors' service agreements etc (see paragraph 9.1 *Directors as employees*): s318.

The accounting records which the company is required to maintain may be held at the registered office or elsewhere, provided that they are open to inspection by the company's officers: s222(1). There is no obligation to give notice to the registrar of their whereabouts.

Regulations are to be made to prescribe, presumably on a uniform basis, how a company must comply with requests to inspect or supply copies of its various registers and documents. This will entail numerous minor changes in the relevant sections imposing these obligations: s723A.

The form in which a statutory register may be kept, ie bound book, loose-leaf or on computer has been explained in connection with the register of members (see paragraph 6.6 *Register of members*). A small company often keeps its very simple statutory registers in a single bound volume, with suitably ruled pages, which can be obtained from a law stationer.

The common seal and other seals

A company may enter into a contract of any type in the same form as is appropriate to a contract made by an individual: Here the majority of company contracts, necessarily made for it by natural persons as agents, are in writing or made by word of mouth or by conduct. A company may also make contracts in the form of a deed executed under its common seal, attested by two signatures as authorised by its articles (see below).

It is now provided however that a company need not have a common seal. Whether or not it has a seal, a document signed by a director and by the secretary or by a second director and expressed to be executed by the company has the same effect as if executed under the common seal. If the document expresses the intention that it is to be a deed, it has that effect. In favour of a purchaser a document bearing the two signatures is deemed to have been duly executed (and to have been duly delivered as a deed if so described): s36A. These provisions are intended to simplify procedure, particularly where a company document is part of the title to property.

A company is required to engrave on its seal (if any) the full name of the company: s350. It rests with the directors to 'adopt' a seal; this is usually one of the formalities completed at the first board meeting after incorporation. An impression of the seal is made in the minutes as a record of its style. A seal is usually a circular die on which the company name, except 'Limited', is engraved around the outside edge and the word 'Limited' runs across the centre (presumably to give it prominence). When a document is sealed, the seal is affixed under pressure to make a permanent impression on the document and witnesses add their signatures.

The articles follow Table A art 101 in providing that the seal shall only be used by authority of the directors or of a committee appointed by the directors. A director and the secretary, or two directors, sign close to the impression of the seal as witnesses to its due application. This practice is recognised by the Law of Property Act 1925 s74(1), which provides that a purchaser may assume that a deed of a company has been duly executed if it is sealed and witnessed in this fashion.

The normal practice is for the board to appoint a 'sealings committee' consisting of any director and the secretary, or of two directors, with authority to apply the seal. A sealings book is kept, in which every document sealed (and the date) is entered and those who have signed, as witnesses, initial the entry in the record. At each board meeting a list of documents sealed is laid before the board. These formalities are important since the company uses its seal on share certificates, debentures and other documents by which it assumes liabilities. The seal, when not in use, is usually held under lock and key.

Public companies which may have a considerable number of share transfers to register (and new share certificates to issue) each month often adopt a second 'Securities Seal', which bears the same legend as the common seal with the addition of the word 'Securities'. This seal is held by the registrar and used only for share certificates: s40. Another modification of procedure is that the articles may dispense with autographic signatures of witnesses to impressions of the securities seal.

Similar modifications may be required if a company has an 'overseas branch register' in a foreign country for the convenience of investors who reside there: s362.

Annual return

Every company is required to deliver to the registrar successive annual returns made up to a date not later than the return date of the company at the time of delivery. The return date is the anniversary date of the company's incorporation, or, if the previous return was made up to a different date, the anniversary of that date. The annual return must be in the prescribed form and be signed by a director and by the secretary: s363.

The purpose of the annual return is to provide a convenient summary of information about the company, such as the address of the registered office, the type of company it is and its principal business activities, the names and addresses of the secretary and the directors (with additional particulars of the latter) and of the shareholders, with particulars of their shareholdings and of the total issued share capital: ss364-364A. There is to be a classification scheme of types of company and of business activity to which the return will relate.

It is only necessary to provide a full list of members and shareholdings once in three years (with particulars of changes in the intervening years' returns) but most large companies find it simpler to provide a complete 'print out' of their register of members each year: s364A(5).

An annual return is a useful source of information about the company to supplement the financial data contained in the annual accounts (see paragraph 14.1). Failure to deliver the annual return at the due time is an offence which may entail liability to a fine. It is also one of the matters to be taken into consideration in determining whether an order for disqualification should be made under the Company Directors Disqualification Act 1986 (Sch. 1 para 4(f) (see paragraph 9.1 *Disqualification of directors*).

However, if the annual return is duly delivered to the registry it may already be somewhat out of date since it is made up to a date four weeks before the due date for filing. Thereafter it becomes steadily obsolescent until replaced a year later by the next year's return.

A new annual return fee of £18, reduced from £32, was introduced by the Companies (Fee) (Amendment) Regulations 1994 (SI 1994/2217).

4

Alteration of Memorandum of Association and Articles

4.1 Alteration of the memorandum

4.2 Alteration of the articles

4.3 Restrictions on alteration of the articles

4.1 Alteration of the memorandum

Introduction

In the early days of company law the memorandum was regarded as the permanent constitution of the company which, unlike its internal regulations (the articles), was to be unalterable in most respects. Practical considerations have dictated extensive modifications of that approach so that almost every part of the memorandum may be altered under an appropriate procedure.

It is a legacy of the original status of the memorandum that there is no general power of alteration, such as applies to the articles (s9). For each clause of the memorandum it is necessary to identify the relevant provision (if any) under which it may be altered and adopt that procedure.

The method of alteration of the standard clauses of a memorandum is explained in its context in this manual as follows:

1. the name of the company (see paragraph 2.2 *Change of company name*);
2. clause stating that this is a public company (see paragraph 1.4 *Re-registration of a public company as private*); insertion of such a clause in memorandum of a private company (see paragraph 1.4 *Re-registration of a private company as public*);
3. country in which registered office is to be situated – this clause cannot be altered;
4. objects clause (see paragraph 2.3);
5. the authorised capital (see paragraph 6.3 *Increase of share capital*);
6. other clauses which might be included in the articles (see paragraph 4.1 *Alteration of optional clauses of the memorandum*).

Alteration of the objects

As already explained (see paragraph 2.3 *The ultra vires principle and CA 1989*) it is normal procedure to consider whether the objects clause in its present form suffices before launching the company into a new venture or a novel type of transaction. If there is any doubt the company then alters its objects clause to incorporate suitable main objects or powers.

A company may by special resolution alter its memorandum with respect to the objects clause: s4.

This simple provision replaces a more elaborate statement of the limit and specified purposes for which alteration was permitted.

It is normal commercial practice to alter the objects whenever an existing or contemplated change in the nature of the company's business or a particular transaction is not sufficiently authorised by the existing objects and related powers. A bank for example would take legal advice on the objects clause of a company customer which had asked for a substantial loan and insist that any alteration was made, which its advisers deemed necessary, before making the loan. If it did not take this precaution its 'good faith' (paragraph 2.3 *Validity of transactions*) might be questioned if it later had to rely on s35A.

The primary safeguard against an injudicious or improper alteration of the objects is the three quarters majority of votes cast which is required to carry a special resolution.

With the new simple procedure for altering the objects clause by special resolution it is unlikely that any member would object to procedural faults. However it is a possibility though, for reasons explained below, the right to object to the court is restricted to the period of 21 days following the passing of the resolution: s6(4).

A minority, who did not vote for the resolution, may object to the alteration on its merits but only within the same period of 21 days. The minority must be at least 15 per cent (by shareholding) of the holders of the issued share capital or a class of it or of a class of debentures giving a right of objection. (This last category, preserved by CA 1948, is now virtually obsolete, ie few if any such debentures now exist: s5(2) and (3).)

The reason for the 21 day time limit in either of these cases is that, after altering its objects, the company will probably proceed with the transaction which made the alteration necessary. If there is going to be an objection, it must be raised and decided within a short period, so that the altered objects are thereafter secure from challenge.

Objections to the merits of the alteration are rare since it is not easy for a minority to satisfy the court that a change which is approved by a substantial majority is unwise. Under the previous law however a few successful objections were made on the ground that the new objects were 'destructive or inconsistent with the existing business': *Re Parent Tyre Co* [1923] 2 Ch 222 and *Re Cyclists' Touring Club* [1907] 1 Ch 269. But if the company entirely changes the nature of its business, it will usually alter its objects clause so as to omit the previous objects and thus obviate any inconsistency.

In its application to the court a 15 per cent minority usually seeks cancellation of the alteration. However, the court may impose or promote other forms of settlement such as the purchase by the company of the objectors' shares or an order for alteration of the memorandum or articles or to entrench some part of the existing memorandum or articles so that it may not thereafter be altered except by leave of the court.

A copy of the memorandum in its altered form must be delivered to the registry. The company first waits 21 days to see whether any application will be made to the court to cancel the alteration (or to declare it invalid). If no such application is made the company then has 15 days from the end of the 21-day period in which to file the altered memorandum. If there is an application, the 15 days runs from the time when it is disposed of.

Alteration of optional clauses of the memorandum

Any condition contained in the memorandum which might have been contained in the articles may be altered by special resolution, but subject to the same right of minority objection to the court, as applies to alterations of the objects: s17(1).

However, this provision for alteration is subject to the following restrictions and exclusions:

1. the company may not alter any part of the memorandum which is subject to a court order for minority protection under ss459–461 (see paragraph 11.2 *The court's powers*);
2. it may not require a member, unless he consents, to subscribe more for his shares than was due when he became a member nor compel him to subscribe for additional shares: s16;
3. the power does not permit alteration of any 'entrenched' provision, ie one which is declared in the memorandum to be unalterable. In any such case alteration can only be made by a scheme of arrangement (see paragraph 12.2) for which court approval is required;
4. for any variation of the class rights attached to shares the correct procedure (see paragraph 3.1 *Variation of class rights – procedure*) must be followed. It is excluded from the scope of s17.

Section 17 is more important for its exceptions than for its powers.

4.2 Alteration of the articles

Apart from having entered into membership of the company in reliance on the statements of the objects and powers in the memorandum of association, the shareholder becomes a member on the terms of membership contained in the articles of association. Just as the memorandum may be altered, so as to redefine the aims and capacity of the company of which they are all members, so may the articles be varied, to alter the rights and relationships of the various members inter se.

Power to alter the articles is given to the company by s9, which states:

'1) 'Subject to the provisions of this Act and to the conditions contained in its memorandum, a company may by special resolution alter or add to its articles.
2) Any alteration or addition so made in the articles shall, subject to the provisions of this Act, be as valid as if originally contained therein, and be subject in like manner to alteration by special resolution.'

In addition the court has power in certain circumstances, such as an alteration of the objects to which objection has been raised (s5(5)), and the grant of a remedy to a minority under ss459–461, to order that the articles shall be altered or alternatively that some existing provision of the articles shall not be altered without the leave of the court.

There are a number of restrictions on the general power of a company to alter its articles. It must respect any prior order of the court (see above). The articles may not be altered so as to conflict with the memorandum or with the Companies Act 1985. An attempt, for example, to shorten the period of notice of general meetings to less than 21 or 14 days (see paragraph 8.1 *Notice of meetings*) would be invalid because s369 overrides it.

As with the memorandum (see paragraph 4.1 *Alteration of optional clauses of the memorandum*) no alteration of the articles may increase the liability of a shareholder on his shares without his consent: s16.

The rights attached to a class of shares, defined by the articles, may at the final stage be varied by altering the articles. But the proper prior procedure (see paragraph 3.1 *Variation of class rights – procedure*) must be followed to obtain any necessary consent before the alteration is made: s125.

Unlike the memorandum, however, the articles may not 'entrench' any article so as to make it unalterable. Devices such as prescribing a larger majority of votes than the three quarters required to carry a special resolution, or entry into a contract by which the company agrees not to alter its articles are simply invalid.

However, in *Russell* v *Northern Bank Development Corporation Ltd* [1992] 1 WLR 588, while accepting the principle that 'a company cannot forgo its right to alter its articles' enunciated in *Southern Foundries (1926) Ltd* v *Shirlaw* [1940] AC 701, the House of Lords affirmed that an agreement outside the articles between shareholders as to how they would exercise their voting rights on a resolution to alter the articles was not necessarily invalid. In *Russell* it appeared that Tyrone Brick Ltd (TBL) and its four shareholders had entered into an agreement, inter alia, that 'No further share capital shall be created or issued in the company or the rights attaching to the shares already in issue in any way altered … without the written consent of each of the parties hereto.' Expressing the views also of the other Law Lords, Lord Jauncey of Tullichettle said:

'Turning back to [the relevant clause] of the agreement it appears to me that its purpose was twofold. The shareholders agreed only to exercise their voting powers in relation to the creation or issue of shares in TBL if they and TBL agreed in writing. This agreement is purely personal to the shareholders who executed it and ... does not purport to bind future shareholders. It is, in my view, just such a private agreement as was envisaged by Lord Davey in *Welton* v *Saffery* [1897] AC 299. TBL on the other hand agreed that its capital would not be increased without the consent of each of the shareholders. This was a clear undertaking by TBL in a formal agreement not to exercise its statutory powers for a period which could, certainly on one view of construction, last for as long as any one of the parties to the agreement remained a shareholder and long after the control of TBL had passed to shareholders who were not party to the agreement. As such an undertaking it is, in my view, as obnoxious as if it had been contained in the articles of association and therefore is unenforceable as being contrary to the provisions of [the Northern Ireland statute]. TBL's undertaking is, however, independent of and severable from that of the shareholders and there is no reason why the latter should not be enforceable by the shareholders inter se as a personal agreement which in no way fetters TBL in the exercise of its statutory powers.'

Again, the statutory requirement of a special resolution to alter the articles is imposed merely to safeguard a minority who may wish to put their opposition to the test. If every member agrees to the change, their agreement is effective even though no meeting has been held to pass the resolution: *Cane* v *Jones* [1980] 1 WLR 1451.

An alteration is valid even though it has the effect of prejudicing the position of an existing shareholder, provided that:

1. it does not purport to deprive him of an already existing financial claim against the company: *Swabey* v *Port Darwin Gold Mining Co* (1889) 1 Meg 385 CA;
2. it does not increase the amount payable on his shares or require him to take additional shares: s16;
3. the alteration is made bona fide in the interests of the company and is not merely discrimination against a minority (see paragraph 4.3 *Discrimination against a minority*);
4. it does not alter class rights without following the correct procedure to obtain the consent of the class (see paragraph 3.1 *Variation of class rights – procedure*).

4.3 Restrictions on alteration of the articles

Freedom of voting

We have seen that at its simplest level, the ordinary member's right to participate in the running of the company finds expression in his ability to take part in the discussion and voting in the general meeting. Resolutions passed in general meeting are therefore the practical result of the collective will of the various members – the majority decision displays the fact that more of the individual members, whatever their many and varied motives may be, have wanted one decision rather than another.

If all this is true, it is quite justifiable for the individual shareholder to exercise his vote in whichever way he wishes, and to take his chance on whether the majority of the other voters agree with him or not. His vote has been regarded, like his share, as his personal property which he can use as he wishes, and even if his action as a shareholder runs contrary to the path he must pursue in some other capacity eg as a director (it being a separate issue whether or not he is in breach of any duties as a director and, if so, what are the effects of the breach).

Thus, in *North-West Transportation Co v Beatty* (1887) 12 App Cas 589, (see paragraph 9.3 *Conflict of interest*) a director was entitled to vote as a shareholder at a general meeting which ratified the purchase by the company from him of a boat at a reasonable price under a contract which was voidable because of his conflict of interest. (See too *Burland v Earle* [1902] AC 83.) Similarly, in *Northern Counties Securities Ltd v Jackson and Steeple Ltd* [1974] 1 WLR 1133, a director who had complied with an obligation to call a general meeting and to advise the members to vote for a resolution which had to be passed if the company were not to be in contempt of court, was nonetheless entitled in his capacity as shareholder to vote against it. Walton J said:

> 'When a director votes as a director for or against any particular resolution in a directors' meeting, he is voting as a person under a fiduciary duty to the company for the proposition that the company should take a certain course of action. When a shareholder is voting for or against a particular resolution he is voting as a person owing no fiduciary duty to the company and who is exercising his own right of property, to vote as he thinks fit.'

He may even enter into a binding contract to exercise his vote in a particular way: *Greenwell v Porter* [1902] 1 Ch 530; *Puddephatt v Leith* [1916] 1 Ch 200; Krüger (1978) 94 LQR 557.

But if a shareholder owes no duties to the company (see paragraph 6.3 *The exercise of shareholders' rights*) (which is of course partly his property), does it follow that he owes no duties to his fellow members? Or, and this is a different point, does it follow that there are no restrictions on the manner in which he may exercise his vote? Certainly, there are a number of specific instances in which majority decisions have been regarded as intolerable because of their effect on certain shareholders, the cases of so-called fraud on the minority, in the sense of abuse of power; the cases are not limited simply to cases of fraud in the usual sense. There may in certain circumstances be some broad duties owed by shareholder to shareholder. In *Estmanco v GLC* Megarry V–C doubted that controlling members had unfettered freedom to pursue policies injurious to the minority and which went against the company's very raison d'etre.

Discrimination against a minority

Relief may also be given, though the extent of this remedy is uncertain, to a minority shareholder who complains of open discrimination against him by the majority, through their control of the company, even though he does not allege misappropriation of its property.

Although shareholders are generally free to vote as they please (see paragraph 4.3 *Freedom of voting*) the court will intervene to restrain the use of voting power for the sole purpose of obtaining some advantage to the majority or of discrimination against the minority, without regard to the interests of the company as a whole.

However, the minority will not obtain relief if the court considers that, despite clear prejudice to the minority, there is also evidence that the majority were bona fide concerned with the interests of the company.

These distinctions are illustrated by a group of cases on alteration of the articles. It will be remembered that, subject to some specific limitations, the articles may be altered by special resolution under s9 (see paragraph 4.2). However, an alteration, otherwise in accordance with legal requirements, will be set aside if not made bona fide in the interests of the company. The following cases are relevant:

1. *Brown* v *British Abrasive Wheel Co* [1919] 1 Ch 290; *Dafen Tinplate Co Ltd* v *Llanelly Steel Co* Ltd [1907] 2 Ch 124. In both cases the articles were altered to give to the majority a power to acquire compulsorily the shares of the minority. In each case the majority had in view considerations bearing on the interests of the company but these were not expressed in the new articles so as to restrict them to that use. The alterations were held invalid.

2. *Sidebotham* v *Kershaw, Leese & Co* [1920] 1 Ch 154. The articles were altered to give power to the directors to require any member who carried on a business competing with that of the company to transfer his shares to them. This alteration was valid since it was expressed in terms which limited its use to safeguarding the company's interests.

3. *Shuttleworth* v *Cox Bros & Co (Maidenhead)* [1927] 2 KB 9. The articles were altered to enable the directors to require any person named in the articles as a 'permanent director' to vacate that office. The purpose of this alteration was to enforce the removal of a particular director who had on numerous occasions failed to account for company money in his hands. He was removed under the new article which was held valid, although it was not expressed to be limited to cases such as his; contrast the decisions in (1) above.

4. *Rights and Issues Investment Trust Ltd* v *Stylo Shoes Ltd* [1964] 3 All ER 628. The articles were altered to increase the voting power of the holders of management shares. This was done to restore the previous strength in votes of those shares which had been diluted by a new issue of shares to other shareholders. The holders of the management shares did not vote on the alteration. It was held valid since its purpose was to strengthen the management of the company (the same factor as prevailed in the *Smith and Fawcett* case on share transfer in paragraph 6.7 *Refusal to register a transfer*).

The most important case in this field was concerned with an alteration of the articles to remove a right of pre-emption given to each shareholder in respect of any shares which another shareholder might wish to transfer (see paragraph 6.7 *Pre-emption rights over transfers*). The majority who voted for the alteration sought to avoid having to offer their shares to the plaintiff (Greenhalgh) before selling them to a non-member. However, the alteration was held to be potentially in the interests of every member, since Greenhalgh too would be permitted to sell his shares to an outsider without having to offer them to the other existing shareholders; *Greenhalgh* v *Arderne Cinemas Ltd* [1951] Ch 286. The case is notable for the analysis of the general principles by Lord Evershed MR, from which the following key propositions are quoted below:

> 'the shareholder must proceed on what, in his honest opinion, is for the benefit of the company as a whole, ie the corporators as a general body ... The case may be taken of an individual hypothetical member and it may be asked whether what is proposed is, in the honest opinion of those who voted in its favour, for that person's benefit ...
> ... a special resolution of this kind would be liable to be impreached if the effect of it were to discriminate between the majority shareholders and the minority shareholders, so as to give to the former an advantage of which the latter were deprived ...
> ... This resolution provides that *anybody* who wants at any time to sell his shares can now go to an outside transferee ... ' (emphasis supplied).

This was the seventh lawsuit, and the fifth to go to the Court of Appeal, between these warring shareholders (see Gower, *Principles of Modern Company Law*, 4th ed pp 624–6 for a fascinating narrative of this prolonged litigation). On the other leading case in the sequence, see paragraph 3.1 *Class rights* for *Greenhalgh* v *Arderne Cinemas Ltd* [1946] 1 All ER 512 on variation of class rights.

A more recent case in the same field was also the product of extreme bitterness between shareholders. The case is significant not so much for its outcome as for the court's formulation of the principles on which relief may be given. In *Clemens* v *Clemens Bros Ltd* [1976] 2 All ER 268 there were two shareholders, aunt and niece, and the articles in this case also contained share transfer pre-emption provisions. Miss Clemens senior had 55 per cent and the niece 45 per cent of the issued ordinary shares. Although the aunt could carry an ordinary resolution she could not carry a special resolution to alter the articles, as she wished to do in order to prevent her shares passing at her death to the younger Miss Clemens.

The articles permitted an increase of authorised capital by ordinary resolution. So the aunt and the working directors, who were in her camp, proposed to increase the authorised capital so that shares might be allotted to the working directors (with due approval for that by ordinary resolution) and to the trustees of an employees share scheme, to be appointed by the directors. If these changes had been effected, the shareholding of the niece would be reduced from the original 45 per cent to 24.5 per cent of the increased capital.

The court cited the above judgment of Evershed MR and also the following passage from the judgment of Lord Wilberforce in *Ebrahimi* v *Westbourne Galleries*.

> (In winding up) 'the "just and equitable" provision ... does, as equity always does, enable the court to subject the exercise of legal rights to equitable considerations of a personal character arising between one individual and another, which may make it unjust , or inequitable, to insist on legal rights, or to exercise them in a particular way'.

On this basis the court held that 'in a case such as the present Miss Clemens is not entitled to exercise her majority vote as she pleases ... it would be unwise to try to produce a principle, since the circumstances of each case are infinitely variable'.

The feature of the *Clemens* case which influenced the court to intervene was that it considered that the resolutions carried at the general meeting had been 'specifically and carefully designed to ensure not only that the plaintiff can never get control of the company but to deprive her of what has been called her negative control' (to block an alteration of the articles). The majority shareholder was to be denied the opportunity of using her position to achieve blatant discrimination against the minority shareholder. In contrast to the reasoning in *Greenhalgh*'s case the alteration could not possibly benefit the younger Miss Clemens, as one of 'the corporators as a general body'.

The other significant point, which will come up again more than once in the context of statutory protection of minorities (see paragraph 11.2) and winding up on the 'just and equitable' ground (see paragraph 12.3 *Just and equitable ground*) is that the court will 'lift the veil of incorporation' (see paragraph 1.3) and take account of a 'quasi-partnership' relationship between a small group of directors or shareholders, if their participation in the company is based upon relations of trust and confidence. If that personal element is not present it is much more difficult for the minority to persuade the court that its case for relief should be upheld.

A minority usually has votes but not enough to carry a resolution. However, a shareholder who has no votes at all, since he holds only non-voting shares, is not on that account disentitled to relief. Even if (as in the *Estmanco* case mentioned in paragraph 11.1 *Introduction: the general rule* the voteless objectors outnumber the controlling shareholder, they are a 'minority' in terms of influence on the company's policy. That was also the situation in the *Harmer* case (see paragraph 11.2 *The court's powers*), where relief was granted under statutory powers.

5

Company Formation

5.1 Promoters and pre-incorporation contracts

5.2 Flotation

5.3 Liability for defects in listing particulars and prospectuses

5.1 Promoters and pre-incorporation contracts

Definition of promoter

The best description of a promoter is that of Bowen LJ in *Whaley Bridge* v *Smith* (1880) 5 QBD 109, 'The term promoter is a term of business not of law, usefully summing up in a single word a number of business operations familiar to the commercial world by which a company is generally brought into existence.'

Cockburn CJ in *Twycross* v *Grant* (1877) 2 CPD 469 defined a promoter as 'one who undertakes to form a company with reference to a given project and to set it going, and who takes the necessary steps to accomplish that purpose'.

The definition is very wide and practically anyone who performs various functions with a view to incorporating a company will be a promoter. The term may also cover individuals who arrange for someone to become a director, procures capital, negotiates preliminary arrangements, and registers the memorandum and articles of association.

Those who act in a purely ministerial capacity, eg solicitors, accountants, valuers, will not be considered promoters merely because they have agreed to become directors or find others who will be: *Re Great Wheal Polgooth Co Ltd* (1883) 53 LJ Ch 42. In this area of the law, the courts have not attempted to define more clearly who is a promoter and the definition is only by reference to the person's work. Note that a promoter may be an amateur or a professional such as a merchant bank.

The advantage of having such a flexible definition is that it ensures that any person who fulfils such a function will be subject to the rules, duties and obligations of a promoter. However, the danger is that a person acting as a promoter according to the definition, does not know that there are certain obligations he has to fulfil.

Professional promoters were particularly prevalent during the latter part of the nineteenth century and much of the case law is from this period. Typically, they would act as a syndicate and purchase land said to contain valuable minerals. They would then form a company and sell the land to the company at an inflated price. Members of the public would have been invited to subscribe for shares in the company only to find at a later date that the land was less valuable than claimed and that the promoters had moved on. Today such cases are extremely rare. The vast majority of companies begin life as private companies and those that promote them also become the directors. So, unlike the professional promoters of the nineteenth century, they continue to have a vested interest in the company after the promotion has ended.

Who are the promoters?

In seeking to find out who are the promoters of a company, it is helpful to ask the following questions:

1. Who had the idea to form the company for the purpose in question?
2. Who drafted the memorandum and articles or gave instructions to solicitors to prepare them?
3. Who paid for the registration of the company and cost of preparing the documents?
4. Who arranged for persons to become the first directors?

This is only a guide and is by no means decisive; a person may have done none of these things and yet be a promoter: see further JH Gross, 'Who is a Company Promoter?' (1970) 86 LQR 493.

The duties of the promoter

The promoter owes a fiduciary duty to the company which has something in common with the obligations imposed on a trustee towards the cestui que trust and on an agent towards his principal. Professor Pennington, *Pennington's Company Law*, 6th ed, p524, considers that the closer analogy is with the relationship between agent and principal and points out that (on the authority of *Omnium Electric Palaces Ltd* v *Baines* [1914] 1 Ch 332) there is no absolute prohibition against a promoter making a profit out of his transaction. It is the making of a *secret* profit that is forbidden. There cannot be a contractual relationship because the company does not exist when the promotion begins.

In formulating remedies to fit particular cases the courts have also apparently imposed on a promoter a duty to promote the interests of the company: *Jacobus Marler Estates Ltd* v *Marler* (1913) 85 LJPC 167.

However, two developments have made it difficult to develop an analysis in terms of common law or equity. First, prospectus law (see paragraph 5.2) has imposed on promoters statutory obligations of disclosure and responsibility for the issue of a misleading prospectus. Secondly, in modern practice the events leading up to the flotation of a public company are closely supervised by merchant banks which, with their advisers, take great pains to avoid any infringement of their clients' obligations. Hence, there is little modern case law on promoters' defaults.

To sum up, a promoter must comply with statutory duties of disclosure. Secondly, at common law he must account for any profit which he may make from his transactions, unless he has made disclosure of his interest and of his profit (if any) to the company, as explained below.

To whom disclosure must be made

In *Erlanger* v *New Sombrero Phosphate Company* (1878) 3 App Cas 1218 the court held that disclosure should be to an independent board of directors. The appellant acquired the lease of an island for £55,000. A company was formed and the lease was sold to the company for £110,000. The appellant was a director of the company. The House of Lords held that the company was entitled to rescind the contract and to recover the purchase money from the appellant as there had been no disclosure by the promoter of the profit he made. Lord Cairns LC said that 'what he could not do was to make a profit without the knowledge of the company'. He should take care that he sells the property to the company through the medium of an independent board of directors.

This rule was found to be too strict since an entirely independent board of directors would be impossible in the case of most companies, and it was held in *Lagunas Nitrate Co* v *Lagunas Syndicate Ltd* [1899] 2 Ch 392 that disclosure to the members would be equally effective. Lindley J in that case said disclosure was deemed necessary 'to all available members of the company'.

The position, therefore, seems to be this: disclosure must be to:

1. an independent board of directors; or
2. existing and potential members as a whole (potential members via the prospectus).

Disclosure to directors who are mere nominees of the promoter will not be sufficient to relieve the promoter of liability, however. In *Gluckstein* v *Barnes* [1900] AC 240 a syndicate headed by the appellant bought land and resold it to a newly formed company. The profit made on the transaction was disclosed in the prospectus. However, the additional profit made by way of reimbursement of outstanding charges on the land which the syndicate had bought at a discount was not disclosed. It was held that the promoters were liable to account to the company for the profit made on the charges. Lord MacNaughten said: 'Disclosure is not the most appropriate word to use when a person who plays many parts announces himself in one character what he has done and is doing in another; to talk of disclosure to a company where there are no shareholders as yet is a mere farce'. In such a case the information should be given in the prospectus. See *Re Leeds & Hanley Theatre of Varieties* [1902] 2 Ch 809 where the defendant company purchased two music halls and had them conveyed to its nominee. The purchase price was £24,000. The defendant company then promoted the plaintiff theatre company and sold the two music halls to it for £75,000. The original board of the plaintiff company was not independent and the prospectus issued to the public failed to disclose the interest of the defendant company or the profit it was making. The Court of Appeal held that the prospectus should have disclosed its interest and profit and the defendant company was in breach of its fiduciary duty. The company was liable in damages.

Remedies for breach of promoter's duties

Rescission

The equitable remedy of rescission is available to the company in respect of any contract entered into as a result of non-disclosure or misrepresentation. The remedy must be exercised on normal contractual principles; the company must not ratify the agreement and this remedy is not available if the company is in liquidation. The remedy may be unavailable to the company if any of the bars to rescission apply:

1. affirmation (subject to the rule preventing ratification of breach of duty by way of fraud on the minority: *Atwool* v *Merryweather* (1867) LR 5 Eq 464n);
2. lapse of time;
3. intervention of a third party right;
4. inability to make restitutio in integrum, ie substantially restoring both parties to the original position: *Re Cape Breton Co* (1885) 29 Ch D 795 (facts given below);
5. the court's discretion under s2(2) Misrepresentation Act 1967 to declare the contract subsisting and award damages in lieu of rescission.

Accounting for the undisclosed profit

Unless a promoter can be held accountable on some other basis, eg that in buying the property he was acting as the company's agent (and for this purpose the company must then have been formed so that it is an existing principal), it is not generally possible for the company both to retain the property and reduce the price paid by calling on the promoter to account for his profit. The primary remedy, if the profit is not disclosed, is rescission and a financial remedy (if any) is usually a claim for damages, if there is the basis for claiming damages at all. *Re Cape Breton Co* (1885) 29 Ch 795 illustrates the obstacle to making a simple claim for the promoter's profit.

In *Re Cape Breton* six partners purchased coal mines for £5,500 and mined them during the partnership. The company was formed and two of these same partners became directors. The company purchased the mines for £42,000. The vendor was one of the original partners who sold the mines as trustee for all the six partners including the two directors. The company went into liquidation and therefore rescission was impossible so the company attempted to sue the directors for the secret profit made on the transaction. The court dismissed the claim. The court distinguished the *Erlanger* case (above) on the ground that, in that case, the appellant purchased the property in order to sell it to the company and so the mines were purchased for the company.

The position, therefore, seems to be this: if the company finds out that the promoter has made a secret profit, it can:

1. rescind the contract where the property belonged to him before he started acting as a promoter (unless the company is in liquidation as in *Re Cape Breton*); or
2. affirm the contract and claim damages if the promoter was the agent of the company.

Damages

Promoters may be liable for damages for misrepresentation inducing a contract and not for breach of fiduciary duty as such. In *Re Leeds and Hanley Theatre of Varieties* (1902) (see paragraph 5.1 *To whom disclosure must be made*) the court held that, since the defendant company owed a fiduciary duty towards the theatre company, and it had breached that duty, it was liable to an action in damages which was assessed as the difference between the market price and contract price, ie the amount of the profit. In *Re Jubilee Cotton Mills* [1920] Ch 100 the promoter was held liable in damages for taking an allotment of shares as consideration for the sale of his property which was over-valued. It may also be possible to base a claim for damages on the principle that a promoter owes a duty of care to the company.

Other remedies

A promoter could be held liable in damages for negligent mis-statement on the principles laid down in *Hedley Byrne* v *Heller & Partners Ltd* [1964] AC 465 and *Mutual Life and Citizens' Assurance Co Ltd* v *Evatt* [1971] AC 793 for false statements about the company in the prospectus.

There is also a remedy in damages under s2(1) Misrepresentation Act 1967.

Where the company is in liquidation, the liquidator may recover secret profits and damages from the promoter even if what is recovered is used to pay off all the company's debts.

Compensation for loss or damage caused to a subscriber of the company's shares on the faith of an untrue statement in the prospectus of which the promoter was a party is also available: as explained in the section on prospectus issues (see paragraph 5.3).

Remuneration of promoter

The traditional way for promoters to obtain their reward was in the form of profit made on property sold to the company or some other ancillary transaction, provided disclosure was made. Where the promoters have only provided services and incurred expenses then difficulties may arise when considering how promoters are to be renumerated for this.

Perhaps the best way to ensure renumeration for promotional services and reimbursement for expenses is for the articles to contain a provision allowing the directors a discretion to pay such sums. There is no such provision in the current Table A, although there was in the old Table A of 1948. Of course, such a provision does not create a binding obligation but there will not usually be a problem where the company promoters become its first directors.

Another possibility is for the company, once it has been formed, to contract with the promoter to pay for his services and expenses. This will have to be a deed contract to be enforceable because the promoter will already have performed his services to the company. Therefore this will amount to past consideration, ruling out a simple contract.

A purported contract, to pay for a promoters services and expenses, between the company and the promoter before the company is formed, will have no effect for it is not possible to contract with a person who does not exist. Similarly, after formation it is not possible for the company to ratify the contract. This is because ratification takes effect from the time the contract was made and at this time the company would not yet have been formed. These points are developed further under the following heading, 'Pre-incorporation contracts'.

Finally, mention should be made of remunerating promoters by issuing them with shares in the company. Historically, this was a popular method whereby promoters would take deferred or founders' shares in the company which often gave them favourable dividend and voting rights. Such shares are now uncommon. Public companies by virtue of s99(2) are prohibited from accepting services in exchange for shares. Details of any renumeration together with who it is to be paid must be disclosed in any prospectus the company issues.

Pre-incorporation contracts

A pre-incorporation contract is a contract purported to be made by or on behalf of a company which has not yet been formed. The question which arises is who is liable on such contracts? Is the company liable or is it the promoter who incurs liability?

At common law the following rules were established.

1. Until a company is formed it has no legal existence. A company comes into being from the date in its certificate of incorporation: s13 and *Re Jubilee Cotton Mills* [1920] Ch 100. Prior to this a pre-incorporation contract cannot be enforced by or against the company, for it is not possible to contract with a non-existent person.

   This is illustrated by the leading case of *Kelner* v *Baxter* (1866) LR 2 CP 174. In this case Baxter and two other promoters agreed to buy some wines and spirits from Kelner and signed the order on behalf of an hotel company which they had not yet formed. When the company was formed, the wines and spirits were consumed but the company failed before Kelner was paid. It was held that the company was not liable for the wines and spirits. Erle CJ said:

   > 'When the company came afterwards into existence it was a totally new creature, having rights and obligations from that time, but no rights or obligations by reason of anything which might have been done before.'

2. An attempt to ratify the contract by the company after it has been formed will not save the contract. This is because ratification has retrospective effect and

attempts to give authority to a person at the time the contract was made. Since a company will not have been formed at this time it cannot be given the necessary authority: *Kelner* v *Baxter* (1866) LR 2 CP 174, *Natal Land Co Ltd* v *Pauline Colliery Syndicate Ltd* [1904] AC 120.

3. If the company is not liable on the contract, the promoters may be personally liable: *Kelner* v *Baxter* (1866) LR 2 CP 174.
4. Where the promoter does not sign the contract as an agent, but merely to authenticate the company's signature then no contract exists at all: *Newborne* v *Sensolid (Great Britain) Ltd* [1954] 1 QB 45.
5. A company may have rights and obligations under the contract where there has been a novation. This consists of the substitution of a new contract, once the company has been formed, for the pre-incorporation contract. The difficulty is deciding whether there actually is a new contract, as merely ratifying or adopting the old one will not suffice: *Re Northumberland Avenue Hotel Co Ltd* (1886) 33 Ch D 16, CA.

A fresh contract was found to exist in *Howard* v *Patent Ivory Manufacturing Co* (1888) 38 Ch D 156 where an important term of the pre-incorporation contract, namely the price, was changed after incorporation and this was held to be sufficient.

The common law position outlined above was altered in 1972 as a result of our entry into the European Community. On entry we had to comply with the First EEC Council Directive 68/151, Article 7 of which states:

> 'If, before a company being formed has acquired legal personality, action has been carried out in its name and the company does not assume the obligations arising from such action, the persons who acted shall, without limit, be jointly and severally liable therfor, unless otherwise agreed.'

This was originally implemented in s9(2) of the European Communities Act 1972 and can now be found in s36C(1) of the Companies Act 1985. It provides that:

> 'A contract which purports to be made by or on behalf of a company when the company has not been formed has effect, subject to any agreement to the contrary, as one made with the person purporting to act for the company or as agent for it, and he is personally liable on the contract accordingly.'

The result is that the promoter is now personally liable irrespective of the capacity in which he contracts and any subtle distinctions raised by *Kelner* v *Baxter* and *Newborne* v *Sensolid* are rendered irrelevant by s36C(1). However, despite the presence of this section, it still took a Court of Appeal decision to put the matter beyond doubt.

In *Phonogram Ltd* v *Lane* [1982] QB 938 the defendant signed the contract 'for and on behalf of Fragile Management Ltd', a company which was not yet formed. The plaintiffs sued for the return of an advance payment repayable under the terms of the agreement, claiming that the defendant was personally liable under what is now s36C(1). The Court of Appeal found for the plaintiffs. Lord Denning felt that the section had 'obliterated' fine distinctions which had been created by the way promoters signed the contract. The words, 'subject to any agreement to the contrary' require an express agreement and cannot be inferred by a promoter signing as agent for the company.

In recent years the main issue of concern has been the application of s36C(1) to non-existent and wrongly named companies. In *Oshkosh B'Gosh* v *Dan Marbel Inc and Coase* (1988) 4 BCC 795 the Court of Appeal held that the section did not apply to make a director personally liable where the company was waiting for a new certificate of incorporation to reflect a change of name. The company had ordered goods under its new name before the new certificate of incorporation bearing the new name had been issued. Could it be argued that the company had not yet been formed and that therefore the director who purported to make the contract on behalf of the company was personally liable? Nourse LJ held that the section had no application as the company was formed at the time the contract was made, despite the fact that it was acting and trading under an incorrect name. Nourse LJ also held that the issue of a new certificate of incorporation to reflect a name change under ss28(6) and (7) does not affect the continued existence of a company.

In *Cotronic (UK) Ltd* v *Dezonie* [1991] BCC 200 the Court of Appeal again excused a defendant from personal liability under the section. In this case a contract was entered into at a time when, unknown to both parties, the company had been struck off the register five years earlier and therefore did not exist. On discovering this a new company was formed with the same name. However, it was held that this was not enough to make the defendant liable under s36C(1) because at the time of signing the contract the formation of the new company had not been contemplated. The contract was therefore void since the company did not exist and the new company was not in the course of formation, however, a claim for quantum meruit was allowed. See also *Badgerhill Properties Ltd* v *Cottrell* [1991] BCC 463

Finally, it is important to note that there are limits to the operation of s36C(1). First, it says nothing about the company's liability, only that of the promoters. Therefore the common law rules are still applicable when considering the company's position. Secondly, the section does not make it clear whether the promoter can *enforce* a pre-incorporation contract; it mentions only liability. It would be a strange result, however, if a promoter was liable on such a contract but could not enforce it. Lastly, the section will not apply where, following the pre-incorporation contract, the company is eventually formed outside the United Kingdom, for example in Guernsey: *Rover International Ltd* v *Canon Films Ltd* [1989] 1 WLR 912 CA.

Quasi-contract and tort

The law of restitution enables a contracting party who has delivered goods to a company which, after incorporation, makes use of them, to recover a reasonable amount for the goods. If the contracting party requires return of the goods and is refused, he can bring a claim in tort for conversion.

5.2 Flotation

Introduction

The syllabus includes 'The Prospectus' and 'Commissions and Discounts' among the subjects on which questions may be set. A prospectus is an offer to the public of shares or debentures of a company for subscription or purchase: s744. Only a public company may lawfully issue a prospectus. Commissions and discounts are payments (or reduction in issue price) made to reward underwriters and brokers who give services in support of prospectus issues. 'Securities' in this section means shares and debentures.

However, it is not possible to study these subjects effectively unless the student also has a broad understanding of the methods by which companies raise the capital which they need for their businesses. Prospectus issues are a part only of that process. It is also necessary to look at the system by which the financial markets, in which securities are traded and new capital is raised, since prospectus law has recently been reformulated by the Financial Services Act 1986 and it is now an integrated part of the system of market regulation.

Raising capital

Every company, with the minor exception of companies limited by guarantee, is likely to issue shares to its members and must receive consideration for the shares of a value at least equal to the nominal value of the shares. The basic rules and procedure of the issue of shares are described in detail later (see paragraph 6.3 *Allotment of shares*) since it is only the offer of shares to the public which is a prospectus and a private company may not (with minor exceptions) issue a prospectus at all.

Companies, public and private, usually obtain their capital, ie the resources which they need in their business or other activity, from a variety of sources. The issue of share capital is only one such source of capital. Among the others are the following:

1. *Loan capital.* This is borrowed money. If it is raised on a fixed, usually long-term, basis it will take the form of *debentures* or *debenture stock*, with characteristics described in Chapter 7. Money may also be borrowed from the banks or other lenders on a short-term basis so that it is repayable on demand. The obvious case is borrowing through bank overdraft.
2. *Goods and services supplied on credit.* Again the terms of payment vary widely. Plant or machinery may be obtained under hire-purchase contracts by which payment is spread over a fixed period. Most trade suppliers of consumable materials etc expect payment within a short period after delivery.
3. *Bills of exchange* and the like are a method of obtaining credit which is not 'borrowing' in the technical sense though it creates liabilities.
4. *Retained profits* are a particularly attractive method of augmenting the resources of a company since they create no external liabilities but are 'reserves' or

'shareholders funds'. The cost is of course borne by the shareholders whose dividends are reduced to the extent that profits are retained within the business.

The appropriate mixture of sources of company finance must vary according to the circumstances of the company. Most companies make use of more than one type. The balance sheet, included in the annual accounts, discloses – to the expert eye at least – what the company's policy is and whether it is prudent and well-chosen.

The growth of a company

There is nothing in company law to prevent the formation of a new public company which immediately issues a prospectus inviting the public to subscribe for shares or debentures, thus providing cash to be used in establishing a new business. In practice it would be virtually impossible to raise investment capital in this way. It is too risky.

The more typical sequence in the growth of a company is as follows:

1. a private company is formed to found or acquire a small business. It may raise loan capital, eg by bank overdraft, but it has an initial share capital of a small amount subscribed by a group of shareholders who are also often the directors of the company and its working managers. The majority of companies do not expand beyond this structure though their scale of operations may become larger;
2. the needs of the growing company and the ambitions of its proprietors require that it shall be converted to a public company in order to raise more capital from financial institutions or from the investing public. It is not yet large enough to satisfy the conditions (and meet the expense) of a full Stock Exchange listing for its securities. But, as explained later, there are intermediate securities markets in which a fledgling public company will be at home for a time. The company may well take advantage of its new status to issue shares (or less often debentures) both to raise additional fixed capital and to widen the market for the shares;
3. the final stage in the growth of a very successful company is a Stock Exchange listing. Thereafter it will expand by making 'rights issues' of new shares (as explained below) or by offering its shares (or cash) to acquire the entire share capital of other companies. There are many possible variants of this outline but it is sketched here to illustrate the kinds of 'prospectus issue' for which the securities markets exist.

A company may of course be formed to acquire a large established business, usually from another company, or to effect a reconstruction of an existing enterprise. In those cases the company may seek a Stock Exchange listing, and perhaps raise additional capital, as soon as it has been launched.

The word 'flotation' which is adopted as the general title of this section is not a technical term. It is generally understood to denote the point at which a company, as in stage (2) of the outline above, first seeks to raise capital by offering securities on an established market.

Over the past hundred years there has been a significant change of emphasis in the market approach to securities offered by companies. In the late nineteenth century accuracy and completeness of the prospectus information was the main requirement. Nowadays, however, the investor looks back over the record of the company for a period of years and considers its forecasts, to assess its prospects of continued success and sound management in the future.

A Stock Exchange listing is therefore more than an incident of a successful prospectus issue since the company must, as a condition of its listing, enter into 'Continuing Obligations' to the Stock Exchange, which are intended to prevent sharp practice and above all to elicit from the company a regular flow of accurate information about the company's affairs. Good information, available to everyone, is the basis of a sound and fair market in the shares of a company. In this way prospectus law has been absorbed into a wider system of financial market regulation.

The markets in securities

In addition to the shares or debentures of companies the market deals in the loan stocks issued by public bodies such as the central and local government and some other, less ordinary financial investments.

The business of dealing in securities is now regulated by the Financial Services Act 1986 which distinguishes between 'listed securities' subject to Pt IV of the Act and 'unlisted securities' which are subject to Pt V. Listed securities are those which have been admitted to the Official List of the Stock Exchange. To get a listing on the Stock Exchange the company concerned must have a trading record of at least three years, have a market value of its shares to be listed of at least £700,000 and 25 per cent of any class of its shares must be held by members of the public, rather than institutional shareholders. At the end of 1994, there were 2,534 companies listed on the Stock Exchange, including 464 overseas companies.

There are several markets for unlisted securities.

1. The *Unlisted Securities Market* ('USM') which is a 'junior league' of the Stock Exchange, established in 1980 to provide a regulated market for securities of companies which could not yet satisfy the conditions for a full listing and permission to deal on the Stock Exchange. There is no minimum market value of shares required and the company need only have a two year trading record. Only 10 per cent of any class of its shares needs to be in public hands. As at 31 December 1994 there were 207 companies quoted on the USM and new applications to this market also closed on that date. It is proposed to abolish the market at the end of 1996. The popularity of the USM has been declining and companies often prefer to wait the extra year to satisfy the three year trading record, and then seek a listing on the Stock Exchange for the additional prestige that it brings.

2. The *Over the Counter Market* which is operated by authorised dealers in securities as an alternative to the Stock Exchange markets.
3. The *Third Market* which was established by the Stock Exchange in 1987 in an attempt to draw into its ambit the securities dealt in on the 'over the counter market'. The Third Market did not live up to expectations and was abolished on 31 December 1990.
4. *The Alternative Investment Market* (AIM) is a new market which is the successor to the USM. Trading on this market is due to start on 19 June 1995. There are no conditions on the market value of shares, length of trading record or as to the percentage of shares in public hands. However, the company will have to submit a prospectus, complying with Regulations to be published in March 1995, appoint and retain a nominated advisor and broker, and meet a number of continuing obligations such as the prompt disclosure of price sensitive information to the Stock Exchange. Shares on the AIM are to be traded on a new trading system called SEATS PLUS, which comes on line in June 1995.

The control of listed securities

Listed securities are subject to regulation by the Stock Exchange, whose 'Yellow Book' (*The Admission of Securities to Listing*) now has the status of legal regulations made under FSA. Conventional prospectus law, contained in Part III and Schedule 3 of the Companies Act 1985 does not now apply to listed securities, although some features of it reappear in the FSA system. In September 1993 the Stock Exchange published a new Yellow Book and gave it a new title, *The Listing Rules*. These replace the old rules contained in *Admission of Securities to Listing*, and came into effect on 1 December 1993.

The outright transfer of responsibility to the Stock Exchange is the culmination of a long process of change. Until 1984 normal prospectus requirements did apply to listed securities. However, it was always an essential part of a prospectus issue by an established public company that the new securities, when issued, should have a Stock Exchange listing. Admission to this premier securities market at least doubled the market price of the securities because they could be much more readily bought and sold. The Stock Exchange insisted on seeing the draft prospectus before it was published and, as a condition of its approval, demanded that it should include more detailed information than the prescribed particulars (for a prospectus) contained in the current Companies Act. The prospectus as published complied with Stock Exchange as well as statutory requirements, but the former were more demanding.

In 1984 formal control was given to the Stock Exchange by the Stock Exchange (Listing) Regulations 1984. This change was made to comply with European Community requirements for a system of regulating to securities markets, which is a wider concept than the control of prospectus issues. The system introduced under FSA Pt IV is an improved model of the 1984 regime (and the 1984 regulations have been repealed).

A significant difference between the 1984 and the FSA system of control is that the latter applies to issues of securities for a non–cash consideration. As a result 'take-over bids' on the basis of share exchange are now subject to the same requirements of accuracy and completeness of information as prospectus issues for cash.

There are two main elements in the system of control:

1. *listing particulars* must be published before securities are listed. A copy of these particulars must also be delivered to the registry (FSA s149) for filing, just as under the old system a copy of a prospectus had to be delivered under s64 of the Companies Act 1985. Hence listing particulars are a form of prospectus although not described as such;
2. *continuing obligations* (set out in detail in the Yellow Book) are imposed on the company as a condition of its listed status. As one example among many these obligations define in detail how a listed company shall make 'preliminary announcements' of its half-year and year-end financial results for the period.

Section 145(1) of the Financial Services Act 1986 allows the Stock Exchange, in accordance with the listing rules, to discontinue the listing of any securities if satisfied that there are special circumstances which preclude normal regular dealings in the securities. A recent example of this can be seen in the case of *R* v *International Stock Exchange of the UK and the Republic of Ireland Ltd, ex parte Else* (1982) Ltd [1993] 2 WLR 70. The Court of Appeal in the same case held that shareholders have no right to be notified or to make representations at a hearing before a committee of the Stock Exchange to delist a company's shares.

Control of unlisted securities

The old prospectus law (Companies Act 1985 Part III) continues to apply to unlisted securities until such time as FSA Pt V comes into effect. However it is of little practical importance since most offers of unlisted securities are subject to elaborate USM regulations. The remainder of this section summarises the effect of FSA Pt V, which in due course will give legal force to USM rules.

Here the control is confined to '*offers* of unlisted securities' (the title given to FSA Pt V). Broadly it is an updated version of the previous system for control of the issue of a company prospectus and the word 'prospectus' is applied to it. Overall responsibility for administration rests with the DTI but there are two alternative methods of control:

1. 'an approved exchange', such as the USM, may be given power to authorise (under FSA s159) the issue of the prospectus, ie decide what it shall contain, before it is delivered to the registry for filing and before it is published as an advertisement of securities offered to the public;
2. regulations made by the DTI will in any other case determine what the prospectus shall contain.

The apparent weakness of the residual control in (2) is that it does not require a 'pre-vetting' of a prospectus in draft by the regulatory body of an organised market in securities. Experience in the past has shown that this preliminary dialogue between the market and the company is the best way of ensuring full disclosure of all the relevant facts.

There is, however, a duty imposed on those who produce the relevant document relating to listed or unlisted securities, to ensure that it gives 'all such information as investors and their professional advisers would reasonably require and reasonably expect to find there, for the purpose of making an informed assessment' of the financial position of the issuing company and of the securities themselves: FSA s146 (listing particulars) and s163 (prospectus for unlisted securities). The responsibility for including all such information is therefore placed on those who prepare the document and it is no answer, if information is omitted, that there was no 'pre-vetting' or that those who examined the document did not call for the pertinent information. Those who know, or should know, must tell all.

The question of liability for the issue of a document which is misleading or incomplete has been little affected by the recent changes in the regulatory system (see paragraph 5.3).

Methods of issue of securities

The explanation above has incidentally mentioned some methods by which the public may be invited to subscribe for securities. A summary may be useful at this point:

1. *Direct invitation to the public.* This is the original form of prospectus. It is still used in such cases as 'privatisation issues' of the share capital of major enterprises, such as British Telecommunications or British Gas. Anyone may apply for as many shares as he wishes and copies of the prospectus are widely distributed and also published in the newspapers.

2. *Rights issue.* This is the standard method by which an established public company raises additional capital. It issues to each of its members a provisional letter of allotment by which he is entitled on payment of the issue price, to be registered as the holder of new shares. The number of shares so allotted is related to his existing holding. If, for example, it is an issue on the basis of one (new) share for every two existing shares, the holder of say 1,000 shares would be provisionally allotted 500 at a price rather below their current market value. If he does not wish to subscribe for additional shares he may renounce the letter and sell his right to subscribe for 500 shares (nil paid) on the market at a price related to the discount of the issue price on the market value. Because the shares may in the end be taken up by anyone, the initial offer to existing shareholders is treated as a prospectus.

3. *Offer for sale.* Under this procedure the company allots a large block of new shares to an 'issuing house' and the latter re-sells the shares by offering them to

the public. This is treated as a prospectus for which both the company and the issuing house have responsibility. This method would commonly be used by a company which was being 'floated' ie launched as a listed or USM company for the first time. It is a requirement of flotation that a substantial number of shares shall be made available for new investors. The company usually wishes to raise additional capital for expansion at this point. The issuing house is normally a merchant bank, which advises and supports the company in this way. Without that support the company, as a newcomer to the market, would have difficulty in making a successful issue (including getting it underwritten in advance as explained later).

4. *Placing.* Under this procedure the new securities are allotted in the first instance in substantial blocks to a small number of financial institutions ('the placees') with the intention that the latter should, when they can re-sell at a profit, dispose of some if not all their holdings to the public. This method is particularly suitable for the issue of debenture stock.

5. *Offer by tender.* This is a variant method in which the company or issuing house does not announce in advance a fixed issue price. Instead it invites tenders for specified numbers of shares at a price (usually above a specified level) to be selected by each bidder. The shares are then allotted to the highest bidders taken in descending level of their bids to the point at which all the shares have been taken up.

Securities of private companies

The securities of private companies may not be 'listed' on the Stock Exchange: FSA s143(3).

It is also the long-established policy that private companies should raise capital by arrangement with persons connected with them and should not make general offers of their securities to the public. Under the law in force until 1986 (Companies Act 1985 s81) there was a simple prohibition, against prospectus offers, imposed on private companies. However, there was a problem of definition – how widely might a private company publicise its efforts to raise capital without going over the line and making what was 'an offer to the public'? Renunciation by the original offeree was permitted if confined to persons connected with him.

In the new FSA system there is a general prohibition against a private company issuing an advertisement offering its securities: FSA s170(1). However, the DTI has power by regulation to make exceptions for specified categories (FSA s160(6)):

1. advertisements of a private character, including cases where the company and the persons to whom they are addressed are connected;
2. advertisements which deal with investments only incidentally;
3. advertisements addressed to persons who appear to the DTI to be sufficiently expert to understand the risks involved.

The DTI may extend the exemption to other types of advertisement.

Underwriting commissions and brokerage

The company or issuing house cannot be certain in advance that sufficient applications will be received from the public to take up all the securities which it is proposed to issue. Many practical difficulties would result if the issue were 'under-subscribed' (and these were recognised in the previous prospectus law).

It has therefore long been standard practice to insure against the risk by arranging for every public issue to be underwritten. The effect of an underwriting agreement is that the underwriter undertakes irrevocably to subscribe for all the securities, or for a given proportion of the issue, to the extent that public response (in applications) is insufficient. If the issue is 'over-subscribed' the underwriter is not called upon to take up any part of the issue.

For his services the underwriter is paid a commission on the number of shares etc, which he underwrites. These are payments out of capital money, ie the proceeds of the issue of shares, and are restricted by s97 (as amended by FSA Sch 16 para 16). The payment must be authorised by the articles and may not exceed a maximum of 10 per cent of the share price; in practice it is always much less.

The heavy risk incidental to underwriting a large issue is illustrated by the cost, in tens or hundreds of millions of pounds, to the underwriters of the British Petroleum sale which was devastated by the market crash of October 1987. They were required to take up at the issue price shares whose market value was much less. It is normal practice therefore for the underwriters to enter into sub-underwriting contracts with others to sub-contract the risk. In return the underwriters share their commission with the sub-underwriters. However, that is a matter of private arrangement between them which is of no direct concern to the company.

Brokerage is a payment to a person who finds others to subscribe for securities of the company but does not himself undertake to do so. A bank or a stockbroker might undertake to circularise its clients in support of an issue of securities and thereby earn a commission.

5.3 Liability for defects in listing particulars and prospectuses

Introduction

The issue of company securities is a form of contract for which the common law remedies of rescission for misrepresentation and damages for various forms of loss are available. In applying these principles to prospectus issues however, these remedies were found to be inadequate, notably in the celebrated decision in *Derry* v *Peek* (1889) 14 App Cas 337. Since 1890 therefore the common law remedies have been supplemented, as regards defects in prospectuses, by a statutory right to obtain compensation for loss suffered. The common law remedies have also been modified by the Misrepresentation Act 1967.

The statutory remedy of compensation has itself recently been modified by FSA ss150 and 166, of which a summary is given below. It is also necessary to consider the common law remedies, since whatever their problems they have a wider potential application. The statutory remedy does not apply to give protection where persons have suffered loss in connection with securities issued by private companies as a result of their misleading statements.

There is very little modern case law on the common law prospectus remedies. The very searching examination of draft prospectuses by merchant banks and by the Stock Exchange, the so-called 'pre-vetting' procedure, brings to notice and eliminates many of the errors or deceptions which plagued the nineteenth century company prospectus issues. However, examination questions on prospectus liability call for a sound knowledge of the nineteenth century case law and reference should now be made to *Al-Nakib Investments (Jersey) Ltd* v *Longcroft* [1990] 1 WLR 1390.

The limits of the remedy

It is generally necessary to consider: (1) what is the basis of claiming the remedy; (2) who is liable; (3) who may claim; (4) what is the measure of damages or compensation awarded; (5) what defences may be available.

Paragraph *The basis of statutory compensation* to *Defences to a claim for statutory compensation* is concerned with the statutory remedy of compensation given by FSA. Paragraph 5.3 *Criminal Liability* deals with criminal penalties, which are also statutory. The remainder of this section then considers the older common law principles.

The basis of statutory compensation

Compensation may be awarded in respect of 'any untrue or misleading statement ... or the omission of any matter required to be included'. This formula applies to listing particulars (FSA s150) and to prospectuses relating to unlisted securities (FSA s166).

Unlike Part III of the Companies Act 1985, now replaced, there is a single remedy for both what is wrongly stated and what is wrongly omitted. In connection with omissions those who issue listing particulars or a prospectus (for brevity 'a document' in the following passage) have an obligation to include 'all such information as investors and their professional advisers ... would reasonably require and reasonably expect to find' in the document. This is a catch-all provision to supplement the numerous specific points for disclosure prescribed by the relevant market or statutory regulations applicable to the document.

The claimant is not required to show that he read and relied on the document. This is reasonable since he may have relied on the opinion of experts who had considered it in detail and formed their published judgment in reliance on it. However, he cannot recover compensation in respect of things of which he had actual knowledge, because he was not then misled: FSA ss151(5)/167(5).

Who is liable to pay statutory compensation

Liability, unless they can establish an available defence (see paragraph 5.3 *Defences to a claim for statutory compensation*), is on the persons responsible for the issue of the document. Under FSA ss152(1)/168(1) they include:

1. the person who issues the securities, ie the company as a legal person;
2. if the issuer is a corporate body, its directors (including any person who has agreed to be named in the document as such) at the time when the document is submitted to the Stock Exchange or delivered to the registry for filing as the case may be;
3. any person who, with his authority, is stated in the document to accept responsibility for the whole or part of it, and any person who has authorised all or part of the document. This brings into the net the expert, such as an accountant or valuer, whose report is cited in the document.

Who is entitled to compensation

A claimant must show that he has 'acquired' the securities to which the document relates and has suffered loss in respect of them as a result of an untrue or misleading statement or wrongful omission: FSA ss150/166.

'Acquisition' for this purpose includes entering into a contract to acquire, eg as a purchaser, or having an interest in the securities. 'Acquire' has a wider meaning than 'subscribe for' (used in the corresponding s67 of the Companies Act 1985). It is arguable therefore that a person who purchases the securities in the market will be able to claim compensation but the point is not free from doubt. The defence in paragraph 5.3 *Defences to a claim for statutory compensation*, (4), implies that a claim might arise some time after the time of issue of the securities, though that is not quite the same point.

The measure of compensation

Compensation is recoverable for 'loss suffered'. It is thought that this retains the previous limit of the difference between the price paid and the value of the securities when the true position is realised. There is no reference to breach of contract or to damages for it, which would provide a basis for a claim for loss of the profitable bargain which the claimant hoped to obtain.

Defences to a claim for statutory compensation

The defendant must first satisfy the court that, at the time of issue of the document, he reasonably believed (after making any enquiries which it was reasonable to make) that the statement was true and not misleading or, as the case may be, that material which should have been included was properly omitted. He must show that:

1. he continued in that belief until the claimant acquired the securities; or
2. it was not practicable for him to bring a correction to the notice of those who acquired the securities before they had in fact done so; or
3. he had taken all reasonable steps to bring a correction to their notice before they acquired the securities; or
4. the securities were acquired by the claimant after such a lapse of time that the defendant ought in the circumstances to be reasonably excused.

Criminal liability

There are no longer specific criminal penalties for offences in connection with prospectuses but FSA contains two sections imposing liability for publishing inaccurate information which could be applied in prospectus cases:

1. making a statement, promise or forecast which is misleading, false or deceptive, if the person who makes it knows of its falsity etc or makes it recklessly. It is also an offence to conceal dishonestly material information: FSA s47;
2. furnishing, knowing its falsity or acting recklessly, information required under FSA, which is false or misleading in a material particular: FSA s200.

It is an offence under s19 of the Theft Act 1968 for an officer of a company:

1. knowingly to make a statement which is false, misleading or deceptive
2. with intent to deceive the members or creditors of the company.

The effect of (2) is to confine liability for a prospectus to cases where, as in a rights issue, it is issued to existing members or debentureholders. This provision, in an earlier form, was the basis of the successful prosecution of a company chairman in *R v Lord Kylsant* [1932] 1 KB 442.

In certain cases the court has power (Powers of Criminal Courts Act 1973 s35) to order a convicted person to pay compensation for loss or damage resulting from the offence of which he has been convicted.

Common law remedies

'Common law' is here used to denote remedies developed by the courts: rescission is historically an equitable remedy.

A contract which is induced by misrepresentation is voidable, whether the misrepresentation is fraudulent, negligent or entirely innocent. That is the basis of the remedy of rescission. It can only be exercised against the company if it has allotted securities directly to subscribers. In an offer for sale the rescission of the contract of sale is a remedy against the issuing house, though the latter is likely to have a similar remedy against the company.

Rescission is an inadequate remedy for a misleading or incomplete prospectus, since the right to rescind has usually been lost before it can be exercised. To recover damages the holder of securities, who has been misled by the prospectus, must establish one of the available legal bases of claim. As will be seen there are several grounds, particularly deceit, negligent mis-statement and liability under the Misrepresentation Act 1967.

The problem which confronts a claimant here is to produce the required evidence of dishonesty or at least of carelessness on the part of the defendant. Claims for damages are generally against the individuals who issued the prospectus rather than against the company, unless its vicarious responsibility is established.

The statutory remedy of compensation was introduced so that the claimant's burden of proof was limited to showing the fault in the prospectus. Those who had issued it were then liable to compensate him unless they could exculpate themselves (see paragraph 5.3 *Defences to a claim for statutory compensation*). They know the circumstances in which the prospectus was issued and so it is fairer to require them to produce evidence on that subject.

Rescission

Where a person has been induced to subscribe for or purchase shares on the basis of a misrepresentation of fact (whether fraudulent, negligent or wholly innocent), he may claim rescission of the contract, to be put back into the position in which he was when it was made and to be indemnified against any expenses incurred. A statement of opinion which the maker did not hold will also found a claim for rescission.

Rescission is available against the company where:

1. the company has actual or constructive knowledge that the contract is made on the basis of the representation;
2. the misrepresentation has been made by a person with the authority of an agent of the company (see Chapter 3): *Lynde* v *Anglo-Italian Hemp Spinning Co* [1896] 1 Ch 178. If the company has not been formed when the promoter makes his misrepresentation, he is not then its agent. However the person misled may rescind if at the time of allotment the company is aware of the promoter's misrepresentation: *Re Metropolitan Coal Consumers Association, Karsberg's Case* [1892] 3 Ch 1. But a subscriber to the memorandum who has been misled cannot rescind his undertaking therein to subscribe for shares: *Re Metal Constituents Ltd, Lord Lurgan's Case* [1902] 1 Ch 707, since s22 applies.

    (Note also that a company is liable for statements made on the basis of an expert's report unless it expressly makes clear it does not verify the report's accuracy: *Re Pacaya Rubber Co* [1914] 1 Ch 542);
3. the misrepresentation is made in a prospectus or listing particulars deemed to be issued by the company.

With regard to (2) there will be no doubt in cases where the company has complied with the correct procedure of applying for a listing or issuing a prospectus relating to the issue of unlisted securities. The area of doubt is where an invitation is issued or information supplied, which constitute 'an advertisement offering securities' as defined by FSA s158(4) but the correct procedure has not been adopted. The company and its officers would then be guilty of an offence. The company could not escape civil liability to rescission because it had behaved unlawfully. The situation is most likely to arise where the representation is made by an agent, as described in (1) above.

Loss of right to rescind

In the following circumstances the right to rescind is lost.

1. Affirmation: If the plaintiff affirms with knowledge of the truth, eg by accepting dividends, voting at meetings or trying to sell his shares: *Central Railway Co of Venezuela* v *Kish* (1867) LR 2 HL 99; see also *Lonrho plc* v *Fayed (No 2)* [1991] 4 All ER 961.
2. Intervention of third party rights. Thus, if the company goes into liquidation, the supervening rights of the creditors bar rescission: *Oakes* v *Turquand* (1867) LR 2 HL 325.
3. Impossibility of restitutio in integrum, of restoring the status quo. But this is of little practical importance here.
4. Lapse of time. In cases of fraud, time runs from discovery of the misrepresentation.
5. Note: where rescission is otherwise available and has not been barred, the court may exercise its discretion to award damages in lieu of rescission in cases of non-fraudulent misrepresentation (s2(2) Misrepresentation Act 1967) (see below).

Damages recoverable by reason of a defective prospectus or listing particulars

As already indicated (paragraph 5.3 *Common law remedies*) there are a number of possible grounds for claiming damages. These circumstances may constitute an infringement of the regulatory system imposed by FSA or entitle the company, if it is liable, to compensation from the responsible officer. The claim for damages may on the other hand be against an individual, and not against the company. Each of these questions has to be considered separately in the context of the type of liability to pay damages.

Damages for deceit

The tort of deceit consists in knowingly making false statements by which the plaintiff suffers loss. In the context of prospectus etc issues it overlaps with 'fraudulent misrepresentation'. In the leading case (*Derry* v *Peek* above) the House of Lords held that to constitute fraud the false statement must have been made either (1) with knowledge that it was untrue or (2) without believing it to be true or (3) recklessly, careless whether it be true or false.

In *Derry*'s case the directors had stated truthfully in the prospectus that under a private Act of Parliament the company might operate a steam-tramway service in Plymouth. They did not say, however, because they failed to appreciate its significance, that the company would have to obtain a licence from the Board of Trade before it might substitute steam trams for horse-drawn trams, which was the original project. A claim against the directors for damages failed because there was no fraud in the sense defined above. At that time damages could not be recovered for negligent misrepresentation.

The difficulty of proving 'fraudulent intent' plus the obstacle presented by the '*Houldsworth* principle' below makes it unlikely that damages will be recovered under this head of liability. Other pertinent case law points to note are:

1. If the plaintiff is not the person, or one of the class of persons, intended to rely on the false statement, he cannot bring an action in deceit. Thus, a person who buys shares in the market cannot sue on the basis of a mis-statement in a prospectus made to induce persons to subscribe for shares: *Peek* v *Gurney* (1873) 6 HL 377. But he can do so where a statement in a prospectus is meant to mislead subsequent purchasers or if a later misrepresentation re-activates a statement in the prospectus: *Andrews* v *Mockford* [1896] 1 QB 372.
2. The plaintiff must in fact have been influenced by the misrepresentation. Even in the absence of specific evidence, that result is readily inferred if the misrepresentation relates to a matter of obvious importance. If, however, the plaintiff made his own enquiries and relied on those, he cannot claim that he was misled by an admittedly inaccurate statement: *Jennings* v *Broughton* (1853) 5 De GM and G 126. But the misrepresentation need not be the sole ground for the plaintiff's decision to apply for the securities: *Edgington* v *Fitzmaurice* (1885) 29 Ch D 459.
3. From 1880 to 1990 it was held, as a matter of principle, that a shareholder could not sue the company for damages for deceit because it would be unfair to creditors that he should thereby diminish the remaining assets of the company (probably by now insolvent). He was not so debarred if he first terminated his membership of the company to become a creditor himself. But by the time he was aware of the deceit it was usually too late to rescind, and so he could not sue: *Houldsworth* v *City of Glasgow Bank* (1880) 5 App Cas 317. However this technical point has now been overruled by a new s111A (s131 CA 1989) which declares that present or past membership shall not be a bar to obtaining damages or other compensation from a company.

The *Houldsworth* principle only applied to members and so it never impeded a claim by debentureholders, based on a fraudulent prospectus, but the better course for them, in most cases, was to enforce their claims as creditors under the debenture.

Damages for non-fraudulent misrepresentation
Damages cannot be awarded at common law for a misrepresentation which is neither fraudulent nor negligent. In such a case the plaintiff must seek rescission plus an indemnity (see below).

A common law action for damages for negligent mis-statement can be maintained against a defendant owing a duty of care to the plaintiff under the principle of *Hedley, Byrne & Co Ltd* v *Heller & Partners Ltd* [1964] AC 465. The scope of the *Hedley Byrne* principle is unclear, despite subsequent judicial elaboration but its application is by no means excluded from cases where the plaintiff is relying on a statement in a prospectus or by a director. Resort may have to be had to it wherever there is no better remedy available.

If he relies on the *Hedley Byrne* principle the plaintiff has to show both that the defendant owed him a duty of care and also that he was negligent. It is doubtful whether such a duty is owed by a company or its directors to subscribers for its securities. However, in the *Hedley Byrne* case some members of the House of Lords thought that there might be such a duty, especially in a 'rights issue' where the invitation to subscribe is addressed to existing shareholders. Another decision (*JEB Fasteners Ltd* v *Marks, Bloom & Co* [1981] 3 All ER 289) extends the duty of care to persons who are likely to be affected by the consequences of negligent mis-statement.

An action on this ground is best reserved for cases where no better remedy is available. Generally the statutory remedy (see paragraph 5.3 *The basis of statutory compensation*) or a claim for negligent misrepresentation (see *Damages in lieu of rescission*, below) will be easier to pursue.

Section 2(1) Misrepresentation Act 1967 only applies to a pre-contractual statement made by one contracting party to another. Of course, the contract for the issue of shares is between the member and the company but not an officer (eg a director). It provides an action for damages for negligent mis-statement and a better one than the common law action, for the burden of proof (of the absence, rather than the existence) of negligence is thrown on the defendant.

Damages in lieu in rescission

Where the remedy of rescission (see paragraph 5.3 *Rescission*) is available for non-fraudulent misrepresentation, the court had a discretion not to grant it but to declare the contract subsisting and to award damages in lieu of rescission, under s2(2) Misrepresentation Act 1967. Such damages cannot be sued for by a plaintiff. They may only be awarded as part of the court's discretion in refusing rescission. But they are prima facie available wherever rescission may be granted and has not become barred.

Common law damages for breach of statutory duty

As there is now an entitlement to statutory compensation in respect of *omission* of material from a prospectus etc (see paragraph 5.3 *The basis of statutory compensation*), a claim for damages is unlikely to be made under this head. Under the previous law there was no such entitlement.

Damages for breach of contract

Although a contract for subscription for shares may be entered on the basis of the terms of the prospectus, it is generally taken to be the case that this contract is replaced completely by novation on allotment by the agreement contained in the articles (Chapter 3), so mis-statements in a prospectus will not generally justify an action for breach of contract. Nor is such an action likely, on the authority of *Houldsworth*, while the plaintiff remains a member or even an allottee: *Re Addlestone Linoleum Co* (1887) 37 Ch D 191, particularly as his claim for breach of contract will be designed to secure damages for loss of profits, in addition to dividends he may receive along with the other members. And the device of allowing an action for damages for breach of collateral warranty or contract is unlikely to succeed nowadays (cf *Heilbut, Symons & Co* v *Buckleton* [1913] AC 30).

But where the difficulties of maintenance of capital and equal rights of membership are not present, an action for loss of expected profits may succeed: ie against a transferor of shares who is in breach of contract. Such an action is of course unlikely to be available against officers of the company as they are unlikely to enter into a contract with a subscriber for or purchaser of shares.

Action for damages

An action for damages will not lie where a shareholder has relied on alleged misrepresentations in a prospectus to purchase shares in the company through the stock market: see *Al-Nakib Investments (Jersey) Ltd* v *Longcroft* [1990] 1 WLR 1390.

6

Capital

6.1 Company capital

Introduction

The word 'capital' is used both in a general economic sense and in a more technical legal sense. In paragraph 5.2 *Raising capital* the methods have been described by which a company may obtain resources for use in its business. It issues shares to its members for which they must provide consideration, in cash or otherwise. It usually borrows, either on a long-term basis by the issue of debentures or as short-term finance, eg in the form of a bank overdraft, or both. It may obtain plant, materials or services which it needs on deferred payment terms. In these contexts the capital of a company is the total fund of resources at its disposal.

Share capital is the proprietors' contribution to and stake in the company. It differs from other forms of resource obtained from outside the company because share capital is not a liability though borrowing and resort to credit do create liabilities. However, it is not possible to match shares and external liabilities with the existing resources of the company. If it trades profitably and if its assets increase in monetary value, it is likely to accumulate 'reserves' in one form or another. When it pays dividends to its shareholders or if it suffers trading losses etc, its resources are diminished.

Company law recognises real value for some purposes, such as the prohibition against issuing shares at a discount on their nominal value and in defining what profits may be distributed as dividends. In other respects however, the treatment of share capital is rigid and rather artificial. This is partly a reflection of the fact that shareholders usually have the protection of limited liability. They provide the agreed consideration for their shares and have no further liability for the company's debts. The price of limited liability is that creditors have the first claim on the assets and capital may only be returned to shareholders (the principle of 'maintenance of capital') if debts have been paid in full (see paragraph 6.4).

Share capital – basic terms and principles

An important concept is authorised capital, the amount of capital a company is entitled by its memorandum to raise. The divisions of this amount (ie the shares) are units of nominal value. It represents the amount of capital that may prima facie be raised by issuing shares. A public company must have at least £50,000 nominal or 'authorised' capital: s11, s118.

The amount of capital that is in fact raised is the issued share capital. This represents in principle the liability of the members of the company. They are liable to the extent of the nominal (par) value of their shares, which means that the company is entitled to use the full amount of the sum received for the shares in order to satisfy claims against it. A public company must issue shares to a value of at least £50,000 before starting business: s117. If the issued shares are only partly paid for, claims are first satisfied out of this paid up capital. If that is not enough, the company can make calls on the members up to the unpaid amount. Uncalled capital is not usual nowadays as shares are generally full paid up, particularly as shares are often worth more than their nominal amount. Section 101 requires shares in a public company to be paid up at least to 25 per cent. Where it exists, the company may resolve that uncalled capital be treated as reserve capital, ie capital which is only to be called up on a winding-up: s120.

Allotted share capital is that to which the allottees have acquired an unconditional entitlement, with the right to be entered in the company's register of members as the holders of the shares: s738. That stage is usually reached when the company has received the whole amount payable on the shares at the time of allotment and the directors have formally resolved to allot the shares. Issued share capital is not a defined term but is usually taken to be share capital where allotment has been followed by delivery to the allottee of the share certificate to which he is entitled under s185, a provision which does not apply to a company to the extent that it has uncertificated shares.

As likely as not, shares will be issued at a *premium*, ie for a price or other consideration (eg a transfer of assets: *Henry Head and Company Limited* v *Ropner Holdings Limited* [1952] Ch 124) which is in excess of their nominal value. Thus, a shareholder may have to pay £3 for a £1 share. If so a sum equal to the aggregate amount or value of the premiums (the excess over the nominal value) must be transferred to a separate share premium account: s130.

Par value is an alternative expression for nominal value. 'Par' is the Latin word for 'equal' and it is used in relation to shares to indicate that the nominal value sets a minimum level of actual value of consideration to be provided for the share. For a £1 share the minimum issue price is £1, which is its par value. It may not be issued at a discount: s100.

Market value is a measure of the shareholder's proprietary interest in the assets of the company by reason of his shareholding, so that on a winding-up, he should be able to share in the assets if their value exceeds the nominal value of his shares and he will be able to claim a proportion of the sum represented by his shareholding after claims against the company have been satisfied. A better measure of the market value of his shareholding will be the price he can get on selling it to someone else, although this is essentially a private matter between seller and buyer, except in so far as they are dealing in shares quoted on a stock exchange.

One means by which the true worth of the company and its capital can be represented is to capitalise the amount in the reserve fund or the share premium account. In other words, the amount of capital not represented by shares can be used to pay for shares and these bonus shares issued to the existing shareholders. The value of their original shares will be reduced, but their loss will be nil as the amount represented by the sum capitalised is merely turned into more shares.

Conversely, by the purchase (and cancellation) of some of its own shares (ss162–166) a company may distribute surplus funds amongst its shareholders (see paragraph 6.4 *Purchase by a company of its own shares*).

6.2 Membership

Introduction

A person may become a member of a company if (1) he agrees; and (2) his name is entered in the register of members: s22. The three common methods are:

1. by being a subscriber to the memorandum of the company on its formation (see paragraph 6.2 *Subscribers to the memorandum*);
2. by applying for and being allotted shares of the company (see paragraph 6.6 *Allotment*);
3. by being entered in the register of members as transferee of shares (or by transmission) (see paragraph 6.7).

Subscribers to the memorandum

The memorandum of a company about to be formed must be subscribed by at least two persons (in practice only two) and each of them must state the number of shares for which he agrees to subscribe (in practice always one only): s2(5).

'The subscribers of a company's memorandum are deemed to have agreed to become members of the company, and on its registration shall be entered as such in its register of members': s22(1). Accordingly the company should, without allotment of the shares – which is not necessary or appropriate in this case – enter the names of the subscribers in the register of members as holders of their subscribers' shares. They are then liable to pay for their shares in cash: s106.

They may of course apply for the allotment of additional shares if they wish.

However, the subscribers' obligation is waived by the company if it forthwith allots all its shares to others; *Mackley's Case* (1875) 1 Ch D 247. Even in that situation, however, the subscribers' obligation is revived if the company later increases its authorised share capital so that shares become available for them: *Re London, Hamburg and Continental Exchange Bank, Evans' Case* (1867) LR 2 Ch App 427.

6.3 Shareholders' rights

General

Statutory rights arising from shareholdings, eg to requisition a general meeting (s368) are described elsewhere. The basic legal principles are as follows:

1. The shareholder may be said to have acquired, by virtue of his share, an interest measured by a sum of money and made up of various rights contained in the contract of membership (see paragraph 3.1 *The effect of the memorandum and articles*), including the right to a sum of money, so far as that sum has not been spent by the company or is subject to being drawn on to satisfy claims by the company's creditors on liquidation: *Borland's Trustee* v *Steel* [1901] 1 Ch 279. His share is an item of property and by virtue of it he has an interest in the company, albeit no proprietary right in the company's property.

2. In the absence of contrary provision in the memorandum or articles, it is presumed that the rights of all shareholders are equal. These include rights to equal liability to calls (where shares are not fully paid up) dividends (however much is paid up on each share: *Oakbank Oil Co* v *Crum* (1882) 8 App Cas 65) attendance and voting at meetings and return of capital on an authorised reduction or a winding up.

Class rights – preference shares

But where there exists more than one class of share (ie where there is one or more classes of preference shares), obviously there cannot be equality. In such a case the position seems to be as follows.

1. There is no implied condition that all shares must always rank equally. Therefore, a company may alter its articles to enable it to issue preference shares: *Andrews* v *Gas Meter Co* [1897] 1 Ch 361.

2. Where shares are preferential in one or more respects, the presumption of equality continues to apply to those respects where there is no preference (eg a right to a preferential dividend does not exclude the right to equal participation in assets on a winding-up): *Birch* v *Cropper* (1889) 14 App Cas 525.

3. Where preference shareholders have specified preferential rights as to dividends, those rights are deemed to be exhaustive: ie, they are not entitled after receiving their preferential dividend to participate in the remaining profits distributable by way of dividend: *Will* v *United Lankat Plantations Co Ltd* [1914] AC 11.

4. Where preference shareholders have a preferential right on a winding up to the return of the capital subscribed by them, that right is prima facie exhaustive as to return of capital and does not entitle them to participate in the return of the remaining capital: *Scottish Insurance Corporation Ltd* v *Wilsons & Clyde Coal Co Ltd* [1949] AC 462; *Re Isle of Thanet Electricity Supply Co Ltd* [1950] Ch 161.

5. Where undistributed profits are capitalised, they are to be treated as capital on a winding-up, to be paid to those entitled to participate in return of capital, and not as undistributed dividends, to be distributed amongst those entitled to dividends as payments to preferential shareholders of preferential dividends, if any: *Dimbula Valley (Ceylon) Tea Co Ltd* v *Laurie* [1961] Ch 353.

6. If there is a reduction of capital resulting in the preferential shareholders being paid off and the preference shareholders are not entitled to participate in surplus assets, they are only entitled to receive the nominal value of their shares, even if the market price is higher: *Re Chatterley-Whitfield Collieries Ltd* [1949] AC 512; *Re Saltdean Estate Co Ltd* [1968] 3 All ER 829.

7. Entitlement to a preference dividend merely gives the right to that dividend, eg 6 per cent on the nominal value of the shares, out of such profits as the company may decide to distribute in dividend to its members. It does not confer a right to insist that the company, if it has distributable profits, shall declare the dividend: *Bond* v *Barrow Haematite Steel Co* [1902] 1 Ch 353. Passing the dividend may of course, under the terms of issue of the shares, give to the preference shareholders additional or new rights, eg to vote at general meetings or to have the company put into liquidation. Alternatively the terms of issue may provide that, if the distributable profits are available, the company is required as a contractual obligation to pay the dividend: *Evling* v *Israel & Oppenheimer Ltd* [1918] 1 Ch 101.

It may be concluded that a person investing in preference shares should do his best to ensure either that he has his rights particularised in all situations in which they may differ from those of the ordinary shareholder (and not just in some particulars, for they will be exhaustive) or that certain of his rights (eg as to return of capital) are not particularised at all, so that they rank equally with those of ordinary shareholders.

Other special rights which may attach to shares

Apart from financial rights, eg to dividends or return of capital, attached to shares, there may be other important rights, such as the right to vote and to initiate or oppose company action.

The articles (Table A arts 54–63) always define what rights (if any) to vote at general meetings are given to the holders of shares and how they are to be exercised (see paragraph 8.1 *Proceedings at meetings*). However, a company might exclude Table A in its entirety without making adequate substitution for its basic provisions. To cover that kind of case it is provided that if the articles make no other provision every member of a company which has a share capital has one vote for each share or £10 stock which he holds: s370(6).

If a company has share capital every member, whose shares entitle him to attend and vote, has a statutory right to appoint a proxy (see paragraph 8.1 *Attendance at meetings*): s372. The articles cannot deprive him of this right.

There is, however, no legal requirement that every member shall have equal voting rights or any rights at all in respect of his shares and the rights given may be 'weighted' to give the holders of some shares more votes than others: *Bushell* v *Faith* [1970] AC 1099.

It is also possible to attach to a share special rights, such as the power to appoint and remove directors from office. It is not uncommon to find in the articles of a subsidiary a power to the holding company to appoint and remove its directors. When British Petroleum was privatised the British Government retained a single 'Gold Share' giving it a veto on decisions taken in general meeting.

In a number of passages (see paragraph 10.2 *Specific statutory rights* also) in this textbook there is mention of a statutory right given to shareholders to object to the court if they disagree with a decision taken in a company meeting, such as an alteration of the objects clause under s5 (see paragraph 4.1). These statutory rights are not attached to particular shares but are given to shareholder(s) if he or they have shares (usually voting shares) making up in the aggregate a specified minimum percentage. These are instances of statutory protection of minorities in particular situations (apart from the more general protection given to them as described in (Chapter 11).

The exercise of shareholders' rights

The basic principle is that a shareholder may exercise the rights which he has by virtue of his shares in whatever fashion he judges to be in his own interest. He has no fiduciary duty to the company or to other members (see paragraph 4.3 *Freedom of voting*). Even if he is also a director, his fiduciary duty in that capacity, does not usually inhibit his rights as a shareholder: *North-West Transportation Co Ltd* v *Beatty* (1887) 12 App Cas 589. However, the principal of 'minority protection' (Chapter 11) may alter the position in that respect in appropriate cases.

The rights attached to shares are defined in the articles (or less often in the memorandum) and both documents may be altered under specified procedures (see Chapter 4). The effect of the alteration may be to deprive a shareholder of existing rights or to modify them or to make them less valuable. These topics are considered later (see paragraphs 6.5 and 6.7).

Shareholders' liability to the company

Shares impose on the holder a liability to pay to the company the issue price, in cash or other agreed consideration, fixed at the time of issue. The company may not, without the shareholder's consent, increase that liability or require him to subscribe for additional shares: s16.

If, therefore, issued shares are fully paid, which is the normal case, the holder has no further liability to the company (assuming that it is a limited company). If, however, his shares are partly paid he is liable to pay the amount outstanding, and that liability passes with the shares if they are transferred to the next holder.

A public company must obtain at least one quarter of the nominal value and the whole of any premium due on its shares at the time of allotment: s101. For all companies the lateset time for payment of any sum still due on shares is when it is in liquidation; at that point the liquidator calls for payment of all unpaid capital.

The terms of issue of shares may include a timetable for payment of the subscription money, if it is not wholly paid in applying for the shares. For example, the privatisation of British Gas in late 1986 entailed the payment by investors of such a huge sum (in aggregate) that the 25p (nominal) shares were issued on terms which required 50p on application, 45p on 9 June 1987 and a final instalment of 40p per share on 19 April 1988. If there is a timetable of this kind the allottee has a contractual liability to pay on the due dates, which arises from his application (offer) for the shares.

In the past companies sometimes tried to make the issue of their shares more attractive to investors by deferring the time for payment of part of the issue price until such date(s) in the future as the directors might fix by making 'calls' on the shares. This practice, like partly paid shares themselves, is no longer popular and so it is obsolete. However, the standard articles (Table A arts 12–22) still include provisions for making calls on shares, and for forfeiture in case of default (see paragraph 6.4 *Forfeiture, surrender and cancellation of shares*). It is also usual to provide that the company shall have a lien (see paragraph 6.4 *A company's lien on its own shares*) on partly paid shares as security for payment of calls (or fixed instalments). The subject is no longer of any practical importance but it must be remembered that if the company did ever exercise any of these rights, it must be careful to observe strictly the terms of its articles.

In tightening up the rules on consideration for shares of public companies (see paragraph 6.3 *Allotment of shares*) recent statutory changes have provided that if there is default in providing agreed non-cash consideration, a liability arises to pay the value in cash: eg s103(6). The re-registration of an unlimited company as limited (see paragraph 1.4 *Re-registration of limited companies as unlimited and vice-versa*) may entail certain liabilities. These, however, are sanctions against evasion of normal liabilities.

Increase of share capital

A limited company which has a share capital must state in its memorandum, at the time of incorporation, the amount of the share capital with which it proposes to be registered: s2(5)(a). This sets the limit of its authorised share capital for the time being, ie the maximum amount of share capital which it may issue. It may however, if its articles provide for it and under the procedure prescribed by the articles, increase its authorised capital: s121. This may only be done by resolution passed in general meeting (s121(4)) and articles in standard form (Table A art 32) require an ordinary resolution.

Since the authorised capital is divided into shares of specified nominal value, the capital is increased by resolving to create additional shares. Within 15 days the company must give notice of the increase to the registrar and deliver a copy of its memorandum showing the increased capital: s123.

A company has a similar power to consolidate or divide its shares into shares of larger or smaller value, to convert fully paid shares into stock or vice versa, or to cancel unissued shares. Notice to the registry must be given within one month: s122.

Reduction of share capital

If so authorisied by its articles (which may themselves be altered to provide the necessary authority), a company limited by shares may by special resolution reduce its share capital in any way and may, if and so far as is necessary, alter its memorandum by reducing the amount of its share capital and its shares accordingly: s135. For example, it may:

1. extinguish or reduce the liability on any of its shares not paid up; or
2. either with or without extinguishing or reducing liability on any of its shares, cancel any paid up share capital which is lost or unrepresented by available assets; or
3. similarly, pay off any paid up share capital which is in excess of the wants of the company (the repayment may be other than in cash and the value of such assets may exceed the nominal value of the shares): *ex parte Westburn Sugar Refineries Ltd* [1951] AC 625.

The resolution by itself is ineffective unless the company applies to the court for an order confirming the reduction. A reduction carried out without the court's confirmation will not be approved retrospectively; see *Re Barry Artist* [1985] 1 WLR 1305, where the court approved a written resolution by all the members although no special resolution had been passed. Note, however, this decision is unlikely to be followed should a similar situation arise again (see paragraph 8.1 *Proceedings at meetings*).

If the court directs, or where the reduction involves diminution of liability in respect of unpaid share capital or the payment to any shareholder of any paid up share capital:

1. every creditor can object to the reduction;
2. the court shall list the creditors entitled to object and may publish notices of the time within which any other creditor must object; but
3. the court may dispense with a listed creditor's consent if the company sets aside a sum which will cover his claim whether it is admitted or not or if it obtains a reliable guarantee, eg from a bank, that all debts of the company will be paid,

and the court may exclude (1)–(3). as regards any class or classes of creditors: s136.

If the court is satisfied that creditors entitled to object have consented, or that their claims have been paid or secured, it may make an order confirming the reduction on such terms as it thinks fit: s137(1).

As a matter of impression, it might be argued that the company seeking the court's consent should demonstrate the merits of the proposed reduction or that it is fair as between the parties immediately concerned. The majority of cases, however, seem to confine the court's role in declining to confirm the reduction to cases where the minimum rights of those entitled to object have been infringed. Hence, if shareholders have been treated in accordance with their class rights, the reduction will normally be upheld (*Scottish Insurance Ltd* v *Wilsons & Clyde Coal Corporation Ltd* [1949] AC 462 – preference shareholders paid off in anticipation of liquidation; *Prudential Assurance* v *Chatterley-Whitfield Collieries* [1949] AC 512 – preference shareholders entitled only to priority of capital and arrears of dividends on winding-up paid off before compensation received for nationalisation of its coal mines). In both the cases cited, however, the nationalisation of coal mining, as well as creating entitlement to compensation, did clearly reduce the scope of the companies' undertakings. Provided the rights of preference shareholders to prior repayment are upheld, class meetings are not required (see paragraph 3.1 *Class rights*): *Re Saltdean Estate Co Ltd* [1968] 1 WLR 1844. The court has also upheld a reduction where class rights were first varied to facilitate it: *Carruth* v *Imperial Chemical Industries Ltd* [1937] AC 707. This may be done either acc ¹ing to the rules as to variation of class rights (see paragraph 3.1 *Variation of class rights – procedure*) or under a scheme of arrangement under ss425–427 (see paragraph 12.2).

In general the courts have approved what the company has done if it accords with the strict legal requirements and they do not generally add to those requirements, eg to impeach a reduction because of an ulterior motive (such as to obtain compensation which will accrue to the company). In such cases, the answer seems to be that potential preference shareholders should only take up their shares if satisfied with the explicit rights which they carry (see paragraph 6.3 *Class rights – preference shares*).

But, although the court will normally accept that what has been done has been fairly done, it may (and should) decline to confirm a reduction which is demonstrably unfair. In *Re Holder's Investment Trust Ltd* [1971] 1 WLR 583, it was proposed to reduce capital by cancelling cumulative redeemable preference shares in exchange for unsecured loan stock. The majority (90 per cent) preference shareholders held 52 per cent of the ordinary stock and shares. The reduction was approved by a special resolution of the company and an extraordinary resolution of a separate class meeting of the preference shareholders but not confirmed by the court on the grounds:

1. that there was no effectual sanction for modifying the class rights because the majority of the preference shareholders acted in their own interests as ordinary shareholders (in which capacity they stood to gain); and
2. the company had not discharged the onus of showing that the proposed reduction was fair – moreover, the minority had shown it was unfair because the advantages of conversion were not greater than the compensation for the disadvantages (see paragraph 3.1 *Variation of class rights – statutory right of objection*).

The court will not confirm a reduction if it amounts to a variation of class rights and the procedure to vary has not been followed: *Re Northern Engineering Industries plc* [1993] BCC 267 (see section 3.1 Class rights).

Where the court does confirm the reduction, it may order the words 'and reduced' to be added to the company's name and may order publication of details of, including reasons for, the reduction: s137(2). In practice, however, it does not exercise this power.

The company obtains from the court an order approving the reduction and a minute showing the capital of the company as reduced. Copies of these documents are delivered to the registrar for registration and the reduction is thereupon effective and may be implemented: *Re Castiglione Erskine & Co Ltd* [1958] 1 WLR 688.

The effect of the approved reduction is that each shareholder's liability is reduced to the amount (if any) by which the reduced nominal value of his shares exceeds the amount paid up thereon. However, if a creditor has been omitted from the list of creditors entitled to object (see (2) above) to the reduction by reason of his ignorance of the application to the court, he may claim from those who were members at the time of the reduction the amount which they would have had to contribute to the payment of his debt, if there had been no reduction: s140.

A limited company which has a share capital may, if authorised by its articles (eg Table A art 3), issue redeemable shares: s159. However, in normal circumstances such shares may only be redeemed out of the proceeds of a new issue of shares or by use of distributable profits, from which a corresponding amount is transferred to a capital redemption reserve. Where such shares are redeemed out of profits, it reduces the amount of the issued share capital but the fixed capital, not available for payment of dividends, remains unchanged owing to the offsetting sum now held in non-distributable capital redemption reserve. This subject is discussed in more detail in connection with the purchase by a company of its own shares, to which the same restrictions apply (see paragraph 6.4 *Introduction and redemption of shares*).

Allotment of shares

A company which has a share capital will duly issue shares. On its formation the subscribers to the memorandum, of whom there are usually only two, will have undertaken to subscribe for at least one share each. When the company is incorporated their names should forthwith be entered in the register of members as holders of their subscribers' shares: s22(1). It is not necessary to allot shares to them.

Most companies will also find it necessary to issue shares in larger quantities as a means of raising basic fixed capital. For this purpose intending shareholders apply to the company, and often tender the subscription money with their applications. In terms of the law of contract, their application is an offer to subscribe. The company, through its directors, allots shares to the applicants. That is an acceptance of their offer. They are liable to pay the issue price of the shares, if they have not already done so. The company enters their names in the register of members, with particulars of their shareholdings: s352(2)(a). Within two months the company must deliver to each shareholder a share certificate: s185(1). The company is also required within one month to deliver to the registry a return of allotments: s88. The return of allotments procedure is incidentally the means by which the 1 per cent capital duty is collected on a Form PUC.

The procedure for allotting shares must be strictly followed. Where an allotment takes place in breach of the company's articles or the Companies Act 1985, rectification of the company's share register may be granted by the court, on the application of a member. The case of *Re Thundercrest Ltd* [1994] BCC 857, is a good example. Rectification of the company's share register was ordered which involved cancelling an allotment of 5,000 shares each to two members of the company. The plaintiff was the only other member and argued that, (1) the letter of provisional allotment did not allow at least 21 days in which acceptance could take place as provided for by s90(6) CA 1985, and (2) that the letter was not properly served, despite a provision in the company's articles which provided that a pre-paid, properly addressed letter was deemed to have been served on the recipient. On the service point, His Honour Judge Baker QC, held that, the deeming provisions in the articles did not apply when it was obvious that the letter had not been posted. It had been returned by the Post Office to the company before the allotment of shares had been made. See Chapter 15, paragraph 15.4, for further details.

As the allotment of shares is a form of contract, an allottee who has been misled may have the normal remedies for misrepresentation etc. That subject has been considered in connection with prospectus issues by public companies, since most of the case law relates to prospectus issues. However, it should be understood that an allottee of shares of a private company has the same comon law remedies though he does not have the rights given by statute (FSA Parts IV and V).

In all allotment of shares by a company, public or private, the same basic legal principles apply, though the detailed rules applicable to public companies are stricter. This is mainly because public, but not private companies, fall within the scope of the European Community Second Directive on Company Law, which was implemented in the UK by the Companies Act 1980 (now re-enacted in parts of the 1985 Act).

The first overriding principle is that a company may not have more issued shares (in total nominal value) than the amount of its authorised capital declared in its memorandum. It may therefore be necessary for the company to increase its authorised capital as a preliminary step to making an issue of shares (see paragraph 6.3 *Increase of share capital*). Before proceeding to allot shares the directors should always consider the amount (if any) of unissued share capital in relation to the proposed issue (and any commitments such as options to subscribe, convertible debentures etc which may be outstanding).

The second principle requires that proper authority shall have been given and be still available for the issue. Until the law was altered in 1980 it was considered that sufficient authority was given by the wide, general delegation of powers of management to the directors (Table A art 70 gives to the directors 'the powers of the company' and this is the general model). There had, however, been cases in which the allotment of existing unissued shares by the directors had been successfully challenged in the courts on the grounds that the directors' exercise of their powers was invalid because it was not for 'a proper purpose'. That limitation still applies but it is deferred for consideration in a later chapter dealing with the directors' duties and powers generally (see paragraph 9.3 *Exercise of powers for proper purpose*).

Partly to remove the uncertainty of this doctrine and partly in compliance with the EC Directive statutory provisions (now s80) were enacted so that the directors may only allot shares if authorised:

1. by the articles of association in specific terms; or
2. by the company in general meeting.

In either case the authority given must be for a specified period not exceeding five years and relate to the issue of a specified number of shares. This rule may be relaxed by elective resolution of a private company (paragraph 8.1 *Proceedings at meetings, elective resolutions*): s379A(1)(a).

A newly formed company may include in its articles a power to the directors to allot all shares comprised within the original authorised capital. But the power, if given in that way, must be limited to a period not exceeding five years from incorporation. If the authorised capital is increased meanwhile, the opportunity may be taken to give the directors power to allot the existing unissued and additional new shares within the ensuing five years. However, whenever the authority given expires or is exhausted (by the issue of shares) the directors will have to seek a renewal of their authority by ordinary resolution passed in general meeting.

The authority given may be limited to making a specific issue or be subject to conditions, and it may be revoked before it has expired.

It has become common practice at each annual general meeting, especially among public companies for which calling an extraordinary general meeting is an expensive operation in printing and postal expenses, to seek renewal of the directors' power to allot all existing unissued shares in the period up to the next annual general meeting, when the process will be repeated. In this way the authority is given for only a year at a time but it is routine AGM business. This of course is entirely a matter of convenience, permitted but not required by law.

If no authority has been given or if it has expired the position is that, whenever the directors may wish to allot shares, they must first convene a general meeting and seek authority for the issue.

These restrictions on allotment do not apply to the subscribers' shares (mentioned above) nor to shares to be allotted under an employees' share scheme. The latter is likely to be submitted to shareholders for approval at a general meeting when the scheme is first established (for a limited period of years). Hence, it is a more apparent than real exception. The above restrictions do apply to the issue of options to subscribe for shares, and in particular to debentures carrying a right to convert into shares (see paragraph 7.1 *Rights of debenture holders*). That is a necessary safeguard against evasion.

There is another statutory restriction on the directors' power to allot (s89) which applies to the issue of ordinary shares (and any participating preference shares) for a cash consideration. In such cases the company must, subject to exceptions, offer the shares to existing shareholders on a 'rights issue' basis, ie in proportion to their existing holdings. Only to the extent that the shareholders do not exercise their 'pre-emption rights' may the shares then be offered to others. There is a procedure and timetable for this offer.

It is possible, however, by special resolution to 'disapply' these rights, either for a period or in respect of a particular issue. It is common practice, if companies regularly give to their directors annually renewed power to allot shares, to disapply the pre-emption rights at the same time: s95; as to private companies, see Schedule 15A, para 3, inserted by s114(1) of the Companies Act 1989. The directors then have unrestricted rights to allot shares subject to the common law principles referred to above.

A private company may by its memorandum or articles permanently exclude the pre-emption principle from any issue of the company's shares: s91. However, the statutory system, when it applies, does not override but supplements any different pre-emption rights, eg to ordinary shareholders only, given by the memorandum or articles of the company.

The third principle applicable by law to the allotment of shares requires that the company shall always obtained as consideration a value at least equal to the nominal value of the shares. This is expressed as a prohibition against issue of shares at a discount: s100.

There is generally no problem when the consideration is in cash. If shares are allotted for a cash consideration which is less than the nominal value, the allottees must pay sufficient to make up the total to a sum equal to the nominal value: *Ooregum Gold Mining Company of India* v *Roper* [1892] AC 125.

In Scotland, at least, where a person has incurred expenditure to approximately the value of the shares issued to him, the company, with the agreement of all those interested, has accepted liability to repay that expenditure to him and it was in consideration of the release of that liability for reimbursement that the shares were issued to that person, the shares will have been issued for adequate consideration: *Park Business Interiors Ltd* v *Park* [1990] BCC 914. In England, it seems, the company's agreement would have to be under seal if the consideration was past: ibid.

If the company accepts a non-cash consideration, a private company is not restricted from placing an enhanced value on it above its normal market value, provided that the directors act in good faith: *Re Wragg Ltd* [1897] 1 Ch 796. Unless the court detects blatant evasion it does not seek to review the directors' opinion of the value to their company of the property, if they declare it to be at least equal to the nominal value of the shares.

Public companies, however, are required:

1. to obtain at least one quarter of the nominal value and the whole of any premium before allotting shares: s101(1). If the consideration is not wholly cash the terms of acquisition by the company must require that the property is to pass to the company within five years of allotment of its shares and it must be transferred within the specified period: s102;
2. to have the consideration valued by an independent valuer who must be, or be selected by, a person qualified to act as the company's auditor: see, eg, *Re Bradford Investments Ltd (No 2)* [1991] BCC 379. The valuer's report on the consideration permits its value to be compared with the nominal value of the shares. However, there are exceptions, including a case where the company makes a 'take-over bid' offering its own shares in exchange for the shares of another company: s103. This is because the value placed on the shares of a 'target company' in a takeover bid cannot reasonably be tested by normal criteria of market value.

These rules on value are part of the system of 'maintenance of capital' described in a comprehensive manner in paragraph 6.4.

The grant of options to subscribe for shares, usually but not exclusively in connection with the issue of debentures carrying a right to convert into shares is subject (in ss80 and 89) to the same restrictions as apply to shares. It is also not permissible to issue convertible debentures with an immediate right of conversion into shares on such a basis that the company receives (through the debenture issue) less cash than the nominal value of the shares (see paragraph 7.1 *Rights of debenture holders*).

6.4 Maintenance of capital

Introduction

The ambiguity of the concept of 'capital' has already been explained (paragraph 6.1 *Introduction*). A company usually obtains capital from other sources in addition to the proceeds of issuing share capital. Even the assets, net of external liabilities, which it owns bear no precise relation to the nominal value of issued share capital.

However, the 'capital' which must be maintained, so far as possible, is a precise concept. It is most clearly expressed in s264 (dividends of public companies) where it is stated that a public company may not pay dividends unless 'the amount of its net assets is not less than the aggregate of its called up share capital and undistributable reserves'.

The underlying idea of maintenance of capital in this sense is that, as the price of limited liability of its members, a company should preserve the capital which it obtains for its shares, plus any surplus which it is required by law to credit to an undistributable reserve. This is to be a 'creditors' buffer', ie a fund which it is hoped will be available to pay their debts. No one of course can ensure that the company's entire net assets will equal this defined 'capital'. It may suffer trading losses or other setbacks. But this amount of capital may not be returned to shareholders except by special means which safeguard the priority claims of creditors. The link between maintenance of capital and limited liability is illustrated by the fact that unlimited companies are generally not restricted by the rules on maintenance of capital.

There are a number of topics connected with maintenance of capital which are so basic to the general system of company law that they require description in their own context in this textbook. The standard, but cumbersome, procedure for reduction of capital with the approval of the court has been described (see paragraph 6.3 *Reduction of share capital*). Reduction of capital may include the cancellation of shareholders' liability to pay capital not yet paid up on their shares and also a return of capital to shareholders. Either diminishes the company's resources for the payment of its debts. If a company issues shares at a premium (see paragraph 6.1 *Share capital – basic terms and principles*), the premium must be credited to a non-distributable share premium account. The concept of 'distributable profits' available for the payment of dividends (see paragraph 6.5) and the priority given to payment of debts in a liquidation are examples of legal principles whose main purpose is to safeguard the rights of creditors. Most of the others are described in the following paragraphs of this section.

Redemption of shares

If its articles (eg Table A art 3) provide for it, a company may issue shares which are redeemable: s159. It must also have non-redeemable shares in issue both at the time when it issues redeemable shares and at the time of redemption, so that its capital may not consist entirely of redeemable shares. The shares must be described as redeemable at the time of issue, ie they cannot be made into redeemable shares after issue, and they must be fully paid and redeemed in cash. The terms of redemption must be fixed by the articles at the time of issue, though some flexibility is permitted, eg by calling for redemption at a time to be chosen later by the company or within a period of years: s159A.

Until 1981 companies were only permitted to issue redeemable preference shares. If a company established before 1981 plans to issue redeemable ordinary shares, its articles may require alteration to widen them so as to cover the proposed issue of that type of shares.

The provision for redeemable shares (and also the power given to a company to purchase its own shares) is intended to promote greater flexibility in capital structure. As one example (of many possible uses) a company may purchase a business and agree to pay a price in excess of the value of the net tangible assets of the business since it will be buying the future profits ('purchased goodwill'). If it pays for the goodwill with redeemable preference shares, it can then accumulate profits from which to redeem the shares at the agreed time. In effect it makes deferred payment for profits out of the profits themselves.

The 'maintenance of capital' principle is expressed in the rules on redemption of redeemable shares:

1. as a general rule the redeemable shares may be redeemed only out of (a) the proceeds of a new issue of shares; or (b) distributable profits of the company. If both are insufficient a private company may resort to capital; this method (also available in a purchase by a private company of its own shares) is described later (see paragraph 6.4 *Resort to capital in redemption or purchase of shares*);
2. if the terms of redemption include the payment of a premium, ie a higher redemption price than the nominal value of the shares redeemed, the premium must generally be provided out of distributable profits only. But it is permitted to draw on share premium account if the shares were themselves issued at a premium in the first place;
3. if distributable profits are applied in redemption of shares, a sum corresponding to the nominal value of the shares redeemed must be credited to a non-distributable capital redemption reserve so that the fixed capital, to be maintained, is not reduced by the redemption;
4. if shares are redeemed out of the proceeds of a new issue of shares, and the nominal value of the latter is less than the nominal value of the shares redeemed, the difference must be credited to the capital redemption reserve: s170;
5. the shares redeemed must be cancelled but the authorised capital is unaffected: s160(4).

General principles of company law also apply. The number of members must not be reduced below the minimum of two by the redemption. If a public company, in redeeming its shares, reduces its issued capital below £50,000, it must re-register as a private company (see paragraph 1.4 *Re-registration of a public company as private*).

Purchase by a company of its own shares

The same basic principles of maintenance of capital apply to purchase by a company of its own shares as to redemption. What has been summarised above is therefore equally applicable, except that a company may purchase shares which were not issued as redeemable (and also redeemable shares on terms other than the redemption terms) and the authority to purchase, although it must be found in the articles at the time of purchase, relates to the purchase to be made at that time, ie it is not laid down when the shares are issued. Section 162 extends the statutory redemption conditions to purchase of shares. In particular the requirements on financing the purchase out of proceeds of a new issue or distributable profits (with a transfer to capital redemption reserve) apply to purchase also.

The most important part of the statutory procedure for purchase of shares is found in ss163–166 which prescribe the manner of obtaining authority to purchase shares. There are three alternatives:

1. *market purchase* where the shares are bought on 'a recognised stock exchange'. In practice only a public company could resort to this procedure since shares of private companies are not dealt in on the Stock Exchange or the USM;
2. *off-market purchase* is any purchase (even if made through stock exchange channels) which is not effected under standard market procedure;
3. *contingent purchase* is a purchase by exercise of an option, ie the original agreement for purchase is not a binding commitment but only an option given to one or both parties. In other respects it is similar to an off-market purchase.

These procedures are intended mainly to safeguard the interests of shareholders which may be affected by the purchase. They do not relate to maintenance of capital. However, it is convenient to deal with them at this point.

The essential aspect of a market purchase is that the vendor of shares to the company and the exact price cannot be known in advance. Approval is given by ordinary resolution, which fixes the maximum number of shares which may be purchased, the maximum and minimum price which may be paid and the duration of the authority to purchase which may not exceed 18 months: s166. The company then makes purchases in the market through its brokers. The company makes a return to the registry of shares purchased within 28 days of delivery of the shares: s169.

A public company which had spare cash might decide that buying in its own shares would be the best use of the money, and would increase the value of the remaining issued shares. But the pros and cons would have to be carefully weighed up and explained to shareholders. At all events it is a possibility extended to such companies as an option.

For an off-market purchase a written contract is prepared which identifies the vendor(s) and states the price. A copy of the contract must be available for inspection by members at the registered office for at least 15 days ending with the date of the meeting and at the meeting itself. The contract must be approved by a special resolution, on which the vendor(s) may not vote on a show of hands nor cast votes attached to the shares to be sold, if there is a vote on a poll. A copy of the contract must be held at the registered office for ten years from the completion of the purchase(s): s169. In this case also there is a return to the registry within 28 days of shares purchased.

A contingent purchase contract is approved in the same manner as an ordinary off-market purchase contract. The approval of the contract suffices for a purchase, in exercise of the option given by the contract, at any time: s165.

Resort to capital in redemption or purchase of shares

This is a procedure to supplement, not to replace, the use of distributable profits or the proceeds of a new share issue, in redemption or purchase of a private company's shares.

The maximum amount of capital ('the permissible capital payment') is the difference between the price to be paid for the shares and (if less) the whole of the distributable profits and any proceeds of a new share issue. To complete the transaction the company must therefore exhaust its entire distributable profits and reserves, which is often a disincentive: s171.

The use of capital requires approval by special resolution. There is the same restriction on voting by the vendor(s) as in approving an off-market purchase: s174.

The directors are required to make a statutory declaration (s173) to the effect that after making the capital payment the company will still be able to pay its debts and to continue carrying on its business as a going concern for at least a year. An auditors' report on the calculation of the permissible capital payment and on the basis of the directors' declaration is also required.

Within a week of the passing of the resolution the company must given notice of it in the *London Gazette* and either give notice of it in a national newspaper or notify each creditor of the company. Members or creditors of the company may, within five weeks of the passing of the resolution, apply to the court to cancel the resolution. The court has power to order the company to buy the shares of the objectors.

The purchase, using capital, may be made within the period of five to seven weeks after the resolution has been passed to approve it (or such other period as the court may substitute after dismissing objections).

Uses of off-market purchase of shares

The procedure for off-market purchase is intended to facilitate investment in small private companies by making it easier to withdraw capital. If, for example, A, B and C have built up a profitable company and, after the death of A, his executors wish to sell his shareholding, the company may find it easier to raise the money for this purpose than the other shareholders.

The contingent purchase contract is intended to cover long-term arrangements, such as the employment in a family company of a professional manager who is not a member of the family but who wishes to be a shareholder while he is working for the company. He and the family shareholders may agree, when he joins the company, that he is to acquire shares but that these are to return to the company (at a current value) when he leaves. The option is exercised when he retires.

To prevent the misuse of this facility to gain improper tax advantages there are stringent conditions of tax law which tend to impede its ready use.

Financial assistance by a company for the purchase of its own shares

The giving of financial assistance by a company to enable someone else to purchase its shares is clearly a way in which a company's capital may be reduced. This will be prejudicial to the interests of the company's creditors as it will diminish the company's capital, which is the fund used to pay off the debts of the creditors. Shareholders and the company itself may also require protection from financial assistance schemes. Where a controlling shareholder uses company assets to fund his share purchases, this will be to the disadvantage of the company's other shareholders, who have not benefitted from the scheme. It may also not be in a company's best interests for its shares to be purchased in this way. Finally, when a company gives financial assistance to a party so that it can acquire its shares, this may lead to the market in the company's shares being manipulated, though this is now specifically prohibited by the Financial Services Act 1986.

The provisions dealing with the giving of financial assistance by a company for the purchase of its own shares are contained in ss151–158. Section 151 lays down the general prohibition against the giving of financial assistance and it implements Article 23 of the Second Company Law Directive, which contains a similar prohibition, but only in relation to public companies.

The original provisions were contained in s45 of the 1929 Companies Act, following the recommendations of the Greene Committee, who were concerned about abuses such as may arise on a take-over, whereby the target company provided the bidder with a loan in which to buy the shares of the target company. The loan was then repaid out of the assets of the company which had been taken over.

Financial assistance is prohibited if given before, at the same time as, or after the acquisition of a company's shares and covers gifts, guarantees, securities, indemnities, loans, etc: see s151(2). In *Charterhouse Investment Trust Ltd* v *Tempest Diesels Ltd* [1986] BCLC 1, Hoffmann J, as he then was, said of the term 'financial assistance':

'The words have no technical meaning and their frame of reference is in my judgment the language of ordinary commerce. One must examine the commercial realities of the transaction and decide whether it can properly be described as the giving of financial assistance by the company, bearing in mind that the section is a penal one and should not be strained to cover transactions which are not fairly within it.'

So, it seems that the courts will not try and strain the meaning of the term financial assistance in order to bring an arrangement within the prohibition contained in s151. Instead they will look at the commercial realities of the arrangement.

Exceptions to the prohibition

Section 153 sets out a number of exceptions to the general prohibition. They include the distribution of a company's assets by the payment of a lawful dividend. This would allow those who have taken over a company to finance the costs of doing so by paying to themselves a dividend authorised by their new company. Also included is assistance given to finance the purchase of bonus shares and shares issued pursuant to an employees share scheme. A sensible exemption is also given to companies whose ordinary business consists of lending money so, for example, a bank would be able to give financial assistance in the form of a loan, to customers who wished to purchase its shares.

In the case of public companies, financial assistance for the purposes of an employees' share scheme or under the money lending companies exemption will only be allowed if its net assets are not thereby reduced. If they are reduced, then the assistance must be provided for out of distributable profits.

The most difficulty has been encountered in the exemptions contained in s153(1), which allows a company to give financial assistance for the purpose of acquiring its shares if:

> '(a) the company's principal purpose in giving that assistance is not to give it for the purpose of any such acquisition, or the giving of the assistance for that purpose is but an incidental part of some larger purpose of the company, and
> (b) the assistance is given in good faith in the interests of the company.'

Section 152(2) provides a similar exemption when the financial assistance has already been given. The House of Lords decision in *Brady* v *Brady* [1989] AC 755 discussed at length the meaning of this 'larger purpose' exemption.

The facts of *Brady* were very complex but in outline the business of Brady Ltd was that of a soft drink manufacturer and road haulier. It was run by two brothers, Jack and Bob. The company began to make losses after the management became deadlocked. This was caused by a breakdown in the relationship between Jack and Bob, who were unable to work with each other. A plan was devised whereby the business would be split up, with Jack taking the haulage side and Bob the drinks side of the business. To off-set the difference in value between the two sides of the business, it was agreed that Jack's new company, M Ltd, would receive assets from Brady Ltd to help M Ltd pay for the shares in Brady Ltd. It was accepted that this amounted to the giving of financial assistance by Brady and this was relied on by Bob when he was sued by Jack, who wanted specific performance of their agreement. Jack claimed that the transaction fell within the larger purpose exemption. The House of Lords held that the larger purpose exemption did not apply to the arrangement, but ordered specific performance on the ground that it came within the private company exemption contained within ss155–158. As Gower points out, *Principles of Modern Company Law* (5th edn, p233), it was 'incredible' that Brady's advisors did not recognise this possibility earlier!

Lord Oliver felt that the scheme was in good faith in the interests of the company. Failure to implement the scheme would return the company to its former position with management deadlock resulting in probable liquidation of the company. It was also of benefit to Brady's corporate and commercial interests as well as the interests of its employees. Viewed objectively, it was then, in the company's interest.

Despite this finding, Lord Oliver was unable to find any larger purpose to which the giving of the financial assistance was merely incidental. He said that it was necessary to distinguish between the *purpose* and the reason for giving the assistance. In this case the only purpose for the giving of the assistance was to help Jack to acquire the shares in Brady. The *reason* was to promote the re-organisation of the family business so that it could be split between Jack and Bob and allow them to go their separate ways. Their Lordships considered the advantages which the scheme produced were mere 'by-products' and that Jack could not therefore rely on the larger purpose exemption in s153(2).

Most commentators agree that this is a narrow interpretation of the wording of s153, as it failed to take into account the wider commercial considerations of the scheme. It is now very difficult to think of a clear example of when the larger purpose exemption would apply and its scope is very uncertain.

In addition to the express exemptions to s151, Millet J, in *Arab Bank plc* v *Mercantile Holdings Ltd & Anor* [1993] BCC 816, held that s151 does not apply if the assistance is given by a foreign subsidiary of an English parent company for the purpose of purchasing the parent company's shares. Section 151 only prohibits English companies who give financial assistance. Millet J did though concede that, read literally, the wording of the section did encompass foreign subsidiaries but that this would give s151 an extraterritorial effect contrary to the principles of private international law.

Financial assistance and the private company exemption

A private (but not a public) company may lawfully give financial assistance, in circumstances which would otherwise be unlawful, if it follows the procedure prescribed by ss155–158. The procedure is sometimes referred to as the 'whitewash' or 'gateway' procedure. The assistance must not reduce the company's net assets or if it does then it is to be made out of distributable profits available for the payment of dividends. In this way the position of creditors is protected.

The following conditions and procedure must be satisfied before the giving of the assistance. The salient steps are as follows.

1. The company must pass a special resolution (or written resolution under s381A: See paragraph 8.1 *Proceedings at meetings*) approving the assistance.

2. The directors must make a statutory declaration that the company will be able to pay its debts as they fall due for the year following the date on which the assistance was given.
3. The auditors must state in a report attached to the statutory declaration that the directors opinion is reasonable. The statutory declaration and the auditors report must be available for the members inspection at the meeting at which the special resolution is passed. The resolution must be passed within one week of the directors statutory declaration being made.
4. The assistance must not be given before the end of a four week period after the resolution is passed. This is to allow objecting shareholders their right to apply to the court to have the special resolution cancelled under s157. Only the holders of 10 per cent or more in nominal value of the company's issued share capital or any class thereof can apply, and they must do so within 28 days of the passing of the resolution and they must not have voted in its favour. Creditors have no right of objection.
5. The assistance must be given within eight weeks of the statutory declaration being made.

Consequences for breach of the provisions.

Section 151(3) provides that a breach of s151 renders the company liable to a fine and every officer liable to a fine and/or imprisonment. No mention is made of the civil consequences which are dealt with by the common law.

An agreement to give financial assistance, in breach of the provisions is unenforceable by either party (*Brady* v *Brady* (above)). Despite this, the transaction for which the financial assistance is given is not affected by the illegality. Gower (*Modern Principles of Company Law* (5th edn, p237)) gives the example of a takeover-bidder who has been given financial assistance by the company. He says that it would be absurd if the bidder could refuse liability to perform the share purchase contracts by relying on the illegal financial assistance

The position may be different if the obligation to acquire shares and the financial assistance forms part of a single composite transaction. Here if the terms of the financial assistance can be severed from the obligation to purchase the shares, then on the authority of *Carney* v *Herbert* [1985] AC 301 PC, the share purchase obligation can be enforced.

Where the unlawful financial assistance has already been given, the transaction will be void. The effect will depend on what form the assistance took. If it was assistance in the form of a mortgage, guarantee or indemnity, the party to whom it was given cannot sue on it. See *Heald* v *O'Connor* [1971] 1 WLR 497.

If the assistance was in the form of a loan or a gift then the company will have to take steps to recover it. Directors will be in breach of their duties if they have authorised the giving of financial assistance and third parties will hold the proceeds of such assistance as constructive trustees on behalf of the company.

Reform

The DTI, in its consultative document, 'Company Law Review: Proposals for Reform of ss151–158 of the Companies Act' (October 1993), has identified six criticisms of the financial assistance provisions. These may be summarised as follows.

1. The uncertain effect of s151. There may be potential financial assistance whenever a company puts someone in funds who, at around the same time, purchases shares in the company. This may lead to the company incurring the cost of taking legal advice.
2. Section 151 may prohibit innocent transactions.
3. The private company exemption in ss155–158 is too complex and burdensome.
4. The criminal penalties for a breach of s151 are inappropriate
5. The consequences of giving financial assistance for innocent third parties who may be deprived of their rights.
6. The unclear and ambiguous wording of some of the provisions in ss151–153. The DTI give as an example the doubt about whether the word 'subsidiary' in s151 prohibits financial assistance by a foreign subsidiary to purchase shares in its English parent company. This has recently be cleared up by Millet J, in *Arab Bank plc* v *Mercantile Holdings Ltd & Anor* [1993] BCC 816, who held that s151 does not prohibit such assistance.

In response to these criticisms the DTI suggested three types of possible reform. Firstly, to amend the current provisions, secondly, to replace the provisions with Article 23 of the Second Company Law Directive, and thirdly to restructure the provisions entirely. The third option is preferred by the DTI and they have suggested a two-tier restructure.

The first tier prohibition would only apply to public companies and would mirror the prohibition contained in Article 23 of the Directive. Companies coming within tier one, would not be eligible for the 'whitewash' exemption in ss155–158.

The second tier prohibition would apply to all private companies and to some public companies not caught by tier one. The whitewash procedure would be available under this tier and would therefore apply to some public companies as well as all private companies.

Both tiers would contain the exemptions in s153(3) and (4), covering assistance given in order to facilitate an employee share scheme and assistance given by money lending companies in the ordinary course of their business respectively.

In addition, the DTI raise the possibility of two further exemptions. The first is an attempt to deal with the *Brady* decision, by amending s153(1) and (2) so that financial assistance would be allowed where the 'predominant reason' for it is to benefit the company. This term would replace the term 'principal purpose' currently used and would have saved the scheme devised in Brady. Secondly, the DTI consider that financial assistance which does not materially reduce the net assets of a company should be allowed by way of a de minimis exemption. Both of these exemptions have good arguments for and against them. For example, the difficulty with a de minimis exemption would be to define what would amount to a material reduction in net assets.

Finally, one result of the DTI's proposals would be the extension of the 'whitewash' procedure to public companies. The consultative document considers simplifying this procedure, for example, by only requiring an ordinary, rather than a special, resolution.

Despite the DTI's consultative document and the call for reform by practitioners and by such bodies as the Law Society, immediate reform in this area is not expected. In the meantime the uncertainty surrounding the provisions, as evidenced by the *Brady* decision, will continue.

Prohibition against shareholdings

A limited company which has a share capital is subject to a general prohibition against acquiring its own shares by purchase, subscription or otherwise: s143(1). There are of course a number of exceptions (s143(3)) including redemption or purchase under the above procedure or, in various circumstances, by order of the court in order to give appropriate relief to a minority of objecting shareholders who wish to be bought out. A reduction of capital may incidentally entail an acquisition by the company of its shares though this is not usual. A company may also acquire its shares by forfeiture (see paragraph 6.4 *Forfeiture, surrender and cancellation of shares*).

The statutory rules do not prevent a company from accepting a gift, eg a bequest under the will of a shareholder, of its own shares: *Re Castiglione's Will Trusts* [1958] Ch 549. In such a case the shares must be registered in the name of a nominee since a company may never be a member of itself.

The same principle is extended to prohibit a subsidiary from being a member of its holding company, unless it holds the shares purely in a trust capacity for some third party or on a short-term basis as a Stock Exchange dealer: s23.

A different situation arises if Company A becomes the holding company of Company B which already holds shares of Company A. To avoid complex problems it is normal practice in such cases for Company B to dispose of its shareholding in Company A to a third party. A disposal by Company B though is not a condition, as the case of *Acatos and Hutchinson plc* v *Watson* (1994) The Times 30 December shows.

In this case, Acatos and Hutchinson plc (AH), wanted to purchase the entire issued share capital of Acatos Ltd (A). A's sole asset was a substantial shareholding in AH. The agreement had been negotiated at arms length and the independent directors of AH had been separately advised, by solicitors and accountants, that the transaction was in the best interests of AH and its shareholders. Lightman J held that the transaction did not breach the rule in *Trevor* v *Whitworth* (1877) 12 AC 409 and s143 CA 1985, which prohibits a company from acquiring its own shares.

His Lordship observed that under the rule AH could not have purchased the shareholding in AH held by A. The issue was whether the rule could be side-stepped by purchasing instead the issued share capital of A, which would have the same economic consequences. The defendant argued that the veil of incorporation should be lifted to treat AH as acquiring its own shares, as this would prevent the rule and s143 being circumvented.

Lightman J reasoned that if a takeover of a target company was prohibited when it held shares in the bidding company, this would provide the target company with a good defence. It was plain that the rule did not have this remarkable and far reaching effect. Furthermore, s23 of the CA 1985 put the matter beyond question, for this expressly allowed A, after the acquisition, to keep its shareholding in AH. (Under s23, A's voting rights are suspended during the ownership.) Finally, his Lordship added that due to the potential for abuse, the court would look carefully at the transaction to see if the directors of the acquiring company had fulfilled their fiduciary duties to safeguard the interests of shareholders and creditors. See Chapter 15, paragraph 15.4, for further details.

Forfeiture, surrender and cancellation of shares

The articles always provide (Table A arts 19–22) for forfeiture by a company of any shares on which the holder fails to pay the amount due to the company. The company may then re-sell the forfeited shares without prejudice to the company's claim against the defaulter.

The company may also accept a voluntary surrender of shares in place of forfeiture if the holder is genuinely unable to pay the amount due on them: *Bellerby v Rowland & Marwood's SS Co Ltd* [1902] 2 Ch 14.

The European Community Second Directive requires that a public company shall not retain indefinitely any shares which have been forfeited by or surrendered to it. Problems can also arise if a public company has a beneficial interest in its own shares held by a nominee, either as a result of its giving financial assistance for the acquisition of the shares or otherwise. The company has the option of disposing of these shares or, if it fails to do so, cancelling them. The period allowed is three years, except where financial assistance has been given, when the period of grace is reduced to one year: s146. Failing disposal, the company must then cancel. If a company redeems or purchases its own shares (see paragraph 6.4 *Redemption of shares*) they are cancelled automatically when acquired: ss160(4) and 162(2).

A company's lien on its own shares

A lien is in the nature of an equitable mortgage. It is possible for a company to have an interest in its own shares under a lien to the extent that the articles provide for it (Table A arts 8–11).

The articles of a private company may give it a lien on its own shares as security for any sum owed by the shareholder to the company, whether as subscription money due on the shares or otherwise. However, a public company is only permitted to have a lien in the following cases:

1. if the shares subject to the lien are not fully paid and the lien is only to give security for the money owing on the shares; or
2. if the ordinary business of the company is the lending of money and the lien arises from a transaction entered into in the course of that business. Thus, a bank might accept from a customer a charge on his holding of shares in the bank to secure a bank advance to him: s150.

These are not important exceptions since both are uncommon sets of circumstances.

The modern practice, in framing the articles of private companies, is to confine the company's lien to case (1) above: Table A art 8.

Any right to a lien given by the articles is subject to normal principles of priority of mortgages. The articles may provide for a 'first and paramount lien' (as in Table A art 8) but, if the company has notice of the interest of another person in the shares before its own claim against the shareholder arises, that claim will rank after the other interest of which prior notice has been given: *Bradford Banking Co Ltd* v *Henry Briggs Son & Co Ltd* (1886) 12 App Cas 29.

Loss of capital of a public company

If the directors of a public company become aware that its net assets are half or less (in value) of the amount of its called up capital, they are required within 28 days to convene a general meeting of the company: s142.

This is a procedure introduced into English company law in compliance with the European Community Second Directive. It presents a number of practical difficulties. How are the assets to be valued in such a case, ie on a going concern or a break-up basis? What is the purpose of the meeting? Will not the summoning of the meeting precipitate a crisis in the company's affairs by publicising its financial difficulties?

It is thought that in an admitted state of financial crisis such as this the directors would probably prefer, and be well advised in their own interest, to resort to one of the procedures of the Insolvency Act 1986, such as inviting a secured creditor to appoint a receiver or applying to the court for an administration order. However, if the situation occurs, their duty to convene a general meeting is categorical.

6.5 Dividends

Introduction

There are three main elements in the law applicable to dividends ie (1) what profits may be distributed as dividends (see paragraph 6.5 *Distributable profits* to *Distribution and undistributable reserves*); (2) how dividends are declared and paid (see paragraph 6.5 *The right to dividends*); and (3) the consequences of an irregularity in the payment of dividends (see paragraph 6.5 *Liability in respect of unlawful distributions*).

Distributable profits

Until the law was reformed in 1980 the rules which defined the profits which a company might distribute as dividend were found in a number of decisions of the courts on particular situations. As a result there was considerable laxity. When the Companies Act 1980 was enacted its purpose was to introduce into English company law various requirements of the European Community Second Directive. However, the provisions on dividends (now ss263–281 of the 1985 Act) were extended, on basic points, to private as well as public companies (only the latter are affected by the Directive) in order to tighten up the general law on distributable profits.

The overriding principle, as a means to the maintenance of capital, is that dividends may not be paid out of capital: *Re Exchange Banking Company, Flitcroft's Case* (1882) 21 Ch D 519. The facts in *Flitcroft's Case* were that for some years the directors laid before the company in general meeting annual accounts from which it appeared that the company was making profits. The shareholders, on the basis of those accounts, approved the declaration of dividends. In fact, as the directors well knew, a number of loans which the company had made in its banking business were irrecoverable. If proper provision had been made for these bad debts, it would have been evident that the company had been incurring losses. The court held that the dividends had been unlawfully paid out of capital and that the directors must make good the loss of capital to the company. It was immaterial that the accounts had been approved in general meeting. No resolution passed in general meeting can validate an unlawful act of the company (see paragraph 2.3 *Validity of transactions*).

The same issue (though not in connection with dividends) arose in the more recent case of *Re Halt Garage (1964) Ltd* [1982] 3 All ER 1016. The company had been trading at a loss but it had continued to pay directors' remuneration, authorised by the articles, to the two directors, who were husband and wife and the shareholders of the company. Owing to ill health the wife had performed no duties of any kind in her capacity of director. The court held that the fees paid to her were an unlawful return of capital to a shareholder, since the company had no profits to distribute, and the payments were not for services and could not be treated as expenses by misdescribing them as directors' fees. She was required to repay these sums. The payments to the husband were properly treated as an expense of the company, and so part of its overall loss, since he had worked as a director.

The principle that payments may not be made out of capital to shareholders, unless they fall within one of the recognised exceptions, requires that a distinction shall be drawn between what is capital and what is not. The latter must be profits. Hence, a satisfactory definition of profits is required to ensure that capital is not improperly paid away.

Under the law as it was before 1980 it was held that a profit of the current year might be treated as distributable without need to make good losses suffered in earlier years: *Ammonia Soda Co Ltd* v *Chamberlain* [1918] 1 Ch 266. It was also permissible to calculate profits without making provision for depreciation of fixed assets depleted by use during the year: *Lee* v *Neuchatel Asphalt Company* (1889) 41 Ch D 1. If assets which the company retained had fallen in market value, no provision need be made against that unrealised loss in determining what profits were distributable: *Verner* v *General and Commercial Investment Trust* [1894] 2 Ch 239. If on the other hand an asset retained by the company had increased in value, a dividend might be paid out of that unrealised profit: *Dimbula Valley (Ceylon) Tea Company Ltd* v *Laurie* [1961] Ch 353. However, if unrealised profits were to be brought into the reckoning the current value of all, not merely selected, property of the company must be considered: *Foster* v *New Trinidad Lake Asphalt Company Ltd* [1901] 1 Ch 208.

These cases serve to illustrate the practices which the current statutory code now holds in check. Except for *Foster*'s case, to which no exception could ever be taken, all the other instances would now be unlawful. One should also add that the decisions which have now been superseded by statutory rules were related to particular facts which afforded some justification for the judicial decisions in those cases.

The current statutory law prohibits a company from making a distribution, typically by paying a dividend, unless it comes from distributable profits which are 'accumulated, realised profits ... less accumulated, realised losses': s263. The formula also provides that all previous dividend payments and any capitalisation of profits (to pay up bonus shares) and any losses written off by reduction or reorganisation of capital duly made are to be taken into account.

Accumulated, realised profits and losses

The effect of the word accumulated, for both profits and losses, means that the company's profit and loss account, although made up annually for each year's accounts, is a running total. Each year's accounts bring in the opening figure of profit or loss from the previous year and add the year's profits or loss to it (or offset a profit against an accumulated loss brought forward or vice-versa). Any dividend(s) paid out of the profits are deducted and a closing balance is carried forward to the next year. It is not now possible to transfer a debit balance from the previous year into a suspense account to get it out of the reckoning, as was done in *Chamberlain*'s case.

The effect of the word realised, applied to profits and losses, is to exclude from the category of distributable profits any unrealised appreciation or diminution of value of retained assets (but on this see also paragraph 6.5 *Distributable profits of public companies*). It is now obligatory for a company to make a depreciation provision in respect of an asset which has a limited economic life, so that its cost is written off over that period: Schedule 4 para 18. The amount of the depreciation provision made is treated as a realised loss, which must be debited in calculating the year's profit (though there is a remission if the asset has been revalued above its original cost): s275(1)). If a surplus arises from a revaluation of assets, it must be credited to a revaluation reserve: Schedule 4 para 34. It may be used in paying up bonus shares, ie it may be capitalised, but it may not be distributed as dividend.

Distributable profits of public companies

A public company which may have distributable profits calculated as described above is subject to an additional restriction imposed by s264.

1. If the amount of its net assets does not exceed the aggregate of its called up share capital and undistributable reserves, it is not permitted to make a distribution at all.
2. Any distribution which it makes may not reduce the amount of its net assets below the aggregate of called up share capital and undistributable reserves.

In effect a public company is required to retain otherwise distributable profits to the extent that it has any deficiency of fixed capital or would create one by making a distribution.

The practical consequence of this rule is that a public company is required to take account of the unrealised loss resulting from a fall in market value of a retained asset. It may set off against it any surplus arising from an increase in value of other retained assets. But, if, when the calculation has been made for all assets, there is a deficiency profits must be retained to offset it.

There are also special rules applicable to investment companies (s265) and to certain insurance companies (s268) to deal appropriately with their special circumstances.

Relevant accounts

The directors have a common law duty to prepare and consider proper accounts before deciding whether there are profits from which they may declare or recommend a dividend: *Re Oxford Benefit Building and Investment Society* (1886) 35 Ch D 502. In *Foster*'s case (see paragraph 6.5 *Distributable profits*) the court declined to approve a dividend out of the appreciation in value of a single asset treated as 'a windfall in the nature of an unexpected profit'. The proper course 'depends upon the result of the whole accounts for the year'.

This principle is now reinforced by statutory recognition of 'relevant accounts' (s270) in calculating what distributable profits there may be. These accounts are generally the latest annual audited accounts of the company. But there are alternative provisions for 'initial accounts' of a recent formed company and for 'interim accounts' which may be considered in mid-year, eg to declare an interim dividend. If the auditors find it necessary to make a 'qualified report' on the accounts, indicating reservations, the possible effect of that qualification on the amount of profits available for payment of a dividend has to be considered: ss271–273. In certain respects more stringent requirements are imposed on public than on private companies over initial and interim accounts.

Distribution and undistributable reserves

Much of the statutory code explained above depends on the meaning of the words 'distribution' and 'undistributable reserves'.

A distribution means any transfer of the company's assets to its members except: (1) a bonus issue of shares (see paragraph 6.1 *Share capital – basic terms and principles*); (2) payment for shares redeemed or purchased (paragraph 6.4 *Redemption of shares*); (3) a payment etc to shareholders in a properly authorised reduction of capital (see paragraph 6.3 *Reduction of share capital*) and a distribution of assets in liquidation (see Chapter 13). The effect of this rather cumbersome definition is that a 'distribution' normally means a dividend.

The undistributable reserves of a company are defined (s264) to include (1) its share premium account (see paragraph 6.1 *Share capital – basic terms and principles*); (2) its capital redemption reserve (see paragraph 6.4 *Redemption of shares*); (3) its revaluation reserve (see paragraph 6.5 *Distributable profits*); and (4) any other reserve which the company may not by law distribute.

It will be clear how much the modern statutory rules on maintenance of capital intermesh and support each other.

The right to dividends

The right to dividends and the rules as to how they are to be declared and paid depend on the articles. The articles generally devolve power on the matter to the directors, although their powers have to be exercised according to the procedure laid down by the articles: *Nicholson* v *Rhodesia Trading Company* [1897] 1 Ch 434; and they should be exercised bona fide: *Dodge* v *Ford Motor Company* (1919) 170 NW 668. However, the courts will not substitute their own business judgment for that of the directors.

Generally speaking, the directors may set aside out of profits reserves for the purposes of the company and may declare interim dividends; otherwise, they may recommend declarations of dividends to the general meeting (annually) which can declare dividends up to the recommended amount: Table A Arts 102–103.

Apart from rights to different assessments of dividends dependent on different classes of shares (eg shares with a preferential dividend), members are entitled to participate equally in dividends regardless of the amount paid up on their shares: *Oakbank Oil Company* v *Crum* (1882) 8 App Cas 65; subject to their liability to calls on shares not fully paid.

Once it is declared and the date for payment has passed, the shareholder can sue the company for payment of the amount owed as a debt based on the terms of his membership and the company cannot avoid its liability to make cash payments by issuing a debenture (a deferred debt) to him: *Wood* v *Odessa Waterworks Company* (1889) 42 Ch D 636. However, modern articles (Table A art 105) usually provide for payment in this form as a possibility.

If a dividend is not declared, it is not payable unless the terms of issue make it payable irrespective of a declaration so long as profits are made, as will generally only be the case with preference shares: *Re Bridgewater Navigation Company* [1891] 2 Ch 31. It is possible that arrears might be claimed on a winding-up even though profits have not been made: *Re New Chinese Antimony Company Limited* [1916] 2 Ch 115. A subscriber for cumulative preference shares should ensure that his rights in these respects are clearly spelt out or that he will not have them (see paragraph 6.3 *Class rights – preference shares*).

Payment of dividends may be restricted or prohibited by statute (see Counter Inflation Act 1973; Dividends Act 1978 now repealed).

The memorandum or articles may prohibit payment of dividends; this is usually so for companies with charitable or quasi-charitable objects (see paragraph 2.2 *Omission of the word 'Limited' from a company name*).

If the shareholder dies or changes his address without giving notice to the company it can happen that his dividend warrants sent through the post do not reach him. As the dividend is at that point a debt (see above) he may claim it (or his executors may do so) at any time before it becomes statute-barred by limitation, which in this case is a period of 12 years.

Even if 12 years has elapsed he may try to assert his claim if he can show that the company's balance sheet during the period has included the usual 'unclaimed dividends' item among its liabilities. But to establish that his claim has been extended by a 'written acknowledgement' he must also show that the copies of the accounts have reached him from the company. This is unlikely to be the case: *Re Compania de Electricidad de la Provincia de Buenos Aires Ltd* [1978] 3 All ER 668.

Liability in respect of unlawful distributions

Since the initiative in preparing accounts and recommending or declaring dividends rests with the directors, the liability usually falls on them to make good to the company any loss of capital caused by payment of an unlawful distribution: *Flitcroft's Case* (above).

A sharehold is not permitted to retain a dividend paid to him out of capital, if he knows or has reasonable grounds for believing that it has been paid in breach of the statutory rules of ss263–264; s277. He may not in these circumstances maintain an action against the directors: *Towers* v *African Tug Co* [1904] 1 Ch 558 CA.

6.6 Company shareholdings

Introduction

The main subject of the previous chapter was the methods by which a company obtains permanent capital from its proprietors by issuing share capital. In most companies members are automatically also shareholders, since the company has a share capital and so holding at least one share is an incident of membership. However, it should be remembered that most companies limited by guarantee do not have a share capital (see paragraph 1.4 *A company limited by guarantee*) and so the members of such companies are not shareholders. This is not an important exception though it will be mentioned where appropriate in this chapter, which is concerned with shares and shareholdings.

A limited company which has a share capital is required to state the amount of its authorised capital divided into shares, ie units of ownership, of defined nominal amount: s2(5)(a). Hence, a shareholding is one or more shares issued to a member, in return for payment or other consideration at least equal in value to the nominal value of the shares, or acquired by him as successor to a previous shareholder. His shareholding is a measure of his interest in the company (and if the shares are not yet fully paid of his liability to subscribe share capital).

To establish who are its shareholders every company is required to show in its register of members the particulars of their shareholdings: s352. This register, which is open to public inspection, demonstrates the shareholder's legal title to his shares (see paragraph 6.6 *Register of members*).

A company is also required to issue to each shareholder a share certificate containing details, extracted from the register, of his shareholding (see paragraph 6.7 *Share certificates*). However, no share certificate need be issued in respect of holdings temporarily registered in the name of SEPON, which is the Stock Exchange nominee company used to facilitate dealings in listed shares: s185(4).

A share certificate is only prima facie evidence of the shareholder's title but he produces it in the course of a transfer of his shares or other dealings such as the creation of an equitable mortgage. It is therefore an important document, on which the shareholder may sometimes rely if in dispute with the company.

Shares usually carry with them defined rights to dividends, return of capital and voting at general meetings. These rights are not conferred by statute law but are specified in the articles (or less often in the memorandum) of the company. In this way each company law may have a capital structure which suits its needs. In particular it may issue shares with different rights, such as preference shares and ordinary shares.

Entry in the register of members merely establishes legal ownership of shares. The registered shareholder may be a trustee for or nominee of some third party. However, an English company is prohibited (s360) from entering in its register any notice of beneficial interests in its shares of persons who are not also holders of the shares on the register. This prohibition does not apply to Scottish companies and there are circumstances in which an English company must respect the rights of third parties, properly disclosed to it (see paragraph 6.4 *Loss of capital of a public company*) or protected by a 'stop notice', in its shares (see paragraph 6.6 *Stop notices*).

The passage above is written to introduce some rules and practices in relation to shares which are explained in more detail later in this chapter or elsewhere in this textbook.

Stock

Throughout the Companies Act the word 'share' includes 'stock' unless a distinction between them is made in the context in which they appear: s744. 'Stock' is a carry-over from a procedure which is now largely obsolete. However, some companies still have stock instead of shares and so an explanation is needed.

In theory every share in the capital of a company is a distinct unit which must be identified by a serial number. If, for example, the capital is £1 million divided into a million £1 shares, each share should have a number in the range 1–1,000,000 to distinguish it from all other shares. However, in practice this system becomes very inconvenient if, over a period of time, transfer of shares leads to division of holdings, so that the holding of any one shareholder is no longer an unbroken numerical sequence.

To avoid this difficulty it is provided that a company, if authorised by its articles, may convert its shares into stock (or back again into shares) provided that the shares at the time of conversion are (1) issued; and (2) full paid: s121. In the example above on conversion the capital of £1 million in shares would become a single aggregate of £1 stock. It would still be registered in the names of different holders and be transferable in 'stock units' but the holdings would not be made up of identifiable units on the register.

However, the need to convert shares into stock may now be avoided (in respect of issued and fully paid shares) by resolving to 'denumber' the shares, so that identifying numbers disappear: s182(2). This is now the more usual practice. The power to denumber is exercised by resolution of the directors at a board meeting.

Share warrants

A share warrant is not just an alternative to a share certificate. In contrast to a certificate it is in itself a document of title to shares.

A company limited by shares may, if so authorised by its articles, issue, with respect to any fully paid up shares, a share warrant, stating that the bearer thereof is entitled to the shares specified therein; those shares may be transferred by delivery of the warrant: s188. On the issue of a share warrant, the company strikes the name of the member off its register of members and substitutes:

1. the fact of the issue of the warrant;
2. a statement of the shares included in the warrant; and
3. the date of the issue of the warrant: s355.

For the purposes of the Uncertificated Securities Regulations 1992, any share warrants issued to bearer under s188 are regarded as forming a separate class of certificated shares.

Section 355(5) makes it clear that a shareholder with a share warrant is not necessarily a member of the company, with all that entails. Share warrants are freely transferable. They are negotiable instruments and may be transferred, free from equities, by delivery.

Subject to the articles, the bearer is entitled, on surrendering the share warrant for cancellation, to have his name entered on the register of members.

Until UK exchange control was suspended from operation in 1979 it imposed requirements on holders of share warrants which deprived them of much of their attraction to UK residents. That obstacle no longer exists but UK company managements prefer to have a system of registered shareholders since, even if the latter are nominees of the real owners, it affords a (rather imperfect) means of approaching the owners and of observing changes in ownership. On the other hand share warrants are popular among investors in other countries of the European Community. With the trend towards international markets in securities of large companies British companies sometimes provide for the issue of share warrants in order to encourage foreign investment in their shares.

Allotment

Refer back to paragraph 6.3 *Allotment of shares* at this point and re-read the description of the basic law and procedure for allotment.

In a simple case the applicant tenders a letter of application for the shares, with a cheque in payment of the entire issue price and the directors, provided that they have the necessary authority, allot the shares and arrange for the name of the allottee to be entered in the register of members as the holder of the new shares. In due course a share certificate (see paragraphs 6.6 *Introduction* and 6.7 *Share certificates*) is issued to him: s185(1).

Public companies as a normal practice, and private companies (if prospectus law (see paragraph 5.2 *Securities of private companies*) does not impede them) occasionally, issue 'renounceable letters of allotment', so that the original allottee, if he does not wish to take up the shares allotted to him, may dispose of his rights. A standard letter of this type includes an attached form of renunciation to be signed by the allottee and a form of application for registration to be signed by the person (if any) who ultimately applies to the company to be registered as the holder of the new shares.

Until 1986 a letter of this type could be renounced so as to transfer the rights thereby given, without payment of stamp duty, which is payable on transfer of registered shares. The renounced letter was simply handed over to the transferee. That exemption has now been ended (and a letter of allotment which is renounced bears 1.5 per cent stamp duty on issue). However, as a legacy of the previous exemption it is normal practice still to limit the period of renunciation to six weeks from the issue of the letter.

By concession the registrar permits companies, which have issued renounceable allotment letters, to postpone the delivery of a return of allotments (s88) until the expiry of the renunciation period so that the return shows the names of the persons entered in the register, if different from the original allottees.

The purpose of the renunciation system is to encourage an active market in newly issued shares, since they are transferable by mere delivery of the letter as a provisional document of title. During the renunciation period persons who may have failed to secure, on allotment, all the shares for which they applied, can buy shares from allottees who do not wish to retain the shares allotted to them. The register thus 'settles down' to normal stablility after these adjustments have been made.

If new shares are allotted under a rights issue, so that the issue price is payable by the registered holder, and no application for registration is made by the allottee or his renuncee, the right to the shares usually lapses (and may pass to the underwriters). If, however, new shares are issued as a 'bonus issue' so that they are issued as fully paid by capitalisation of profits (see paragraph 6.1 *Share capital – basic terms and principles*), the normal practice is always to enter the name of the allottee in the register unless meanwhile his renuncee has applied for registration having purchased the shares from him.

Within a month of making an allotment of shares (unless the issue of renounceable allotment letters justifies an extension) a company is required to deliver to the registrar a return of allotments, giving the details, on a Form PUC and to pay capital duty at the 1 per cent ad valorem rate on the consideration received: s88. If, however, there is a non-cash consideration, a signed contract or particulars of it must be attached to the return.

Register of members

Every company must keep a register of members and enter thereon the name of each member, a statement of the number of shares (or amount of stock) held by him and the dates on which he was registered and on which he ceased to be a member: s352. The register must also indicate the classes of shares held by each member. We saw above that the name of the bearer of a share warrant is not entered on the register: s355.

The court has power to rectify the register where a name is wrongly inserted or omitted: s359. A person whose name wrongly appears (because it should never have appeared or because he has rescinded his contract with the company) should have his name removed or he may be estopped from denying he is a member, by letting his name remain. The share register may also be rectified where a bonus issue of fully paid shares is declared void on the grounds of common mistake: *Re Cleveland Trust plc* [1991] BCLC 424. Subject to this right of correction the register is prima facie evidence of its prescribed contents: s361 (but not of any additional matter).

The register must be held within the country in which the company is incorporated, ie the register of an English company must be at a place in England or Wales: s353(1).

The register may be held either at the registered office of the company or at the place where it is made up, eg the premises of the company transfer office or of the professional registrar to whom the transfer work is contracted out. If held elsewhere than at the registered office, the address must be notified to the registry within 14 days of moving the register to it (and it is also shown in the annual return).

If the company has more than 50 members an index must be maintained with the register. But this is not required if the register itself is in alphabetical order of members, eg loose-leaf form: s354.

A register of members may be kept in the form of a bound book, which is the normal practice of a small private company, or it may be in loose-leaf form or on computer: ss722–723.

If in loose-leaf form, adequate precautions must be taken to prevent and to discover any falsification. Typically, the loose-leaf sheets are held in a locked folder of which the company registrar or secretary holds the key.

If the register is held on computer there must be facilities for inspection (by print-out on demand).

Any person may inspect the register which must be open for this purpose for at least two hours on every working day. Anyone who is not a member of the company may be required to pay a small inspection fee. Every person is entitled to receive from the company within ten days of demand a copy of the register or part of it, eg a list of holders of 100 or more shares, on payment of a fee not exceeding 10p for each 100 words: s356.

If the members of a company which has no share capital are divided into classes, eg voting and non-voting members, the register must show the class to which each member belongs. In distinguishing between classes of shares (see above) it is usual to make separate entries on different pages for a member who holds shares of more than one class.

Where, with his consent, a person's name is entered on a company's register of members, he is a member of the company for the purposes of s22 of the 1985 Act: *Re Nuneaton Borough Association Football Club Ltd* [1989] BCLC 454.

Section 352A of the 1985 Act, as inserted by the Companies (Single Member Private Limited Companies) Regulations 1992, provides that if the number of members of a private company limited by shares or by guarantee falls to one there must be entered in the company's register of members with the name and address of the sole member:

1. a statement that the company has only one member, and
2. the date on which the company became a company having only one member.

If the membership of such a private company increases from one to two or more members there must be entered in the company's register of members, with the name and address of the person who was formerly the sole member, a statement that the company has ceased to have only one member together with the date on which that event occurred. If a company makes default in complying with these requirements, the company and every officer of it who is in default is liable to a fine and, for continued contravention, to a daily default fine.

Interests in shares

The prohibition against making an entry in the register of members of a trust (s360) provides a means of concealing the true identity of the beneficial owner of shares. Section 360 has effect with respect to the appropriate register for an uncertificated security: Uncertificated Securities Regulations 1992.

All companies, however, are subject to rules (ss324–328) which require a director to disclose to the company his interests and dealings in shares or debentures of the company, or of any other company of the same group (see paragraph 9.1 *Publicity about directors*). This requirement extends to the interests and dealings of the director's spouse and minor children (s327) and 'interests' are widely defined (Sch 13). The company is required to enter in a separate register the information on these subjects which it receives and the register is open to inspection, as in effect an extension of the register of members. If the company is listed on a recognised stock exchange, the information must be passed on to that body: s329.

The other disclosure system relates to the shares of public companies carrying unrestricted voting rights at general meetings. It requires disclosure of interests (and of dealings) in substantial shareholdings only, currently set at 3 per cent or more of the capital. The very complicated rules on this subject (ss198–220) may be summarised as follows. Interests in substantial shareholdings must be notified to the company on acquisition, relinquishment or where the percentage level of a substantial holding changes by 1 per cent. These events must be recorded by the company on an additional register (s211) open, of course, to inspection. The company need not stand by waiting for information to arrive: s212 empowers it to require information from members and others.

Interests disclosed in the course of such investigations are to be registered: s213. By s214 a minority shareholder may compel an investigation. Criminal penalties are made available by ss210 and 216: *Re Geers Gross plc* [1988] 2 All ER 224.

In order to prevent abuse of voting power by a single member controlling 'puppet' companies, nominees or trustees who hold shares for him, a wide class of interests count towards the 3 per cent. The interests of spouses, infant children and controlled companies, beneficial interests under trusts, the benefit of contracts to purchase shares or other rights to call for shares, or to vote, must be aggregated with any direct sole or joint shareholdings to determine whether a holding is 'substantial': ss203 and 208. Certain charitable and professional holdings are to be disregarded: s209.

Further, in order to prevent circumvention of these provisions by groups of members acting in concert – 'concert parties' – the interests of concert party members are cumulative. Each such member has a duty to inform the company if his interest combined with the others' exceeds the threshold, and to keep other concert party members informed of his own holdings: ss204–207.

For the purposes of Pt VI (ss198–220) and ss324, 325, 326, 328 and 346 of the 1985 Act and Schedule 13 thereto, an entitlement to a unit of a security is not an interest in a share and the interest which an account holder has in an entitlement to a share is an interest in the share itself: Uncertificated Securities Regulations 1992.

Stop notices

Although in general a company takes no heed of trusts affecting shares, it is possible to guard against the company registering a transfer of shares against the beneficial interest of, for example, an equitable mortgagee, by serving a stop notice. This obliges the company to notify the person serving it of any proposed transfer affecting the interest. Fourteen days' grace is then available before the company may register the transfer, in which an injunction may be sought: O.50, Rules of the Supreme Court. It is possible to obtain an order imposing a similar standstill on the payment of dividends.

Special types of member

Problems may arise in dealings with any of the following categories of member:

Minors

Because of his very limited contractual capacity a minor, if he becomes a member of a company, may treat his membership and shareholding as a voidable contract during and within a reasonable time after minority: *Steinberg* v *Scala (Leeds) Ltd* [1923] 2 Ch 452. If he repudiates the shares the minor cannot recover any sum which he has paid to the company as subscription money unless the shares have at all times been completely worthless, which is unlikely. On the other hand the termination of his status as shareholder deprives the company of its right to call on him for any unpaid capital on partly paid shares.

As partly paid shares are now uncommon, this is not a problem which arises very often nowadays. It is possible for a company to include in its articles a prohibition against a minor ever being a member. This is a precaution adopted mainly to strengthen the company's claims against any person who transfers partly paid shares to a minor without disclosing his age. The case law in this area is rather obscure and conflicting.

Deceased members

The death of a member terminates his membership, so that he may no longer be reckoned in counting the number of members. But his shareholding remains as an asset of his estate, to which his personal representatives become entitled on obtaining a grant of representation in respect of the estate. The company is not obliged to recognise their position until they produce for inspection the grant which has been made to them. Thereafter the company is required to treat them as legal owners of the shares (s187) and to deal with any transfer of the shares, signed by them, which they may present for registration, in accordance with its normal procedure (but subject to any restrictions in the articles of association): s183(3) and Table A art 30.

On production of the grant the company usually makes a suitable entry against the deceased member's shareholding shown in the register of members. This is not prohibited by s360 since it does not amount to entry of notice of a trust. However, the shares remain in the name of the deceased member unless the personal representatives by letter of request apply to have the shares registered in their names, so that they become members in their own right. As an inducement to them to do so (it suits the convenience of the company) the articles (Table A art 31) may deny to them the full rights of membership unless the shares are re-registered in their names. But it is still an option to them and not an obligation. If they prefer they may leave the shares in the name of the deceased member until they have occasion to transfer them on sale or to a beneficiary.

Bankrupt members

The trustee in bankruptcy of a member has broadly the same rights and options as personal representatives of deceased members. In addition bankruptcy law (Insolvency Act 1986 s315) gives to the trustee power to disclaim 'onerous property' which might be used if the bankrupt held partly paid shares.

Companies

One company may be a member of another if its objects clause gives it a suitable express power to acquire shares of another company. It cannot, however, be a member of itself nor usually of its holding company (see paragraph 6.4 *Prohibition against shareholdings*).

Ceasing to be a member

Since membership arises on being entered in the register of members (see paragraph 6.2 *Introduction*) it follows that membership ceases when the member is no longer on the register.

In the case of a company which has a share capital membership ceases when the member no longer has shares registered in his name, usually because he has transferred his entire holding. As explained above a minor may repudiate his shares and a trustee in bankruptcy may disclaim them; an individual ceases to be a member if he dies; a corporate member ceases to be a member if it is dissolved as the final stage of liquidation. The company itself may forfeit or accept the surrender of shares (see paragraph 6.4 *Forfeiture, surrender and cancellation of shares*).

If the company is dissolved its former members are no longer members.

Membership of a company with no share capital

The articles of a company limited by guarantee, which has no share capital, follow the model of Table C: s8(4).

These articles provide that membership is obtained by (1) being a subscriber to the memorandum on formation of the company and (2) approval by the directors of an application for membership. Membership ceases on death and on the expiry of seven days' notice of withdrawal. Membership is not transferable.

6.7 Transfer and transmission of shares

Introduction

A shareholding is personal property (in the technical sense) and so it is by its nature transferable, subject to:

1. the relevant provisions of the Companies Act 1985, which require a 'proper instrument of transfer' in writing (s183, which does not apply to shares in uncertificated form) and of the Stock Transfer Act 1963, which introduced a simplified standard form of share transfer;
2. the articles of association which always require that the transferor's share certificate shall be surrendered to the company for cancellation (Table A art 24) and usually that a separate form of transfer shall be used for different types of shares, eg when the transferor is transferring both preference and ordinary shares there must be a separate transfer of each. If the company is a private company its articles often give to the directors a power in their discretion to reject share transfers and may confer on other members a right of first refusal of any shares which a member wishes to transfer. All companies include in their articles a power to reject a transfer of partly paid shares, to prevent evasion of liability for unpaid capital by transfer of shares to a person who cannot pay.

Much of the procedure for transfer of shares is also suitable for a transfer of registered debentures (see paragraph 7.1 *Ownership and transfer of debentures*) but the legal basis differs in some respects.

'Transfer' is the term used when a shareholder by his own act passes the ownership of shares to another person. 'Transmission' by operation of law is the term used when ownership passes as a result of an event such as the death or bankruptcy of a member, as described above (see paragraph 6.6 *Special types of member*).

Transfer procedure

There is a basic procedure which is suitable for a transfer of fully paid shares of a private company, where the transferor is transferring his entire shareholding by a single transfer. That is described first, before coming to variations adapted to other situations.

At one time companies included in their articles a prescribed form of share transfer. As a result of the Stock Transfer Act 1963 however:

1. the standard form of transfer set out in the Act may always be used, as an alternative to any form required by the articles, for a transfer of fully paid shares. As a result only the standard form is now used;
2. the form of transfer need only be signed by the transferor (not attested or sealed) and it need not be signed by the transferee, unless the shares are partly paid. However, the name and address of the transferee must be shown on the completed transfer.

The standard sequence of transfer procedure is therefore:

1. the shareholder partially completes a standard form of transfer by inserting the particulars of the company and of the shares to be transferred and signs it. He hands the signed transfer, with his share certificate, to the transferee. If it is a sale the latter usually pays the price in exchange for these documents;
2. the transferee inserts his name and address, or the similar particulars of the person to whom he intends to transfer title to the shares, the price and the date. He then presents the transfer to the Stamp Office and pays the stamp duty, usually at an ad valorem rate on the price (currently 0.5 per cent on each £100 or part thereof, eg £3.50 on a price of £650);
3. the transferee then delivers the stamped transfer and the transferor's share certificate to the company at its transfer office. The company has a maximum period of two months (s185 and s183(5)) in which it must either deliver to the transferee a share certificate showing that the transfer has been registered, or a notice of its refusal to do so (see paragraph 6.7 *Refusal to register a transfer*);
4. as a matter of routine the company registrar will check that the transfer is in order and relates to shares registered in the name of the transferor. The old share certificate is cancelled. The transfer is submitted to the board of directors, or a committee of the board or other person(s) authorised by the directors to deal with transfers. If the transfer is approved, the necessary entries are made in the register of members to record a transfer out of the holding of the transferor and into the name of the transferee (see paragraph 6.6 *Register of members*). A new share certificate in the name of the transferee is made out and sealed by the company for issue to him.

Certification

If a shareholder transfers only part of his shareholding or if he wishes to transfer the entire holding divided between different transferees, he varies the above procedure by sending his share certificate to the company with the transfer(s). The company retains the share certificate for cancellation, indorses the transfer(s) with the words 'Certificate lodged' or its equivalent, over the signature of a responsible officer, and returns the transfer(s) to the transferor.

The subsequent procedure is as described above (see paragraph 6.7 *Transfer procedure*) except that a transferee will accept a certified transfer as an assurance that the company holds the transferor's certificate and so will not expect him to produce it with the transfer.

If the transfer is of part only of the transferor's entire holding, the company will in due course issue to him a 'balance certificate' in respect of his holding as reduced by the transfer.

Certification is 'a representation by the company to any person acting on the faith of the certification that there have been produced to the company' a share certificate for the shares to be transferred: s184.

There is a risk that the company will return a transfer duly certified without having obtained the share certificate, or (as in *Longman* v *Bath Electric Tramways Ltd* [1905] 1 Ch 646) will by oversight send the certificate back to the transferor. Such a mistake gives to the transferor the opportunity to make two sales of the same shares (1) by the certified transfer; and (2) by a transfer supported by his share certificate. The priority of claims between the two transferees depends on which of them delivers his transfer to the company for registration first. The other will have his transfer rejected as the shares are no longer available for transfer. If it is the holder of the certified transfer whose application is rejected, he may recover the price of the shares from the company as damages for a loss suffered by relying on an inaccurate certification. If, however, the claim falls to be made by the holder of the uncertified transfer, plus share certificate, he may have no claim against the company since the transferor's share certificate is merely 'prima facie evidence' (s186) that the transferor to whom he paid the price had good title to the shares. The company is in this case entitled to show that, although the share certificate reflected the state of the register when it was issued, subsequent events have rendered it out of date. Section 186 does not have effect in relation to a certificate issued with respect to uncertificated shares.

Thus far the explanation, following case law established by decisions of the courts many years ago, is based on an analysis of the rights given, or not given, by documents processed under transfer procedure. In recent years there has been a tendency to extend the duty of care, which is the basis of liability for negligence, to persons who may be adversely affected by want of care over company documents: *Arenson* v *Casson, Beckman, Rutley & Co* [1977] AC 405; *JEB Fasteners Ltd* v *Marks, Bloom & Co* [1981] 3 All ER 289. It may be that if the situation described above came before the courts now, where a transferee holding a transfer (not certified) and a share certificate, was refused registration because the shares were no longer in the name of the transferor (as a result of negligence in certification of the other transfer) the transferee could claim damages for negligence.

Stock Exchange transfer procedure

In dealings in listed securities on the Stock Exchange (or other recognised exchange such as the Unlisted Securities Market) the standard transfer procedure is unsuitable because the same shares may be sold more than once in rapid succession within the same 'account period' (usually two weeks) and it would not be practicable to enter each successive transaction in the company's register and issue a certificate to the buyer. Yet there is need of means to establish that the seller in each transaction has good title to the securities which he sells. ('Securities' includes debentures as well as shares – the procedure is the same.)

The Stock Exchange procedure is a matter of practice rather than law and it is not found in the Companies Act 1985. The Act does, however, modify its standard rules, eg by exemption from the normal requirement of issue of a share (or debenture) certificate (s185(4)) to a Stock Exchange nominee (see below), to facilitate dealings under Stock Exchange procedure.

In outline a sale of listed securities by a registered holder is completed by a transfer (duly registered) to a Stock Exchange nominee company (SEPON). No certificate is issued to SEPON. If there are further dealings in the same securities during the account period, the seller relies on his beneficial ownership of the holding registered in the name of SEPON. At the end of the account period, SEPON transfers the securities to the ultimate buyers and, on registration of the transfers, certificates are then issued by the company. An incidental consequence of this system of 'pooling' is that it becomes impossible to match a buyer with an identified seller. That is one reason why the Criminal Justice Act 1993 (see paragraph 10.3 Civil remedies) does not impose a civil (only a criminal) liability. It would be impossible for a buyer to show that the securities which he had purchased were those sold by the insider dealer.

An attempt was made to make the transfer of listed securities paperless by developing an electronic system of transfer. This was known as TAURUS (transfer and automated registration of uncertified stock). The task proved to be too difficult, however, and a project that began over a decade ago was abandoned in 1993.

The Bank of England is currently working on another electronic securities settlement system called CREST. This system is due to start operating in the latter part of 1996. It will allow those who wish to hold or transfer their shares in electronic form to do so. Using CREST will be voluntary and changes to the law governing the transfer of securities will need to be made to allow the system to operate. Section 207 CA 1989 provides for such changes to be made by regulations, which are currently in draft form. CREST will be owned and run by CRESTCo, a limited company having a £12m share capital and owned by 69 firms from the securities industry. Until the inauguration of the system, the Bank of England will continue to manage and control CREST.

Competing claims to the same shares

The prohibition (s360) against entry of notice of any trust in the register of members requires the company to recognise the legal rights of the registered holder of the shares – and no one else. Registered debentures are always issued on terms which, as a contract, extend the principle of s360 to the debentures.

Where there are competing claims to securities, normal principles of equitable priority apply subject, as in the case of land, to relevant procedure in establishing title.

As a general rule the registered holder has priority over any other claimant because he has the only legal title. However, equity does not permit him to obtain priority over equitable interests existing at the time when he acquires his legal title if he has knowledge of those interests. To take a simple example a person who accepts a transfer of securities into his name as nominee of the beneficial owner, or as trustee under an existing trust, holds the securities subject to those obligations of which he had notice from the outset. The company is precluded (s360) from disputing his title, but the beneficial owner may assert his rights, and protect them by serving a stop notice (see paragraph 6.6 *Stop notices*) on the company.

The registered holder will, however, be postponed to a person whose equitable interest is created after his own if he is estopped by his own conduct from asserting his legal rights. This situation arises if the registered holder delivers a signed transfer (on which the transferee's name has been inserted) and his share certificate to an agent, with limited authority to use the documents to raise a loan on mortgage, and the agent exceeds his authority: *Colonial Bank* v *Hepworth* (1887) 36 Ch D 36 at p54. However, each such case has to be decided on its facts and there are instances where the registered holder has successfully argued either (1) that the agent was not given complete documents so as to constitute apparent authority to carry out the transaction; or (2) that it was not the principal who created the apparent authority.

Equitable interests in securities may arise under a trust, or an equitable mortgage by deposit of the share certificate or by reason of a transfer not being registered. The general rules which determine priority between competing equitable interests are:

1. the basic principle is that an earlier equitable interest has priority over a later one. If, for example, a trustee improperly creates an equitable mortgage over trust securities, the prior interest arising under the trust will prevail over the subsequent interest of the mortgagee even though he does not know of it;
2. registration of a transfer, by creating a legal title, gives to the transferee priority over an earlier equitable interest provided that he does not have notice of the prior interest before registration of his transfer, or the expiry of a reasonable time for registration, if earlier: *Moore* v *North Western Bank* [1891] 2 Ch 599;
3. the priority normally given to the person entitled to an earlier interest is lost if he, by action or inaction, induces the owner of a subsequent interest to believe that the securities are not subject to a prior interest. The simplest case is where an equitable mortgagee fails to obtain and retain the mortgagor's share certificate, thus permitting the mortgagor to contract a second mortgage: *Farrand* v *Yorkshire Banking Co* (1888) 40 Ch D 182. If the second mortgagee then has the securities registered in his name principle (2) above will apply.

The position between seller and buyer of securities pending registration of the buyer as holder is usually fixed by the terms of the contract of sale (including any relevant market practice). Unless so agreed the position is that, as soon as the contract has been made and the seller has identified the securities to which it relates (if that is not already clear), equitable ownership passes to the buyer. He is then entitled to dividends paid thereafter, even if declared before the sale, and is liable to indemnify the seller against any calls made on partly paid shares. However, until the purchase price is paid the seller is entitled to vote at general meetings as he sees fit.

When listed securities are sold, the sale is explicitly made 'ex div' or 'cum div' as the case may be to remove all doubt.

A legal mortgage of securities is effected by a registered transfer into the name of the mortgagee. An equitable mortgage is usually by deposit of the mortgagor's share certificate with the mortgage. In either case the parties will agree upon dividends, redemption and other incidental matters.

Forged transfers

A forgery is a nullity and if the name of the holder of shares is removed from the register as a result of a forged transfer he may require the company to restore his name as registered holder.

Generally a person defrauded by a forged transfer (and a stolen transferor's share certificate) has no remedy against the company or the holder of the shares. His sole remedy is against the person who defrauded him. If, however, the transfer to him is genuine but the transferor's title is defective, the share certificate may give to the claimant rights against the company (see paragraph 6.7 *Share certificates*).

A person who presents a transfer to the company for registration impliedly warrants that it is genuine. If it is a forgery, however, he has no claim against the company in respect of the share certificate issued to him and is liable to compensate the company for any loss it may suffer: *Sheffield Corporation* v *Barclay* [1905] AC 392.

Share certificates

The obligation of a company to issue share certificates has been mentioned above (see paragraph 6.6 *Introduction*). The certificate is a statement by the company that at the time of issue of the certificate the person named in it was the registered holder of the shares specified.

The company is estopped as against a person relying on a statement contained therein from denying the representation it made thereby.

Hence, if the person relying on the certificate sues the company, the company is estopped from pleading in its defence that the statements therein were untrue. Thus, if a third party buys shares in reliance on a statement in the certificate as to the name of the registered shareholder but another person's name is restored in its place to the register, the third party can claim damages from the company on the basis of the market price of the shares he was purchasing: *Re Bahia & San Francisco Railway Co* (1868) LR 3 QB 584. The cause of action arises because of its wrongful refusal to place or keep on the register the name of the person who is entitled to assume his right to be so entered: *Re Ottos Kopje Diamond Mines Ltd* [1893] 1 Ch 618. Alternatively, it could be that the plaintiff is entitled to damages because of a negligent misrepresentation in a document intended to be relied on by third parties, to whom the company has breached a duty of care (cf *Ministry of Housing and Local Government* v *Sharp* [1970] 2 QB 223); but that would not explain why the company was estopped where it was not negligent.

The company will also be estopped from denying the truth of the false statement where it is acting against the person relying. The latter has a defence to calls where the share certificate states that the shares are fully paid up: *Burkinshaw* v *Nicolls* (1878) 3 App Cas 1004.

In appropriate circumstances, even the person to whom the certificate is issued may rely on the estoppel. For example, where A sells shares to B and then purports to sell them to C, if C has a share certificate issued to him and makes use of it to sell the shares to D, whom the company refuses to register, thereby causing C to have to compensate D, C can claim damages from the company: *Balkis Consolidated Co v Tomkinson* [1893] AC 396. Similarly, where the company makes calls on the person to whom the certificate is issued, the certificate stating that they are fully paid up: *Bloomenthal v Ford* [1897] QB 156.

But it will be difficult for such a person to rely on the estoppel for the following reasons:

1. a person cannot rely on the estoppel if he has not relied and acted on the representation in the share certificate. In particular, this will not be so when he is aware of the truth;
2. a person who has put forward a forged transfer cannot rely on a statement made by the company (as a consequence of it) on the certificate;
3. the company is not estopped by a statement contained in a forged share certificate (*Ruben v Great Fingall Consolidated* [1906] AC 439) unless it is represented as true by a person or persons with authority to bind the company (see paragraph 2.5).

Refusal to register a transfer

If a transfer is properly completed and stamped, and is delivered to the company with the transferor's share certificate (or the transfer has previously been certified) the company is required within a period of two months (or less if the shares are listed and Stock Exchange procedure applies) either to register the transfer and issue a share certificate to the transferee or to give him notice of its refusal to do so: ss185 and 183(2).

A company may only refuse to register a transfer (if it is in order) if the articles give a power to do so and that power is effectually exercised. Public companies do not usually (and a listed company is not permitted to) include any such restriction in their articles. Private companies are no longer required, as they were until 1980, to include such a power of refusal in their articles, but many still do so. The 1985 Table A model articles do not include a power of refusal (though the 1948 Table A Pt II did have it for private companies) and so a special article may now be required if the power is to be taken.

Modern practice (following the 1948 Table A) is to word a power of refusal so as to provide that 'the directors may, in their absolute discretion and without assigning any reason therefor, decline to register any transfer of any share, whether or not it is a fully paid share'. However, the earlier case law establishes that, if the articles limit the power to specified grounds, it may only be exercised on those grounds. If, for example, there is power to reject a transfer to a person whose admission to membership would be contrary to the interests of the company, it may not be used to refuse a transfer of a single share because the directors disapprove of the transfer itself: *Re Bede Steam Shipping Co Ltd* [1917] 1 Ch 123.

The directors may be asked, where grounds of refusal are specified in the articles, what were the grounds of their refusal. They have no obligation to elaborate their reasons in a detailed explanation, unless the articles impose it on them. The Table A formula ('without assigning any reason') merely expresses what would otherwise be implied. If, however, the directors do volunteer an explanation, it may be used as a basis for any challenge in the courts of their refusal of the transfer. Hence, it is the normal practice that reasons are never given in the notice of refusal.

Much of the case law on challenges to directors' refusal of a transfer relates to the principle that any exercise by the directors of their powers of any kind is valid only if they do so in what they (subjectively) regard as the best interests of the company (see paragraph 9.3 *The director's duties*). However, it is readily assumed in favour of the directors that their decision, even if it yielded some advantage to them eg in strengthening their position within the company, was taken bona fide in the interests of the company. This was the reason for upholding the directors' decision to refuse a transfer in order to secure to the managing director voting control of the company: *Re Smith and Fawcett Ltd* [1942] Ch 304.

The directors' power of refusal lapses if it is not exercised within a reasonable time, not exceeding two months, of the delivery of the transfer to the company: *Re Swaledale Cleaners Ltd* [1968] 3 All ER 619. Moreover, it must be a positive exercise of a power of refusal by board resolution. A mere failure to approve, or even to consider, the transfer is not an exercise of a power of refusal: *Re Hackney Pavilion Ltd* [1924] Ch 276. In such cases the transfer must be registered since the power to refuse it has not been exercised.

A person who disputes the refusal of a transfer has his remedy in an application to the court for rectification of the register of members under s359. Directors will be personally liable for the costs of proceedings to rectify the register of members where they wrongfully refuse to register a transfer of shares. It makes no difference that they act in what they believe to be the interests of the company, based on advice received from their solicitors: *Morgan* v *Morgan Insurance Brokers Ltd & Ors* [1993] BCC 145.

Pre-emption rights over transfers

The articles of private companies sometimes include provisions by which any shareholder who wishes to transfer his shares must first offer them (through the company) to other members at a fair price. This is strictly construed against all parties as a form of pre-emption contract. If therefore a shareholder agrees to sell his shares to a third party and accepts the price, but remains on the register as nominee of the purchaser, that will be treated as a case of wishing to transfer the shares: *Lyle and Scott Ltd* v *Scott's Trustees* [1959] AC 763.

The other members on their side may only exercise their rights of pre-emption if they, and the company on their behalf, follow the exact timetable and procedure set out in the articles.

The 'fair value' provision usually calls for the assistance of the auditors as valuers. This may lead to disputes about the value placed on the shares and to claims against the auditors (see paragraph 14.2 *Auditors as valuers of shares*).

The court will not enquire into the valuation unless there is evidence it was improperly made (a controversial exercise of discretion is insufficient) or unless reasons for the valuation are given which are patently wrong: *Dean* v *Prince* [1954] 1 Ch 409; *Baber* v *Kenwood Manufacturing Co Ltd* [1978] 1 Lloyd's Rep 175. However, a valuation which on its face demonstrates an erroneous calculation may be challenged notwithstanding that:

1. it is expressed to be 'final, binding and conclusive' in accordance with the articles; and
2. the shares have already been transferred; *Burgess* v *Purchase & Sons (Farms) Ltd* [1983] 2 WLR 361.

In *Jones* v *Sherwood Computer Services plc* [1992] 2 All ER 170 the Court of Appeal said that, in the absence of fraud or collusion, an expert's determination could only be challenged on the ground of mistake if it was clear from the evidence that the expert had departed from his instructions in a material respect. In reaching this conclusion, their Lordships refused to follow *Dean* v *Prince* and doubted, at least, the judgment of Nourse J in *Burgess* v *Purchase & Sons (Farms) Ltd*

Shares should normally be valued at their market price (*Short* v *Treasury Commissioners* [1948] AC 534) although it is conceivable that a block of shares will be worth more per share if the buyer of them is thereby enabled to obtain control of the company through the strength of his voting power.

Purchase of shares and misrepresentation

Where a party is induced to purchase shares by fraudulent misrepresentation, damages are assessed by the difference between the price paid and the price the shares would have fetched on the open market, had the market *not* known about the fraud. They are not to be assessed on the basis of the price that would have been paid had the market known about the fraud.

In *Smith New Court Securities Ltd* v *Scrimgeour Vickers (Asset Management) Ltd and Another* [1994] 1 WLR 1271, the plaintiff purchased 28,141,424 shares in a public company at 82.25p. The plaintiff was induced to make this purchase as a result of a misrepresentation that it was in competition with other bidders for the shares, which was untrue.

The judge at first instance held that the plaintiff was entitled to recover damages because of the misrepresentation. He measured the damages on the difference between the price paid and the true value of the shares on date of purchase, which was 21 July 1989. He then went on to find that due to another fraud, which was unconnected and then undiscovered, the value of each share at that date was 44p. The difference between the purchase price (£23,146,321) and the value of the shares at 44p each (£12,382,226) was £10,764,005, and judgement was awarded for this amount. On appeal, Nourse LJ held that the correct measure of damages was the difference between the price paid (82.25p per share, amounting to £23,146,321) and the price which the shares would have fetched on the open market, in the absence of the misrepresentation, on 21 July 1989 (78p a share amounting to £21,950,311). The damages were accordingly reduced to £1,196,010. See Chapter 15, paragraph 15.4, for further details.

7

Debentures

7.1 Debentures and debenture stock

7.2 Charges on company property

7.3 Registration and priority of charges

7.4 Receivership

7.1 Debentures and debenture stock

Introduction

In explaining how a company obtains the resources needed in its business (see paragraph 6.1 *Introduction*) we mentioned incidentally that, in addition to share capital, a company often makes use of borrowed money ('loan capital' is the technical term).

Borrowing is a form of contract to which the normal conditions apply. If a company borrows for an ultra vires purpose, the loan will usually be irrecoverable unless the lender can rely on s35 (see paragraph 2.3). The articles may impose on the directors a maximum amount which they may borrow for the company, eg twice the amount of the paid up share capital and reserves, without obtaining the approval of the company in general meeting. If the directors make unapproved borrowings in excess of their powers, the question will arise whether the loan contract is binding on the company (see paragraph 2.5).

The conditions of a loan are usually set out in writing. Any such document is a debenture: s744. It is normal practice for a company to execute a debenture under its common seal since this gives to the debentureholder certain additional rights. The use of the seal is controlled by the directors and so a debenture which has been sealed records a transaction decided on by the directors. If the debenture under seal is secured, it constitutes a mortgage by deed to which s101 of the Law of Property Act 1925 applies.

The form and terms of the debenture vary as agreed between the company and the lender. If, for example, the company gives security to its bank for its overdraft, the bank will usually require the company to execute a single debenture in the standard form supplied by the bank. If the shareholders of a private company decide to supply part of its capital in the form of loans, so that this money may be withdrawn later without the formality attached to repayment of share capital, they may arrange that the company shall issue to each of them one of a series of uniform debentures, ranking equally (pari passu) in priority of claims against the company. If a public company raises a large amount of loan capital, the standard practice is to execute a debenture trust deed, under which an independent corporate trustee is appointed to represent the interests of debenture holders and a debenture stock is raised, transferable in units. References in this chapter to 'debentures' include debenture stock, unless otherwise stated and 'debenture holder' includes debenture stockholder and also the trustee (so far as relates to remedies). One of the advantages of appointing a trustee for debenture holders is that the trustee may hold the security, eg charges on company property, which cannot be directly vested in numerous debenture holders.

Section 744 expressly provides that in company law the term 'debenture' includes both secured and unsecured debentures. However, the financial world usually reserves the term debenture for a secured loan and distinguishes other borrowing as 'unsecured loan stock' and the like. The term 'mortgage debenture' usually means that the debenture is secured by a charge on company land or buildings.

A debenture may be irredeemable, ie have no fixed date for repayment. In that event it is repayable only if the company makes default in the terms, eg by failing to pay interest when due, or if the company goes into liquidation, since the liquidator's duty is to pay all debts so far as the funds suffice. However, in these days, when the value of money tends to decline due to the effect of inflation, it is unusual to find irredeemable debentures. The terms of a standard debenture include a fixed date or determinable date for repayment.

Shares and debentures

A person who leads money to a company repayable at a distant date may well consider that he is investing rather than lending. As will be seen (see paragraph 7.1 *Ownership and transfer of debentures*) he is likely to be given a debenture stock certificate in respect of his loan which is transferable in much the same way as a shareholding. Like a preference shareholder he will receive fixed income, ie interest at the agreed rate in his case, at half-yearly intervals.

However, there are also essential differences between a shareholder and a debentureholder. The former, even if he holds preference shares, is a proprietor. The debentureholder on the other hand is a creditor whose rights are based on his contract with the company. The agreed interest on his debenture is payable at the due date, whether or not the company has made sufficient profits to pay it. In any return of capital in liquidation the debentures must be repaid in full before anything may be paid to shareholders.

Ownership and transfer of debentures

A debentureholder owns a debt payable to him by the company. Unless, as is often the case, the terms of the debenture provide for registered title, the holder of a debenture may assign his rights to it like any other debt. A legal assignment must be in writing with written notice to the debtor company: Law of Property Act 1925 s136.

It is possible for a company to issue bearer debentures which are negotiable instruments transferable merely by delivery.

The more usual situation is that a company issues a series of uniform debentures, each of which is a separate unit, or it issues a debenture stock under a trust deed, divided into transferable units. In either case the terms of the debenture will stipulate that the company is to maintain a register of debentureholders and to issue to each of them a debenture certificate (or individual debenture if it is a series and not a stock). In making a transfer the registered holder executes the same form of transfer as is used for shares and the same transfer procedure is followed (see paragraph 6.7 *Transfer procedure*).

Although a company is not (in order to allow flexibility) legally required to maintain a register of debentureholders, if there is such a register it must be held, open for inspection, with some related documents on charges, either at the registered office or, as regards the register, at the place where it is made up of which notice must then be given to the registrar and shown in the annual return: s190 (see paragraph 3.2 *Statutory registers, etc* and paragraph 7.3 *Late delivery of particulars*).

The terms of the debenture provide that legal ownership of the debenture is established by entry in the register. The company is required to give exclusive recognition to the rights of the registered holder and obtains a valid receipt from him in respect of all payments of interest or capital on the debenture. In this way the ownership of registered debentures is put on the same basis as the ownership of shares. It has, however, to be expressed in the terms of the debentures since s360, which prohibits the entry of trusts on a share register (see paragraph 6.6 *Interests in shares*), does not apply to debentures.

Rights of debenture holders

Normally a debenture carries the right to interest, payable at fixed dates, and to repayment at a fixed or determinable date, eg at a date within a period of years to be selected by the company.

To strengthen the position of the debenture holders, the company may be required to set aside a sum of money each year in a sinking fund to finance eventual repayment or to redeem a proportion of the debentures each year, by purchase in the market or by repayment of debentures selected by drawing lots.

The terms of the debenture contract may give to the debenture holders additional special rights, eg to appoint one or more directors or to attend and vote at general meetings. Rights of that category are usually embodied in the articles as part of the company's constitution. They are comparatively rare nowadays.

If the debentures are secured by a charge on the company's assets, the debenture will provide for the occasions on which the charge becomes enforceable. Failure to pay interest or to repay capital, in accordance with the terms of the debenture, are standard defaults which 'trigger' the charge and also render the capital of the debenture immediately repayable. The debenture may also require the company to keep its property fully insured and/or to retain its property without making substantial disposals and even to maintain its profits or net assets above a specified level. The effect of these 'covenants' is that default renders the debenture immediately repayable, so that the debenture holders may expect to recover their money before the company's financial decline becomes acute and perhaps irreversible.

An unsecured loan stock may carry similar safeguards, plus a prohibition against the company creating any charge on its assets which would take priority over the claims of the loan stockholders.

A convertible debenture gives to the holder the option, to be exercised at fixed dates, of converting his holding into shares of the company at a specified price. In effect there are two stages, ie the repayment of the debenture and the application of the money, while still in the hands of the company, in payment for shares. The terms of conversion must not be such as to permit immediate issue of shares at a price below their nominal value: *Mosely* v *Koffyfontein Mines Ltd* [1911] 1 Ch 73 (see paragraph 6.3 *Allotment of shares*).

Enforcement of debenture holders' rights

If the company defaults in payment of interest or repayment of capital of its debentures, the obvious remedy is for the debentureholders (or their trustee if it is a debenture stock) to sue the company on its personal liability for debt. If that fails, or is inadequate, a petition may be presented for the compulsory winding-up of the company so that its assets are realised and applied in paying its debts.

If the debenture is secured by a charge on the company's assets, the more satisfactory remedy is to enforce the security. In theory there are four possible methods of enforcement, ie taking possession of the charged property, applying to the court for an order for foreclosure, appointing a receiver and selling the property. In practice secured debentureholders usually appoint a receiver, who has power to sell the property which is subject to the charge if it seems the best course. These remedies are considered in a later section (see paragraph 7.3).

As a debenture will often impose on the company a variety of ancillary 'covenants', breach of which makes the loan capital repayable at once, a company may get into a situation of default in repayment of capital long before the contractual date for repayment.

A rather different problem arises when the company's articles embody some right given by the debenture, eg to appoint one or more directors, and the company alters, or proposes to alter its articles to remove these provisions. A related problem has already been considered (see paragraph 3.1 *The articles and contracts with the company*) in connection with managing directors. To recapitulate, the company's statutory power (s9) to alter its articles cannot be restrained by a contract with a third party though he retains his rights against the company for breach of contract: *Southern Foundries (1926) Ltd* v *Shirlaw* [1940] AC 701.

As a general principle the court would not grant an injunction to enforce a contract of employment, and so that issue does not arise in connection with managing directors. Is it then a remedy which the debentureholder can obtain to preserve his rights under the articles? He cannot of course assert that the articles themselves are a contract with him: *Eley* v *Positive Assurance Co Ltd* (1876) 1 Ex D 88 CA (see paragraph 3.1 *The effect of the memorandum and articles*). But does his separate contract (the debenture) give him any leverage in obstructing the alteration of the articles?

In *Shirlaw*'s case, when it was before the House of Lords, Lord Porter made an obiter dictum that no injunction would be granted in any circumstances to restrain an alteration of the articles. It was only an obiter dictum because Shirlaw had sought, and been awarded damages in his progress to the House of Lords. The issue in *Shirlaw*'s case was whether the statutory power to alter the articles deprived him of all remedies for breach of contract incidental to the alteration. It was held that it did not.

Although the grant of an injunction was not an issue in *Shirlaw*'s case (and could not have been since he had a contract of employment) there are earlier cases in which the courts had granted or contemplated the grant of an injunction, or making a declaration, in favour of debentureholders who were about to lose their rights expressed in the articles: *British Murac Syndicate Ltd* v *Alperton Rubber Co Ltd* [1915] 2 Ch 186; *Baily* v *British Equitable Assurance Co* [1904] 1 Ch 374.

It is generally considered that Lord Porter's ruling is of general application and overrules these earlier decisions. However, that is not quite the end of the matter. In *Cumbrian Newspapers Group Ltd* v *Cumberland & Westmoreland Herald Newspaper & Printing Co Ltd* [1986] 2 All ER 816 the court said obiter that an injunction might be granted to restrain a company from issuing a notice to convene a general meeting to consider an alteration of the articles (in breach of a separate contract) unless the company was at that stage already under a statutory obligation, eg under s368 (see paragraph 8.1 *Persons able to convene meetings*), to issue the notice. However, if that is correct, it is easy enough for the company to arrange that members holding 10 per cent of the shares shall requisition a general meeting under s368.

The other possible loophole is that the alteration of the articles, which cannot be prevented, is usually only the first step. If, for example, the company alters its articles to remove a power given to debentureholders to appoint a director, it will then proceed under s303 to remove their nominee from the board. It has been suggested that, as this is the actual breach of contract, the debentureholders might obtain an injunction to restrain the company from proceeding under s303. The situation would be analogous to that in *Re A & BC Chewing Gum Ltd* [1975] 1 All ER 1017 where the court granted equitable relief (of a different kind) following a removal of a director in breach of contract.

7.2 Charges on company property

Introduction

The effect of a charge on company property (cf *Mettoy Pension Trustees Ltd* v *Evans* [1991] 2 All ER 513) is to give to the creditor who holds the charge a priority right to recover payment of his debt from that property if the company defaults in payment.

Many companies do not have occasion to create such charges. If a company which has no outstanding charges on its property goes into insolvent liquidation, the liquidator will apply the assets, remaining after payment of liquidation expenses, in payment of a small category of preferential debts, and the balance is shared proportionately by the unsecured ordinary creditors. To take a simple example, if the non-preferential debts total £500,000 and the remaining assets produce £200,000, every creditor will be paid 40p in £1 of his debt.

If, however, one creditor has obtained a charge on property worth £50,000 are security for a debt of £30,000, he will recover his debt in full from the security and hand over the balance of £20,000 to the liquidator. The other creditors, whose debts total £470,000, will share assets worth £170,000, and so they receive about 36p in £1 of their debts. Competing claims of creditors may be much more complicated than this example. The rules on 'priorities' are explained later (see paragraph 7.3 *Memorandum of a charge ceasing to affect property of the company*).

If the company borrows money, eg from its bank or by the issue of debentures, it may well have to charge its property as security. It is much more difficult for trade creditors to insist on having security for their short-term debts which are paid in the ordinary course within a few weeks. Hence, in recent years suppliers of goods have, to an increasing extent, introduced into their supply contracts a 'retention of title clause' (colloquially called a *Romalpa* clause – see paragraph 7.3 *Retention of title clauses*). The effect of such a clause is that goods etc supplied to the company remain the supplier's property until he is paid. If the company becomes insolvent while his debt is outstanding he recovers his property from the possession of the company.

A creditor of a company may obtain a third-party guarantee of its debt to him, eg from directors or shareholders. A guarantee gives to the creditor a right to recover his debt, up to the amount guaranteed, if the company defaults. It is a form of security but is not a charge on company property. Hence, it is not necessary to describe the law of guarantees here as it is not part of company law.

It is an essential condition of the priority given by a charge that persons dealing with the company should have the means of discovering its existence. With only minor exceptions a charge on company property created by the company itself gives priority over other creditors only if the particulars of the charge are registered at the registry and open to inspection on the file.

Before coming to registration and priorities of charges (see paragraph 7.3), it is necessary to consider the two kinds of company charges, ie fixed and floating charges.

Fixed charges

A fixed charge is a mortgage, legal or equitable, of company property to which much of the general law of mortgages applies. The following points have been covered by sections of the Companies Act 1985:

1. Debentures may be irredeemable (see paragraph 7.1 *Introduction*) or be repayable only after a long period of years: s193. This excludes companies as mortgagors from the principle of mortgage law which requires that the mortgagor's right to redeem shall not be impeded by a remote repayment date. Companies need to raise loan capital on a long-term basis and that is the more important consideration: *Knightsbridge Estates Trust Ltd* v *Byrne* [1940] AC 613.
2. Section 193 preserves to companies, as to other mortgagors, the right to recover property, on redemption of the mortgage, without being subject to continuing advantages in favour of the debentureholder, unless these were conceded as part of a reasonable commercial bargain: *Kreglinger* v *New Patagonia Meat and Cold Storage Co Ltd* [1914] AC 25.
3. An order may be made for specific performance of a contract to subscribe for debentures of a company: s195.
4. A company may re-issue redeemed debentures unless it has cancelled them or, as is often the case, the debentures were originally issued on terms prohibiting re-issue: s194.

Like any mortgage a fixed charge attaches to the property charged as from the moment of creation of the charge. If therefore the company sells the charged property while the charge is outstanding, it passes with the property as an incumbrance on it to which the rights of the transferee are subject. Obviously this situation would be unacceptable to a purchaser of goods from the company in the course of trade.

For that reason a company cannot in practice create fixed charges over its current assets. Fixed charges are confined to fixed assets, such as land, buildings, plant etc which the company will probably retain over its useful life. If the company wishes to sell such property, it usually arranges to discharge the debt out of the sale proceeds so that the property can pass unencumbered to the new owner.

Siebe Gorman v *Barclays Bank Ltd* [1979] 2 Lloyd's Rep 142 established that it is possible to create a fixed charge over a future book debt owing to the company, provided that the charge requires the company to receive payment of the debt into a bank account, from which it may not withdraw the money except with the consent of the holder of the charge. But the effectiveness of the restrictions on the company's ability to deal with the money will be closely examined since the general trend is still towards treating a charge on book debts, however expressed, as a floating charge: *Re Armagh Shoes Ltd* [1982] NI 59; *Re Brightlife Ltd* [1986] BCLC 418.

Although the *Siebe Gorman* principle is narrowly restricted in its effect, the banks have tended to include fixed charges on book debts in their standard debentures to be executed by company customers. This is because a fixed charge, unlike a floating charge, has priority over preferential unsecured debts.

The latest development on whether a fixed charge over book debts is possible is the Court of Appeal decision in *Re New Bullas Trading Ltd* [1994] BCC 36. In this case the court reiterated the principle that whether a charge is fixed or floating depends upon the intention of the parties. However, the label given to a charge is not conclusive and may be upset if other provisions in the debenture are inconsistent with the label given. Nourse LJ, with whom Russell LJ and Scott Baker J agreed, held that a charge over books debts, which was expressed to be a fixed charge, was in fact a fixed charge while the debts were uncollected and became a floating charge when the debts were realised. This is an important and new extension of the law in this area.

Floating charges

The characteristic of a floating charge is that it does not immediately attach to the property charged but floats over it until the moment of crystallisation (see paragraph 7.2 *Crystallisation of floating charges*).

There is some debate as to the nature of a floating charge. It may be regarded either (1) as a charge which exists from the moment of creation but subject to a license given to the company to dispose of the property free from incumbrance; or (2) as a future mortgage which will attach to assets owned by the company at the time of crystallisation. The choice between these alternatives has some bearing on the automatic crystallisation dispute (see paragraph 7.2 *Crystallisation of floating charges*). See Pennington (1960) 23 MLR 630.

Because it does not impose an immediate incumbrance on the property charged, a floating charge may apply to current assets. If expressed, as is usual, to apply to the 'undertaking and assets' of the company a floating charge takes in both fixed and current assets. It is also possible to create a floating charge over a class of assets.

Normally a floating charge is created by the use of the words 'floating charge'. However, it has been held (in the words of Romer LJ) that a charge, however expressed, is a floating charge:

1. 'if it is a charge on a class of assets of a company present and future;
2. if that class is one which, in the ordinary course of the business of the company, would be changing from time to time; and
3. if ... it is contemplated that, until some future step is taken by ... those interested in the charge, the company may carry on its business in the usual way as far as concerns the particular class of asset': *Re Yorkshire Woolcombers Association Ltd* [1903] 2 Ch 284 (reported as *Illingworth* v *Houldsworth* [1904] AC 355 in the House of Lords).

The advantage of a floating charge is principally that it takes in the current assets which may be the most valuable assets of the company.

The disadvantages of a floating charge fall mainly under two heads. First, there can be no certainty as to the assets, and their value, to which the floating charge will attach when it crystallises. Secondly, a floating charge ranks behind unsecured preferential debts in most cases and may also rank after a fixed charge on fixed assets subject to the floating charge. The questions of priority are considered later (see paragraph 7.3 *Memorandum of a charge ceasing to affect property of the company*).

The courts have often had to decide whether, upon its true construction, a charge is fixed or floating. This will obviously depend on the wording of the individual debenture. A example is the case of *Re Cimex Tissues Ltd* [1994] BCC 626, in which the court had to decide whether or not a charge over plant and machinery was fixed. The central issue of the case was whether a licence to deal with the charged property, in favour of the borrower, is inconsistent with the charge being fixed. On the facts of the case it was held that the charge was fixed despite a clause allowing the borrower to deal with the assets charged. On this point, Mr S J Burnton QC (sitting as a deputy High Court judge), said:

> 'The extent to which the licence to deal is incompatible with a fixed charge must depend on all the circumstances of the case, and in particular on the nature of the charged property. Where the charged property is stock, or book debts – ie where the assets are naturally fluctuating – the court will readily conclude that a liberty for the chargor to deal with the charged assets is inconsistent with a fixed charge. Where, as in the present case, the assets are specific and do not necessarily fluctuate, some liberty to release the charged assets may not be inconsistent with a fixed charge. Conversely, however, on this basis a floating charge over present goods, not extending to future goods, is not a conceptual impossibility.'

So, it would seem that a licence to deal with the charged property does not necessarily mean that the charge is a floating charge. It depends on the extent of the licence and also on the nature of the assets charged. The case is also interesting for it highlights the importance of having a well drafted debenture and one which is appropriate for the borrower's type of business. In *Re Cimex* the wording of the debenture was criticised as being 'defective' and the judge identified the debenture as apparently deriving from the precedent for a debenture to secure bank lending at p145 of vol 4 of the *Encyclopedia of Forms and Precedents* (5th edn). This was wholly inappropriate as the business of the company was that of a toilet roll manufacturer! See Chapter 15, paragraph 15.5, for further details.

Crystallisation of floating charges

The essence of a floating charge is that so long as the company continues to carry on its business in the usual way, it may dispose of assets within the class(es) to which the charge relates free of incumbrance by the charge.

The following passage explains the position in mid-1990. Section 410 CA 1989 provides for regulations to be made for the compulsory notification of events leading to crystallisation. These regulations by their nature will alter the substantive law established by the judicial decisions cited below. See paragraph 7.3 *Other points of registration procedure.*

As soon as the company ceases to carry on its business in the usual way the holder of the charge is entitled to withdraw his consent to the unfettered disposal of assets and to enforce his charge against the assets which the company then has: *Re Griffin Hotel Co Ltd* [1941] Ch 129 and see, eg, *Armour* v *Thyssen Edelstahlwerke* AG [1990] 3 WLR 810. At that point the charge is said to crystallise and it becomes a fixed charge.

In a review of the law on this subject the Cork Committee (Insolvency Law and Practice etc Cmnd 8558 of 1982 para 1571) said that:

'it is well settled that a floating charge crystallises:
1. on the company going into liquidation;
2. on the debentureholder intervening by appointing or obtaining the appointment of a receiver or by taking possession of the assets subject to the charge; or
3. (probably) on the happening of an event defined in the debenture as a crystallising event.'

As regards (2) it is the actual appointment of the receiver which causes crystallisation. If the debenture provides for the appointment of a receiver on the occurrence of certain events, those events do not cause the charge to crystallise until the receiver is actually appointed: *Government Stock and Other Investment Co* v *Manila Railway Co* [1897] AC 81.

It often happens that by the time a secured creditor has acted and appointed a receiver, some other creditor has obtained priority over him. If, for example, the floating charge prohibits the company from creating other charges with priority over the floating charge and the company breaches that prohibition by creating a fixed charge in favour of another creditor who is unaware of the prohibition (see paragraph 7.3 *Memorandum of a charge ceasing to affect property of the company*), the fixed charge will take priority and the floating charge may be worthless as regards the asset subject to both charges.

To counter this risk to his position the holder of a floating charge may include in it a provision that the charge shall crystallise automatically as soon as the company does anything which would entitle the holder of the floating charge to enforce his security and that crystallisation is to occur immediately prior to that action, so that the floating charge takes priority before the company's breach itself affects the asset in question. That is category (3) of the Cork analysis above.

The Cork Committee qualified proposition (3) because the law on this point is uncertain. The Cork Committee itself (para 1572) conceded that there was 'no conceptual difficulty' in automatic crystallisation. In New Zealand there has been a clear judicial decision in favour of its validity: *Re Manurewa Transport Ltd* [1971] NZLR 909.

The New Zealand High Court was here following judicial pronouncements in two English cases: *Davey & Co* v *Williamson & Sons Ltd* [1898] 2 QB 194 and *Evans* v *Rival Granite Quarries Ltd* [1910] 2 KB 979. However, in *Evan's* case the

Court of Appeal was divided in its views on the question. It is also arguable that in both cases the facts were such that a ruling in favour of automatic crystallisation was only an obiter dictum. On the other hand going into liquidation brings about crystallisation without need of intervention by the debentureholder and so does ceasing to carry on business, since a floating charge only permits the company to dispose of assets in the course of its business: *Re Woodroffes (Musical Instruments) Ltd* [1985] 3 WLR 543. In this last case Nourse J explicitly held that automatic crystallisation had occurred. In *Re Brightlife Ltd* [1986] BCLC 418 Hoffmann J also treated automatic crystallisation as legally possible if the charge was appropriately worded, though the point was not the main issue in that case.

Both Gower and Pennington regard automatic crystallisation clauses as valid. The argument of principle is that, if a floating charge is regarded as an immediate charge subject to a licence to the company to dispose of its property until crystallisation, there is no reason why the chargeholder should not stipulate that his licence terminates at the moment before some act of the company which conflicts with the terms of the charge. In an early case the charge was expressed to float 'until default': *Re Horne and Hellard* (1885) 29 Ch D 919. If on the other hand a floating charge is considered to be a mortgage of future assets, owned by the company at the moment of crystallisation, it cannot by its terms take effect so as to gain priority over third party rights obtained before the mortgage is created by crystallisation.

The Cork Committee (paras 1575–1580) based its strongly argued objections to automatic crystallisation on practical grounds. If it may occur by reason of a specified event, without intervention by company or creditor, there could be crystallisation of the charge of which both parties were unaware, since they did not realise what had happened, eg when the company's transactions caused it momentarily to exceed a limit on borrowings set by the debenture (Cork para 1577) and thus constituting a breach of covenant (see paragraph 7.1 *Rights of debenture holders*). Yet once the charge has crystallised, the company can no longer dispose of current assets unencumbered by the charge, so that grave difficulties would arise in its normal dealings with customers. The Cork Committee (para 1580) therefore recommended that crystallisation should occur only when specified public events had happened, ie the appointment of a receiver or administrator (see paragraph 7.4) or the commencement of liquidation (see Chapter 13).

The crystallisation of a floating charge in favour of a bank, will complete the assignment of the charged property to the bank, thus defeating the claims of local authorities to levy distress over the property to recover unpaid business rates. On crystallisation the property no longer belongs to the company, and so the goods will not be the company's to seize by the local authority. See *Re ELS Ltd* [1994] 3 WLR 616 (Chapter 15, paragraph 15.5).

7.3 Registration and priority of charges

Registration of charges

The statutory rules on registration of charges (Part XII of CA 1985) will be entirely replaced by Part IV of CA 1989 which substitutes new ss395–408 in the 1985 Act. This complete revision follows from the Diamond Report and is intended to improve the machinery and procedure of registration, without however altering the basic features of the system.

There are four systems of registration of charges which may apply to the property of a company. These overlap, so that due compliance with one does not relieve the company of its obligations, nor suffice as a substitute, in respect of any other which is applicable. They are:

1. within 21 days of creating a charge over property of specified types (see paragraph 7.3 *Registrable charges*) a company is required to deliver particulars to the registry to obtain registration. This procedure applies to property in any part of the world;
2. if a company acquires property which is already subject to a charge which, if created by the company itself would require registration under 1. above, the company is required within 21 days of acquisition to deliver particulars to register the existing charge (as a charge on its property);
3. at its registered office a company is required to maintain a comprehensive register of all charges of any kind over its property, with copies of the instrument creating or evidencing the charge. See paragraph 7.3 *Company register of charges*;
4. a fixed charge on identified company land may be registrable under either the Land Registration Act 1925 or the Land Charges Act 1972. A floating charge, although it affects company land, is not registrable under these statutes, since it refers generally to classes of assets and not to specific lands. Any charge of either kind on company land must be registered at the Companies Registry (see paragraph 7.3 *Registrable charges*).

The purpose of these registration requirements is to disclose the charges to persons who may inspect the registers. Failure to register a charge, where required, renders the company and its officers liable to fines. Among company charges ((1) to (3)) above only failure to register a charge in category (1) has the effect of making the charge void for certain purposes, though it does not extinguish the debt for which the charge is intended to provide security.

Registrable charges

Under s395 any of the following charges, if created by a company, require registration at the companies registry within 21 days of creation;

1. a charge on land or any interest in land, except a charge to secure rent etc;
2. a charge on goods or any interest in goods, with exceptions where the chargee has possession of the goods or of a document of title to them. The exception keeps out of the registration system arrangements, usually of very short duration, by which goods, bills of lading etc are pledged as security in the course of trading;
3. a charge on intangible property, such as business goodwill, intellectual property, book debts, and the uncalled share capital of the company or sums owing to the company by members for calls on their shares which they have not yet paid;
4. a charge created to secure an issue of debentures;
5. a floating charge on the whole or part of the company's property.

An unpaid vendor has a lien on the property, so long as he retains it, which is created by law. If that is all, the charge is not registrable, since it is not created by the purchaser company: *London and Cheshire Insurance Co Ltd* v *Laplagrene Property Co Ltd* [1971] Ch 499. On the other hand a deposit of its title deeds by the company, unless otherwise stipulated, eg deposit for safekeeping only, is treated as an equitable mortgage, which does require registration: *Re Wallis & Simmons (Builders) Ltd* [1974] 1 WLR 391. If in the course of buying property, the purchasing company agrees that the vendor may retain the title deeds until the price has been paid in full, that is an equitable mortgage, in which the vendor's lien is merged. If therefore the charge is not registered the vendor can no longer rely on his lien, which did not by itself require registration: *Capital Finance Co Ltd* v *Stokes* [1968] 3 All ER 625.

In *Re Weldtech Equipment Ltd* [1991] BCC 16 it appeared that conditions of sale purported to create an assignment to the company of debts incurred by purchasers of equipment sold by the company. Applying *Tatung (UK) Ltd* v *Galex Telesure Ltd* (1989) 5 BCC 325, Hoffmann J held that the wording of the clause made it clear that the assignment was intended to be by way of charge and that it was void for want of registration under s395 of the 1985 Act. Where an agreement is not a sham, in determining whether it is one of sale or charge the court will have regard to its substance rather than the labels put on it by the parties: *Welsh Development Agency* v *Export Finance Co Ltd* [1992] BCC 270.

The DTI may by regulations vary the list of charges which require registration.

Retention of title clauses

In a contract of sale the seller may stipulate that the title to property shall not pass to the buyer until the purchase price has been paid. Where the purchaser is a company, this arrangement is not a charge on the property of the company, requiring registration, since by the terms of the contract of sale title has not yet passed to the company: *Aluminium Industrie Vaassen BV* v *Romalpa Aluminium Ltd* [1976] 2 All ER 552; see also *Armour* v *Thyssen Edelstahlwerke AG* [1990] 3 WLR 810.

However the relevant clause of the contract should be correctly drafted, so that it does not by its wording transfer the legal title of the goods etc to the company, reserving rights of the vendor which amount to an equitable charge void unless registered: *Re Bond Worth Ltd* [1979] 3 All ER 919. After this and related legal points had been explored in a number of decisions on the particular contract provisions, the effectiveness of properly drafted '*Romalpa* clauses' was reaffirmed by the Court of Appeal in *Clough Mill Ltd* v *Martin* [1985] 1 WLR 111.

The Cork Committee on insolvency, in Chapter 37 of its report, recommended that there should be disclosure of retention of title clauses, by requiring their registration. This recommendation has not so far been implemented.

Registration procedure

The registrar is required to maintain for every company a register of charges on its property, and to include in it the particulars and other information delivered to him: s397(1) and (2). This is a modified procedure which should make it easier and safer to extract information on making a search for registered charges on the company's property.

Any person may require the registrar to provide a certificate stating the date on which particulars or other information relating to the charge were delivered to him: s397(3). This replaces the previous procedure by which the registrar received the original instrument of charge and returned it with a certificate of registration attached. He will no longer see the original charge (or a copy); it was a useless formality since the registry staff did not, and could not be expected, to study the charge in detail. Everything now depends on the particulars provided, on a prescribed form. The particulars provide only a summary of the charge. It is all the more important that this information should be complete and accurate as far as it goes.

The registrar's certificate, signed or sealed by him, is conclusive evidence that the particulars or other information was in fact delivered to the registry not later than the date stated on the certificate: s397(5).

The major change made here is that the registrar's certificate is no longer conclusive evidence, as it was before, that all statutory requirements as to registration had been complied with. As a result the courts are no longer prevented from considering whether the registration of the charge is defective on grounds such as the following:

1. the prescribed particulars etc were not in fact delivered in the correct form or detail within the permitted period of 21 days: *R* v *Registrar of Companies, ex parte Central Bank of India* [1986] 2 WLR 177 (where incorrect documents received within the 21 days period were returned for correction and a corrected version was accepted after the 21 days had expired);
2. the date of creation of the charge shown on the documents was not the true date: *Re C L Nye Ltd* [1971] Ch 442;
3. the property charged was not correctly stated: *National Provincial Bank Ltd* v *Charnley* [1924] KB 431;

4. the amount secured by the charge was not correctly stated: *Re Mechanisations (Eaglescliffe) Ltd* [1966] Ch 20.

In addition there are other related changes whereby such defects may be corrected (see paragraph 7.3 *Failure to register within 21 days, Late delivery of particulars* and *Errors or omissions in the particulars*). It is also possible to deliver further particulars, to supplement or vary the previous registered particulars, but in this case the chargee's signature, as well as that of the company, is required on the form: s401. If however property is added to the security, that must be treated as the creation of a new charge, for which separate original particulars must be delivered.

On receiving and registering the original or further particulars, the registrar sends to the company, to the chargee and to any other person who appears to be interested in the charge, a copy of the particulars which he has registered, with the date of delivery which he has recorded: ss398(5) and 401(4). This is an additional safeguard to the chargee, who under the old procedure, could in theory be unaware of the content of the registered particulars. In practice it is the chargee who, in his own interest, attends to the due registration of the particulars.

It is still primarily the legal duty of the company to register the particulars within the 21 days period. However it is also provided that any other person, usually the chargee, may attend to this for the company and recover from the company any costs of so doing it: s398.

Where the company acquires property subject to an existing charge the basic procedure is the same as for a charge which the company has created, but the legal consequences of failure to register are different. As already stated, the 21 day period for registration in this case runs from the date of acquisition: s398.

The effect of registration

Registration is notice to any person who takes a charge over the company's property of matters disclosed in the registered particulars insofar as they require registration: s416(1).

In the one case of registered charges, the general abolition of constructive notice of documents on file at the registry, does not apply: s711A(4). In consequence a person who takes a charge on the property of the company without making a preliminary search at the registry, which is standard practice, is still affected by a prior registered charge which he could have discovered if he had made the search.

A person other than a subsequent chargee might also be affected by constructive notice if he failed 'to make such inquiries as ought reasonably to be made': s711A(2). See paragraph 2.3 *Validity of transactions* for earlier discussion of this point. If, for example, an unsecured creditor of the company in his dealings with it became aware that the company had handed over the title deeds of property to a third party in circumstances suggesting a loan transaction, and he did not ask for an explanation nor seek further information of any kind, he might have constructive notice of a registered charge, created by the deposit of which he did know.

A court cannot go behind a certificate of registration of a charge and delete or rectify the registration: *Exeter Trust Ltd* v *Screenways Ltd* [1991] BCC 477.

Negative pledge clauses

A registered charge is notice only of matters requiring registration. In the past it became common practice for chargees holding floating charges to include in the terms of the charge a prohibition against the company creating any other charge, usually a specific charge, over the same property which would take priority over the floating charge (see paragraph 7.3 *Priority of charges*). This restriction was called a 'negative pledge clause'. Under the previous registration system, there was no requirement that such a clause should be disclosed in the particulars presented for registration. However the chargee often did include it among the particulars.

A person who makes a search at the registry, as a normal but optional precaution before acquiring an interest in company property, would by this means have actual notice of the negative pledge clause. If however he made no search and remained unaware of the negative pledge clause, its inclusion among the registered particulars did not affect him with constructive notice: *Wilson* v *Kelland* [1910] 2 Ch 306.

The DTI now has power by regulation to vary the prescribed particulars of charges requiring registration. It is expressly provided that particulars of 'negative pledge causes' may be added by this procedure: s415(2)(a).

Failure to register within 21 days

It has been stated that failure to register entails liability to fines: s398(3). In the case of a charge created by the company, failure to register within 21 days renders the charge void against;

1. an administrator or liquidator of the company; and
2. any person who for value acquires an interest in or rights over the property subject to the charge, provided that the 'relevant event' occurs after the creation of the charge, whether before or after the expiry of the 21 days period allowed for registration. The relevant event is insolvency in case (1) and the acquisition of the interest or right in case (2): s399. This provision eliminates the anomalous distinction made in *Watson* v *Duff Morgan and Vermont (Holdings) Ltd* [1974] 1 All ER 794 (where the first charge, although unregistered, retained priority over a subsequent registered charge created on the same day and so within the 21 days allowed for registration of the first charge).

If the relevant event occurs on the same day as the creation of the charge, it is presumed to occur after that creation, so that it takes priority over the charge, unless evidence is produced that it preceded it: s399(3).

As under the previous procedure, failure to register in time (or to deliver correct particulars (see paragraph 7.3 *Errors or omissions in the particulars*), renders the debt secured by the charge immediately repayable on demand: s407.

However if a person acquires property, or a charge on it, on the express terms that the charge, not in fact registered, is to take priority over his interest, it preserves its priority in spite of the failure to register. This alters the previous law under which it was held that registration was the only effective notice of a charge requiring registration: *Re Monolithic Building Co* [1915] 1 Ch 643.

Late delivery of particulars

It is no longer necessary to apply to the court, as it was under the old procedure, for permission to register out of time, by delivery of the particulars after the expiry of the 21 days period: s400(1). This is not a major change since, under the old procedure, it was generally possible, except where there had been deliberate concealment of the charge, to obtain a court order for registration out of time, but only on the basis that the late registration would cause the charge to rank in priority after any charges or other interests arising in the interval. However, the court would not exercise its discretion to extend the time for registration unless evidence was submitted as to why the charge was not registered or, where the application to register late was only made after further, unsuccessful, attempts to secure another charge: *Re Telomatic Ltd* [1993] BCC 404.

The court would not generally sanction late registration if the company was insolvent, or on the verge of insolvency. Under the revised procedure the charge remains void against an administrator or liquidator, in spite of late delivery of particulars, if two conditions are shown to have existed:

1. at the date of delivery of the particulars the company was unable to pay its debts or became unable to do so by reason of the transaction under which the charge was created; and
2. insolvency proceedings began with the 'relevant period', which is six months, extended to one year in the case of a floating charge (or two years for a floating charge in favour of a person connected with the company (see paragraph 13.6 *Avoidance of floating charges*). The relevant period runs from the date of delivery of the particulars: s400.

Errors or omissions in the particulars

As explained in paragraph 7.3 *Registrable charges* difficulty might arise from errors or omissions in the particulars delivered and accepted for registration, since the instrument creating the charge was not, and still is not, on the file at the registry for scrutiny in detail in the course of a search.

Under the new procedure incomplete or inaccurate particulars renders the charge void (against the persons mentioned above in connection with failure to register within the 21 days) but only in respect of those aspects of the charge which would have been disclosed by complete and accurate particulars: s402(1). This provision does not apply to a unit of an uncertificated debenture: Uncertificated Securities Regulations 1992.

It is however possible to apply to the court for an order to make the charge fully effective. In deciding whether to make the order the court should consider whether prejudice, as defined by s402(4) and (5), has resulted from registration of defective particulars.

Memorandum of a charge ceasing to affect property of the company

A memorandum in the prescribed form and signed both by the company and the chargee may be delivered to the registry, to give notice that a registered charge has ceased to affect all or part of the property subject to it: s403(1). This action is appropriate when the secured debt is repaid or part or all the charged property is released from the charge.

Regulations may be made to prescribe the evidence which will be required in support of the memorandum: s413(3).

This procedure puts the chargee in a better position than the previous system, under which the company without giving him notice or securing his participation could give notice to the registry that the charge had been discharged, wholly or in part. If the memorandum was inaccurate, it did not prejudice his rights, but it could cause difficulties and disputes.

The previous procedure of action by the company alone was based on the fact that, in some cases, no action was taken for a period of years to 'clear' a registered charge, which had in fact been discharged. When the matter came to light, perhaps on the sale of the property after many years, it could be difficult to find the chargee, or his successor, if his signature was required. Hence the matter was previously left to the company alone. But that position has now been reversed.

If the memorandum as delivered under the new procedure is later found to be incorrect, the charge is void to the same extent as described in paragraph 7.3 *Failure to register within 21 days*.

On receiving the memorandum for registration, the registrar sends a copy, by way of notice of registration, to the company, the chargee and any other person interested: s403(4).

Other points of registration procedure

1. if a company has created a charge to secure an issue of debentures, it must within 21 days of issuing any debentures deliver for registration particulars of the debentures taken up: s408. Thus if the company executes a debenture trust deed, which creates a charge on its property, that would require registration. Later, when the debentures or debenture stock had been issued, particulars of that issue would also be registered, so that there is a complete record of the position on the file;
2. due notice must be given to the registry of the appointment of a receiver under a charge and of his vacating office (paragraph 7.4 *The appointment of a receiver*): s409;

3. the DTI may make regulations requiring notice to be given to the registrar of the crystallisation of a floating charge, ie of an act or event whereby a floating charge is converted into a fixed charge on the property of the company: s410. (See paragraph 7.2 *Crystallisation of floating charges.*)

Company register of charges

There is an entirely distinct legal requirement on a limited company that it shall at its registered office maintain a register of charges, fixed or floating, on all or any part of its property. The company must also hold a copy of the instrument by which each charge is created, though a specimen copy will suffice for debentures issued as a series: s411.

Intentional failure to comply with s411 entails liability to a fine for the company officer who is at fault. But it does not affect the validity of the charge.

Any person may inspect the register and the copies of charges etc. This right gives him the opportunity to examine the details of the charges, which is not possible by a search at the registry, since no copies are held there.

Unless the person making the inspection is a member or creditor of the company, he may be required to pay a fee.

Any person may require the company, on payment of a fee, to supply him within ten days of the request, with a copy of entries in the register or of an instrument creating a charge: s412.

Priority of charges

Much of this complex branch of law is explicable by reference to one or other of two basic principles:

1. *priority of time*: as between charges of equal validity the charge which attaches first to company property takes priority over a charge on the same property created later;
2. *notice by registration*: a registrable charge which is not registered within 21 days (or in some instances a longer period allowed by the court) loses its priority over a subsequent charge on the same property if that charge has been duly registered.

Proposition (1) means that if a company first creates a floating charge on property and later a fixed charge on some part of that property, the latter charge will often obtain priority, since it attaches first unless the floating charge has already crystallised (see paragraph 7.2 *Fixed charges* and *Crystallisation of floating charges*): *English and Scottish Mercantile Investment Company Ltd* v *Brunton* [1892] 2 QB 700.

On the use of negative pledge clauses, to preserve the priority of a floating charge over a subsequent fixed charge see paragraph 7.3 *Negative pledge clauses*.

On the priority between charges when the second is expressed to be subject to the first, which is not registered, see paragraph 7.3 *Failure to register within 21 days* and s405 above.

Proposition (1) also means that if there are two successive floating charges over the company's assets generally the first in time will take priority over the later one, if both are duly registered: *Re Benjamin Cope & Co Ltd* [1914] 1 Ch 800. However, a floating charge by its nature gives to the company, pending crystallisation, power to dispose of particular assets free of incumbrance by the charge. If therefore a company first creates a floating charge on all its property and then a floating charge on some class of assets, such as book debts, the later charge may have priority over the earlier one: *Re Automatic Bottle Makers* [1926] Ch 412.

Another cause of conflict is where a company, in the course of buying property, creates a mortgage over it, usually as security for money borrowed to finance the purchase. It may be, but need not be, a mortgage in favour of the vendor to secure a part of the price allowed to remain outstanding. The effect of granting such a charge on the property is that it comes into existence just before the transfer of ownership to the company is completed. It is therefore an incumbrance in being at the time of acquisition. It ranks ahead of any general charges on the company's property even if they prohibit the creation of charges in priority to themselves: *Security Trust Co* v *Royal Bank of Canada* [1976] AC 503.

Where the holders of a floating charge and a fixed charge enter into a deed of priority that the floating charge shall rank in priority to the fixed charge, then the order of payment out is:

1. liquidation expenses;
2. preferential creditors;
3. floating charge holders;
4. fixed charge holders.

Re Portbase (Clothing) Ltd [1993] BCC 96.

Re Portbase was distinguished in *Griffiths* v *Yorkshire Bank plc* [1994] 1 WLR 1427, on the ground that there was no deed of priority present in *Griffiths*, which is an excellent example of the competing claims to company property which are often made by secured creditors, in the event of default by the company.

In *Griffiths*, Skainmead Ltd ('the company') granted the Yorkshire Bank plc ('the bank') a debenture secured by a fixed and floating charge on 13 January 1977. A second debenture was granted to APH Industries Ltd (APH), which was also secured by a fixed and floating charge, on 12 August 1985.

On 23 June 1986 APH demanded sums due to it under the 1985 debenture, amounting to £64,000. At the same time it also served a notice on the company under a clause contained in its debenture. In its notice, the company specified all stock in trade and book debts as being converted to a specific fixed charge. Earlier that same day, on 23 June, the bank had demanded £91,500 owed to it by the company and on 24 June appointed receivers.

The assets subject to the 1977 floating charge realised £99,500. The question for the court to decide was whether the notice served by APH under the 1985 debenture converting the floating charge to a fixed charge gave priority to APH. If it did then APH would receive its £64,000 in full, the remaining £35,500 would be paid to the preferential creditors and the bank would get nothing. If APH did not get priority, then the preferential creditors would be paid off in full, the bank would receive the balance in part payment of its debt, and APH would get nothing.

It was held, by Morritt J, that APH did obtain priority and they were therefore entitled to be paid first out of the £99,500 realised from the assets subject to the 1977 floating charge. By serving notice on 23 June 1986, APH crystallised its floating charge over stock and book debts into a fixed charge having priority over the floating charge contained in the 1977 debenture. This priority was not lost the following day when the 1977 debenture crystallised on the appointment of the receivers, for there was no agreement as to priority requiring that result. See Chapter 15, paragraph 15.5, for further details.

Effect of insolvency

The appointment of a liquidator (usually but not always in a situation of insolvency) or of an administrator avoids any existing charge which is unregistered (see paragraph 7.3 *Failure to register within 21 days*): s399. See also paragraph 13.6 *Avoidance of floating charges* to *Transactions at an undervalue* on the effect of such an appointment on a registered charge, which in some cases will be avoided: ss238–245 IA 1986.

7.4 Receivership

The role of a receiver

Any creditor of a company, even though he has no security for his debt, may sue the company for debt or petition for a compulsory winding-up order. In this way the company's assets may be applied in payment of its debts.

The secured creditor, typically a debentureholder, may in addition enforce his security by taking control of the property of the company which is subject to the charge created in his favour. He may thus apply the income or the capital value of the property in satisfaction of his debt, with priority over other creditors who do not share his claims to that property.

In theory a security may be enforced by: (1) taking possession; (2) applying to the court for a foreclosure order by which ownership of the property is vested in the creditor; (3) sale; or (4) the appointment of a receiver of the property and its income. In practice only the appointment of a receiver is likely to be satisfactory and free of potential liability to the creditor. Hence, this section deals exclusively with receivership.

A receiver is a financial agent and manager whose task is to control and obtain money from property for which he accounts to those whom he represents. Receivership is not restricted to enforcement of secured debts. A receiver, may for example, be appointed to wind-up the affairs of a partnership in dissolution.

Until recently statute law, eg the Companies Act 1948, contained very little to regulate company receivership. It was left to the debentureholder and the company to agree, in the terms of the debenture, when a receiver might be appointed and what his powers were to be. In case of need the debentureholder might apply to the court for a suitable order. However, the acts of a receiver may significantly affect the shareholders, employees and creditors of a company. Practical difficulties and disputes have produced a large body of case law and will continue to so. Hence, the Insolvency Act 1986 contains a great deal of new material on receivers. Most of the statutory provisions cited in this section are from that Act and are prefixed by 'IA' to avoid confusion with citations from the Companies Act 1985, to which there are no distinguishing prefixes throughout this textbook. Note that the 1986 Act includes, by way of consolidation, all the material previously found in the 1985 Act dealing with receivers (and liquidators also).

There is now a distinction between a receiver appointed under a floating charge on the whole or substantially the whole of the company's property and any other receiver. The former is defined as an 'administrative receiver': IA s29(2). Since he has control of all the company's property he is necessarily responsible for its management (and may be styled 'receiver and manager'). If, as is common, the debenture creates both fixed charges on the company's property and a floating charge as well, the receiver is an administrative receiver, to whom the relevant parts of the Insolvency Act 1986 apply. If, however, a receiver is appointed under a fixed charge on specific assets only, such as land or buildings, his position is regulated by the law of mortgages. What follows in this section relates exclusively to administrative receivers, unless otherwise stated, and for brevity 'receiver' means 'administrative receiver'.

Only an insolvency practitioner (see paragraph 13.2 *Insolvency practitioners*) may act as a receiver. The same restriction applies to liquidators and to administrators appointed by the court (see Chapters 12 and 13). There are certain similarities of method as well as of personnel but the distinction between these categories should be kept clearly in view. A receiver is the representative of a secured creditor, with the task of obtaining payment of what is owing to the latter. An administrator or a liquidator has a different task to perform, although either may well be concerned with the problems of company insolvency.

Who may be a receiver

There are three limitations:

1. a receiver must be an individual and not a corporate body: IA s390(1);
2. only an individual qualified to act as an insolvency practitioner may be a receiver: IA s390(2). This means that he has been authorised by a professional, usually accountancy, body of which he is a member or directly by the DTI, to act in this capacity. In either case he must have suitable expertise and an unblemished record (see paragraph 13.2 *Insolvency practitioners*);

3. he must not have been disqualified by a court order made under the Company Directors Disqualification Act 1986 nor be an undischarged bankrupt, unless the court has granted him leave in the latter case to act as receiver: IA s390(4). On the CDDA see paragraph 9.1 *Disqualification of directors* and and in spite of its title the Act provides for disqualification from acting as receiver etc as well as director or company manager.

The appointment of a receiver

A secured debenture always specifies events, primarily – but not only – financial default in payment of interest or repayment of capital of the debt, on the happening of which the debentureholder (or his trustee if it is a debenture stock) may appoint a receiver. Other specified events would include the appointment of a receiver by some other secured creditor, commencement of liquidation, or breach of various 'covenants' by the company concerning the conduct of its affairs (see paragraph 7.1 *Rights of debenture holders*).

If a secured debenture has been issued under the company's seal, the debentureholder also has a statutory power of appointment as mortgagee under the Law of Property Act 1925 s101(1). There is some doubt (*Blaker* v *Herts and Essex Waterworks Co* (1889) 41 Ch D 399) as to whether this power applies to a floating charge but Pennington (p550) considers that on a proper construction it does. This statutory power is not often used since the debenture is likely to give a wider power. As a 'fall-back' a secured debentureholder may apply to the court to exercise its power to appoint a receiver on his behalf, if principal or interest are in arrear, or the company has gone into liquidation, or the debentureholder's security is 'in jeopardy'.

In *Re London Pressed Hinge Co* [1905] 1 Ch 576 the court held that the debentureholder's security was in jeopardy when a creditor of the company obtained judgment against the company, enforcement of which would include all the assets over which the debentureholder had a floating charge.

In *Re Victoria Steamboats Co* [1897] 1 Ch 158, when a petition was presented for the winding-up of the company, this was considered as placing the debentureholder's security in jeopardy. In *Re New York Taxi Cab Co* [1913] 1 Ch 1 the security was held not to be in jeopardy merely because the assets of the company were insufficient to meet the amount outstanding on the debenture debt; there was no risk of the security being seized to pay off claims and the company was still a going concern.

A receiver is appointed by a written instrument signed by the appointor and delivered to him. He has a day in which to accept or decline the appointment. If he accepts it, the appointment is effective from the time when the written instrument was delivered to him. If he does not accept within a day, the appointment lapses: IA s33.

An insolvency practitioner would decline appointment if the charge, which is the basis of his appointment, had not been registered (see paragraph 7.3 *Effect of insolvency*) or if he anticipated that an ensuing liquidation within a short time might cause the charge to become void (see paragraph 13.6 *Avoidance of floating charges* to

Transactions at an undervalue). If the appointment is invalid, the court may order that the person who made it shall idemnify the receiver: IA s34.

The appointment of a receiver must be suitably publicised:

1. every invoice, order for goods or business letter issued by or on behalf of the company must state that a receiver has been appointed (eg 'XYZ Ltd in receivership'): IA s39(1);
2. the person by whom the receiver is appointed must within seven days give notice of the appointment to the registrar. On vacating office the receiver himself gives notice of it to the registrar: s409.

Action after the receiver's appointment

Much of the action taken by the receiver following his appointment is a matter of good practice and commercial efficacy rather than of law. He has, however, certain legal obligations:

1. forthwith upon his appointment he must give notice of it to the company and call for a statement of affairs from its representatives (see below);
2. unless the court relieves him of the obligation he is required within 28 days to send notice to all creditors of the company of whose addresses he is aware: IA s46.

The statement of affairs gives particulars of the assets, liabilities and creditors of the company. The receiver demands it from those officers, employees etc whom he judges able to provide the information. They have 21 days, or such longer time as the receiver allows, in which to submit it to him: IA s47.

Within three months of his appointment (or such longer time as the court may allow) the receiver is required to make a report on the events leading up to his appointment, his progress and plans for disposal of assets and carrying on the business, and the estimated amounts likely to be available to the debentureholders whom he represents and to other creditors of the company.

The report is distributed to the registrar, to the debentureholders (and their trustee if any) and possibly to unsecured creditors of whose addresses the receiver is aware. Alternatively he may publish a notice inviting unsecured creditors to apply for copies of the report.

Unless the court relieves him of the duty he must call a meeting of the unsecured creditors on 14 days' notice and lay his report before them. The meeting may resolve to establish a creditors' committee to obtain information from the receiver from time to time: IA ss48–49. The unsecured creditors are thus given statutory rights to obtain information of the progress of the receivership but they have no right to intervene, so long as the receiver behaves in proper manner.

An abstract of receipts and payments is made up for each complete year of the receivership, and for the final period until its termination. This must be delivered to the registrar within two months of the date to which the accounts are made up: Insolvency Rules 1986 r.3.32.

Directors and employees

The directors remain in office during a receivership but their powers of management are suspended in respect of all parts of the company's enterprise, usually the whole, which come under the receiver's control. Their formal powers and duties, eg to convene general meetings are not affected.

It is open to the receiver to invite the directors to work under his control. He may appoint one of them to be 'manager'. But, if he deems it necessary, he may instruct them not to enter the company's premises without his leave. As the receiver has authority to apply the common seal to documents, he should take it over from them: IA Sch. 1 para 8.

The directors may none the less take action to protect the company's interests insofar as the receiver may fail to do so. Where the directors initiated legal proceedings against the debentureholder for breach of contract, since the receiver understandably was unwilling to do so, it was held that they were entitled to do this but any damages which they might recover would be added to the company's funds under the receiver's control: *Newhart Developments Ltd* v *Co-operative Commercial Bank Ltd* [1978] 2 All ER 896. However, directors have no power to bring proceedings on behalf of the company where the receiver's position would be prejudiced by their decision: *Tudor Grange Holdings Ltd* v *Citibank NA* [1991] 4 All ER 1. Indeed, in *Tudor* Sir Nicolas Browne-Wilkinson VC said that, although he was bound by the decision, he had substantial doubts whether *Newhart* had been correctly decided. He continued:

'The decision [in *Newhart*] seems to ignore the difficulty which arises if two different sets of people, the directors and the receivers, who may have widely differing views and interests, both have power to bring proceedings on the same cause of action. The position is exacerbated where, as here, the persons who have been sued by the directors bring a counterclaim against the company. Who is to have the conduct of that counterclaim which directly attacks the property of the company? Further, the Court of Appeal in the *Newhart* case does not seem to have had its attention drawn to the fact that the embarrassment of the receiver in deciding whether or not to sue can be met by an application to the court for directions as to what course should be taken, an application now envisaged in s35 of the Insolvency Act 1986.'

If the receiver is appointed as agent of the company under the terms of the debenture (see paragraph 7.4 *The receiver's status within the company*), which is the normal case, his appointment does not automatically terminate any contract of employment of company staff, unless the duties of an employee, typically a managing director, are inconsistent with the receiver's assumption of control: *Griffiths* v *Secretary of State for Social Services* [1974] QB 468. Even in *Griffiths* case it was held on the facts that it was open to the board at any time to limit the managing director's power (see *Caddies'* case in paragraph 9.1 *The managing and other working directors*). The appointment of a receiver had been such a change and so it was not so inconsistent with the managing director's position as to terminate it.

A sale of the business by the receiver, without a transfer of the employees to the service of the purchaser, is an act which terminates the service of company employees: *Re Foster Clark Ltd's Indenture Trusts, Loveland* v *Horscroft* [1966] 1 All ER 43.

If the receiver is appointed by the court, or as agent of the debentureholders, that constitutes such a change in the employing company as to terminate the contracts of its employees: *Reid* v *Explosives Co Ltd* (1887) 19 QBD 264.

If the receiver 'adopts' the contracts of company employees, he is bound by them (see paragraph 7.4 *The receiver's status within the company*).

The receiver's status within the company

The receiver:

1. is deemed to be the agent of the company unless and until it goes into liquidation;
2. is personally liable on any contract made by him in the course of his duties, unless the contract otherwise provides, and on any contract of employment which he adopts; and
3. is entitled to an indemnity out of the assets of the company: IA s44(1).

It is also provided (s44(2)) that the receiver is not to be deemed to have adopted a contract of employment by reason of anything done or not done within the first 14 days of his appointment. His retention of existing company employees for up to a fortnight does not therefore make him personally liable to them, if he dismisses them within that period. Insolvency practitioners are working out a standard practice for avoiding liability to employees whom they may retain after the first 14 days. It generally entails the issue of a letter to each of them explaining the intended legal position of their retention in the company's service.

The powers of the receiver are usually set out in full in the debenture. However, there is now a statutory list of powers given to all receivers, subject only to any inconsistency with the debentures: IA s42 and Sch. 1. The statutory powers include carrying on the business and selling the property of the company, as well as more technical powers which experience suggests the receiver may require.

The directors as managers of the company have no power, without the authority of a general meeting, to present a petition for the compulsory winding-up of the company. A receiver, insofar as he is a company manager in the place of the directors, is in the same position. However, his powers as receiver under the debenture include what is incidental or conducive to enforcing the security. Those receiver's powers do enable him to present such a petition on his own authority: *Re Emmadart Ltd* [1979] 1 All ER 599.

A receiver is not an 'officer' of the company who can be made accountable by an action for misfeasance under IA s212: *Re B Johnson & Co (Builders) Ltd* [1955] Ch 634 (see paragraph 13.6 *Other uses of liability*).

A receiver appointed by the court is an officer of the court: *Moss SS Co* v *Whinney* [1912] AC 254.

The statutory provision that the receiver is to be the agent of the company continues past practice in the wording of debentures. Debentureholders arranged that their receiver should be deemed to be the agent of the company so that they would not be liable for his wrongful acts. However, *Standard Chartered Bank Ltd* v *Walker* [1982] 2 All ER 938 established that a receiver, in his disposal of company property, owed a duty of care to guarantors whose personal liabilities would be increased by his negligence. The case also decided that the debentureholder who intervened, by instructing his receiver how to act, constituted the receiver his agent (in addition to his being the agent of the company) so that the debentureholder was liable as principal for what the receiver had done. In brief the bank as debentureholder had instructed the receiver to sell company assets at the earliest (and disadvantageous) time, with the result that the guarantors became liable to contribute more than they would otherwise have had to pay. They successfully resisted the bank's claim against them under the guarantee.

The receiver may also claim an independent status in his dealings with the company on the ground that he has fiduciary duties to the debenture holder, and so is not a mere agent of the company, whose rights are derived solely from that fact: *Gomba Holdings UK Ltd* v *Minories Finance Ltd and Others* [1988] 1 All ER 261; *Re Aveling Barford Ltd and Others* [1988] 3 All ER 1019.

The duties of a receiver were usefully reviewed in the Privy Council decision in *Downsview Nominees Ltd & Anor* v *First City Corporation Ltd & Anor* [1993] 2 WLR 86. Giving judgment, Lord Templeman was mindful of the warnings of the House of Lords against extending the ambit of negligence and said that a receiver did not owe a duty of care in negligence to the company or to debenture holders. However, a receiver must exercise his powers in good faith and for a proper purpose. These are equitable duties and are not based on negligence principles. They are owed to the company and also to subsequent encumbrancers. So, where a receiver and manager appointed under a first debenture embarks on a course designed, not to enforce the security under his debenture but to prevent the enforcement of a second debenture holders security, then he will be in breach of his duty and liable in damages to the second debenture holder.

The decision in *Downsview* would appear to overrule the decision in *Standard Charter Bank Ltd* v *Walker* (above), although the case was not cited in argument.

In dealing with the company's assets the receiver should follow the prescribed order of priority of discharge of obligations. In particular a receiver, like a liquidator, is required to pay unsecured preferential debts out of assets subject to a floating charge: IA s40 (see paragraph 13.5 *Preferential unsecured debts*).

His remuneration is usually fixed by the debenture under which he is appointed. However, if the company goes into liquidation, the liquidator may apply to the court to fix the receiver's rate of remuneration: s36. Where a receiver is appointed by the court, his remuneration is fixed by the court and the court may disallow excessive claims made by him, or claims arising from any of his actions which were improper or misguided, but his right to be indemnified out of assets extends to all the assets subject to the receivership, regardless of possession of them: *Mellor* v *Mellor* [1992] 4 All ER 10.

Where a receiver appointed by a debenture holder has paid the debenture holder in full and all that remains before the termination of the receivership is payment of his own remuneration, but the company disputes the figure claimed, the company can obtain an interlocutory injunction to restrain the receiver from selling any further property pending the determination of the question of the disputed remuneration which would reveal whether there was any need to realise any further sums: *Rottenberg* v *Monjack* [1992] BCC 688.

If the receiver wishes to sell assets which are subject to a charge, he may apply to the court for authority to sell the assets free of the charge. However, he must show that it is advantageous to do this and the proceeds of sale (or the market value if higher) must be applied towards discharge of the debt which the charge secured: IA s43.

The receiver and the contracts of the company

The position over contracts of employment has already been considered. On taking up his appointment the receiver will find some outstanding commercial contracts made before his appointment and will probably have to arrange for additional contracts to be made if he decides to carry on the business.

He is not bound by contracts made before his appointment and can induce the company to break them, though the company incurs liability to pay damages for breach of contract. Contracts will be broken if he, for example, closes down or sells off the business of the company. But if he decides to carry on the business he should not breach contracts so as to destroy the goodwill, without obtaining the approval of the court for his policy. In the leading case the receiver found on his appointment that the company's output had been sold for a year ahead at prices which were now below the market level. He therefore sought leave of the court to repudiate these contracts so that he might then re-sell the output at higher prices, thus obtaining a greater cash flow with which to pay off the secured debt. However, the court refused leave saying to the receiver that 'it is his duty to do … everything reasonable and right for the protection of the property as an undertaking for the benefit of all persons interested in it': *Re Newdigate Colliery Ltd* [1912] 1 Ch 468.

On the other hand the court will not refuse leave to the receiver to abandon contracts if they are unprofitable and can only be completed by borrowing additional money: *Re Thames Ironworks, Shipbuilding & Engineering Co Ltd* [1912] WN 66.

A person who is owed a debt by the company or who will have a claim against it for damages if his contract is broken, cannot obtain an injunction to restrain the receiver, as the company's agent, from applying the assets so that his claim will not be met: *Airlines Airspares Ltd* v *Handley Page Ltd* [1970] Ch 193. An injunction against the company is not necessarily binding on the receiver: *The Cretan Harmony* [1978] 3 All ER 164.

The receiver's management powers give him ample capacity to enter into new contracts if he wishes to do so. To avoid personal liability a receiver usually, as a minimum precaution, keeps his transactions within the limit of the company's available cash resources so that prompt payment is made as each debt is incurred.

However, that policy will not suffice to avoid for example liability (for the receiver) arising from defects in the company's products. The more comprehensive modern practice for avoiding liability is therefore to 'hive down' the business into a subsidiary, of which the receiver is managing director but not receiver. The company's employees remain in its service but work for the subsidiary. The receiver has no personal liability on contracts which he makes for the subsidiary.

In theory the receiver may avoid personal liability on the contracts which he makes by including in them a disclaimer of liability. But the other parties to the contract would resist such a scheme. By subrogation they can claim against the company's assets insofar as the receiver has an indemnity out of the assets. If he has no liability, he has no right to indemnity.

Suppliers of goods on credit allegedly sold subject to a retention of title provision to a company which goes into receivership are adequately protected by an undertaking given by the administrative receivers that, should the suppliers vindicate their claim to title, the receivers will pay them the value of any goods used or sold during the receivership: *Lipe Ltd* v *Leyland Daf Ltd* [1993] BCC 385.

Privilege against self-incrimination

A director of a company is subject to an overriding statutory duty to assist the receivers of that company in their functions when summoned to appear before the court to be examined under s236 of the Insolvency Act 1986 and he cannot therefore refuse to answer questions put to him by the receivers on the ground that his answers might incriminate him: *Re Jeffrey S Levitt Ltd* [1992] 2 All ER 509.

The court has a general discretion whether to make an order under s236 and it should be exercised by carefully balancing the reasonable requirements of the office-holder (ie, an administrator, administrative receiver, liquidator or provisional liquidator) in carrying out his task against the need to avoid making an order which is wholly unreasonable, unnecessary or oppressive. An order would not necessarily be unreasonable because it caused the addressee inconvenience or a lot of work or might expose him to further claims, although these are factors which the trial judge could take into account in performing the balancing exercise: *British and Commonwealth Holdings plc* v *Spicer & Oppenheim* [1992] 4 All ER 876.

The effect of liquidation

If the company goes into liquidation, the receiver ceases to be its agent. But he may still dispose of assets under his control by virtue of his continuing powers as receiver: *Sowman* v *David Samuel Trust Ltd* [1978] 1 All ER 616.

If the charge under which the receiver was appointed remains valid, he will continue to have control of all assets subject to the charge. In the typical case of a floating charge covering the whole undertaking and property of the company, the receiver's continuing powers leave little for the liquidator to deal with so long as the receiver is in office.

There is no legal objection to the appointment of a receiver after the commencement of liquidation, which will cause a floating charge to crystallise and provide grounds for a receivership. The receiver then takes control, from the liquidator, of property subject to the charge.

If on the other hand the effect of liquidation is to render the charge void, the receiver vacates office and hands over to the liquidator the remaining company property in his charge. If he can account satisfactorily for his past dealings, he has no liability for assets of which he has properly disposed. However, it is an uneasy situation and few insolvency practitioners will accept appointment as receivers if they see it coming.

The charge will become void on liquidation if it has not been registered within 21 days of its creation: s395. There are other circumstances, explained in paragraph 13.6 *Avoidance of floating charges* to *Transactions at an undervalue* in which liquidation may render a charge void.

It is possible for the same individual to act both as receiver and as liquidator and in the past such appointments have been made. However, the professional accountary bodies have advised their members to avoid such combined appointments since there is often a conflict of interest between them.

The interaction of an administration order and receivership is considered in paragraph 13.1 *Administration orders*.

8

Meetings

8.1 Meetings and resolutions

8.2 The powers of the directors

8.1 Meetings and resolutions

Types of meeting

Actions decided upon by the company's shareholders are taken in meetings of the members. The following types of meeting may, or must, be held:

General meetings and class meetings
As a rule, a general meeting is one in which all shareholders may take part and which decides on matters binding the whole membership. Class meetings may be held by particular classes of shareholder and decide matters relating to that particular class; they are not necessarily governed by the same rules as general meetings (see paragraph 3.1 *Variation of class rights – procedure*). There may also be class meetings of debenture holders or other creditors.

Annual general meeting (AGM)
Every company must in each calendar year hold a general meeting as its annual general meeting: s366. It may hold other meetings but is usually content with the AGM as its annual ordinary meeting. The ordinary business of the AGM includes declaring a dividend, the consideration of the accounts, balance sheets, and the reports of the directors and auditors, the election of directors in the place of those retiring and the appointment of, and the fixing of the remuneration of, the auditors. A private company may by elective resolution dispense with holding AGMs (see paragraph 8.1 *Proceedings at meetings, Elective resolutions*): s379(1)(c).

Extraordinary general meetings (EGM)
There are meetings other than annual general meetings, and may be called when the necessity arises.

Types of resolution

The following types of resolution may be passed:

Ordinary resolution

This is passed by a simple majority of votes cast by those present, entitled to vote and voting. It is used for matters not required by statute or the company's regulations to be passed by either of the following two types of resolution.

Special resolution

This is passed by a majority of three quarters of votes cast by those voting and requires 21 days' notice; s378(2). It is used for deciding fundamental issues such as altering the regulations or varying class rights.

Extraordinary resolution

This is passed by a majority of three quarters of votes cast by those voting. Notice must be given but need not be of a specified length: s378(1).

Where no period of notice is specified it is usually 14 days as the minimum for any general meeting (see paragraph 8.1 *Notice of meetings*).

Either a special or an extraordinary resolution must be identified as such in the notice of the meeting.

Unanimous resolutions of private companies

A private company may also by unanimous consent of its members (1) adopt a resolution without holding a meeting and (2) dispense with some statutory regulations otherwise applicable to the company (see paragraph 8.1 *Proceedings at meetings, Resolutions in writing* and *Elective resolutions*).

Resolution in writing of a public company

A public company may by its articles (Table A art 53) provide for a resolution in writing to be signed by all its members instead of holding a meeting to pass it. But the membership of most public companies is too large to make this a practicable procedure.

Persons able to convene meetings

Directors

Directors are generally empowered to convene meetings by the articles: Table A art 37.

Shareholders

Directors must call an extraordinary general meeting on the requisition of members holding not less than one tenth of the paid-up capital carrying voting rights. The requisition must state the objects of the meeting. If the directors do not within 21 days duly convene a meeting, requisitionists representing more than half of their total voting rights may themselves convene a meeting: s368

It may happen that the number of directors required to constitute a board meeting, to convene a general meeting, is not available. Therefore the articles (Table A art 37) usually provide that a single director or one (or two) members may in that case convene a general meeting. As a further 'fall back' against the absence of suitable powers in the articles for convening meetings, there is a statutory provision (usually non-operative because there are alternative provisions in the articles) by which two or more members holding at least one tenth of the issued share capital may convene a general meeting if the articles make no other provision: s370.

Department of Trade

If default is made in holding the annual general meeting, the Department of Trade may, on the application of any member, call such a meeting and give such ancillary or consequential directions as it thinks expedient including fixing a quorum (see paragraph 8.1 *Proceedings at meetings*) of one person in case of difficulty: s367.

The court

If for any reason it is impracticable to call a meeting or to conduct one in the prescribed manner, the court may, either of its own motion or on the application of any director or of any member who would be entitled to vote, order a meeting to be called, held and conducted in such manner as the court thinks fit, and may give such ancillary or consequential directions as it thinks expedient: s371. See, eg, *Re Sticky Fingers Restaurant Ltd* [1991] BCC 754; cf *Re Downs Wine Bar Ltd* [1990] BCLC 839. In addition, the court has an inherent power to call meetings for particular purposes eg, it may order that a general meeting be held to ascertain the views of members on some proposal or matter in dispute. Again it may fix the quorum at one person in case the other member(s) of the company cannot or will not attend.

In *Re Whitchurch Insurance Consultants Ltd* [1994] BCC 51, the company consisted of two people, I and R, who had previously lived together and who were the only shareholders and directors. I held the majority of the shares. Their business relationship had broken down and meetings could not be held as R would not turn up to them. Harman J, held that the court could order a meeting to be held under s371 so that the minority shareholder, R, could be removed as a director. This was despite the fact that R had presented a s459 petition (see paragraph 11.2 *Unfair prejudice*) the day before the hearing of the s371 application. The court could take into account the existence of the s459 petition, but it was right that this company should be able to hold a board meeting to deal with the inquorate state of all of its meetings.

In *Harman & Anor* v *BML Group Ltd* [1994] 1 WLR 893, the Court of Appeal refused to order a meeting under s371. The company's shareholding consisted of A and B ordinary shares. They entered into a shareholders agreement that no meeting would be quorate unless a B shareholder or proxy was present. The applicants only held A shares and Dillon LJ, held that it was not right to use s371 to override the class rights of the B shareholder in the shareholders agreement. See Chapter 15, paragraph 15.6, for further details.

Auditor

Where an auditor's notice of resignation contains a statement as to the circumstances of his resignation which he considers should be brought to the notice of the members or creditors, he may requisition the directors to call an extraordinary general meeting for considering his explanation: s392A(2).

Serious loss of capital

Where it becomes known to any of the directors of a public company that there has been a serious loss of capital the directors must convene an extraordinary general meeting to consider whether any and if so what measures should be taken to deal with the situation: s142 (see paragraph 6.4 *Loss of capital of a public company*).

Notice of meetings

A meeting will not be properly held unless proper notice has been given to persons entitled to receive it. The question of notice is usually determined by the articles but is subject to statutory provisions, in particular that notice must be served on every member in the manner required by Table A except in so far as the company's articles have made alternative provision: s370(1).

Twenty-one days' notice is prescribed for an annual general meeting or a meeting for the passing of a special or elective resolution, and fourteen days' notice for other meetings: s369. But an AGM called on shorter notice is duly called if all members entitled to attend and vote agree; so will other meetings agreed to by a majority entitled to attend and vote holding not less than 95 per cent of the shares of such members: s369. This percentage may by elective resolution of a private company (see paragraph 8.1 *Proceedings at meetings, Elective resolutions*) be reduced to not less than 90 per cent: s366A.

The notice must specify the date, time and place of the meeting (which must be reasonable ie not designed to prevent members from attending) and state the statutory right of members, if entitled to attend and vote at a general meeting, to appoint a proxy who need not be a member (see paragraph 8.1 *Proceedings at meetings*). If it is an AGM the notice must describe it as such. The text of any extraordinary or special resolution must be set out verbatim (s378) and it is good practice always to set out in full the text of any ordinary resolution unless it is ordinary business of an AGM (see paragraph 8.1 *Types of meeting, Annual General Meeting (AGM)*).

Special notice must be given to the company of a resolution: *go to p. 207*

Peter as man. director

1. to remove a director: s303(2) (see paragraph 9.1 *Removal of directors under s303*);
2. to elect or reappoint a director over the retiring age in a public company if s293 applies (see paragraph 9.1 *Section 303 – some practical considerations*);

3. in certain cases of of a change of auditors (see paragraph 14.2 *Vacation of office*): ss388(3) and 391A.

Special notice must be given at least 28 days before the meeting and the company must then give notice to the members: s379. But this section does not confer on an individual member a right to compel the inclusion of a resolution in the agenda (*Pedley* v *Inland Waterways Association Ltd* [1977] 1 All ER 209 considered in paragraph 9.1 *Section 303 – some practical considerations*).

Members representing at least one twentieth of the voting rights or 100 or more members each holding shares on which an average £100 per member is paid up may require the company to give to members entitled to receive notice of AGM notice of any resolution which it is intended to move and to circulate a statement on business to be discussed to those members: ss376–377. However, directors have the tactical advantage with circulars as they have better opportunity to prepare them and, if prepared for the benefit of members, to finance their circulation from company funds: *Re Dorman Long & Co* [1934] 1 Ch 635. But they must be truthful: *Tiessan* v *Henderson* [1899] 1 Ch 861.

Whether any notice given is satisfactory depends on the requirements of the statute and of the articles and, generally speaking, on whether in the particular circumstances it is reasonably adequate to enable an ordinary member to decide whether or not he ought to attend the meeting to safeguard his interests. Irregularity or inadequacy of information in a notice renders the proceedings of the meeting void: *Kaye* v *Croydon Tramways Co* [1898] 1 Ch 358. It may be advisable to supplement the notice with an explanatory circular.

Attendance at meetings

To constitute a meeting at least two persons (or such larger number as is specified by the articles as the quorum (see paragraph 8.1 *Proceedings at meetings*) must be present: *Sharp* v *Dawes* (1876) 2 QBD 26.

The directors have the advantage in any battle of circulars of being able to despatch, with the notice of the meeting, forms by which a member may appoint a proxy to vote for a particular proposal. Even if the form enables the member to appoint a proxy who can in the alternative vote against the proposal (stock exchanges require quoted companies to use two-way proxies), members often appoint in favour of the directors' views and seldom use their general power to revoke their proxy's authority in favour of the contrary view, either formally or by voting personally: *Cousins* v *International Brick Co Ltd* [1931] 2 Ch 90.

Any member of a company with a share capital entitled to attend and vote at a meeting is entitled to appoint another person (whether a member or not) as his proxy and instead of him to attend and vote (though only on a poll, not on a show of hands): s372.

A member which is another corporation may be resolution of its own directors authorise another person to act as its representative and exercise its powers at a meeting of the company of which it is a member: s375.

If the hall reserved for the meeting is too small to accommodate all the members who wish to attend the meeting, the chairman may adjourn the meeting but only to such other time and place as will afford to all members a reasonable opportunity of voting in person or by proxy: *Byng* v *London Life Association Ltd* [1989] 1 All ER 560.

Proceedings at meetings

Quorum

Whether or not requirements as to a quorum are satisfied often depends upon the articles of a particular company and their effect upon common law and statutory rules. Generally speaking, two members should be present. Only exceptionally would a meeting be quorate with only one member present: ss367(1), 371(2). Under Table A art 40 a quorum is required throughout the meeting but under the 1948 Table A a quorum at the outset suffices.

Notwithstanding any provision to the contrary in the articles of a private company limited by shares or by guarantee having only one member, in the case of such companies one member present in person or by proxy is a quorum: Companies (Single Member Private Limited Companies) Regulations 1992.

Chairman

Responsibility for the conduct of the meeting is in the hands of the chairman who, in the absence of express provision for his appointment in the articles may be elected by the members present from one of their number: s370(5). Otherwise the chairman of the board or another director will often act (see paragraph 9.1 *The chairman*).

Moving and discussion of resolutions

A member may move any resolution of which the general nature of the subject matter has been indicated in the notice calling the meeting (even if the resolution differs from a specific resolution actually set out verbatim in the notice) unless the resolution had to be set out verbatim in which case that particular resolution is the one to be moved. However, an amendment may be moved if it is in the scope of the notice but this depends on the leeway allowed by the wording of the notice. A reasonable opportunity must be extended to members to speak on the motion or any permissible amendment. Thereafter, it may be put to the vote. Any special or extraordinary resolution may only be passed as set out in the notice: *Re Moorgate Mercantile Holdings* [1980] WLR 227.

Voting

In the first instance, voting will be on a show of hands. This will be a rough guide as it will generally be on the basis of one vote per person, whatever the size of his actual shareholding and voting rights: Table A art 62. But a poll may be demanded and the articles cannot nullify such a demand where made: by five or more members entitled to vote, or by members representing not less than one tenth of the voting rights of all members present and entitled to vote, or by members holding shares conferring a right to vote being shares on which an aggregate sum has been paid up equal to not less than one tenth of the total sum paid up on all the shares conferring that right. Nor can they forbid a demand for a poll on any question other than election of the chairman or an adjournment: s373.

The chairman should exercise his powers to demand a poll so as to give effect to the real sense of the meeting: *Second Consolidated Trust Ltd* v *Ceylon Amalgamated Tea & Rubber Estates Ltd* [1943] 2 All ER 567. On a poll, each member will be able to exercise all the votes he has (normally one per share) though he need not exercise all his votes, nor need he cast all the votes exercised in one way: s374. A proxy may vote on a poll: s372(2).

Adjournment and dissolution

Meetings may be adjourned and the business completed at a later date. Motions for closure of discussion, adjournment or dissolution of the meeting may generally be passèd by ordinary resolution (see also s381). If the meeting ceases to be quorate Table A art 40 requires that it be terminated or adjourned.

Minutes

Minutes of meetings must be kept by the company and may be inspected by members: ss382–383 (see paragraph 3.2 *Statutory registers, etc*).

Resolutions in writing

All the members, or all the members of a class, of a private company may by signing a resolution in writing do anything (with two exceptions) which would otherwise require the holding of a meeting to pass a resolution: s381A. The signatures need not all be on the same copy, so that separate copies may be sent to members simultaneously for signature and return if that is convenient.

The two exceptions to which this procedure does not apply are the removal of a director (under s303) or of an auditor (under s391) from his office (see paragraph 9.1 *Removal of directors under s303* and paragraph 14.2 *Vacation of office, Removal*).

In every case a copy of the signed resolution is to be sent to the auditors who, if it concerns them, may within seven days by notice to the company state their opinion that the resolution should be considered by a meeting. The resolution does not become effective until the auditors have given notice that the resolution does not concern them or that it need not be considered at a meeting or the seven day period has expired without any notice from the auditors: s381B.

A copy of the resolution is to be preserved in the same way as the minutes of a meeting: s382A. This statutory procedure prevails over any contrary provision of the memorandum or articles: s381C. For written unanimous resolutions there are some consequential modifications of the procedure under ss95, 155, 164–167, 173, 319 and 337.

Where a private company limited by shares or by guarantee has only one member and he takes any decision which may be taken by the company in general meeting and which has effect as if agreed by the company in general meeting, he must (unless that decision is taken by way of a written resolution) provide the company with a written record of that decision. If he fails to comply, he is liable to a fine, but failure to comply does not affect the validity of the decision: Companies (Single Member Private Limited Companies) Regulations 1992.

On possible but unlikely public company procedure see paragraph 8.1 *Types of resolution, Resolution in writing of a public company.*

Elective resolutions

An elective resolution is one passed at a general meeting of a private company, convened by a 21 day notice, setting out the terms of the resolution and stating that it will be proposed as an elective resolution: s379A(2).

Such a resolution is carried only if every member of the company entitled to attend and vote at the meeting agrees to it by voting for it either in person or by proxy: ibid.

A copy of the resolution and of any ordinary resolution whereby it is revoked must be filed at the registry within 15 days: s380.

An elective resolution may be revoked by passing an ordinary resolution to that effect. It automatically ceases to have effect if the company is re-registered as a public company. The procedure for passing and revoking an elective resolution prevails over any contrary provision of the articles: s379A(5).

By an elective resolution the members of a private company may elect to dispense with any of certain standard legal requirements in respect of the company as follows:

1. the directors' authority to allot shares may be given for an indefinite period or a period in excess of the standard maximum of five years (see paragraph 6.3 *Allotment of shares*): ss80–80A;
2. the directors may be exempted from the normal requirement (see s252 and paragraph 14.1 *Laying and delivering accounts*) of laying annual accounts before a general meeting;
3. the company may dispense with holding an annual general meeting (see paragraph 8.1 *Types of meeting, Annual General Meeting (AGM)*): ss366 – 366A;
4. the requisite majority for agreeing to short notice in holding an EGM (s369) or a meeting to pass a special resolution (s378) may be reduced from the normal 95 per cent to a lesser figure not less however than 90 per cent (see paragraph 8.1 *Notice of meetings*).
5. the retiring auditors may be automatically reappointed for another year without the need of express reappointment (see paragraph 14.2 *Appointment*): s386.

If the second and third elections listed above are made they must be disclosed in each annual return (see paragraph 3.2 *Annual return*).

Irregularities

The statutory procedures described in *Resolutions in writing* and *Elective resolutions* above recognise that a unanimous agreement of members should prevail over the normal requirements of procedure at meetings, which are intended to protect a dissentient minority.

The courts had already accepted that in such situations a unanimous agreement of members, obtained without holding a meeting or at a meeting invalidated by some irregularity of procedure, should be treated as a binding decision of the company: *Re Duomatic Ltd* [1969] 2 Ch 365; *Cane v Jones* [1980] 1 WLR 1451. It would serve no purpose to insist that a second meeting should be held to regularise the decision: *Bentley-Stevens v Jones* [1974] 1 WLR 638.

However more recently the courts had begun to have doubts over this practice, especially if there had been a failure to observe express statutory directions for passing a resolution at a properly convened meeting: *Re Barry Artist Ltd* [1985] 1 WLR 1305.

With statutory means of curtailing certain formalities, the courts may no longer accept informal unanimous agreement of members as a sufficient substitute. It remains to be seen.

Registration and publicity

Details of resolutions in meetings are generally the private concern of the company and its members. However, certain resolutions which may affect third parties must be registered, ie a signed printed copy must be delivered to the registry where it is enclosed on the company file for public inspection: s380. They include special resolutions, extraordinary resolutions, elective resolutions, resolutions which have been agreed to by all members which would otherwise have had to have been passed as special or extraordinary resolutions, resolutions binding particular classes of shareholder, and resolutions for voluntary winding up. Such resolutions are thereafter annexed to the articles and become part of the company's public documents: s380.

8.2 The powers of the directors

Introduction

The directors have such powers as are given to them by the articles. The question which then arises is whether the shareholders voting in general meeting can either exercise those powers directly or issue binding instructions to the directors as to the exercise of the powers delegated to them.

The directors' general powers of management

It is the established practice, to which almost all companies conform, to include in the articles a widely drawn delegation of general powers to the directors. Table A art 70 is as follows:

'Subject to the provisions of the Act, the memorandum and the articles and to any directions given by special resolution, the business of the company shall be managed by the directors who may exercise all the powers of the company. No alteration of the memorandum or articles and no such direction shall invalidate any prior act of the directors which would have been valid if that alteration had not been made or that direction had not been given. The powers given by this regulation shall not be limited by any special power given to the directors by the articles and a meeting of directors at which a quorum is present may exercise all powers exercisable by the directors.'

The effect of this form of words is that the directors may undertake any transaction which is within the limits set by the objects clause of the company unless the Companies Act 1985 or some limitation contained in the memorandum or articles prohibits them from so doing. As examples s121(4) provide that an alteration of the company's authorised capital (see paragraph 6.3 *Increase of share capital*) must be effected by resolution passed in general meeting; the articles often fix a limit on the amount which the directors may borrow without obtaining authority from a general meeting.

The other key point in this formula is that the directors may be instructed in the exercise of their powers by special resolution. But no such instruction (or any alteration of the memorandum or articles) is to invalidate what the directors have already done, provided that it was valid before the instruction or alteration was made. This part of art 70 is intended to remove the ambiguity of the corresponding 1948 Table A art 80 which referred to 'regulations made in general meeting'. It was not clear whether these 'regulations' were merely the articles of the company or special instructions.

Control of the directors by a general meeting

For many years to come companies, formed before 1985, will retain articles which follow the wording of the 1948 Table A. Moreover, some of the controversy, to which we shall now come, is over the status of the directors and their inherent relationship with the members in general meeting, regardless of the exact definition of their powers in the articles.

From 1906 onwards there have been judicial statements to the effect that the articles, defining the directors' delegated powers, are a contract by which those powers are given to the directors to be exercised in the interests of the company as the directors think best. On that basis it would be a breach of contract if the members took decisions on matters within the directors' competence or gave instructions to the directors on matters within their delegated powers. Among various statements we have:

'They (the members) cannot themselves usurp the powers which by the articles are vested in the directors any more than the directors can usurp the powers vested by the articles in the general body of shareholders.' (*Shaw* v *Shaw* below)

'These resolutions are absolutely inconsistent with the articles; in truth this is an attempt to alter the terms of the contract between the parties by a simple resolution instead of by a special resolution.' (per Farwell LJ in *Salmon*'s case below)

On the other hand there are some cases (see paragraph 8.2 *When the general meeting can intervene*) where, in special circumstances, a decision of a general meeting to act directly and thus by-pass or override the directors has been upheld although it fell within the limits of the powers delegated to the directors.

It is best to look at the caselaw in historical sequence. In the nineteenth century the courts had not yet reached the clear concept of a contractual division of powers between directors and general meeting and were sometimes disposed to treat the directors as simple agents of the company, subject to instructions from the company in general meeting as their principal. However, there was then a sequence of cases, as set out below, which established that, in normal circumstances a general meeting cannot give instructions to the directors, unless (as in the 1985 Table A art 70) the articles expressly provide for it. The cases are:

1. *Automatic Self-Cleansing Filter Syndicate Co Ltd* v *Cunninghame* [1906] 2 Ch 34 in which the Court of Appeal upheld the directors' refusal to carry out a sale of corporate property in defiance of a simple resolution passed in general meeting which authorised the sale.
2. *Gramophone & Typewriter Co Ltd* v *Stanley* [1908] 2 KB 89 concerned the tax liability of an English company. Buckley LJ said (obiter), 'The directors are not servants to obey directions given by shareholders.'
3. *Quinn & Axtens* v *Salmon* [1909] AC 442 in which Lord Loreburn stated (obiter) that the word 'regulations' in article 80 was synonymous with the articles. See also paragraph 3.1 *The effect of the memorandum and articles, Contract between the company and its members* for the facts.
4. *Shaw* v *Shaw* [1935] 2 KB 113 where the question was whether or not proceedings should be brought in the name of the company. Green LJ said that the effect of the articles was that power and control over the financial affairs of the company and the powers of management should be vested in the directors alone.
5. *Scott* v *Scott* [1940] Ch 794 where the majority shareholders attempted to declare interim dividends and have the company investigated by outside auditors. It was held that this was an unauthorised intrusion into management of the company, which under article 80 was exclusively that of the directors.
6. *Breckland Group Holdings Ltd* v *London & Suffolk Properties Ltd* [1989] BCLC 100 where a 51 per cent shareholder initiated action in the name of the company against the other 49 per cent shareholder. Harman J held that this was only within the competence of the board of directors by virtue of the company's management article, which was similar to article 80. Following this decision Farrar, 'Farrar's Company Law', 3rd ed at p366, says that 'it is unlikely that there is any point in continuing to press the minority interpretation of article 80,' the minority position is that it is possible for the general meeting to interfere in the management of a company by passing only an ordinary resolution, as opposed to a special resolution, which article 70 of the 1985 Table A requires.

When the general meeting can intervene

Before coming to the particular cases in which intervention by the general meeting has been upheld, one may note that there are two slightly different views of the underlying principle which justifies them. It can be argued (and some commentators in learned journals have done so) that the nineteenth century approach was fundamentally correct, ie the directors, as mere delegates, must be subject to the overriding control of those whom they represent. The second view, which is much narrower in its scope, is that in some matters the powers undoubtedly delegated to the directors do not give them exclusive powers. On the contrary it is said (eg Pennington *Company Law*, 5th ed, p650) that some powers are concurrent, so that the general meeting may exercise them in certain cases. The latter seems to be the better view and easier to reconcile with the actual cases:

1. *Marshall's Valve Gear Co Ltd* v *Manning, Wardle & Co Ltd* [1909] 1 Ch 267. There were five directors of the company, one of whom was also the controlling shareholder. The other four directors decided that the company would not sue another company, in which they were personally interested, for infringement of the company's patents. The controlling shareholder, as representative of the company in general meeting, then began proceedings in the company's name. The other directors sought to have the action dismissed. It was held that, as the board of directors had failed to exercise their power to take legal action to protect the company's interests, a representative of the general meeting might do so. A more recent case (on a different point) explicitly recognised that the directors have power to bring legal proceedings to protect the company's interests: *Re Emmadart Ltd* [1979] 1 All ER 599.

2. *Barron* v *Potter* [1914] 1 Ch 895. The articles gave to the directors power to co-opt additional members to the board (as in Table A Art 79) but the two directors had reached deadlock on this. A general meeting then elected additional directors and this election was held to be valid.

3. *Alexander Ward & Co Ltd* v *Samyang Navigation Co Ltd* [1975] 2 All ER 424. At a time when the company had no directors two individuals began legal proceedings on its behalf to recover debts. Later, when the company was in liquidation, the liquidator purported to ratify and adopt the action. It was objected that it had been begun without authority since only the directors had power to do this. This contention was rejected.

In the *Alexander Ward* case, Lord Hailsham LC commented that 'the company could have done so either by appointing directors or as I think by authorising proceedings in general meeting which in the absence of an effective board *has residual authority* to use the company's powers' (emphasis supplied).

It will be noted that in all these cases there was a failure of the board to act for the company, and that in two cases the action taken was to protect the company's interests by necessary legal action. One can hardly deduce a principle from these instances, but they do indicate the criteria which the courts are disposed to apply in making exceptions from the normal rule that the directors' delegated powers are exclusive to them and that the general meeting cannot overrule them. In the *Shaw* case (see paragraph 8.2 *Control of the directors by a general meeting*) the issue was whether a resolution passed in general meeting could instruct the directors to discontinue legal proceedings which they had begun. In that instance the issue was not protecting the company's interests, but a challenge to the directors' judgment of where those interests lay – and it failed.

There are also cases, such as *Bamford* v *Bamford* [1970] Ch 212 where the directors have taken the initiative in seeking ratification by a general meeting of their action, making use of their powers, since it would otherwise be invalid. There is no doubt that the general meeting has power to do this (see paragraph 9.3 *Exercise of powers for proper purpose*).

9

Directors

9.1 Management of the company

9.2 Duties of directors

9.3 Performance of duties

9.4 Breach of duty

9.1 Management of the company

Introduction

One of the essential differences between a company and a partnership is their management structure. In a partnership every partner is the agent of the firm and of the other partners for the purpose of carrying on the business and he is entitled to take an active part in the management of the firm: Partnership Act 1890 ss4 and 24. These basic terms may be, and sometimes are, modified by special agreement. However, essentially a partnership draws no distinction between ownership and management. The same group of individuals are both owners and managers. Such a system is unworkable unless the number of persons involved is relatively small and so it is provided by s716 of the Companies Act 1985 that a partnership shall not have more than 20 members (though considerable exceptions have been made in this respect for professional partnerships to which special considerations apply).

The difference of management structure between a company and a partnership is due to other factors besides size. Even a small, 'one-man' company has the same basic structure as a huge public company. The fundamental reason is that a company is separate from its proprietors and cannot manage itself. It must have directors even if, as is often the case in small companies, they are also the shareholders. Professor L C B Gower's ingenious attempt to promote a hybrid incorporated firm (A New Form of Incorporation for Small Firms – A Consultative Document: Cmnd 8171 of 1981) has attracted little support. An earlier attempt was the limited partnership, in which there are general (managing) partners and limited partners, whose limited liability is conditional on their abstaining from taking any part in the management. In the 80 odd years since the Limited Partnership Act 1907

191

introduced this category there have been, and still are, only a handful of limited partnerships in the entire country.

The new system of relaxing procedural requirements by elective resolution (paragraph 8.1 *Proceedings at meetings, Elective resolutions*) and also the less demanding rules on accounts of small companies (paragraph 14.1 *Exemptions from statutory requirements*) are intended to reduce the formalities affecting small businesses managed as companies.

The private company is the preferred structure for the small business and the public company for the large one. Although their management systems may differ in detail, particularly in the content of their accounts, they are essentially the same.

It will be seen that in a company there are three distinct elements, ie the company itself, its management (board of directors) and its proprietors (shareholders). The relationship between these elements is complex:

1. the directors have control of the company assets and business and they have obligations (called 'duties') towards the company which have some features derived either from the law of trusts or from the law of agency, but which do not correspond exactly with either. They are not answerable to the shareholders as proprietors though modern statute law requires directors to provide them with much detailed information. The directors are, however, answerable to the company in general meeting in a number of respects and the shareholders control the general meeting;

2. the shareholders usually appoint the directors but may not instruct them as to how they should exercise their powers (see paragraph 8.2). The shareholders may, however, restrict the directors' powers by altering the articles and may remove the directors from office (s303 (see paragraph 9.1 *Removal of directors under s303*)). Recent developments in statute law have added to the specific matters on which directors are obliged to seek approval in general meeting for the exercise of their powers. However, the essential point is still that the directors are (to some extent) agents of the company and are not agents of the shareholders.

The structure has also to provide for resolving internal differences among directors and among shareholders. Although a private company need not have more than one director, it usually has two or more: s282. Public companies must have at least two directors and usually have several. All companies are required to have at least two members and public companies may have memberships of tens of thousands. The board meeting and the general meeting serve various purposes, including reaching decisions on matters which are in dispute (see paragraph 9.1 *Board meetings* and paragraph 8.1).

The working of the system of management and control of companies has been affected by the application of equitable principles to the exercise of legal rights: *Ebrahimi* v *Westbourne Galleries Ltd* [1973] AC 360. The common law protection of minorities has been supplemented by statute: ss459–461. A member may apply to the court to dissolve the company on 'just and equitable' grounds: Insolvency Act

1986 s122. That theme is not pursued in this chapter but in its context elsewhere in this textbook (see paragraph 13.3 *Just and equitable ground*).

The Cadbury Committee

On 1 December 1992, the Cadbury Committee, named after its chairman Sir Adrian Cadbury, published a report called *The Financial Aspects of Corporate Governance* (London: Gee 1992). It was set up by the Financial Reporting Council, the London Stock Exchange, and the accountancy profession. The reasons for setting up the Committee are evident from the report itself at paragraphs 2.1 and 2.2 which state that the Committee's sponsors:

'2.1 ... were concerned at the perceived low level of confidence both in financial reporting and in the ability of auditors to provide the safeguards which the users of company reports sought and expected. The underlying factors were seen as the absence of a clear framework for ensuring that directors kept under review the controls in their business, together with the looseness of accounting standards and competitive pressures both on companies and on auditors which make it difficult for auditors to stand up to demanding boards.
2.2 These concerns about the working of the corporate system were heightened by some unexpected failures of major companies and by criticisms of the lack of effective board accountability for such matters as directors' pay ...'

The report included a Code of Best Practice, which the committee recommended that the boards of all listed companies should follow, although it also encourages as many other companies as possible to follow the Code. The Stock Exchange has made it a continuing obligation of listing that listed companies should include a statement of compliance with the code in its annual report and accounts. The statement must also be reviewed before publication by the auditors.

The Code itself consists of a number of recommendations under four headings: The Board of Directors; Non-Executive Directors; Executive Directors; and Reporting and Controls. Annexed to the Code are a number of further recommendations in the form of Notes, which, although they do not form part of the Code, are considered to be good practice. The Code has become a very important part of a listed company's system of corporate governance and its provisions are referred to throughout this chapter where relevant.

The directors

The following are the main features of law and practice in relation to directors:

Appointment

The first directors are named, with their consent, in one of the documents presented to the registrar to form the company (see paragraph 2.1 *Documents*) and they are automatically appointed when the company is formed: s13(5). Subsequent appointments (and also termination of office) of directors are regulated by the articles.

In the standard system (Table A arts 73–80) directors (unless they also hold executive office as managing director etc) retire by rotation at the annual general meetings but may be immediately reappointed. New directors are co-opted by the existing directors but retire and seek reappointment at the next annual general meeting. Notice must be given to the registrar of any changes within 14 days: s288(2).

The Code of Best Practice says that the appointmentand selection of non-executive directors should be a formal process, decided by the whole board, for a specific term, and that re-appointment should not be automatic (paragraphs 2.3 and 2.4). Notes 6 and 7 to the Code further provide for their duties, term of office and remuneration, to be set out in a letter of appointment, and that a nomination committee, consisting of a majority of non-executive directors and preferably chaired by the chairman, carry out the selection process and then make their proposals to the full board.

Share qualification

A director is not required to hold shares of the company unless the articles so provide (Table A no longer does so). If he is required to hold qualification shares he must become the registered holder of the required shares within two months of appointment or such shorter time as the articles may allow: s291. If he fails to do so or ceases at any time to be qualified he immediately vacates office automatically.

Age

Directors of public companies and of their subsidiaries may be required to retire from office at the annual general meeting following their 70th birthday. However, this rule may be excluded by an express provision of the articles: s293. This is one of the situations where special notice may be given to secure exemption from the age limit which otherwise disqualifies a director from re-election (see paragraph 8.1 *Notice of meetings*).

Bankruptcy

An undischarged bankrupt may not act as director or take part in the manage of a company except by leave of the court: Company Directors Disqualification Act 1986 s11.

Mental illness, etc

In addition to statutory grounds of disqualification, the articles may provide for vacation of office on account of mental illness, absence from board meetings for a specified period etc: Table A art 81. A director on his side may always resign by notice to the company.

The appointment of a receiver or the making of a court order for compulsory liquidation of the company may also terminate the directors' appointments.

Powers

The directors' powers are defined by the articles (see paragraph 8.2). These are collective, not individual powers, and are exercisable at board meetings. However, the articles (Table A art 72) permit the delegation of powers, including the appointment of managing and other directors to hold executive office (see paragraph 9.1 *The managing and other working directors*).

The Cadbury Code of Best Practice, in paragraph 1.1, provides that:

> 'The board should meet regularly, retain full and effective control over the company and monitor the executive management.'

The Code goes on, in paragraph 1.4 and Note 2, to provide that a schedule of matters specifically reserved for decision by the full board should be given to the directors on appointment. The aim of this is to ensure that 'the direction and control of the company is firmly in its hands'.

Categories

Law and practice have produced a number of special terms which should be understood:

1. Although there is no useful legal definition of director it is accepted that a director is a person who attends board meetings as of right and takes part in its decisions. Any person, even if called a 'director', eg a 'sales director', is not a company director if he is not a member of the board.
2. The articles (Table A arts 65–69) may permit each director to appoint a substitute to attend and vote for him as alternate director at board meetings. An alternate director is usually regarded as a director to whom the relevant legal rules apply.
3. A shadow director is any person in accordance with whose directions the directors of the company are accustomed to act: s741. This brings into the net the person who exercises management control of the company without being formally and openly appointed a director. Many rules of company law apply to him as a director. Shadow directors and de facto directors are mutually exclusive terms and must therefore be distinguished from one another. In *Re Hydrodan (Corby) Ltd* [1994] BCC 161, Millet J, distinguished between three types of director: de jure directors who have been validly appointed; de facto directors who act as directors without either having been validly appointed or appointed at all; and shadow directors who fall within the definition in s741. Unlike a de facto director, a shadow director does not claim or purport to act as a director and is not held out by the company as being a director. In *Re Moorgate Metals Ltd* [1995] BCC 143, the business of the company was that of metal merchants, reselling container loads of scrap metal. Warner J, in director disqualification proceedings against two directors, H and R, held that R was a de facto director. R was not formally appointed as a director as he was an undischarged bankrupt. His Lordship identified a number of facts that led to this finding:

a) the company only came into existence as a result of R asking H to join him in a business he was thinking about starting;
b) R and H shared responsibilities in managing the company;
c) R was in sole charge of the company's trading with no limit on the extent to which he could bind the company;
d) R and H received equal remuneration;
e) H consulted R on all important decisions, such as the appointment of bankers and solicitors.

Warner J, concluded by saying that 'In my view Mr Rawlinson was a director in all but name.' See Chapter 15, paragraph 15.7, for further details.

4. A director who also holds a management post (see paragraph 9.1 *Directors as employees*), eg as head of a department, in the company is sometimes called a 'working director' or executive director in contrast to a director who has no such other duties who is called a 'non-executive director'. This is a practical rather than a legal distinction. Both are directors for legal purposes, although the actual responsibilities of the former must be greater than those of the latter, if only because he has a deeper knowledge of the company's affairs than can be gained by attending board meetings (see paragraph 9.1 *The managing and other working directors*). The role of a non-executive director is really to act as an impartial observer and advisor to the board of directors. This is apparent from the Cadbury Code of Best Practice, paragraph 2.2, of which provides:

> 'Non-executive directors should bring an independent judgement to bear on issues of strategy, performance, resources, including key appointments, and standards of conduct.'

The Code recommends in Note 1 that a minimum of three non-executive directors be appointed. The independence of non-executive directors is a continuing theme of the Code so they should not participate in their company's share option schemes, their service should not be pensionable by the company, and their fees should reflect the time actually spent on company business.

Directors as employees

As indicated above a director may also be an employee of the company. The following points deserve mention:

1. there should be provision in the articles, as there always is (Table A art 84), for a director to combine the two roles, since as an employee he has a personal interest in conflict with that of the company as employer. He requires release from his strict fiduciary position as director to permit him to be in this position (see paragraph 9.3 *Conflict of interest*);
2. it is sound practice, but not essential, for the company and the working director to enter into a formal 'service agreement' to regulate the terms of his

employment. If a director undertakes management work, without being formally employed, it is a question of fact, depending on the circumstances, whether he is an employee: *Parsons v Albert J Parsons & Sons Ltd* [1979] ICR 271. In the *Parsons* case a major shareholder and director took part in the management of the business but did not take his remuneration or otherwise behave in the appropriate manner for an employee. The High Court concluded that he was and the Court of Appeal that he was not an employee;

3. directors' employment is subject to a number of statutory rules of company law:

   a) A contract for the director's services (even as a self-employed consultant) requires approval by the company in general meeting unless the company is free to terminate it without penalty within five years: s319. If it is not approved in this way it is still a valid agreement but the company may terminate it at any time by reasonable notice.

   b) A director's service agreement (subject to some limited exceptions) must be available for inspection by members: s318.

   c) The annual accounts must disclose specified information about the aggregate salaries of directors for management services: Sch. 5 Pt V (see paragraph 9.1 *Publicity about directors*).

The Cadbury code of Best Practice provides:

'3 Executive Directors.
3.1 Directors' service contracts should not exceed three years without shareholders' approval.
3.2 There should be full and clear disclosure of directors' total emoluments and those of the chairman and highest-paid UK director, including pension contributions and stock options. Separate figures should be given for salary and performance-related elements and the basis on which performance is measured should be explained.
3.3 Executive directors pay should be subject to the recommendations of a remuneration committee made up wholly or mainly of non-executive directors.'

It will be seen that the Code modifies s319 and also the information which must be disclosed under Schedule 5, Part V of the CA 1985. Finally it should be noted that the chairman should be available to answer questions on remuneration principles at the Annual General Meeting of the company (Note 9).

The chairman

for conc. on C see p. 219

The articles provide (Table A art 91) that the directors may appoint one of themselves to be chairman of the board, usually for an indefinite period to hold office so long as he is a director though he may in like fashion be removed or replaced. The chairman only has a casting vote if the articles (Table A art 88) give it to him.

The articles (Table A arts 42 and 50) usually provide that the chairman of the board shall also take the chair at general meetings and shall have a casting vote at those meetings.

The duties of the chairman are further described in paragraph 9.1 *Board meetings* and paragraph 8.1 *Proceedings at meetings*. He has an important role to play both at board and at general meetings but statute law has little to say about him. His position is regulated to a considerable extent by common law on meetings. In brief he derives his authority from the meeting and owes it a duty to conduct its proceedings in an impartial and orderly fashion, so far as he is able to do so.

not impartial perhaps in connection with Peter so maybe chairman in breach of duty no. 3 y215

The managing and other working directors

There is no legal requirement that a company shall appoint a managing director and in consequence no definition of his duties. The articles (Table A art 72), in providing for the delegation by the board of its powers mentions a managing director as one instance of permitted delegation but leaves it to the board to define his powers and duties.

In a very small company the directors may be the only working executives engaged in running the business. In such cases delegation of powers is not a significant issue, though each individual director in his own activities is theoretically acting as a delegate of the board.

Delegation is more formal in a company whose business is organised into departments, each assigned to a manager who may, but need not be, also a director. For example, a company may have a finance, sales, production, technical, etc director. Their powers and duties as managers of their departments are not, in the legal sense, any different from those of managers who are not also directors.

A managing director, if appointed, does, however, by virtue of his office have a special position. As the title implies a managing director must also be a director. If he is removed from his directorship, as for example in *Shirlaw*'s case (see paragraph 3.1 *The articles and contracts with the company*) his position as managing director is automatically terminated.

In appointing a managing director the board may confer on him as much or as little actual authority as it thinks fit. In the leading case the board was dissatisfied with the performance of the managing director and resolved that his duties should be limited to the management of one subsidiary. He objected that as managing director of the holding company he had general responsibilities, by virtue of his position, for the business of the entire group. However, that contention was rejected: *Harold Holdsworth & Co (Wakefield) Ltd* v *Caddies* [1955] 1 All ER 725.

A managing director does have apparent authority to carry on the company's business in the usual way and to enter into contracts and other commercial transactions on its behalf. A person who deals with a managing director is entitled to assume that he has the normal powers of his office, unless he is aware that he has not: *Freeman & Lockyer* v *Buckhurst Park Properties (Mangal) Ltd* [1964] 2 QB 480 (see paragraph 2.5 *Holding out*).

Some large companies appoint a 'chief executive', who is usually a member of the board. This expression is not common in company law but denotes authority comparable with that of a managing director.

The Cadbury Code of Best Practice provides that:

'There should be a clearly accepted division of responsibilities at the head of the company, which will ensure a balance of power and authority, such that no one individual has unfettered powers of decision. Where the chairman is also the chief executive, it is essential that there should be a strong and independent element on the board, with a recognised senior member.'

Board meetings

The articles (Table A art 88) provide that 'Subject to the provisions of the articles the directors may regulate their proceedings as they think fit'. By express resolution or by established practice the directors provide for:

Notice of meetings
How long notice is to be given (usually only what is 'reasonable'), to whom is it to be given, what information is it to contain. Table A art 88 provides that notice need not be given to a director who is absent from the UK. It is usual to issue a written agenda setting out the business to be done, but it is not legally necessary to do so. The legal position is that a director must be ready to attend a meeting on reasonable notice to transact whatever business may then arise (unless other, more specific rules are adopted). However, if a meeting is called in breach of the established practice, so that one or more directors do not attend, its proceedings may be invalid.

Quorum
Unless some other minimum attendance is set a quorum is two: Table A art 89. There are also rules which exclude directors who have an interest in items of business from forming part of the necessary quorum for that business and from voting on it: Table A art 95.

Proceedings
As the board is usually a small number of persons, it proceeds informally to reach its decisions by agreement, without taking votes. However, it may sometimes be necessary to take a vote to reach a majority decision on a contentious issue.

Minutes
A written record, in the form of minutes, must be kept: s382. If signed by the chairman these are evidence of the proceedings.

Disqualification of directors

A person does not need any formal qualifications to be a director of a company. It may therefore seem a little odd that there is a whole Act, the Company Directors

Disqualification Act (1986), which is dedicated to the disqualification of directors. The name of the Act is slightly misleading in that the court can make a disqualification order against a person from acting as a director, or a liquidator or administrator, or a receiver or manager, from being concerned in any way with the promotion, formation or management of a company: s1(1).

The courts have stated that the aim of the Act is to protect the public from directors' misconduct and unfitness, and that it is not intended as a punitive measure: see *Re Lo-Line Electric Motors Ltd* [1988] Ch 477. Later decisions, however, have recognised the reality of a disqualification order being made. For example, in *Re Cedec Ltd* [1991] BCC 148 at 153 Balcombe LJ, said:

'While a disqualification order is not of itself penal, it is clearly restrictive of the liberty of the person against whom it is made, and its contravention can have penal consequences under section 13.'

Section 13 makes it an offence if a person contravenes a disqualification order or, acts as a director while an undischarged bankrupt.

In *R v Holmes* [1991] BCC 394, the Court of Appeal (Criminal Division) allowed an appeal by a director against the making of a compensation order of £25,000 to the National Westminster Bank plc under s35 of the Powers of the Criminal Courts Act 1973. H had been convicted of fraudulent trading and part of the sentence included a disqualification order for 12 months together with the compensation order. Delivering the judgment, Tucker J, felt that the two orders were inconsistent with each other. The disqualification order removed H's ability and means to pay the compensation order and as a matter of principle it was wrong. The compensation order was quashed.

The Act applies to directors and shadow directors who are defined in s22(5) as:

'... a person in accordance with whose directions or instructions the directors of the company are accustomed to act ...'

A person will not be a shadow director though merely because he gives the company advice in a professional capacity. This may allow holding companies and so called 'company doctors' to come within the Act as shadow directors: *Re a Company* (No 005009 of 1987) [1988] BCC 424 and *Re Tasbian Ltd (No 3)* [1992] BCC 358.

Grounds for making a disqualification order

The grounds for making a disqualification order are set out in ss2–10 of the Act under three broad headings.

1. Disqualification for general misconduct in connection with companies: ss2–5 CDDA. Under s2 a directors can be disqualified for up to 15 years where he has been of an indictable offence of various kinds. An example occurred in *R v Goodman* [1992] BCC 625, where a director of a public company who was convicted of insider dealing was disqualified for 10 years.

Under s3 the court can make an order for up to 5 years for persistent breaches of company legislation. This covers failure to file annual accounts and returns etc to the registrar of companies: *Re Artic Engineering Ltd & Ors* [1986] 1 WLR 686

Section 4 allows an order to be made for up to 15 years where a director, in the course of the winding up of a company, has been guilty of fraudulent trading or guilty of any fraud in relation to the company or for any breach of his duty.

Finally, disqualification may result under s5 for 5 years, where the director has been convicted of failing to make returns to the registrar on at least three occasions within the last 5 years. This provision is very similar to that contained in s3, except that s5 does not require a separate application to be made to a civil court for disqualification; it can be made at the same time as convicting the director.

2. Disqualification for unfitness: ss6–9 CDDA. This is perhaps the most important ground of disqualification and is dealt with separately below.

3. Other cases of disqualification: ss10–12 CDDA. Under s10 where a court makes a declaration under ss213 or 214 of the Insolvency Act 1986 (fraudulent and wrongful trading) that a person make a contribution to the assets of a company, then it may, at the same time, make a disqualification order for up to 15 years.

It is an offence, under s11, for an undischarged bankrupt to act as a director without leave of the court. In *R* v *Brockley* [1994] BCC 131, the Court of Appeal (Criminal Division) held that s11 was an offence of strict liability. In this case B had acted as a director of a hotel company at a time when he was an undischarged bankrupt. He honestly believed he had been discharged based on a statement made to him by a paralegal employee of his solicitors. Inquirey of the Official Receiver would have shown him not to have been discharged however. Henry LJ, applying the mischief rule, said that if the section required mens rea then:

> 'a bankrupt who lay low, buried his head in the sand, and took part in the prohibited activities, would have a defence and an advantage not available to the responsible bankrupt who took steps to establish his position ...'

Where an individual debtor has failed to comply with an administration order made under Part VI of the County Courts Act 1984 and this leads to the order being revoked under s429 of the Insolvency Act 1986, then the court can make a disqualification order under s12 CDDA.

Disqualification for unfitness

There is a large body of case law decided under s6 of the Act which provides for disqualification of unfit directors of companies that have become insolvent. The court must be satisfied under s6(1):

> '(a) that he is or has been a director of a company which has at any time become insolvent (whether while he was a director or subsequently), and
> (b) that his conduct as a director of that company (either taken alone or taken together with his conduct as a director of any other company or companies) makes him unfit to be concerned in the management of a company.'

If so satisfied the court must make an order for between 2–15 years; the court has no discretion in making an order. The Act (s9) introduced for the first time statutory criteria to determine unfitness and this is contained in Schedule 1. So, the court can, for example, take into account any misfeasance or breach of any fiduciary or other duty by the director in relation to the company. Similarly it can take into account the extent of the directors responsibility for the causes of the company becoming insolvent. Students should refer to the schedule for a full list of matters that are applicable.

The leading case on unfitness is *Re Sevenoaks Stationers (Retail) Ltd* [1991] Ch 164. This case is important for a number of reasons. It was the first case on s6 to go to the Court of Appeal, who laid down guidelines on the length of disqualification orders. The Court of Appeal also cleared up the uncertainty surrounding the position of Crown debts. The case involved a successful appeal by a director against a disqualification order of 7 years which was reduced to 5 years.

Dillon LJ endorsed the suggestion that the statutory disqualification period should be divided into three brackets:

1. the top bracket for periods over 10 years, should be reserved for particularly serious cases, which might include cases where a director who had already had one period of disqualification fell to be disqualified yet again;
2. the bracket of 2–5 years should be applied where, although disqualification was mandatory, the case was relatively not very serious;
3. the intermediate bracket of 6–10 years should apply for serious cases which did not merit the top bracket.

His Lordship also dealt with the words in s6, 'makes him unfit to be concerned in the management of a company'. In *Re Lo-Line Electric Motors Ltd* [1988] Ch 477 at 486, Brown-Wilkinson V-C said that:

'Ordinary commercial misjudgment is in itself not sufficient to justify disqualification. In the normal case, the conduct complained of must display a lack of commercial probity although I have no doubt that in an extreme case of gross negligence or total incompetence disqualification could be appropriate.'

Dillon LJ said he 'deplored' the tendency of the Bar to treat such statements:

'as judicial paraphrases of the words of the statute, which fall to be construed as a matter of law in lieu of the words of the statute. The result is to obscure that the true question to be tried is a question of fact.'

Referring to the test in s6 he said:

'These are ordinary words of the English language and they should be simple to apply in most cases. It is important to hold to those words in each case.'

Contrary to the Vice Chancellor's suggestion in *Re Lo-Line*, it was not necessary for incompetence to be 'total'.

The *Sevenoaks* case also clarified the position regarding Crown debts such as unpaid VAT. There had been conflicting views on whether failure to account for such debts meant that a person was more susceptible to being disqualified. Dillon LJ dealt with this issue by taking the view that owing Crown debts should not automatically be treated as evidence of unfitness but that it is necessary in each case to see what the significance, if any, of the non-payment of the Crown debts is.

It must of course be remembered that companies can fail for legitimate economic reasons without being run by unfit directors. A recent example is the case of *Re Cladrose Ltd* [1990] BCC 11, where two directors ran three companies which all became insolvent, there having being a total failure to file annual returns or accounts. The business of the three companies was different in each case and was carried on in different areas of the country. The case is interesting for the sympathy shown to the directors by Harman J. He recognised that the first company was affected by a serious slump in the market for its products, agricultural business machinery. He also felt that the business of the second company, as motor dealers, was seriously hampered by the withdrawal of a sub-agency agreement by the company's principal who supplied the company with its stock of cars to sell. In relation to the third company, whose line of business was air taxi and aircraft dealing, the directors had been 'strung along' by a person who was purporting to bid for the whole company at a price which would have yielded a very substantial profit. Harman J described the person as 'insubstantial and unreal'. Unfortunately the bid never materialised and the company became insolvent. The conclusion was, 'That there were misjudgments, but they were not incompetent, nor were they gross incompetence.' The first director who was not professionally qualified escaped a disqualification order, but the second director, who was a chartered accountant was disqualified for the minimum 2 year period. This was almost entirely due to the fact that no annual returns or audited accounts were ever filed. It was also reasonable in the circumstances, according to Harman J, for the non-professional director to rely on the accountant director to attend to the Companies Acts requirements. For a more recent example of a refusal to make a disqualification order see *Re Wimbledon Village Restaurant Ltd* [1994] BCC 753, in which the court refused to disqualify two executive directors and one non-executive director of a restaurant business. See Chapter 15, paragraph 15.7, for further details.

Examples of behaviour meriting 10 year disqualification orders can be seen in the cases of *R* v *Goodman* [1992] BCC 625 and *Re T & D Services (Timber Preservation and Damp Proofing Contractors)* [1990] BCC 592. In the former case it will be remembered that a chairman of a public company was convicted of insider dealing and was disqualified for 10 years. He also received an 18 month prison sentence, with 9 months suspended. In the latter case four companies had become insolvent. There was evidence of failure to keep proper accounts, sales of property at undervalue and preferential payments being made. Again a 10 year disqualification order was deemed to be appropriate.

Less serious examples of disqualification can be seen in the cases of *Re Swift 736 Ltd* [1992] BCC 93 and *Re Cargo Agency Ltd* [1992] BCC 388. The former case involved a husband and wife who between them had managed some 16 companies, some of which were 'phoenix' type companies. There were breaches of Companies Acts requirements such as the keeping of proper books and records and there was also failure to submit accounts and returns. However, there had been no personal gain by the directors and they had lost their personal fortunes resulting in the husband being declared bankrupt. The husband was disqualified for 3 years, the wife for 2 years. In the latter case a director was disqualified for 2 years after managing a company which had always traded at a loss and went into liquidation owing £224,000. The director had received an unreasonably high salary, but had also lost his own money. In addition trading had taken place when he should have realised the company was insolvent.

The court will also have to consider unfitness if the Secretary of State applies for an order under s8 of the Act following an investigation into the affairs of a company by inspectors. Inspectors can be appointed in a variety of situations under ss431–441 CA 1985. The first reported case under s8 is *Re Samual Sherman plc* [1991] 1 WLR 1070. In this case a former director of a public company was disqualified for 5 years, following an investigation into the affairs of the company. The director had, inter alia, failed to file accounts and annual returns, acted as the sole director and secretary and, failed to keep the company registers up to date.

When must a director be unfit?

It may be that the disqualification hearing does not take place until a number of years after the company, which the person was a director of, has become insolvent. In *Re Pamstock Ltd* [1994] BCC 264, the court disqualified a director who provided venture capital for small, and often newly formed companies, for two years. Since 1988, the director had not been concerned in the affairs of any company that had become insolvent. He had also ensured that a chartered accountant was appointed secretary to all companies he had been concerned with since and that annual accounts and return were properly filed. Despite this, Vinelott J held that the court had to take into account past conduct, even if it was now satisfied that the director was behaving responsibly. Vinelott J said:

> '... it [cannot] be said that his subsequent conduct justifies the conclusion that his past misconduct should be overlooked upon the ground that there is no reason today for saying that a disqualification order is needed for the protection of the public. A disqualification order must to some extent express the view of the court as to the seriousness of past misconduct.'

See Chapter 15, paragraph 15.7, for further details.

In the first case in which the Secretary of State appealed against a refusal to make a disqualification order, the court was again faced with having to decide whether unfitness had to exist at the time of the hearing. In *Secretary of State for Trade and Industry* v *Gray and Another* (1994) The Times 24 November, the Court of Appeal allowed an appeal by the Secretary of State and held that the director should have been disqualified after the judge at first instance had found that he had:

(1) made preferences contrary to s239 IA 1986, (2) traded at a time when he knew the company was unable to pay its debts, (3) failed to keep proper accounting records, and (4) failed to file the 1987 accounts on time.

Hoffmann LJ, held that it was not necessary for the court to be satisfied that the director was unfit at the time of the hearing. If this was the position his Lordship explained there would be no need to make disqualification under s6 mandatory. Further, the judge was wrong to allow, in mitigation, the fact that the remedy for making preferences lies with the liquidator pursuing a claim on behalf of the creditors. To allow this would be to deny the specific reference to preferences in Schedule 1 of the CDDA (which deals with matters that the court is to take into account when making a disqualification order) any effect. See Chapter 15, paragraph 15.7, for further details.

Consequences of a disqualification order

Despite the making of a disqualification order, it is always open for a person to apply for leave to act as a director under s17. Where leave is given conditions will almost certainly be imposed. In *Re Majestic Recording Studios Ltd* (1988) 4 BCC 519 a director of five insolvent companies owing £649,175 was given leave to act as a director for a named company during his 5 year disqualification order, provided that an independent chartered accountant approved by the court acted with him as co-director and also that the previous year's accounts were properly audited. Mervyn Davis J, took into account the fact that the director was 'the moving spirit' behind the company and that without him, his livelihood and the jobs of 55 people would be at risk.

In *Re Gibson Davies Ltd* [1995] BCC 11, Sir Mervyn Davies was faced with the first appeal against a decision to refuse leave to act as a director under s17 of the Act. The appeal was successful after his Lordship was satisfied that there was a need to make the order and, more importantly, that the public would receive adequate protection from the safeguards offered by the director. The need to make the order was based largely on the fact that the director was the 'guiding light' of the company, that his name appeared on the publicity material, and that without him the company would fail and jobs be lost. The safeguards offered by the director included the joint signing of company cheques, a maximum of £380 per week for directors emoluments, and a promise to file annual accounts and returns as well as the preparation of monthly management accounts. See Chapter 15, paragraph 15.7, for further details.

Although the Act makes no express provision regarding appeals, the Court of Appeal for the first time in *Secretary of State for Trade and Industry* v *Ettinger* [1993] BCC 336, held that Secretary of State may appeal against the length of a disqualification and increased the order from 3 to 5 years. This case is also interesting for the very powerful statement by Nichols V-C that limited liability is a privilege that should not be misused.

A person who acts as a director in contravention of a disqualification order commits an offence and may be personally liable to pay for the company's debts:

ss13 and 15. The registrar keeps a register of disqualified directors which can be inspected by members of the public free of charge: s18. The Court of Appeal has also recently allowed an appeal by the Secretary of state, against a refusal to make a disqualification order at all. See *Secretary of State for Trade and Industry* v *Gray and Another*, discussed above.

Procedural points

In *Re Carecraft Construction Co Ltd* [1994] 1 WLR 172, Ferris J adopted a summary procedure for disqualification cases. When the procedure applies, the need for a fully contested hearing is avoided. The director enters what is in effect a guilty plea. There must be an agreed schedule of facts, the director must accept that the court is likely to find him unfit to take part in the management of the company, and there must be agreement on the relevant bracket into which the disqualification period falls. This procedure has recently been applied in *Re Aldermanbury Trust plc* [1993] BCC 598.

Where the application to disqualify is made on the basis that the director is unfit, the Secretary of State or the Official Receiver has two years in which to make the application beginning on the date of the company's insolvency. This time limit can be extended with leave of the court: s7 CDDA. The court will not stay disqualification proceedings, however, pending the outcome of parallel private litigation between the company and the director concerning the same conduct that the Secretary of State is relying on in the disqualification proceedings: *Re Rex Williams Leisure plc (In Administration)* [1994] 3 WLR 745. See Chapter 15, paragraph 15.7, for further details.

In *Re Working Project Ltd; Re Fosterdown Ltd; Re Davies Flooring (Southern) Ltd* [1995] BCC 197, Carnworth J, had to decide whether disqualification proceedings in the County Court were possible after the liquidation of the companies was complete. Under s6(1) of the CDDA 1986, it was 'the court' which had to make the disqualification order. On a strict reading of s6(3)(a) and (b) of the Act, the County Court only remained the court as long as the company 'is being wound up'. Applying the literal rule, it was argued that when the winding up was complete, the court lost its jurisdiction. Sensibly, it was held that it would be patently absurd if proceedings had to be aborted simply because the liquidator had completed his task. The correct interpretation was that the County Court should retain jurisdiction as long as it had jurisdiction at the time of commencement of proceedings. See Chapter 15, paragraph 15.7, for further details.

Conclusion

The Act has proved to be a very useful tool in taking directors who are unfit or who have conducted themselves in a less than satisfactory manner out of circulation. It is to be hoped that the Act may also be going some way to improving the standard of skill and care that directors are exhibiting towards their companies. That said, the National Audit Office published a report in 1993 by the Comptroller and Auditor General entitled 'The Insolvency Service Executive Agency: Company Director Disqualification.' Among the report's findings were that by March 1993 some 2,900 applications for disqualification had resulted in 1,700 disqualification orders and that there was a lack of awareness among directors of the provisions or even the existence of the Act! Also, the perception of directors is that the Act does not deter unfit conduct.

Removal of directors under s303

Members of the company have power by ordinary resolution to remove a director from office and to appoint another director in his place: s303. However, special notice must be given of intention to propose such a resolution (see paragraph 8.1 *Notice of meetings*). In theory this power is an effective means by which members may exert pressure on the board of directors. In practice it is rather more complicated. This section will explain the basic procedure under ss303–304. This will be followed (see paragraph 9.1 *Section 303 – some practical considerations*) by some comments on practical constraints on its use.

Peter as man. director

A shareholder who wishes to propose a resolution under s303 first gives special notice to the company under s379 at least 28 days before the meeting. Under the statutory procedure the board then informs the members of the resolution in the notice issued to convene the meeting. It also delivers to the director, whose removal is proposed, a copy of the special notice. He has the right to have a written statement in his own defence circulated to members, or if that cannot be done in time, to address the meeting before the resolution is put to the vote.

what Peter can do

If the removal of the director is a breach of contract (service agreement) between him and the company, he may claim damages for breach of contract.

The existence of this statutory power of removal by a simple majority vote on an ordinary resolution does not prevent the company from including in its articles some simpler alternative procedure, though it cannot by its articles override the statutory power. If those who wish to remove the director can command a three quarters majority of votes, which may well be the case in the context of a private company dispute, they may use their votes to include in the articles a simple power to remove a director summarily by extraordinary resolution, which does not affect s303, and then pass an extraordinary resolution.

no X

Section 303 – some practical considerations

On receiving special notice the directors will consider whether they are required to include in the notice convening the meeting the resolution for the director's removal. Unless the person who gives special notice, with his supporters, has at least one twentieth of the voting rights or is a group of at least 100 members, the directors may reject the resolution and it cannot then he debated or put to the vote at the meeting: *Pedley* v *Inland Waterways Association Ltd* [1977] 1 All ER 209.

protection for Peter

A member who cannot command the minimum support required by s376 (above) is unlikely to be able to carry his resolution at the meeting. But he can thus be denied the opportunity of getting his resolution before the meeting for discussion.

It more often happens that a shareholder who has, with his supporters, at least 10 per cent of the voting shares, requisitions a meeting under s368 since he has more control of the situation if he proceeds in that fashion.

A second constraint is the possible cost to the company of removing a director from office in breach of his service agreement. The position in that respect has been improved by s319 (see paragraph 9.1 *Directors as employees*) which prevents directors from obtaining long-term service agreements without the knowledge and approval of the members. (On what may be a breach of contract in these circumstances see paragraph 3.1 *The articles and contracts with the company*).

Finally, if the directors in founding the company wish to secure themselves against removal as a result of a subsequent quarrel, they may resort to the device which was effective in *Bushell* v *Faith* [1970] AC 1099. In that case the articles provided that each of the three shareholders/directors should have three votes for each of his shares on any resolution for his own removal. As the other director-shareholders would still have only the normal ratio of one vote per share, the director resisting removal could outvote them, by 'weighted voting'.

When the case came before the Court of Appeal it was argued that to recognise such a device effectually frustrated the intention of s303. However, the court took the view that s303 required that an ordinary resolution was duly carried, and this had not happened. There is nothing inherently wrong in uneven voting rights.

Publicity about directors

A person who deals with a company needs to know the names of its directors. The members are entitled to information about directors' interests and transactions in connection with the company. These factors have produced an elaborate code of disclosure rules relating to directors.

Every company must maintain a register of directors and secretary (s288) at its registered office. The register must contain various personal particulars and also, with some exceptions, information of directorships of other companies held by each director, currently or within the previous five years. The information in the register is reproduced in the annual return sent to the registry each year: s363 and Sch. 15. The register must be open to inspection by the public during at least two hours of each working day.

It is no longer necessary to list the names of the directors on the company's letterheads. However, if the company opts to do so – as many still do – the list must be complete and not selective: s305.

If there is a change of directors or secretary notice must be given to the registrar within 14 days. The registrar gives notice in the *London Gazette* of receipt of any notification of a change of directors: s711.

A company must also maintain a register of directors' interests in shares or debentures of the company or of any other company in the same group: s325. This register is held with the register of members and is open to public inspection: Sch. 13 Pt IV. The information entered in the register has to be supplied by the director in compliance with elaborate rules designed to enforce disclosure of any indirect and family interests of the director in the securities.

The third major source of information about directors' affairs is the annual accounts and directors' report which the company must send to the registry each year (Chapter 14). These documents give information of salaries, fees and other payments made to directors as a group (with individual particulars for the chairman and the highest-paid director) and their interests and transactions of various kinds.

Directors' transactions

The disclosure requirements described above are part of an increasingly detailed system of regulating transactions of directors by which they might secure personal advantage to themselves. Chapter 9 considers the more general aspects of this problem. At this point, however, we provide a summary of the more important statutory restrictions on directors' transactions.

A director may only hold another office, typically as a manager, in the company, if that dual arrangement is sanctioned by the articles, as it always is: Table A art 72. The board fixes his salary and other terms of employment and he does not vote on this matter: Table A art 94. The amount of directors' emoluments is disclosed in the accounts in aggregate. Fees may only be paid to directors for their services as directors as provided by the articles. Payment of pensions to directors is similarly regulated: Table A arts 82 and 87.

A director, his spouse and minor children may not trade in options to buy or sell shares or debentures of the company or any other company of the group: ss323 and 327.

If a director is directly or indirectly interested in a contract of the company, eg by being a shareholder of another company which is negotiating a contract with the company of which he is a director, he is required 'to declare the nature of his interest' to the board of the company at the first opportunity, so that the other directors are aware of it: s317. He may not vote on it: Table A art 94. A director of a company is bound to declare his interest to the board of directors before agreeing a variation of the terms and conditions of his service contract by virtue of s317. However, the non-declaration of interest, when the period of notice was increased from 3 to 5 years, was only a technical breach which did not invalidate the notice increase: *Runciman* v *Walter Runciman plc* [1993] BCC 223. Disclosure under s317 must be to the board of directors and not just to a committee of directors: *Guinness plc* v *Saunders and Anor* [1988] 2 All ER 940. When the annual accounts are being prepared the board will, among other things, consider whether any director's interest in transactions of the company is material for disclosure in the accounts: Sch. 6.

If a director, or a person connected with him, enters into a substantial property transaction with the company or its subsidiary, it requires approval in general meeting, failing which it may be rescinded by the company: s320. Transactions with a value in excess of £100,000 or one tenth of the company's net assets (subject to a minimum of £2,000) fall under s320. (See also paragraph 9.4 *The nature of the remedy, Conflict of interest* on the new s322A where there is no minimum value though the board of directors must have exceeded their powers in sanctioning the transaction.)

In *Duckwari plc* v *Offerventure Ltd* [1995] BCC 89, the Court of Appeal held that it was a substantial property transaction where D plc had taken over the benefit of a contract for the sale of property from another company, O Ltd. The purchase price was £495,000 and a director of both companies arranged the transaction. Millet LJ was satisfied that D plc had acquired a non-cash asset from the director, via his company O Ltd, and that there had therefore been a breach of s320 CA 1985. See Chapter 15, paragraph 15.7, for further details.

On directors' service agreements for terms exceeding five years see paragraph 9.1 *Directors as employees.*

In principle, though there are several exceptions, a company may not make loans (or enter into similar transactions) with or for the benefit of a director of the company or of its holding company: s330. The restrictions are more extensive if the company is a public company or a member of a group which includes a public company. Any such loan transactions have to be disclosed to the board (s317) and (with minor exceptions) in the annual accounts.

If the company terminates a director's appointment he may have a claim for damages for breach of contract of employment (see paragraph 3.1 *The articles and contracts with the company*). However, the company has no liability to pay compensation to him for loss of office as director, and of the directors' fees incidental to it. If the company makes an ex gratia compensation payment the director may only retain it, if the payment is approved in general meeting: s312. The rule is extended to payments made in connection with the sale of the company's business or a take-over bid for its shares: ss313–314.

Directors and company insolvency

The purpose of the passage which follows is to present a convenient summary of the effect on the personal position of directors of the insolvency of their company. These matters are discussed in more detail in the passages in the textbook to which they are particularly relevant.

As a general principle a director, as much as a holder of fully paid shares, of a limited company, is free of liability for the unpaid debts of the company if it becomes insolvent. On the other hand the directors, who control the management of the company and decide whether it should continue to trade, may have been gravely at fault in permitting the insolvency to occur. Hence, there are two main sanctions, designed to induce in directors a proper concern for the solvency of the company. These are (1) personal liability for the debts of the company and (2) disqualification from acting as directors or managers of companies in future. Each of these penalties is applicable only in specified circumstances but the risk should concentrate the minds of directors at all times.

It is possible for a limited company to impose on its directors unlimited personal liability for its debts (in liquidation): ss306–307. In practice, however, no one is prepared to hold a directorship on that basis.

A particular creditor may impose on company directors liability (often limited to a maximum amount) for the company's liabilities to the creditor by persuading the directors to give personal guarantees to the creditor of those liabilities (see paragraph 7.2 *Introduction*). Banks in their dealings with private companies sometimes obtain such guarantees of the company's overdraft. Guarantees are, however, essentially a matter of contractual obligation and not of company law, which hardly recognises their existence.

If a company is in insolvent liquidation, the court may on the application of the liquidator, order that directors shall make a contribution or compensation payment in consequence of their participation in fraudulent or wrongful trading, or their misfeasance in the performance of their duties (see paragraph 13.6).

The disqualification of directors by court order has been mentioned above (see paragraph 9.1 *Disqualification of directors*). This order may be made on various grounds of which company insolvency is only one. What follows relates to disqualification arising from company insolvency. For this purpose a company is deemed to be insolvent if a receiver is appointed (see paragraph 7.4), or an administration order is made (see paragraph 12.1 *Administration orders*) or if the company goes into liquidation (see Chapter 12) and its assets do not then suffice to pay its debts, and the liquidation costs, in full: Company Directors Disqualification Act 1986 s6(2). The following paragraphs set out the general effect of ss6–10 of that Act, which provide for disqualification of directors of insolvent companies.

The effect of company insolvency, as defined above, is that an authorised insolvency practitioner (see paragraph 13.2 *Insolvency practitioners*) takes office as receiver, administrator or liquidator of the company, as the case may be. The provisional liquidator of a company in compulsory liquidation is the Official Receiver (the head of the DTI Insolvency Service) (see paragraph 13.3 *The conduct of the liquidation*) who performs his functions through a member of his staff. For the purposes of disqualification procedure, these 'officeholders' follow the same essential procedure.

It is the duty of the officeholder, expressed in regulations made under the 1986 Act and in s7 of that Act, to report to the DTI on directors whose conduct makes them unfit to be concerned in the management of any company. It should be noted that a creditor of the company has no direct access to the DTI in this respect. It was concluded that if individual creditors could threaten directors with possible disqualification at their instance, they might have means to exert pressure to get their claims on the company given priority. A creditor may of course complain to the officeholder.

The officeholder in the course of his investigation of the company's affairs will review the manner in which the directors have performed, or failed to perform their task. It is also open to the DTI, which keeps records of directors of all insolvent companies, to instruct the officeholder to make a report on a particular individual. The DTI may also take action following an investigation of the company's affairs by inspectors or by the DTI itself CDDA s8 (see paragraph 11.3).

If the DTI considers, on the basis of information received, that it is proper to do so, it then applies to the court for a disqualification order. In reaching its decision the court is required to have regard to a number of specific topics, relevant to directors' performance, set out in Sch. 1 of the 1986 Act.

Where the DTI decides to discontinue disqualification proceedings it must pay the director's costs: *Re Southbourne Sheet Metal Co Ltd* [1992] BCC 797.

The court may also make an order on its own initiative in connection with proceedings by which a director is ordered to pay a contribution towards the assets of a company in insolvent liquidation on account of his participation in wrongful trading: CDDA s10 (see paragraph 13.6 *Wrongful trading*).

The director against whom these proceedings are taken may appear and make his defence and attempted rebuttal of the matters charged against him.

In case of company insolvency the disqualification order is for a minimum of two and a maximum of 15 years (five years if the order is made by a court of summary jurisdiction) as the court sees fit.

While the order is in force the individual may not be a director, liquidator, administrator or receiver of any company, or be concerned, directly or indirectly, in the promotion, formation or management of a company, except by leave of the court: CDDA s1. If the person disqualified, or any other person acting under his instructions, acts in breach of the order, he is personally liable for the debts of the company, and the person disqualified is also guilty of a criminal offence.

Industrial democracy

It is commonly taken for granted that a person is a member of a company if he is a shareholder and that a reference to the interests of the company is a reference to the interests of the shareholders. Even if this is true, it does not per se take account of the fact that the company must operate within a framework of restrictions (eg those imposed by statute, government departments, stock exchanges, etc) and that the interests of the company may not be furthered if interests other than those of the shareholders are totally disregarded (eg those of creditors – who supply credit or loan capital – or of the employees, whose efforts are essential for making profits).

These points are relevant to the views of those who advocate some schemes of worker participation in the running of the company. Their proposals emerge from a variety of factors: the shift of control from the owners of the shares to the managerial class, and the need to curb its powers; the changing idea of the company from the object of legal ownership to a social or economic enterprise combining capitalists and workers; and the greater importance of plant-level bargaining with labour and of consultation to avoid confrontation.

Two basic philosophies underline the debate. The first is that persons such as the workers, who play a practical part in making the company a success, should be able to participate in the way in which it is run. The suggested means of implementing this philosophy of co-determination is through a pluralist, two-tier, management structure, requiring a supervisory board of directors (elected by shareholders and employees) whose functions are the consideration of policy and the supervision of a management board of directors, which it elects and whose task is the day-to-day running of the company. This is basically the approach which is a key element of the EC draft Social Charter put forward in 1989.

The unitary system is based on the view that the interests of workers will be furthered by the extension of collective bargaining into the company's organic structure. It saw its practical expression in the United Kingdom in the majority report of the Bullock Committee, which advocated a single board of directors comprising equal numbers of directors appointed by trades unions and shareholders respectively (X number of directors each) plus a number (Y) of directors appointed jointly by the 2X directors or, in default of agreement, by an Industrial Democracy Commission (Y being less than X but more than one) – the famous 2X + Y formula. So as to prevent the general meeting depriving it of power, the board would have a certain number of attributed functions (submitting proposals to the general meeting for: winding up; changing regulations; paying dividends; changing the capital or organic structure; and disposing of a substantial part of the undertaking).

The Bullock Report foundered in the face of criticism and opposition from the business world. Whether or not a system of industrial democracy is introduced, and what sort of system it would be, are questions to be decided in the political and parliamentary arena.

However, a number of piecemeal provisions which give some, albeit slight, encouragement to employee participation have appeared on the statute book. Briefly, these include:

1. Sch. 7 Pt V obliges corporate employers of more than 250 employees to include in the annual directors' report a statement on progress made towards employee participation and information arrangements.
2. Sections 151–154 lifts the prohibition on the provision of financial assistance for the purchase of a company's own shares and allows loans to be made to employees and money to be provided to employee share schemes for the purchase of fully paid up shares.
3. Section 309 imposes a duty on directors to have regard to the interests of employees as a whole.

In addition tax legislation offers remissions and inducements of various kinds for employees' share schemes, profit-sharing or profit-related pay schemes, all of which in one way or another are likely to give to employees, if they participate, some interest in and benefit from the profitability of the company for which they work.

The Employment Protection (Consolidation) Act 1978 and related legislation give to employees (whether the employer is or is not a company) various individual and collective bargaining rights and safeguards.

9.2 Duties of directors

The nature of the director's position

There may be several different types of director in a company, depending upon the functions of each director and his function in the company. Two points, however, are reasonably clear. First, that the directors of a company are persons of some importance and with a definite place in the constitutional structure of the company (see paragraph 9.1 *Introduction*). It is they who in practice control the company and upon whom the fortunes of the company largely depend. But this does not mean that they can treat the company as their own, which brings us to the second point, that the directors have certain duties which they are obliged to fulfil. These derive from the various roles which a director does or may play in the company.

Although he may be, he is not necessarily a servant of the company under a contract of employment, so his duties are not necessarily related to a contract of service. He will be in the position of an agent (although the precise nature of the agency will depend upon the particular circumstances) and so will owe the duties of an agent. But his relationship with the company cannot be determined solely by reference to the law of agency, especially as he does not necessarily have all the rights of an agent.

It has been said that directors are in the position of trustees but this is inaccurate except in so far as it suggests, quite rightly, that the director is in a fiduciary position and owes duties of good faith. But, although like a trustee he is under an obligation to exercise due skill and care, the nature of the obligation differs. A trustee must be cautious and safeguard the trust property; the director, however, is engaged in a speculative undertaking and the likelihood of his having to take risks is such that his obligation to refrain from negligence is far less onerous than that of a trustee.

Being of a general nature, the type of duties owed by directors may be owed by non-directors. Thus, an agent of the company will owe similar duties and an employee will owe certain obligations to the company. In fact, anyone who is not specifically designated a director might find himself within the statutory definition of a director (s741) with the relevant consequences of that. But generally speaking, a servant's duty of fidelity may impose lesser obligations than the director's duties of good faith: *Bell v Lever Bros Ltd* [1933] AC 161. It is important to ascertain not so much the type of duty imposed but the degree of compliance necessary to fulfil the obligation.

The director's duties

It is convenient at this stage to summarise the duties of directors. Generally speaking, they are the ordinary duties of agents and fiduciaries so far as they are

P must examine whether all other directors have breached duties 3, 5, 6, 7 & 13 in the way they've acted against him See p.221

applicable in the context of company law. More specifically (and in no particular order of importance), the director must:

1. carry out his duties (as laid down by the articles of association and decisions of the company in general meeting and of the board of directors, etc);
2. carry out his duties personally (he must not generally delegate performance to someone else);
3. not exceed his powers or instructions although, if he does, it does not follow that the company will not be bound: see eg s35A (see paragraph 2.3 *Validity of transactions*);
4. indemnify the company for losses it suffers as a result of his breaches of duty;
5. act in the best interests of the company as a whole;
6. act honestly and in good faith (his overriding duty);
7. exercise his powers for the proper purpose for which they were given;
8. not put himself in a position in which there will or may be a conflict between his duties to the company and the interest of himself and/or a third party; *see p.222*
9. notify the company of his interest in its shares or debentures, or those of an associated company: s324 and Sch. 13 (see paragraph 9.1 *Publicity about directors*);
10. disclose for approval at a general meeting any substantial non-cash transaction with the company: ss320–322 (see paragraph 9.1 *Directors' transactions*);
11. account to the company for any benefits he receives by virtue of his position as a director;
12. exercise due care and skill in carrying out his duties (ie he must refrain from being negligent);
13. have regard to the interests of employees: s309.

wife's (on item 8) *annuity*

— Chairman has conflicting interests ie duty nos 5, 6, 7 and wife's annuity.

Directors ∧ Chairman

In the main, he has duties of a fiduciary nature and of care and skill. Nowhere have the duties been authoritatively codified despite recommendations (eg by the Jenkins' Committee) that they should be (an attempt in the Companies Bill 1978 failing on the loss of the Bill when Parliament was dissolved in April 1979). The Bullock Committee, in particular, recommended that there should be one place where a director, in particular one appointed to represent the workforce under a scheme of industrial democracy, should be able to discover a statement of the duties which he owes.

Nevertheless, it is clear, for example, that it is a breach of fiduciary duty for a company director to wrongfully authorise the transfer of company assets to another company and that his breach lies in the act of signing the transfer forms, not in his failure to make proper enquiries before signing: *Bishopsgate Investment Management Ltd v Maxwell* [1994] 1 All ER 261. On the other hand, the fact that a director took expert professional advice in relation to a highly technical matter may give him a good answer to any allegation of breach of fiduciary duty: see, eg, *Norman v Theodore Goddard* [1992] BCC 14.

In relation to the taking of professional advice, the Cadbury Code of Best Practice provides in paragraph 1.5 that:

'There should be an agreed procedure for directors in furtherance of their duties to take independent professional advice if necessary, at the company's expense.'

Furthermore, this procedure should be set out in a formal document. Note 3 to the Code suggests that it could be contained in a board resolution, the articles, or in a letter of appointment.

To whom are the duties owed?

There are potentially a number of individuals or bodies to whom the director owes duties. Thus, it might be argued that he is responsible for the board of directors, of which he is a member and which may have initially secured his appointment as director. But, although directors may derive power from their activities as a board (their authority to bind the company generally depends on whether or not they act as a board) their duties are not owed to the board (ie to themselves!). Thus, they cannot control the extent and exercise of their duties, or excuse breaches of them, by board decisions (though see *Queensland Mines Ltd* v *Hudson,* below) and quaere whether they can, as shareholders, excuse themselves: *Re Horsley & Weight Ltd* [1982] 3 All ER 1055 (see paragraph 2.3 *Invalid transactions of directors*).

It is not the rule that directors' duties are owed to the persons who appoint them, whether they be their fellow directors or anyone else. Thus, a director appointed by holders of debentures under a power in the debentures owes his duties primarily to the company and not to the debenture holders. This might appear to detract from the protection given to debenture holders, in that their appointee will not be obliged merely to promote their interests, unless it is remembered that the appointee should be able to see, by his membership of the board, that the affairs of the company are properly conducted and in the manner presumably expected by the debenture holders.

Directors appointed by the workforce under a scheme of industrial democracy would owe their duties to the company not simply to the employees whom they represent (rather as Members of Parliament are representatives, and not delegates, of their constituents). Likewise, the members of the management board of directors under a two-tier board system would owe their duties to the company and not to the supervisory board of directors (see paragraph 9.1 *Industrial democracy*).

This is all quite reasonable and does not detract from the supposed purposes in having directors appointed by particular parties if it is accepted that directors must take account of the interests of the company and that this requires taking account of all relevant interests (whether of shareholders, creditors, employees, etc) in deciding what is in the overall interests of the company. In other words, it may be antiquated and misconceived to assume that the interests of the company must be the interests of the shareholders alone (see Davies and Wedderburn (1977) 6 *Industrial Law Journal* 197; cf. Kahn-Freund (1977) 6 *Industrial Law Journal* 65). Of course, it would be naive to assume that directors could in any case act in the best interests of the shareholders if they ignored related interests. Formerly they were only permitted to take account of such interests so far as doing so will benefit the company as a going concern: *Parke* v *Daily News* [1962] Ch 927. But now note s309 and IA s187 (see paragraph 2.3 *Gifts by companies*).

The general rule therefore is that directors owe their duties to the company as a whole and this has traditionally been taken to mean to the shareholders as a collective body; which includes present and future shareholders: *Abbey Glen Property Corp* v *Stumborg* (1978) 85 DLR (3d) 35. They may take account of their own interests as shareholders and of the interests of particular sections of shareholders; they are not required to think of the company as an entity which is completely distinct from its members. But they owe no general duty to individual shareholders.

In *Percival* v *Wright* [1902] 2 Ch 421 a contract could not be avoided for non-disclosure where directors had agreed to buy shares offered to them by certain shareholders at a fixed price, which happened to be below the price offered by another company which had been negotiating (confidentially) with the directors. According to Swinfen Eady J, the directors' duties to the company precluded their disclosure of the other offer and, since the shareholder offerors had knowledge of the directors' power to enter such negotiations, they must have taken the risk of them. However, despite the general rule, particular circumstances may give rise to a duty owed by directors to particular shareholders, such as where they are authorised to act as agents for particular share holders in relation to sale of their shares: *Allen* v *Hyatt* (1914) 30 TLR 444.

The particular facts of a case may give rise to a fiduciary duty to an individual shareholder, especially if the director has a personal interest in the situation and there is a special relationship between the parties, eg where minority shareholders in a small family firm sell shares to the managing director following misrepresentations made by him: *Coleman* v *Myers* (1978) 41 MLR 585; [1977] 2 NZLR 298.

In performing their duties to their company, directors will have to take into account the interests of the company's creditors, at least when it is insolvent. If they fail to do so they will be in breach of their fiduciary duty to the company: *West Mercia Safetyware Ltd* v *Dodd* [1988] BCLC 250, adopting the Australian view laid down in *Walker* v *Wimbourne* [1976] ALJR 446.

In *West Mercia* it was the liquidator who in effect enforced the breach of duty against the director. There has been some debate as to whether the directors owe a direct duty to the creditors so that they could bring an action against the directors themselves. If the company is solvent then the position is clear. Neither the company nor its directors owe any duty to creditors: *Multinational Gas and Petrochemical Co Ltd* v *Multinational Gas and Petrochemical Services Ltd* [1983] Ch 258. If, on the other hand, the company is insolvent then it had been said by Lord Templeman in *Winkworth* v *Edward Baron Development Co Ltd* [1986] 1 WLR 1512 at 1516 that:

'A duty is owed by the directors to the company and to the creditors of the company to ensure that the affairs of the company are properly administered and that its property is not dissipated or exploited for the benefit of the directors themselves to the prejudice of the creditors'.

Winkworth seemed to suggest that a direct duty was owed to creditors, but Lord Templeman's statement sits uneasily with remarks by Lord Lowry in *Kuwait Asia Bank EC* v *National Mutual Life Nominees Ltd* [1991] 1 AC 187 where he said at p217:

'A director does not by reason only of his position as director owe any duty to creditors or to trustees for creditors of the company'.

This question then remains very much a live issue.

9.3 Performance of duties

Duties of care and skill

The standard of care and skill required of a director has been described by Romer J in *Re City Equitable Fire Insurance Co* [1925] Ch 407 as follows:

1. A director need not exhibit in the performance of his duties a greater degree of skill than may reasonably be expected from a person of his knowledge and experience. (Directors are not liable for mere errors of judgment.) See *Re Denham* (1883) 25 Ch D 752 and the *Overend and Gurney* case in paragraph 9.4 *The nature of the remedy*.
2. A director is not bound to give continuous attention to the affairs of his company. His duties are of an intermittent nature to be performed at periodical board meetings and at meetings of any committee of the board upon which he happens to be placed. He is not, however, bound to attend all such meetings, though he ought to attend whenever, in the circumstances, he is reasonably able to do so. See *The Marquis of Bute's Case* [1892] 2 Ch 1.
3. In respect of all duties that, having regard to the exigencies of business, and the articles of association, may properly be left to some other official, a director is, in the absence of grounds for suspicion, justified in trusting that official to perform such duties honestly. See *Dovey* v *Cory* [1901] AC 477.

Such duties are, in practice, even less onerous than the wording might suggest. It has been said that he must do his honest best without having to be competent. Certainly one cannot say whether a man has been guilty of negligence unless one can determine what is the extent of the duty which he is alleged to have neglected. This requires consideration of the nature of the company's business and of the manner in which the company's work is distributed among officials.

Different expectations will be made of different directors (eg of executive and non-executive directors, the latter being potentially useful in being able to bring to the board a breadth of knowledge and experience which the company's own management may not possess and in increasing the element of independence and objectivity in board decision-making: *The Conduct of Company Directors*, Cmnd 7037 (1977), paras 19–21). But differing degrees of skill and care do not justify generally low standards.

The Company Directors Disqualification Act 1986 s9 has tended to tighten up the law on directors' performance by requiring the court, in considering an application for a disqualification order (see paragraph 9.1 *Disqualification of directors*) to have regard to a list of specified shortcomings in determining whether the director has shown himself unfit for office. Although this is most likely to arise in company insolvency (see paragraph 9.1 *Directors and company insolvency*), no director should, in his own interest, neglect his specified responsibilities at any time. The Company Directors Disqualification Act 1986 Sch. 1 is a useful check-list of specified statutory duties.

It was recently held in *Re D'Jan of London Ltd* [1993] BCC 646, that a director was negligent by signing an insurance proposal form, which had been filled in by a broker, without reading it. The form contained inaccurate information allowing the insurance company to avoid indemnifying the company after a fire at its premises. The court went on to hold, however, that the director could be partly relieved from liability under s727 as he had acted honestly and reasonably.

Performance and the duty of good faith

Directors are bound to carry out their duties (to exercise the powers and discretion given to them) but the means by which they do so will not generally be specified. They are, however, obliged to adhere to their overriding duty of good faith and to act in what they consider to be in the best interests of the company, as described above. How they exercise their functions is for them – and not the court or anyone else – to decide, but (where directors act against the company's interest, the court will intervene at the instigation of a member: *Re A Company, FFI (UK Finance) Ltd* v *Lady Kagan* (1982) 132 New LJ 830.)

While it is not a breach of a director's fiduciary duty to form an intention to set up a competing business after his directorship has come to an end, or to fail to disclose such an intention, offering future supplies to one of the company's present customers or future employment to one of the company's present employees could constitute a breach of that duty: *Balston* v *Headline Filters Ltd* [1990] FSR 385.

Thus, the court will not direct a director to exercise his discretion in a mandatory way at the instance of some of the shareholders: *Pergamon Press Ltd* v *Maxwell* [1970] 1 WLR 1167. (Directors must not fetter their discretion but, on the other hand, they cannot exercise it as the fancy takes them. They must exercise it for the purpose for which it is given.)

Exercise of discretion

Just as directors must not, as we shall see (paragraph 9.3 *Conflict of interest*) put themselves in a position where there is such a conflict of interest that they are unable to perform their duties to the company, there are limits to the extent to which they may restrict their freedom to exercise their discretion in the interests of the company.

Thus, they should not delegate their discretion to others, except as empowered by the articles, although they may delegate the task of implementing their decisions to agents or employees.

Similarly they should not, as a rule, bind themselves by contract to vote in a particular way at board meetings, although they might be bound to vote in a particular way if:

1. as shareholders they have entered into a voting agreement (*Ringuet* v *Bergeron* [1960] SCR 672; cf Krüger (1978) 94 LQR 557); or
2. they have entered into a contract on behalf of the company in which they have agreed to take steps to ensure that the contract is implemented: *Thorby* v *Goldberg* (1964) 112 CLR 597.

In *Fulham Football Club Ltd* v *Cabra Estates plc* [1992] BCC 863, approving *Thorby* v *Goldberg*, the Court of Appeal affirmed that there is no general proposition that directors can never make a contract by which they bind themselves to the future exercise of their powers in a particular manner, even though the contract taken as a whole is manifestly for the benefit of the company. In that case their Lordships also concluded that there is no rule of public policy whereby a company (a football club) could ignore the undertakings given by its directors not to give evidence at a local council enquiry concerning a compulsory purchase order and that no rule of public policy or otherwise rendered such an agreement illegal or unenforceable.

Exercise of powers for proper purpose = c'c defence for gifts

Although the directors themselves must decide how to exercise their powers, and although actions taken by them outside their powers may be ratified by the company in general meeting, this does not permit the directors to exercise their powers other than for the purposes for which they are given.

Obviously the exercise of a discretion may require the taking account of many factors and the influence of mixed motives. But the directors will be justified if their main purpose is a proper one. Thus, it was permissible in *Mills* v *Mills* (1938) 60 CLR 150 for directors who were majority ordinary shareholders to capitalise dividends and issue bonus shares to the ordinary shareholders because, although the position of preference shareholders was weakened, the moving purpose was in the interests of the company and, said Latham CJ, 'it would be ignoring realities and creating impossibilities in the administration of companies to require that directors should not advert to or consider in any way the effect of a particular decision upon their own interest as shareholders'.

The court is entitled to look at the situation objectively in order to estimate how critical or pressing, or substantial or insubstantial an alleged requirement may have been. If it finds that a particular requirement, though real, was not urgent or critical at the relevant time, it may have reason to doubt or discount the assertions of individuals that they acted solely in order to deal with it, particularly when the action they took was unusual or even extreme. The extent of the discretion is a question of construction: *Re Smith and Fawcett* [1942] Ch 304.

A common source of difficulty in this context concerns the powers of directors to issue new shares. By s80 the directors may issue shares only under an express authority conferred by the articles or given by the company in general meeting. The power is given essentially to facilitate the raising of capital for the company but provided that the overriding purpose is to benefit the company, the power may be exercised although capital is not especially necessary at that particular time: *Harlow's Nominees Pty Ltd* v *Woodside (Lakes Entrance) Oil Co No Liability* (1968) 42 ALJR 123. What must not happen is for the power to be exercised to enable the directors to entrench themselves in control in the face of take-over bids.

But in *Hogg* v *Cramphorn Ltd* [1967] Ch 254, an issue of shares for such a purpose was held to be ratifiable by the general meeting so long as the new shareholders did not vote – and the issue was subsequently ratified (see also *Bamford* v *Bamford* [1970] Ch 212).

A different approach was taken by the Supreme Court of British Columbia in *Teck Corporation* v *Millar* (1973) 33 DLR (3d) 288. In that case, directors agreed to vest a certain percentage of shares in a company to whom exclusive management rights were granted, thereby depriving of control existing majority shareholders who wished to develop the company's properties. The court stressed that the directors could take account of the reputation, policies and experience of anyone seeking to take over the company and have regard to interests other than those of the shareholders (eg of employees). *Hogg* v *Cramphorn* was not followed, on the basis that the overriding general rule is that the directors must act bona fide on behalf of the company.

And in the *Savoy Hotel* case (see Charlesworth, 12th ed p427) the investigator considered that defensive transfers of property and shares were not proper exercise of directors' powers, despite the directors' (and counsel's) view that the transactions were in the best interests of the company and its members.

In *Howard Smith Ltd* v *Ampol Petroleum Ltd* [1974] AC 821, directors acting, it would seem, honestly (for the sake of raising much-needed finance) allotted shares to a company which wanted to make a take-over bid, the effect being to reduce the majority shareholding of two other companies whose take-over bid had been rejected. The allotment was held invalid because 'it must be unconstitutional for directors to use their fiduciary powers over the shares in the company purely for the purpose of destroying an existing majority, or creating a new majority which did not previously exist. To do so is to interfere with that element of the company's constitution which is separate from and set against their powers.' See also *Re Downs Wine Bar Ltd* [1990] BCLC 839.

Similarly, it is not within the powers of a company's directors, knowing that the shareholders are proposing to appoint new directors, to pass a resolution the effect of which would be to remove all managerial powers from the new directors: *Lee Panavision Ltd* v *Lee Lighting Ltd* [1991] BCC 620.

Conflict of interest

It is part of the fiduciary duty owed by a director to his company that he shall not place himself in a position in which his own personal interest conflicts with the interest of the company, to which he should give his exclusive attention.

Chairman Go to p. 227
If a director is in breach of his duty in this respect, it is no justification to show that the company did not suffer any loss as a result. The breach of duty is in the conflict of interest itself: *Aberdeen Railway Co* v *Blaikie* (1854) 1 Macq 461.

Go also to p. 228
The most common application of this principle is where the director enters into a contract with the company, or becomes indirectly interested in a contract made by the company, eg when he is also a director or shareholder of another company with which the company makes a contract.

Obviously the principle cannot be applied with complete strictness in every case. If, for example, the director is also a working employee of the company, there is a conflict of interest since the director's personal interest as an employee is in conflict with the interest of the company as employer (see paragraph 9.1 *Directors as employees*). Another instance is where the director, or some other commercial concern in which he has an interest, sells goods to or purchases goods from the company at the market price. That was the situation in *Blaikie*'s case above.

There are two methods of relieving the director from a breach of duty in these situations:

1. the articles (Table A arts 84–85) may permit a director to be an employee of the company, or to provide services to it, or to be interested in a transaction of the company; or
2. the company in general meeting may sanction the conflict of interest, usually by approving the relevant transaction.

In either case there are some special requirements to take into account.

A director may only rely on the relieving provisions of the articles if he has made proper disclosure of his interest in compliance with s317 (see paragraph 9.1 *Directors' transactions*). In the *Rolled Steel Products* case (see paragraph 2.3 *Contractual capacity*) one of the objections to the guarantee, approved by the directors, was that one of the two directors, who had a personal interest in it, had not made formal disclosure of his interest. Table A art 85 expressly states this requirement as a condition of the exemptions which follow.

Secondly, a director who has disclosed his interest and obtained exemption under the articles may nonetheless disqualified from being counted in the quorum on this item of business and from voting on it. However, the articles (eg Table A art 94) may authorise a director to vote (and be counted in the quorum) in specified types of conflict of interest.

Approval by the company in general meeting is required if either the articles do not provide adequate exemption or this form of approval is expressly required usually by statute. As stated in Chapter 9 (see paragraph 9.1 *Directors as employees* and *Directors' transactions*) ss319–320 provide that directors' service agreements for periods exceeding five years and substantial property transactions in which a director is, directly or indirectly, interested, require such approval. In the case of a company listed on the Stock Exchange any contract in which a director is interested is a 'Class 4' contract, with the result that the Stock Exchange may require that it be submitted for approval in general meeting. As will be seen, when we come to 'minority protection', approval in general meeting is conditional upon a sufficient disclosure being made of the effect of the transaction (see paragraph 11.1 *Expropriation of the company's property*).

If a contract is submitted to the general meeting for approval, the director may use his votes as shareholder in voting for the resolution to give approval: *North-West Transportation Co Ltd* v *Beatty* (1887) 12 App Cas 589. As shareholder he is not inhibited from the exercise of his normal rights by a conflict of interest which affects him as director. However, if there is fraud his votes will be disregarded (see paragraph 4.3 *Freedom of voting*).

Upon giving up his directorship a director may compete with the company provided that in doing so he is not making use for his own advantage of information gained while he was a director: *Thomas Marshall (Exports) Ltd* v *Guinle* [1978] 3 WLR 116 and *Cooley*'s case in paragraph 9.3 *Prohibition of personal gain by directors*; cf *Balston* v *Headline Filters Ltd* [1990] FSR 385. Such behaviour is not so much a conflict of interest, since he is no longer a director, as an appropriation to his own benefit of information which belongs to the company.

There seems to be no legal obstacle to the same individual being a director of two different companies merely because they compete in the same market. At all events it is not an unusual situation; in the period when there was a subtantial UK investment in numerous small plantation companies, producing rubber and other produce, many individuals held 'multiple directorships' in competing companies of that type. If, however, in a situation of actual conflict, one company seeks to subordinate the interests of another company to its own, it is not proper for the same individual to remain a director of both. These problems were analysed by Lord Denning in his judgment in *Scottish Cooperative Wholesale Society Ltd* v *Meyer* [1959] AC 324 (see paragraph 11.2 *The court's powers*).

Prohibition of personal gain by directors

Unless he has the consent of the company a director may not secure to himself from his office any personal advantage. That prohibition applies in cases where the director obtains his 'profit' without causing loss to the company. It includes the financial gain arising from a profitable contract as well as the appropriation of property.

The principle underlying this rule is that a director, like a trustee, holds office without entitlement to reward, unless of course it is properly authorised.

If a director sells property to the company at a profit or buys property from it at an undervalue (usually measured in either case by reference to market value) there is a conflict of interest, which may be resolved as explained above (see paragraph 9.3 *Conflict of interest*) and there is also a profit made by the director at the company's expense, for which he is accountable unless the company agrees that he may retain it. These situations often overlap with minority protection (see paragraph 11.1 *Expropriation of the company's property*) since the directors either are or have the support of those who are majority shareholders: if that were not so the directors would not retain office.

The facts of *Daniels* v *Daniels* [1978] Ch 406 provide an illustration of the duality of principle. The directors, who were also controlling shareholders, had sold company property to one of themselves at an undervalue. A minority shareholder was granted relief by way of 'minority protection' although no evidence was produced of dishonest intent on the part of the directors. However, it has also been suggested that it was a case of breach by the directors of their duty to apply property of the company 'for the specific purposes of the company ... and to apply it otherwise is to misapply it in breach of the obligation ...': *Selangor United Rubber Estates Ltd* v *Cradock (No 3)* [1968] 1 WLR 1555.

Until 1942 it was generally believed that the prohibition of directors' 'secret profits' was limited in its scope to cases where the profit was gained at the company's expense. The decision of the House of Lords in *Regal (Hastings) Ltd* v *Gulliver* (1942) [1967] 2 AC 134n dispelled that misunderstanding. Here the company had had an opportunity of investment which it could not take up in full because it lacked the necessary cash. The directors contributed the balance required and, when the investment was sold at a profit, they took their share of it. It was held that they were accountable to the company, although it had suffered no loss by their action, since as directors they might only retain a gain obtained in their office if the company agreed. If in fact a general meeting had been called to approve their participation, they would have been entitled to their profit, and as controlling shareholders they might have voted for it (*Beatty's* case: see paragraph 9.3 *Conflict of interest*). But no such meeting was held.

Two general issues have arisen partly as a result of *Gulliver's* case and have been much discussed by learned commentators. The first, which is directly related to the circumstances of the case, is how far the company, without formally releasing the directors from their fiduciary duty not to profit from their office, may by its own actions relieve them. Two Commonwealth cases – *Peso Silver Mines Ltd* v *Cropper* (1966) 58 DLR (2d) 1 and *Queensland Mines Ltd* v *Hudson* (1978) 52 AJLR 399 PC – suggest that if the proposition has been considered and declined by the board of the company, then after a reasonable interval any director is free to take up the opportunity for himself without having to account for his profit. However, there is no English decision to that effect and the Canadian and Australian decisions, although not unreasonable, seem to run counter to the reasoning of *Gulliver's* case.

Subsequent English decisions make it clear that a director cannot by sharp practice evade his duty to account for his profit. If, for example, he resigns from his directorship and then takes up the investment or contract which the company has declined, he is still accountable: *Industrial Development Consultants Ltd* v *Cooley*

[1972] 2 All ER 162. Secondly, if in negotiating compensation for premature termination of his service agreement he withholds from the company material facts about his past breaches of duty, he is in breach of duty over the compensation itself and may be compelled to repay it: *Horcal Ltd* v *Garland* [1984] BCLC 549.

The second question is how far the company in general meeting may relieve directors of their duty, or liability for breach of duty, towards the company. This is considered later (see paragraph 9.4 *Relief from liability*).

Finally, the concept of 'profit', for which the director is accountable, is widely interpreted. In *Gulliver*'s case the directors invested their own money: *Cooley*'s case the director rendered services. In reckoning the profit their own contribution was taken into account, but it did not render the surplus a legitimate profit which they might retain. In a deserving case however, eg *Boardman* v *Phipps* [1967] 2 AC 46, the court is disposed to apply a generous basis to the reckoning of the profit.

Directors' dealings in securities

The directors' duty to disclose their interests, elaborately defined, in shares or debentures of the company, incidentally requires them to disclose their dealings, since they must (Sch. 13 para 22) inform the company within three days of any changes in those interests. A company whose securities are listed on a recognised stock exchange is required to pass on to that exchange any such information on the day following its receipt and the stock exchange may publish it: s329. A director who observes these requirements is thus subject to the constraint of publicity on his dealings. If he fails to comply he is guilty of an offence.

Subject to proper disclosure he is in theory free to deal in the securities of his company like any other investor: *Percival* v *Wright* in paragraph 9.2 *To whom are the duties owed?* In practice, however, he is much affected by the prohibition of insider dealing in the Criminal Justice Act 1993 considered in Chapter 10 *Insider Dealing*. He is undoubtedly 'connected' with his company, by virtue of his position, at all times. If he attends monthly board meetings, at which management accounts are considered, it is difficult to argue that he is not placed in possession of confidential price-sensitive information on each occasion. For good measure, if his company is listed, the Stock Exchange requires a ban on its directors against their dealing in its securities within a two-month period before the announcement of its half-yearly and end-of-year financial results (except after consultation with the chairman or some other director designated to supervise such exceptional cases). There is thus a total ban for four months of the year.

To explain what follows it is necessary to distinguish between (1) traded options and (2) employees' share schemes which may take the form of options or rights to subscribe for company shares. There is an active stock exchange market in traded options. In essence an investor buy a market option to purchase or to sell, or at his choice to do either, a specified number of shares of a company at an agreed price at a date say three months ahead. The option costs him only a fraction of the market value of the shares and he need not exercise it, when the time comes if it would be unprofitable. He speculates on a rise or a fall in market value which would make completion at the option price advantageous to him. A director of a listed company, or of any other company in a group which includes a listed company, is entirely prohibited from dealing in options of this kind: s323.

Section 323 does not, however, have to apply to the grant of options to subscribe for its shares (or debentures) by a company to its directors. If this 'right to subscribe' is granted, however, the company must enter it in its register of directors' interests (see paragraph 9.1 *Publicity about directors*) which is open to public inspection. The grant of the option is also subject to the general restriction on allotment of ordinary shares for cash (otherwise than as a 'rights issue') imposed by s89 (see paragraph 6.3 *Allotment of shares*). The normal practice is that an 'employees' share scheme' as defined by s743, including options for directors and senior executives, is approved in general meeting. There are also complicated tax provisions to be considered.

The impact of the Financial Services Act 1986 on the issue of securities of public companies has been described (see paragraph 5.2). It does not directly affect directors' dealings but the documents published for public information in a flotation or a takeover bid often include, among much else, data on directors' dealings in the recent past in shares of their company or (in a take-over bid) of the target company.

9.4 Breach of duty

Peter can sue other directors as shareholder and other shareholders can sue chairman as the co.

Who may sue for breach of duty

The director owes his duty to the company and so it is normally the company which should take action if he is in breach of his duty (see paragraph 9.2 *To whom are the duties owed?*). This proposition, to which there are exceptions, was laid down in *Foss* v *Harbottle* (1843) 2 Hare 461. In that case Foss and other shareholders tried to sue Harbottle and other directors, who had sold land to the company at an excessive price and mismanaged its affairs. Their action was dismissed, with the observation that they should convene a general meeting so that the company as the only competent plaintiff might decide whether to sue the directors.

There are exceptions to the rule in *Foss* v *Harbottle*, where individual members of a company are permitted to bring proceedings against directors or others, but these instances of 'minority protection' are considered in Chapter 11 (see paragraph 11.1 *Introduction: the general rule*).

The nature of the remedy

The action to be taken against a director or the board of directors must be appropriate to the nature of the breach for which a remedy is sought.

[handwritten: Peter as shareholder can claim]

[handwritten: no]

Excess of powers

It is the duty of the directors to use only such powers as are delegated to them by the articles, which cannot be wider than the limits defined by the objects clause (paragraph 8.2 *The directors' general powers of management*), and to use those powers in a proper manner.

[handwritten: (2) loan]

The appropriate remedy may be an application to the court for a declaration or, if necessary, an injunction to restrain the directors. An example is found in *Parke* v *Daily News Ltd* [1962] Ch 927, where a shareholder successfully prevented the company from distributing its assets to redundant employees (see paragraph 2.3 *Gifts by companies*) – but s719 now gives the necessary power.

[handwritten: excess of powers]

[handwritten: loan (2)]

In addition to preventing such an action the company may have grounds for claiming compensation from the directors for any loss which their action has caused, eg when a dividend is unlawfully paid out of capital, as in *Re Exchange Banking Co, Flitcroft's Case* (1882) 21 Ch D 519 (see paragraph 6.5 *Distributable profits*). On the same principle (but under special statutory provisions) the liquidator may bring misfeasance proceedings against directors or other officers of a company in liquidation to recover compensation under Insolvency Act 1986 s212 (see paragraph 13.6 *Other bases of liability*). In claiming compensation from directors for exceeding their powers, it is unnecessary to show that they have been negligent. Their liability arises from causing a loss to the company by a breach of their duty to act within their powers: see, eg, *Re DKG Contractors Ltd* [1990] BCC 903.

[handwritten: loan (2)]

Negligence

If the directors have not acted with a proper degree of skill and care (see paragraph 9.3 *Duties of care and skill*) they are liable to the company for any loss which their negligence has caused. In practice, however, it is difficult for the company to recover damages for negligence on the part of directors. The company must show that 'no men with any degree of prudence, acting on their own behalf, would have entered into such a transaction': *Overend and Gurney Co* v *Gibb* (1872) LR 5 HL 480. In that case the directors were held not to have been negligent to a culpable degree, although they knew that the business which they bought had an excess of liabilities over assets. However, as a matter of judgment they thought that its prospects were satisfactory. The second difficulty which may arise over evidence is to show just what loss has resulted from the directors' negligence.

[handwritten: Annuity may be rescinded]

[handwritten: Chairman]

Conflict of interest

The normal remedy if a director has become involved in a conflict of interest situation, without being relieved of liability by the consent of the company, is to rescind the contract. This remedy is available both against the director, if he was the other party to the contract, and against a third party, such as another company in which the director was interested: *Blaikie*'s case (see paragraph 9.3 *Conflict of interest*).

As a general rule the company may not both affirm the contract to retain its benefits and recover from the director any profit (unless of a fraudulent nature) which he has obtained from his interest or part in it: *Burland* v *Earle* [1902] AC 83.

A new section 322A deals with transactions in which:

1. one of the parties is a director of the company or of its holding company or a person connected with or a company associated with such a director; and
2. in connection with the transaction the directors have exceeded their powers (see paragraph 2.3 *Invalid transactions of directors*).

The transaction is voidable at the instance of the company, but it ceases to be voidable if restitution has been made or the company has been indemnified or the transaction has been ratified by resolution passed in general meeting or if the rights which a person (not a party to the transaction) has acquired bona fide and without notice that the directors were exceeding their powers would be affected by the avoidance: s322A(5). Whether or not the transaction is avoided the parties in (1) and the directors in (2) are liable to account to the company for any gain and to indemnify it for any loss or damage resulting from the transaction. These statutory provisions supplement, and so do not displace, any common law principles which may apply: s322A(4).

These new provisions should be read with those of s320 (paragraph 9.1 *Directors' transactions*). The common law principle which prohibits conflict of interest transactions generally is supplemented by these statutory procedures applicable to cases where either (1) the amount involved is substantial or (2) the directors exceed their powers in approving the transaction. But they permit ratification and protect the rights of an honest third party who is a purchaser for value of the property involved.

Section 322B of the 1985 Act, as inserted by the Companies (Single Member Private Limited Companies) Regulations 1992, provides that where a private company limited by shares or by guarantee having only one member enters into a contract (other than a contract entered into in the ordinary course of the company's business) with the sole member of the company and the sole member is also a director of the company, the company must, unless the contract is in writing, ensure that the terms of the contract are either set out in a written memorandum or recorded in the minutes of the first meeting of the directors of the company following the making of the contract. Failure to comply with this requirement is an offence, but the contract's validity is not thereby affected.

Director's personal profit
If the director is accountable the company may recover from him his profit, even though it was not made at the company's expense: *Gulliver*'s case (see paragraph 9.3 *Prohibition of personal gain by directors*).

Misappropriation of company property
If a director has disposed of company property to a third party in breach of his fiduciary duty to the company (see *Cradock*'s case in paragraph 9.3 *Prohibition of*

personal gain by directors), the company may only recover it from the other party if it can prove that he received it under a constructive trust, ie with knowledge or grounds for suspecting that the disposal to him was a breach of the director's duty to the company: *Karak Rubber Co Ltd* v *Burden* [1971] 3 All ER 1118. The company has of course a remedy against the director for breach of his duty to deal with the property properly (see paragraph 9.3 *Prohibition of personal gain by directors* and *Guinness plc* v *Saunders and Anor* [1988] 2 All ER 940).

It is a breach of fiduciary duty for a director to withdraw £36,800 out of the company's bank account and deposit it into his own personal savings account. The director will be treated as holding the money as constructive trustee for the company. A subsequently acquired claim for compensation under the terms of a service contract cannot be used as a set-off against the director's obligation to restore the money to the company: *Zemco Ltd* v *Jerrom-Pugh* [1993] BCC 275.

Constructive trust

International Sales and Agencies Ltd v *Marcus* [1982] 3 All ER 551 was decided on the basis of constructive trust. The case has been considered earlier (see paragraph 2.3 *Validity of transactions*) in connection with s35 and the question whether a transaction of a single director can ever be one 'decided on by the directors'. Here one may note that if the recipient of the property has the knowledge which makes him a constructive trustee it will usually be impossible for him to show that he acted in good faith, as required by s35.

Directors' duties to other persons

Employees

In the performance of their functions the directors are required (s309) to have regard to the interests of the company's employees in general, as well as the interests of members. However, this is declared to be a duty owed to the company, with the result that the employees cannot enforce the duty. This last stipulation was intended to prevent trade unions from suing directors, if for example the latter had taken a decision to close down all or part of the company's business, thus making employees redundant.

The intention and effect of s309 is to provide a defence to directors if the shareholders object to a management decision which seems to them unduly favourable to employees, eg not to close an unprofitable plant so as to preserve jobs. The shareholders are unlikely ever to challenge a failure of the directors to consider the interests of employees.

However, the above point needs to be considered in the context of management practice. The managements of companies usually have established negotiating procedures with trade unions or have set up other consultative machinery, such as works councils etc. Moreover, it is usually in the company's interest to promote good industrial relations. Hence, most company boards of directors do give some consideration to the views and interests of employees in the course of prudent management. But, in view of the restrictive wording of s309, it is unlikely that they will ever be challenged in a court for failure to give due weight to employees' interests.

Members

See paragraph 9.2 *To whom are the duties owed?* and in particular *Percival* v *Wright*. However, there are a number of statutory provisions which may affect directors in their dealings with individual members. If for example directors allot shares in disregard of members' pre-emption rights (s89) (see paragraph 6.3 *Allotment of shares*), the members may recover compensation under s92. The purpose of the insider dealing legislation is partly to prevent directors from using their inside information to secure an advantage from other shareholders by covert market dealings in the company's shares.

Peter as shareholder may be able to recover comp.

Creditors and other outsiders

The liability of directors if the company becomes insolvent is explained in detail in connection with liquidation (see paragraph 13.6). See also *Re Welfab Engineers* [1990] BCC 600 where it was alleged – unsuccessfully – that the directors of a company in financial difficulty had acted improperly because, in selling the company's principal asset, they had, inter alia, given priority to job preservation.

In managing the company, while it is still a going concern, the directors have no duty to the outsiders with whom they have dealings on its behalf. If, for example, they decide that the company shall break its contracts, the other parties cannot sue the directors in tort for inducing the breach.

The directors have a normal liability for misrepresentation of various kinds (see paragraph 5.3). Apart from prospectus liability they could be liable for untrue statements made in the course of commercial dealings but it would be necessary to prove fraud in order to make them personally liable.

It is possible to impose on directors statutory unlimited liability for the company's debts: s306. However, no company ever does so (see paragraph 9.1 *Directors and company insolvency*).

Takeover bidders

If, during the course of a contested takeover bid, the directors of the target company make express representations, intending that the bidder will rely on those representations, they owe a duty of care not to be negligent in making representations which might mislead the bidder: see *Morgan Crucible Co plc* v *Hill Samuel Bank Ltd* [1991] 1 All ER 148.

Relief from liability

Although the position of directors is somewhat similar to that of trustees, there is no general power given to the company to release directors from liability, such as beneficiaries may exercise towards their trustees in respect of breach of trust. On the contrary any attempt to exempt company officers from liability in advance is void: s310 (see below).

The company in general meeting does, however, have wide powers to authorise acts of the directors which would otherwise be in breach of their duty to the company. These powers, where they apply, may be exercised prospectively or retrospectively by ratifying what has been done and they cover use of powers for an irregular purpose (*Bamford*'s case); conflict of interest between the director and the company; and directors' personal gains from their office (*Gulliver*'s case) (see paragraphs 9.3 *Exercise of powers for proper purpose* to *Prohibition of personal gain by directors* and 9.4 *The nature of the remedy, Conflict of interest*).

On the other hand the case law shows that in a number of fields the general meeting has no power of ratification or exemption from liability. These include:

1. there is no power to sanction an unlawful act such as a payment of dividend out of capital (*Flitcroft*'s *Case* in paragraph 9.4 *The nature of the remedy, Excess of powers*). It is now possible however for a company to ratify a transaction which is outside the limits set by its objects clause and to relieve the directors of their liability (paragraph 2.3 *Management of the company* which overrules the principle established in the *Ashbury Railway Carriage* case);

2. actions of the directors which are not bona fide (in the minds of the directors) taken in the interests of the company. The facts of *Re W & M Roith Ltd* [1967] 1 All ER 427 provide an example. A director and controlling shareholder had managed his company for 20 years without a service agreement. At a time when his health was failing he entered into a service agreement for the sole purpose of including in it a clause giving a company pension to his widow if he should die in the company's service, as he did shortly afterwards. Plainly his mind was not in any way directed to promoting the interests of the company. The objects clause was altered to provide the necessary express power (see paragraph 2.3 *Gifts by companies*) to grant pensions to directors' widows. In so doing the general meeting was in effect sanctioning the grant of the pension (through the service agreement) but it was later held to be void. This decision turns on its particular facts; the grant of widows' pensions is in other circumstances a proper benefit to offer directors as part of the agreed reward for their work;

3. fraud on creditors or failure to preserve a company's assets for general creditors: see *Aveling Barford Ltd* v *Perion Ltd* (1989) 5 BCC 677;

4. if a three quarters' majority of votes cast at a general meeting is required, eg to carry a special resolution to alter the articles, the meeting cannot by a simple majority of votes authorise an action contrary to the articles: see *Edwards* v *Halliwell* [1950] 2 All ER 1064 (see paragraph 11.1 *Introduction: the general rule*);

5. a majority in general meeting cannot authorise a decision of the directors which is a 'fraud on a minority' or a denial of personal rights of members given to them by the articles (see paragraphs 4.3 *Freedom of voting* and 11.1 *The personal action*).

Section 310(3) now permits a company to take out, at its expense, insurance cover for its officers (and the auditor) against liability. In addition the company may indemnify them against liability:

1. incurred in successfully defending civil or criminal proceedings; or
2. successfully applying for relief under s727.

An officer of a company who becomes involved in legal proceedings for negligence or breach of trust on his part, may apply to the court for relief. If the court is satisfied that he acted reasonably and ought fairly to be excused, it may relieve him of liability: s727. See, eg, *Re Welfab Engineers* [1990] BCC 600; cf *Re DKG Contractors Ltd* [1990] BCC 903. A defence that directors had acted reasonably and honestly does not have to be pleaded in answer to a misfeasance summons; it may be raised for the first time at the trial: *Re Kirby's Coaches Ltd* [1991] BCC 130.

An administrator is an officer of a company for the purposes of s727 of the 1985 Act and he may therefore be absolved from liability in accordance with that provision: *Re Home Treat Ltd* [1991] BCC 165.

10

Insider Dealing

10.1 Introduction to insider dealing

10.2 Criminal provisions in the Criminal Justice Act 1993

10.3 Civil remedies

10.1 Introduction to insider dealing

The 'velvet collar' crime of insider dealing was first made an offence by the Companies Act 1980, after a decade of fierce debate. The provisions were re-enacted in the Company Securities (Insider Dealing) Act 1985 and were in turn amended by the Financial Services Act 1986, the Criminal Justice Act 1988 and the Companies Act 1989. The current law is now to be found in Part V of the Criminal Justice Act 1993. These new provisions were needed in order to comply with the EC Insider Dealing Directive (89/592), which is a minimum standards directive allowing Member States to legislate further if they wish.

On 1 March 1994 two statutory instruments, relating to insider dealing, also came into force. The first of these is the Insider Dealing (Securities and Regulated Markets) Order 1994 (SI 1994 No 187). This Order specifies the 'securities' and 'regulated markets' to which the Act applies. The securities identified are the same as those contained in Schedule 2 of the Act. A schedule to the Order lists 48 European Investment Exchanges, and any market which is established according to the rules of any of them will be a regulated market. Within the United Kingdom, the Order provides that markets established under three investment exchanges will be covered. These are, the Stock Exchange, LIFFE (the London International Financial Futures Exchange), and OMLX (the London Securities Derivatives Exchange).

The second Statutory Instrument is the Traded Securities (Disclosure) Regulations 1994 (SI 1994 No 188), which implements Article 7 of the EC Insider Dealing Directive (89/592). Regulations 3(1) requires companies, whose securities are traded on a regulated market to:

'... inform the public as soon as possible of any major new developments ... which are not public knowledge and which may ... lead to substantial movements in the price of that security'.

233

If disclosure would 'prejudice the legitimate interests' of the company, then it need not be made. The regulations also require that a range of sanctions be available against companies which do not comply, for example, to suspend trading in the relevant securities.

According to the White Paper: 'The Conduct of Company Directors' Comnd. 7037 (1977):

> 'Insider dealing is understood broadly to cover situations where a person buys or sells securities when he, but not the other party to the transaction, is in possession of confidential information which affects the value to be placed on those securities.'

Those most likely to possess such information are company directors, though insider dealing is by no means restricted only to directors. An example of insider dealing is when a director of X plc buys some shares in the company knowing that it is going to announce, say, a 25 per cent increase in its half yearly profits. This is obviously good news and the market will respond favourably. The result will be that when the information is publicly announced the share price of X plc will rise and the director will have made a profit by dealing on the basis of the information before the public announcement.

The main argument against insider dealing seems to be that it affects the integrity of the market. If investors think that others are making improper use of inside information they will be less likely to use the market themselves, therefore damaging the market. Other arguments are that it is unfair, unethical and morally wrong. Insider dealing, however, also has its supporters. They argue that there is no victim of the crime, that it is a reward for entrepreneurial activity and that dealing before the information is made public results in a speedier, more accurately quoted share price. These policy arguments are well documented: see (1974) 90 LQR 494

10.2 Criminal provisions in the Criminal Justice Act 1993

Part V of the Criminal Justice Act 1993 came into force on 1 March 1994. It repeals the Companies Securities (Insider Dealing) Act 1985 and contains some important changes to the law on this subject.

Does the Act apply?

Before the provisions of the Act can be relied on, a number of pre-conditions have to be met.

The Act provides that the offence of insider dealing applies to 'individuals' as opposed to persons. The effect of this is that the company itself cannot commit the offence. However, the company, as a legal person, can only act through agents and the agents will attract liability where the dealing is done in the name of a company. Presumably the agent will have committed an offence by encouraging another person (the company) to deal, within the meaning of s52(2)(a).

Insider dealing occurs when the securities of a company have been dealt in on the basis of price sensitive information which is not public. The Act has increased the range of securities to which the offence relates. Securities are defined in Schedule 2 of the Act and include shares, debt securities (eg debentures), warrants, depository receipts, options, futures and contracts for differences. A person will have dealt in securities if he acquires or disposes of the securities or he procures, directly or indirectly, an acquisition or disposal of securities by any other person: s55. The actus rea of the offence then, is dealing in the securities of a company and merely possessing the price sensitive information is insufficient.

Anna (1)

The information that the insider possesses must be of a certain quality. It must be inside information within s56 which:

> '(a) relates to particular securities or to a particular issuer of securities or to particular issuers of securities and not to securities generally or to issuers generally;
> (b) is specific or precise;
> (c) has not been made public; and
> (d) if it were made public would be likely to have a significant effect on the price of any securities.'

The Act does not give examples of such information, it merely sets out the criteria. However, the Listing Rules of the Stock Exchange provide that a number of events have to be announced to the market because they may be price sensitive. Such events include dividend announcements, board appointments or departures, profit warnings, share dealings by directors or substantial shareholders, acquisitions and disposals above a certain size, annual and interim results, rights issues and other offers of securities.

It is uncertain what degree of share price movement is required to amount to a 'significant effect'. Section 58 of the Act contains a non-exhaustive definition of when information can be said to have 'been made public'.

To come within the Act the person must be have the information as an insider. This he will have if he knows it is inside information, and that he has it, and knows he has it through an inside source: s57(1). Under s52(2) a person has information through an inside source if he has gained it:

> (a) through being a director, employee or shareholder of an issuer of securities; or
> (b) through having access to the information by virtue of his employment, office or profession; or
> (c) where the direct or indirect source of the information comes from a person within (a) or (b).'

This would cover a category of insider that used to be called tippee. An example would be where a managing director, who has inside information, goes home and tells his son, a merchant banker who goes on and deals in the securities of the company. In this example, the son will be an insider within category (c). In this chapter the term tippee will continue to be used to describe category (c) insiders.

Section 57 removes a previous condition that there had to be a connection between the insider and the company. One result of this may now be that a director of X plc, which is about to announce record losses, who buys shares in Y plc, its only competitor, will commit an offence in relation to Y plc. If this is the case, it is an extension of previous liability. The section also extends the categories of insiders to include shareholders, recognising that large influential shareholders may receive preferential treatment relating to inside information.

The acquisition or disposal of the securities must take place on a 'regulated market', such as the Stock Exchange and the Unlisted Securities Market or where a 'professional intermediary' is involved. For this reason the Act, generally speaking, only covers listed or quoted companies but as under the old law purely private deals, even in securities that fall within the Act, are not covered.

The offences

The offence of insider dealing can be committed in three ways which are set out in s52 of the Act. These are:

> '(a) that the individual deals in the price affected securities; or
> (b) that he encourages another person to deal; or
> (c) that he discloses the inside information.'

No offence is committed in (c) if the disclosure is in the proper performance of the functions of his employment, office or profession. To be convicted of (b) it must be shown that the individual knew or had reasonable cause to believe that the person would go on and deal. Encouraging another to deal replaced the offence of 'counselling and procuring' and would probably cover a wider range of behaviour.

The offences can only be committed by 'An individual who *has* inside information ...'. Under the previous legislation, the individual had to *'obtain'* the information. The old form of wording had caused a great deal of concern following the acquittal of an accused who successfully pleaded that he had not obtained the information within the meaning of the Act, when he had been given it without asking for it. This loophole was closed by the House of Lords in *Attorney-General's Reference (No 1 of 1988)* [1989] AC 971, which applied the mischief rule to the Company Securities (Insider Dealing) Act 1985 and held that the word 'obtain' could cover information obtained passively, without purpose or effort. Lord Templeman said at p971:

> 'Parliament cannot have intended that a man who asks for information which he then misuses should be convicted of an offence while a man who, without asking, learns the same information which he also misuses should be acquitted.'

The wording of the new offences in s52 puts the matter beyond doubt by using the neutral word 'has'.

The defences

The defences to insider dealing are contained in s53 of the Act. For dealing and encouraging another to deal, the defences are very similar. They are:

'(a) that the insider did not at the time expect the dealing to result in a profit (or the avoidance of a loss) attributable to the price sensitive information, or
(b) that the insider at the time believed on reasonable grounds that the information had been or, in the case of encouraging, would be, disclosed widely enough to ensure that those dealing without the information would not be prejudiced, or
(c) that the insider would have done what he did even if he did not have the information.'

It will also be remembered that for the offence of disclosing the information, no offence is committed if disclosure is made in the proper performance of an employment, office or profession: s52(2)(b).

There are additional special defences in Schedule 1 of the Act covering market makers, market information and price stabilisation. It will be apparent from the wording of the defences that they are potentially very wide. Under the previous legislation it was decided in *R v Cross* (1990) 91 Cr App R 115 that the prosecution had to make out the elements of the offence and then the burden of proof shifts to the accused to prove, on a balance of probabilities, that a defence applies. The new regime does not alter this. The case itself involved a managing director who left a company while in possession of price sensitive information. The defendant argued that he did not use the information in order to make a profit or avoid a loss, but only dealt in its shares in order to satisfy a share option scheme, the terms of which required him to sell the shares within 30 days of leaving the company. This defence succeeded and the conviction was quashed. This defence would now, arguably, come within (c) above.

Penalties

The penalties are contained in s61 which makes insider dealing an either way offence. On summary conviction, the penalty is a fine not exceeding the statutory maximum and/or up to 6 months imprisonment. On conviction on indictment, the penalty is an unlimited fine and/or up to 7 years imprisonment. To date, only one offender has been sentenced to a term of imprisonment which was for 18 months with 9 months suspended.

Under the previous legislation, any transactions entered into were not void or even voidable by reason only that it was entered into on the basis of inside information. However, in *Chase Manhattan Equities Ltd v Goodman* [1991] BCLC 897, Knox J held that such a transaction is tainted with illegality and was unenforceable by the party convicted of insider dealing. Section 63(2) of the Act now provides that 'No contract shall be void or unenforceable' by reason only of an insider dealing offence. This would appear to make such contracts enforceable and reverse the *Chase Manhattan* decision.

Prosecution and investigation

Proceedings for offences under the Act can only be commenced by or with the consent of the Secretary of State or the Director of Public Prosecutions: s61(2). The wording of the section allows consent to be given to the Stock Exchange to commence proceedings. This is sensible since the monitoring and investigation of suspected insider dealing and the creation of false markets in shares is largely done by the Surveillance Department of the Stock Exchange.

Section 177(1) of the Financial Services Act 1986 provides:

> 'If it appears to the Secretary of State that there are circumstances suggesting that an offence under Part V of the Criminal Justice Act 1993 (insider dealing) may have been committed, he may appoint one or more competent inspectors to carry out such investigations as are requisite to establish whether or not any such contravention has occurred and to report the results of their investigation to him.'

The remainder of the section gives the inspectors extensive powers such as requiring any person to produce documents, attend before them, and also the power to examine any person under oath. Section 178 then sets out the penalties for failure to co-operate with s177 investigations.

These powers were recently applied in *Re an Inquiry under the Company Securities (Insider Dealing) Act 1985*. [1988] AC 660. In this case a journalist had published two articles in national newspapers which accurately predicted decisions of the Monopolies and Mergers Commission about take over bids. It was not suggested that the journalist was dealing as an insider, but it was suspected that there was perhaps an insider dealing ring in operation and that the journalist had received the information from the someone in the ring. Investigators were appointed under s177 FSA and asked him to reveal his source. He refused, relying on s10 of the Contempt of Court Act 1981, which does not make a journalist liable for contempt of court if he refuses to disclose his source, unless disclosure is 'necessary ... for the prevention ... of crime'. The House Lords held that disclosure was required by the journalist as prevention also embraced the detection and prosecution of crimes. He was fined £20,000 under s178 FSA as if he were in contempt of court.

Will the Act work?

Despite some important changes, which are to be welcomed, many of the problems which existed in the old legislation remain. The most quoted criticisms of the law on insider dealing are:

1. The Act only imposes criminal liability and it is very difficult to establish the high standard of proof. Short of an admission, it has proved to be very difficult to secure a conviction.
2. The number of prosecutions brought since 1980 has been disappointing, amounting to around 30 in number.
3. The legislation provides a potentially wide range of defences.
4. The wording of the Act is cumbersome and vague.
5. The courts do not treat 'white collar' crime as seriously as they should do. There is a feeling that the courts are 'too soft' on those convicted of insider dealing and this can be evidenced from the sentences that have been imposed to date.
6. There is no central agency charged with detecting and enforcing insider dealing.

10.3 Civil remedies

Why no civil remedy?

One of the main criticisms of the Act is that it is entirely criminal and does not contain a civil remedy. In 1989 the Department of Trade and Industry issued a consultative document entitled 'The Law on Insider Dealing'. In it, at paragraph 2.12, the reason for a lack of a civil remedy is clear:

> 'While there is at present no explicit civil remedy for insider trading it is however possible that, depending on the facts of the case, an action could be brought by the other party, eg for fraudulent misrepresentation, or by the company, eg for breach of fiduciary duty, or to enforce a duty to account to the company for the profits. The Government is not therefore at present convinced of the need to modify the law in this area.'

However, as will be seen below, this view is surely too simplistic and does not take into account the practical and legal difficulties involved. The possible civil remedies are discussed below.

Breach of fiduciary duty

Directors owe a range of fiduciary duties to their company (See paragraph 9.2 *The director's duties*). If they trade on inside information then they will probably be liable to the company for any profits they have made. Support for this view can be found in the case of *Industrial Development Consultants Ltd* v *Cooley* [1972] 1 WLR 443. In this case it will be recalled that Cooley was an architect and managing director of IDC. Cooley, on behalf of IDC, began negotiations with the Eastern Gas Board about designing and constructing new depots for them. After telling IDC that he was suffering from ill health, Cooley was released from his employment and then took the benefit of design and construction contracts with the Eastern Gas Board personally. Roskill J held that he was accountable to IDC for all the benefits he received under the contract with the Eastern Gas Board. Roskill J said:

[handwritten margin note: Enid]

> 'Information which came to him while he was managing director and which was of concern to the plaintiffs and was relevant for the plaintiffs to know, was information which it was his duty to pass on to the plaintiffs because between himself and the plaintiffs a fiduciary relationship existed.'

Although some commentators have questioned whether price affected information can be considered to be company property, the House of Lords decision in *Boardman* v *Phipps* [1967] 2 AC 46 appears to put the matter beyond doubt. However, on this point there was a strong dissenting speech by Lord Upjohn.

[handwritten margin note: Anna]

A practical difficulty in enforcing this remedy is that the company is not really the loser. It has suffered no loss as such and so it may have no incentive in pursuing the claim. A shareholder who feels aggrieved about the company's refusal to bring an action will no doubt be prevented from doing so himself under the rule in *Foss* v

Harbottle (1843) 2 Hare 461 (see paragraph 11.1 *Rule in Foss* v *Harbottle*), which will deny the shareholder locus standi to sue, in favour of the company which is the proper plaintiff in company litigation.

Directors only owe their fiduciary duty to the company. Therefore an action by a stranger, or another company in the group is not possible against a director who has used confidential information and made profit, or avoided a loss. It must also be remembered that the case of *Percival* v *Wright* [1902] 2 Ch 421 provides that the directors do not owe a fiduciary duty to the shareholders or a group of shareholders. The duty is owed to the company as a whole, that is, the general body of shareholders present and future. This case would seem to bar a claim against a director by a person to whom he had bought or sold the shares.

Anna Where a person other than a director deals on the basis of inside information, then they may be liable to account for their profits to the company on the basis that they hold the proceeds as a constructive trustee: *Belmont Finance Corpn Ltd* v *Williams Furniture Ltd (No 2)* [1981] 1 All ER 393. This principle, if applied, would cover tippees who receive the information from the director.

Misrepresentation

Whether a director could be made liable on the basis of an action for misrepresentation must be doubtful. Generally speaking the parties to a contract are under no duty to disclose all material facts, such as the inside information. Moreover, silence is not enough to amount to a representation. One way around this might be to extend the categories of contract which are said to be uberrimae fidei, that is, of the utmost good faith. The effect of such contracts is that there must be disclosure by both contracting parties of all material facts. Such an extension is unlikely.

Breach of confidence

It is often suggested that another remedy available to the company is an action against the director or other insiders for breach of confidence. It provides:

'... protection against the unauthorised disclosure or use of information which is of a confidential nature and which has been entrusted to a person in circumstances which impose an obligation to respect its confidentiality.': Law Commission Working Paper No 58, 'Breach of Confidence' (1974).

In *Coco* v *Clark (AN) Engineers Ltd* [1969] RPC 41 Megarry J, identified three conditions for a breach of confidence action:

1. the information must have the necessary quality of confidentiality about it;
2. it must have been disclosed in circumstances importing an obligation of confidence and;
3. there must be an unauthorised use of that information to the detriment of the person who disclosed the information.

Most of the breach of confidence cases have been concerned with the unauthorised use of trade secrets, but it is easy to see how this developing tort could be adapted to cases of insider dealing.

Section 35 Powers of the Criminal Courts Act 1973

Theoretically, the 'victim' of insider dealing could be awarded compensation by a court under the above Act. The compensation order is paid by the offender, the insider dealer, and made at the time of sentencing. The difficulty with this remedy is that: 'A compensation order is designed for the simple straight forward case where the amount of the compensation can be readily and easily ascertained.': *R* v *Donovan* (1981) 3 Cr App R 192, per Eveleigh LJ. In cases of insider dealing it may well be impossible to calculate the loss and the courts will not enter into a detailed enquiry.

Breach of statutory duty

The question to ask in the context of this possible head of civil liability is, can an infringement of the Criminal Justice Act 1993 also amount to a breach of statutory duty allowing a plaintiff to recover in tort for any loss caused as a result of the infringement? This is a firmly established remedy in the United States in cases of insider dealing but it is submitted that the English courts would be unwilling to entertain such an action here.

It is a matter of construction whether a criminal statute can also impose civil liability on a convicted person: *Cutler* v *Wandsworth Stadium Ltd* [1949] 1 All ER 544. As a general rule if, on its true construction, a statute provides for the enforcement of its provisions by criminal prosecutions then civil claims are not possible. However, in *Lonrho Ltd* v *Shell Petroleum Co Ltd* [1981] 2 All ER 456, Lord Diplock identified exceptions to this including where the provisions of the statute are for the benefit of a particular class of individuals. Is the Criminal Justice Act for the benefit of a particular class of individual? This remains to be seen but it is unlikely: see Hannigan, 'Insider Dealing' (1988) at p96 where the civil remedies for insider dealing are discussed at length.

Conclusion

The hurdles which have to be jumped before a conviction can be secured under the Act are daunting. Although the new provisions may have improved the position somewhat, the fact remains that many in the city (and elsewhere) believe that this is a crime which is going undetected. The difficulties of imposing criminal liability could be overcome by relying on the civil remedies. Here though, as we have seen, the civil remedies, such as they are, are not tailor made to the problem, so that any effective civil remedy should be provided for by Parliament. As Gower points out, *Principles of Modern Company Law*, 5th ed at p641,

> '... it would be a potent deterrent against insider dealing – and one which would cost the public funds little or nothing'.

Finally, two points must be made about the enormity of the problem of detection. First, the sheer volume of transactions that take place on the Stock Exchange and the USM make it difficult to spot insider dealing. In 1993, for example, 2,916,772 transactions were recorded. Secondly, a civil remedy may in practice be academic, as the victim would only rarely be able to link a sale or purchase by him to an identifiable buyer or seller. The Stock Exchange share transfer procedure (known as the TALISMAN system) would only identify SEPON LTD as the other party to the deal. (See paragraph 6.7 Stock Exchange transfer procedure.) This was in fact another reason why civil liability was not included in the legislation.

11

Minority Protection

11.1 Rule in *Foss* v *Harbottle*

11.2 Statutory rights of a minority

11.3 Inspections and investigations

11.1 Rule in *Foss* v *Harbottle*

Introduction: the general rule

Not infrequently, there will occur a breach of some duty owed to the company whether arising from statute, contract, tort or the fiduciary position of the party in breach. The duty may be owed by a third party, a director or other servant, or even perhaps by a member (eg in the unlikely case of his having to pay calls on shares not fully paid up). Since the duty breached is one owed to the company, which is a separate person in law, the company is the proper person to seek a remedy for the breach. Further, where the majority of members may ratify or excuse a breach, given that the will resides in the decisions of the majority, it would be futile (in the absence of fraud or other inequitable conduct) for the minority to litigate against the wishes of the majority. There is much to be said for the view that any action taken by the company must be taken via the methods provided by its constitutional structure and in that way only. Hence, the so-called rule in *Foss* v *Harbottle* (1843) 2 Hare 461, a case in which individual shareholders were ruled incompetent to bring an action against directors alleged to have misapplied company property, the company, as the victim of the alleged misdeeds, being the proper plaintiff to complain (see also paragraph 9.4 *Who may sue for breach of duty*).

Similarly, the court in *Mozley* v *Alston* (1847) 1 Ph 790 refused to grant to shareholders an injunction to restrain directors who were allegedly improperly appointed, from acting, for if the majority of shareholders wished to complain, they could act against the directors through the medium of the company.

The company will act through whichever of its organs has the authority to act in such situations. Usually the general meeting will have devolved this power on the board of directors. If so, the majority in general meeting cannot generally restrain or compel directors in the exercise of their powers of litigation: *John Shaw & Sons*

(Salford) Ltd v *Shaw* [1935] 2 KB 113 (see paragraph 8.2 *Control of the directors by a general meeting*). If, however, the directors refuse to do so they may sometimes (see paragraph 8.2 *When the general meeting can intervene*) decide to take (or discontinue) proceedings in the company's name: *Marshall's Valve Gear Co Ltd* v *Manning, Wardle & Co Ltd* [1909] 1 Ch 267. Where a company in general meeting resolved to discontinue an action for breach of contract (*Estmanco (Kilner House) Ltd* v *Greater London Council* [1982] 1 All ER 437) the court entertained a 'derivative action' (see below) by a minority shareholder to prevent those controlling the company from pursuing injurious policies. In *FFI Finance Ltd* v *Lady Kagan* (1982) 132 New LJ 830, the court at the suit of a shareholder, restrained directors from directing a plea of 'guilty' on behalf of the company to a conspiracy charge.

In *MacDougall* v *Gardiner* (1875) 1 Ch D 13, Mellish LJ pointed out that:

'holding that such suits must be brought in the name of the company does certainly greatly tend to stop litigation ... If the thing complained of is a thing which in substance the majority of the company are entitled to do, or if something has been done irregularly which the majority of the company are entitled to do regularly, or if something has been done illegally which the majority of the company are entitled to do legally, there can be no use in having a litigation about it, the ultimate end of which is only that a meeting has to be called, and then ultimately the majority gets its wishes.'

The rule, therefore, prevents each and every shareholder from taking whatever form of action he wishes whenever he wishes to complain of an alleged wrong by directors, servants or third parties, in situations where the company itself, either by decision of the board or a resolution of the general meeting, can decide whether or not to take action.

Of course, the rule in *Foss* v *Harbottle* contains seeds of potential injustice. Is the individual shareholder to be deprived by the company of insisting on his right to have its affairs conducted in accordance with the regulations? Can the company act capriciously in disregard of the interests of all but the majority shareholders? Can the directors, by decisions in board meetings and by their ability to control decisions of the general meetings (see above), treat the company as their own and act as they wish, taking account only of their own interests?

According to Jenkins LJ in *Edwards* v *Halliwell* [1950] 2 All ER 1064:

'The cases falling within the general ambit of the rule in *Foss* v *Harbottle* are subject to certain exceptions ...

1) in cases where the act complained of is wholly ultra vires the company ... the rule has no application because there is no question of the transaction being confirmed by any majority ...

2) where what has been done amounts to ... a fraud on the minority [see below] and the wrongdoers are themselves in control of the company, the rule is relaxed in favour of the aggrieved minority who are allowed to bring ... a minority shareholders' action on behalf of themselves and all others ...

3) the rule did not prevent an individual member from suing if the matter in respect of which he was suing was one which could validly be done or sanctioned, not by a simple majority of the members ... but only by some special majority as, for instance, ... a special resolution ...

4) [where the company] has invaded the individual rights of the complainant members, who are entitled to maintain themselves in full membership with all the rights and privileges appertaining to that status.'

Exceptions (1) and (3) recognise the inherent limits placed on the company, and therefore on the majority who control it, by general law, the contractual capacity of the company and its constitution. Exception (2) raises complicated issues which are considered at length later (see paragraphs 4.3 and 11.1). Exception (4) is also a limitation of majority powers by safeguarding 'individual rights' of members. The problem here is to know what is meant by 'individual rights' (see paragraph 11.1 *The personal action*). Certainly they are rights against the company. The borderline case is the member's interest in having the company's affairs managed in accordance with its constitution. *MacDougall* v *Gardiner* above denies to the individual member personal rights of that kind against the company, and the majority. Some authorities, however (Wedderburn (1957) CLJ 194 and (1958) CLJ 93), argue that a member has a contractual right in this field since the memorandum and articles are declared by s14 to be a contract between members and the company.

The general principle underlying the exceptions is that a member may take legal proceedings only in situations where the majority decision is not binding on him. However, the cases (*Hogg* v *Cramphorn* [1967] Ch 254 and *Bamford* v *Bamford* [1970] Ch 212 on directors' irregular allotment of shares conflict with that principle. In those cases the court gave a hearing to members' objections but ruled that any irregularity could be put right by approval in general meeting. These were sensible but anomalous decisions arising from the application of a different principle, ie the power – in some instances – of a general meeting to ratify an irregular action of the directors (see paragraph 9.4 *Relief from liability*).

For an example of an allegation which could not be seen as an allegation within the exceptions to the rule in *Foss* v *Harbottle*, see *Re Downs Wine Bar Ltd* [1990] BCLC 839.

Derivative and representative actions

The derivative action
Here the plaintiff's right of action derives from that of the company.

An individual shareholder may be permitted to vindicate the rights of himself and other potentially aggrieved shareholders, in a situation in which they are complaining of a detriment suffered by themselves as members of the company (the real plaintiff) at the hands of those in control of the company. Such actions are brought by way of exception (2) in Jenkins LJ's list, supra. In *Prudential Assurance Co Ltd* v *Newman Industries Ltd (No 2)* [1981] Ch 257 it was held that a derivative action was appropriate where the board of a company was under the control of directors abusing their powers and that whether or not a derivative action could be brought should be tried, if possible, as a preliminary issue. In *Estmanco* (see above) the disputed decision was that of the majority shareholders. In both these cases it was doubted whether the 'demands of justice' were a practical test as to whether a derivative action should be allowed contrary to the rule in *Foss* v *Harbottle*, rather they are a reason for making an exception to the rule (paragraphs 4.3 and 11.1).

Derivative actions are brought by and on behalf of aggrieved members against the other members, other persons at fault and the company (so that all will be bound by the court's decision).

Provided the relevant organ of the company has not decided not to sue by a majority which is independent of the wrongdoers, the action may be allowed to proceed and the plaintiffs will be entitled to an indemnity from the company for the costs of the suit, although they should secure their position by applying first to a Master to sanction the proceedings; *Wallersteiner* v *Moir* (No 2) [1975] 1 All ER 849; 40 Conv 51.

As may be apparent from Chapters 5 and 9, an action is more likely in the case of alleged breach of fiduciary duty by directors or promoters than for negligence. As their duties of care are so undeveloped, it is not surprising that there has been little litigation on the question of negligence in this context. What little authority there is, however, decides, despite s310, that an action for negligence will not lie in these circumstances: *Pavlides* v *Hensen* [1956] Ch 565; (1956) 19 MLR 538; cf. *Heyting* v *Dupont* [1964] 1 WLR 843. Negligent acts may, of course, be ratified by general meeting.

In *Daniels* v *Daniels* [1978] 2 All ER 89; (1978) 41 MLR 569; [1979] Conv 47 (see paragraph 9.3 *Prohibition of personal gain by directors*) a minority shareholder was held entitled to sue for a breach of duty by directors and majority shareholders to the detriment of the company and the benefit of the directors where those directors had sold company property to a director at an under-valuation. This has been welcomed as evidence of judicial willingness to allow an action for negligence but the case itself does not go further than to condemn the obtaining of a personal advantage from the position of directors. Earlier authorities on the rule in *Foss* v *Harbottle* are usefully reviewed in *Daniels*.

In *Fargo* v *Godfrey* (1986) 130 SJ 524 it was decided that a minority shareholder could seek leave to sue in the company's name where that company was in liquidation and where he claimed that the directors of the company had embezzled the company's funds.

The representative action

In this type of action a member sues as representative of members or a class. The proprietary rights of members are rights of participation in the company, so the courts are reluctant to allow representative actions. In *Hogg* v *Cramphorn Ltd* [1967] Ch 254 (see paragraph 9.3 *Exercise of powers for proper purpose*) a minority shareholder maintained a representative action in respect of a defensive issue of shares; but the case was adjourned to give the company the opportunity to ratify the issue. In the *Prudential Assurance* case the Court of Appeal rejected the argument that the plaintiff was entitled to bring a representative action because the profitability of its shares was diminished. Those losses were primarily the company's losses.

However, where a number of individual members have the right to bring personal actions, one may (but need not) sue in a representative capacity on behalf of himself and the others.

The personal action *by Peter as a ~~member~~ shareholder*

It may happen that, whatever the causes (eg whether it be through the machinations of the directors and/or the general meeting), (the company improperly acts in disregard of the personal rights of a member. It may have acted contrary to its articles or failed to conform with a statutory resolution procedure. It may have acted illegally or ultra vires (see exception (1) in *Edwards* v *Halliwell* (above)).

see p. 257 ← arbitration refusal gives rise to a personal action by Peter

In such a case, the member may be able personally to sue the company.) Thus in *Pender v Lushington* (1877) 6 Ch D 70 the court enjoined the directors from acting on the basis of a resolution not having been carried because votes attached to the plaintiff's nominee shareholdings were improperly rejected. The plaintiff sued in a representative capacity but it was held that he could sue personally in respect of his individual right to have his vote recorded.

(In *Baillie* v *Oriental Telephone Co Ltd* [1915] 1 Ch 503 a member's application succeeded to restrain a company from putting into effect a resolution for which insufficient notice had been given.) *Written res. in Peter's case perhaps insufficient notice applies*

It is, however, possible that the member's ability to exercise his rights may be overtaken by the company acting to correct its previous action (cf *Hogg* v *Cramphorn Ltd* (above)).

Expropriation of the company's property

In the ordinary course a company will assert its rights to its property against anyone who damages or deprives the company of it, unless litigation is judged unprofitable – a matter for decision within the company under its constitution (see paragraph 11.1 *Introduction: the general rule*). If, however, those who have appropriated the property are also in control of the company they will ensure that it does not assert its rights against them. Here 'the claims of justice' should be 'superior to any difficulties arising out of technical rules': per Wigram V-C in *Foss* v *Harbottle*.

The principle is readily understood but is not always easy to apply. It is reconciled with the principle of majority control by a doctrine that a shareholder's vote must be disregarded in so far as it is used to protect his own fraud against the company and other members. A number of points must be established to bring this principle into operation.

Company property

In applying the rule the property of the company is deemed to include not only its existing assets but also the benefit of profitable contracts. For that reason majority votes in general meeting to disclaim any interest of the company in contracts diverted to its majority shareholders have been treated as invalid: *Menier v Hooper's Telegraph Works* (1874) 9 Ch App 350; *Cook v Deeks* [1916] 1 AC 554. Assets would also include any appropriation of property by selling company property at an undervalue (as in *Daniels v Daniels* [1978] 2 All ER 89 (see paragraph 9.3 *Prohibition of personal gain by directors*) or buying it an an excessive price. Any device for 'milking' company assets is an appropriation of them.

Appropriation by the majority

If company property is transferred, eg by sale at an undervalue, to a third party and not to the controlling majority, then clearly it is not a case of expropriation by the controlling majority for their own benefit, which is the basis of the right of objection given to the minority: *Pavlides v Jensen* [1956] 2 All ER 518. The company may of course have grounds for suing the directors for negligence or failure to discharge their duty in respect of the company's property: *Gibb*'s case in paragraph 9.4 *The nature of the remedy*. However, the decision whether to take such proceedings must be taken within the company by majority vote if appropriate and not by minority appeal to the court.

On the other hand the word 'fraud' (as in 'fraud on a minority' or 'fraud on the company' which are applied to these cases) does not require that the majority shall have had any dishonest intent. In the *Daniels* case above the directors had sold property at an undervalue to one of themselves but the pleadings did not allege fraud. On the contrary the company had purchased the property at probate value from the estate of a deceased shareholder and then re-sold it at the same price. If the case had gone to a full trial (none such is reported) it might have been argued in their defence that failure to have the property revalued before selling it was negligence rather than fraud. However, the court held that any transaction in company property by which the controlling shareholders obtained a benefit to themselves fell within the scope of a minority shareholder's right of objection: at all events he was entitled to have the issue investigated at a full trial, *Pavlides* case was distinguished.

Control

Peter can sue as shareholder, board of directors for C's gifts

The justification for making an exception to the principle of majority control in these situations is that those who have appropriated company property may by their control prevent the company from calling them to account. Where a resolution is passed in general meeting to approve what has been done (as in *Cook v Deeks* above) or where the register of members discloses a clear majority (as in *Pavlides* case) the existence of voting control is indisputable.

However, members sometimes cast their votes at general meetings on the basis of information supplied by the directors. In this way a fraudulent minority of shareholders who are also dirctors may be able to attract the support of other shareholders who are not parties to their fraud on the company. That seems to have been the situation in *Atwool v Merryweather* (1867) LR 5 Eq 464 though there were additional reasons for permitting the action against the promoter/directors to continue.

[handwritten margin note: Directors + fraud gifts]

The same issue of 'de facto control' by a combination of minority shareholding and supply of management information to the board of directors and then to the general meeting arose in *Prudential Assurance Co Ltd* v *Newman Industries Ltd (No 2)* (1981) above. In the High Court action Vinelott J was disposed to accept that facts of this kind constituted a sufficient degree of control, ie ability to influence the outcome of a general meeting. However, the Court of Appeal, in a judgment which has been much criticised, overruled this finding. The Appeal Court's reasons were that, when the issue of control or no control is raised as a preliminary point to decide whether it is a case which should proceed to full trial of the alleged misconduct by the majority, the court cannot readily investigate the alleged misinformation of shareholders nor, in fairness to the defendant, should it assume that it existed without proof.

The Court of Appeal suggested that when confronted with allegations of this kind, the court should adjourn the case so that a general meeting may be held at which the truth or falsity of the allegations may be considered by shareholders. It might well lead to the enforced disclosure of relevant facts previously withheld from members. However, a general meeting, probably acrimonious, is not a useful forum for investigation of complicated and disputed facts.

At all events this decision seems to establish that control means having a firm majority of votes. However, Sir Mervyn Davies in *Barrett* v *Duckett & Ors* [1993] BCC 778 held that a 50 per cent shareholder who was complaining about the behaviour of the other 50 per cent shareholder/director, was a minority shareholder for the purposes of a derivative action. The matter is now much less important than it was because the statutory remedy (s459 in paragraph 11.2) has now displaced the common law 'fraud on a minority' avenue into a court hearing for a dissatisfied minority.

The final nail in the coffin of minority shareholder actions under the common law might well be the decision in *Smith* v *Croft (No 2)* [1988] Ch 114. Knox J, held that it is necessary to go beyond establishing wrongdoer control, and see what the views of the majority within the minority are. If the majority of the independent minority shareholders do not want to bring proceedings then the action should be struck out. This decision, if followed, would appear to place yet another hurdle in the way of minority actions and once again illustrates the reluctance of the courts to interfere with company management.

Exoneration of breach of duty

The 'fraud' of which the minority complains is usually an act of the directors, since the management of the company is in their hands. The directors are likely to be controlling shareholders or elected to office by controlling shareholders to represent them (as in *Pavlides* case). A transaction by which the directors wrongly dispose of the company's assets is a breach of the director's fiduciary duty: *Cradock*'s case in paragraph 9.3 *Prohibition of personal gain by directors* and *Daniel*'s case above). Is the majority competent to exonerate the directors from liability by passing a resolution in general meeting to approve what they have done? No. The normal power (see paragraph 9.4 *Relief from liability*) to ratify irregular acts of directors does not extend to fraud in which the majority itself is implicated: *Cook* v *Deeks* in paragraph 11.1 *Expropriation of the company's property*.

11.2 Statutory rights of a minority

Specific statutory rights

In addition to the common law rights of a minority to seek a remedy in the courts against a majority which is abusing its position (see paragraph 11.1) a single member or a prescribed proportion or number of members have a number of statutory rights to bring a specific grievance or objection before the courts. These include:

1. the right of a 15 per cent minority to appeal against an alteration of the objects clause (s5) (see paragraph 4.1 *Alteration of the objects*) or a variation of class rights (s127) (see paragraph 3.1 *Variation of class rights – statutory right of objection*);
2. the right of a 10 per cent minority to apply to the court to cancel a special resolution passed to authorise financial asistance by a private company for the purchase of its own shares (s157 (see paragraph 6.4 *Financial assistance by a company for the purchase of its own shares*) and the right of any member to appeal to the court against a special resolution to resort to capital in payment for the company's own shares (s176) (see paragraph 6.4 *Resort to capital in redemption or purchase of shares*);
3. the right of a 5 per cent minority (or at least 50 members) to apply for cancellation of a special resolution to re-register a public company as private (s54) (see paragraph 1.4 *Re-registration of a public company as private*);
4. the right of a member to present a petition to the court for the compulsory winding up of the company: Insolvency Act 1986 s122 (see paragraph 13.3 *Grounds for compulsory liquidation*).

A 10 per cent minority of members may also requisition a general meeting of the company (s368) (see paragraph 8.1 *Persons able to convene meetings*) or require a public company to exercise its powers to investigate ownership of its shares (s214) (see paragraph 6.6 *Interests in shares*). Various specified proportions of members may apply for a Department of Trade investigation of the affairs of the company or the ownership of its shares (ss431 and 442) (paragraph 11.3).

A minority of 5 per cent (or 100 members) may require the company to introduce business into the notice of an AGM or to issue their circular on general meeting business: s376 (see paragraph 8.1 *Notice of meetings*).

Where a special or extraordinary resolution is prescribed by statute or by the articles, members who hold more than 25 per cent of the voting shares have a veto (see paragraph 8.1 *Types of resolution*). All members have extensive rights to information (see paragraph 3.2) about the company, and in particular to receive a copy of each year's annual accounts (s240) (see paragraph 14.1 *Duties with respect to accounts*). Many transactions of the company, especially those in which a director has a personal interest, require approval by resolution in general meeting (see paragraph 9.1 *Directors' transactions*). The disclosures incidental to seeking that approval may enable a minority to attract the support of other members so as to reject the proposal before the meeting.

The above summary is not completely exhaustive but will serve to illustrate the widespread, and increasing, range of rights given by statute to shareholders who are a minority of the members.

The development of the general statutory protection of a minority

Until 1948 a minority had to resort to the tortuous common law remedies (see paragraphs 4.3 and 11.1) available in case of abuse of their position by the majority. Apart from the technical and procedural difficulties, a minority might well be frustrated by a general assertion that the majority had acted in good faith in the use of their votes and so could not be called to account. The *Greenhalgh* saga (and the other cases cited in paragraph 4.3 *Discrimination against a minority*) are illustrations of that.

The Cohen Committee (Report of the Committee on Company Law Amendment Cmd 6659 of 1945) therefore recommended (para 60) that the law should give to the court, in hearing a petition for winding up on the just and equitable ground (see above) 'the power to impose upon the parties to a dispute whatever settlement the court considers just and equitable'. This was to be an alternative to making an order for winding up and so it would only be available if grounds for such an order existed and winding up was not the most appropriate remedy. This recommendation was enacted as s210 of the Companies Act 1948.

For various reasons s210 failed to provide the relief which had been intended. It was therefore replaced in 1980 (s75 of the Companies Act 1980 now re-enacted as ss459–461) by more flexible provisions. In particular the remedy may be sought without showing that grounds existed for winding up the company, the petition may be based upon a single act or omission, and the test of oppression of members was replaced by unfair prejudice. It is, however, still necessary to show that the petitioner, or those whom he represents, have been affected in their capacity of members.

As a result of these changes there has been, since 1981, a flow of petitions seeking relief. In dealing with them the courts have been able to develop a coherent and more detailed set of guidelines for the use of their discretionary powers.

Unfair prejudice — Peter's shareholding (shareholder)

Under s210 of the 1948 Act it was necessary to prove 'oppressive conduct of the company's affairs' over a period of time. 'Oppressive' was judicially interpreted to mean 'burdensome, harsh and wrongful': *Scottish Cooperative Wholesale Society* v

Meyer [1959] AC 324. Again 'oppression must import that the oppressed are being constrained to submit to something which is unfair to them as a result of some overbearing act on the part of the oppressor': *Re Jermyn Street Turkish Baths* [1971] 1 WLR 1047. In *Meyer's* case the controlling shareholder had diverted business away from the company to its own enterprise so as to deprive the minority of the profits which that business would have brought to the joint company. Oppression meant the deliberate exploitation of majority control to damage the minority and a disregard of their legitimate rights and expectations.

It is generally considered that the courts have a wide discretion to interpret 'unfair prejudice' in relation to the facts of each case. However, there is general acceptance of the basic test laid down in *Re Bovey Hotel Ventures Ltd* (1981)(unreported decision of the Court of Appeal) and cited in *Re R A Noble (Clothing) Ltd* [1983] BCLC 273

> 'if he can show that the value of his shareholding in the company has been seriously diminished or at least seriously jeopardised by reason of a course of conduct of those persons who have had de facto control of the company, which is unfair to the member concerned.'

In *Re Soundcraft Magnetics Ltd, ex parte Nicholas* [1993] BCLC 360 the Court of Appeal decided that the withholding of money owed to a subsidiary company by a parent company that exercised financial control over it constituted acts done in the conduct of the subsidiary's affairs for the purposes of s459 of the 1985 Act. However, although serious damage was thereby caused to the subsidiary, the acts were not unfairly prejudicial because the parent company withheld the payments in order to secure its own survival. It was, said Fox LJ, a price that the subsidiary had to pay.

Directors' negligence

The courts have taken the view that a shareholder must take the risk that the directors and the management of the company may turn out to be of poor quality. They have also been very reluctant to concern themselves with examining commercial decisions that have been taken by the directors, for judges are ill qualified to do this. In *Re Sam Weller and Sons Ltd* [1990] Ch 682 at 694, Peter Gibson J said that he had no doubt that a court would ordinarily be very reluctant to accept that managerial decisions could amount to unfairly prejudicial conduct. So, it was thought that if directors failed in their duty of care, this could not form the basis of a s459 petition. *Gore-Browne on Companies* (44th edn, 1986), vol 2, p28.021 does not put the matter so definitively, saying:

> 'Another aspect of the enforcement of directors' duties by means of a petition under section 459 which remains unclear is the directors' duty of care. It would seem that the Jenkins Committee intended that the reformed statutory remedy might be used in this regard, although the courts decided otherwise in the case of the old section 210.'

The reference to the old case law under s210 supports this view. In *Re Five Minute Car Wash Service Ltd* [1966] 1 All ER 242, decided under the 'oppression' test of s210 of the 1948 Act, it was held that allegations that the chairman and managing director had carried out their duties in an unwise, inefficient and careless manner, could not, without more, amount to oppressive conduct.

In *Re Elgindata Ltd* [1991] BCLC 959, a case decided under s459, allegations of bad management against a director again failed. The petition was ultimately successful though, as the director had used assets of the company for his personal benefit and for the benefit of his family and friends.

While mismanagement may well be conduct which is prejudicial conduct in the interests of the company's members, it is not regarded as being unfair. The point has already been made that this a risk which the shareholders run, when investing in a company.

In the recent case of *Re Macro (Ipswich) Ltd & Anor* [1994] BCC 781, Arden J has held, for the first time, that mismanagement is capable of amounting to unfairly prejudicial conduct. The business of the company was that of landlords of residential property and garages. The petitioner alleged that the sole director and majority shareholder managed the company inadequately by:

1. failing to attend to the affairs of the company during the winter period;
2. between the mid 1930s to 1987 wasting money on building repairs and committing the company to poor lettings;
3. receiving commissions from 1979 to 1988 from builders which he failed to account to the company; and
4. currently leaving the property management to an inexperienced employee.

The court ordered the purchase of the petitioners shares, but the judge declined to appoint another director, as she felt that it would make matters worse, rather than resolving the dispute between the parties.

As the judgement of the case shows, however, the mismanagement must be sufficiently serious. On this point, and relying heavily on *Re Elgindata*, Arden J, said:

> 'With respect to alleged mismanagement, the court does not interfere in questions of commercial judgment, such as would arise here if (for example) it were alleged that the companies should invest in commercial properties rather than residential properties. However, in cases where what is shown is mismanagement, rather than a difference of opinion on the desirability of particular commercial decisions, and the mismanagement is sufficiently serious to justify the intervention by the court, a remedy is available under s459.'

See Chapter 15, paragraph 15.8, for further details.

The decision is a significant extension of conduct which may fall within s459, but it should not come as too much of a surprise. The possibility of serious mismanagement, as opposed to poor management, amounting to unfairly prejudicial conduct, had been alluded to before in the mismanagement cases on s459. It was probably only a matter of time before such conduct was found to be sufficiently serious.

Directors' breach of duty

A majority can usually relieve directors of liability for breach of their duty to the company, unless there has been fraud (see paragraphs 9.4 *Relief from liability* and 11.1 *Exoneration of breach of duty*). This does not of itself constitute 'unfair prejudice' to a dissenting minority. But on facts which are a ratifiable breach of duty by the directors is capable of constituting unfair prejudice: *Re A Company* (No 005287 of 1985) [1986] 1 WLR 281. The same case also decided that an action might proceed although the defendant had disposed of his shares and so was no longer a member.

A proposed sale of a company's business at an undervalue to a company wholly owned and controlled by the directors will be restrained by injunction in s459 proceedings brought by a minority shareholder: *Re Mountforest Ltd* [1993] BCC 570.

Members' interests affected

It was decided under s210 of the 1948 Act that a petition may not be founded on the adverse effects of management decisions on the position of a member in some other capacity, such as employee of the company (*Elder* v *Elder and Watson Ltd* 1952 SC 49) or as its creditor for an unpaid debt: *Re Bellador Silk Ltd* [1965] 1 All ER 667. It seems from the passage quoted above that 'unfair prejudice' must affect the petitioner as member by reason of the fall in the value of his shares. This was explicitly stated in *Re A Company* [1983] Ch 178. However, the courts are disposed to interpret the statutory phrase 'interests of members' to include matters incidental to being a shareholder, even 'the legitimate expectation that he would continue to be employed as a director': *Re A Company* (No 00477 of 1986) (1986) 2 BCC 9, 171. However this interpretation would not extend to a directorship of a public company (*Re Blue Arrow* [1987] BCLC 585) nor to a case where the underlying motive is to extract financial compensation for loss of office: *Re A Company* (No 003843 of 1986) [1987] BCLC 562.

In *Re Tottenham Hotspur plc* [1994] 1 BCLC 655, it was held that a public limited company did not have a legitimate expectation that its owner and controller, the football manager Mr Terry Venables, would participate in the management of Tottenham Hotspur plc, after he was removed as its chief executive. It was argued that this expectation arose out of an oral agreement between the two joint shareholders, Mr Venables, and the entrepreneur, Mr Alan Sugar, who were also both directors. The court rejected this argument. Sir Donald-Nicholls V-C said:

> 'But nothing was disclosed which would suggest to anybody that Mr Venables's rights in relation to his appointment as chief executive were regulated by anything other then the company's constitution and the formal legal documents. There was nothing to suggest that the board of directors did not have the normal right to "hire and fire" the company's chief executive, or, that there was an agreement or understanding that, if Mr Sugar and Mr Venables should fall out, they were nevertheless bound to continue to support each other indefinitely ...'

See Chapter 15, paragraph 15.8, for further details.

The case supports the view that s459 may not be a very effective remedy in the case of a public limited company. In such cases, the courts will probably take the view that investors are entitled to assume that there are no other agreements and expectations in existence, other than those contained in the company's constitution and other documents made available to them.

All or some members

Section 459 requires that the petitioner shall demonstrate prejudice 'to the interests of some part of the members (including at least himself)'. On a strict construction this phrase might exclude a case, most likely to arise in a large public company, where all the members have suffered prejudice by reason of mismanagement by the directors: *Re A Company* (No 00370 of 1987) [1988] BCLC 570 (but the 1989 Act disposes of this point). It is immaterial that the directors may not have voting control of the company since s459 does not limit its remedy to prejudice inflicted by a controlling majority. The formula quoted above refers to 'persons who have de facto control' and that would cover the position of directors in relation to the large and inactive membership of a public company. It is generally considered that 'some part of the members' should be deemed to include all the members in such cases.

The petitioner's grievance must of course be more than a dispute over company policy and management arrangements. The following cases illustrate this point:

1. *Jermyn Street Turkish Baths* case above. There had been two shareholders, one of whom had been guarantor of the company's bank overdraft at the time of his death. Thereafter the controlling shareholder had restored the financial position of the company and enabled it to pay off the overdraft. She had allotted more shares to herself and under a pre-agreed formula most of the profits went to her as management commission. No dividends were paid. This was not 'oppression' of the estate of the deceased shareholder and it would almost certainly not be treated as 'unfair prejudice'. In its decision the court took account of the benefit to the executors of the deceased member by the extinction of their liability under the guarantee.

2. *Noble Clothing* case above. There were two shareholder/directors, one of whom provided most of the capital and the other managed the company's business. It was agreed between them that the managing director would consult the other (the petitioner) over important matters of policy. But he failed to do so and the other appeared for some time to acquiesce. Then they quarrelled and the petitioner alleged that lack of agreed consultation was 'unfair prejudice'. His petition was dismissed.

3. *Re A Company* [1983] 2 All ER 36. The executors of a deceased shareholder proposed that the company should apply its surplus funds to purchase of the shares of the deceased, since they urgently needed the money to support dependants of the deceased. The directors, however, used the money to diversify the business. This was not unfair prejudice to the minority. However an unduly restrictive policy over a long period in distributing profits as dividends may amount to unfair prejudice: *Re A Company* (No 00823 of 1987) (1989) The Times 26 July.

4. *Re Carrington Viyella plc* (1983) 1 BCC 98. The petition was founded on the company's failure to approve the chairman's long-term service agreement under s319 (see paragraph 9.1 *Directors as employees*) and failure of the controlling shareholder to comply with an undertaking given to the DTI (to induce it not to refer a matter to the Monopolies Commission). Neither of these defaults was considered to be 'unfair prejudice' (nor would it be in the sense adopted in the later decisions above).

5. *Re A Company* (No 00789 of 1987) [1990] BCLC 384. Shares had been created at an extraordinary general meeting called without proper notice. Harman J decided that the creation of the shares was ineffective and unfairly prejudicial to the interests of those who had spent money on them. The controlling shareholder was ordered to sell his shares to a subscriber for the new shares.

Fault on both sides

On the other hand a petition may succeed even though the petitioner is somewhat at fault so that, in terms of equity, he does not come to the court 'with clean hands'. In *Re London School of Electronics Ltd* [1986] Ch 211 the petitioner had alleged that the other director/shareholders had diverted part of the company's business to themselves, thereby depriving him of participation in a substantial part of the profits. They had responded by removing him from his directorship. He had then set up his own school and enrolled students of the joint company. In spite of this conduct he was entitled to relief.

Single event

Section 459 provides that 'any actual or proposed act or omission' of the company or on its behalf may be unfairly prejudicial. This form of words is wider than s210 of the 1948 Act, which confined petitions to cases where the grounds alleged were 'conduct' of the company's affairs over a period, so that a petition could not be based on a single decision of the company management: *Elder*'s case above. Under s459 either sustained conduct or a single act or omission may be the basis of the petition. For example, in *Re Milgate Developments Ltd* [1991] BCC 24 it appeared that there was a dispute between individual shareholders. In response to a petition under s459, the petitioner was granted an order restraining the other shareholders from causing the company to be represented in the litigation on the basis that the company's money should not be spent on litigation between shareholders. This decision was followed in *Re A Company* (No 004502 of 1988), *ex parte Johnson* [1991] BCC 234.

Who may petition?

The right to present a petition under s459 is limited to:

1. a member of the company (which includes a person who, with his consent, has been included on the company's register of members: *Re Nuneaton Borough*

Association Football Club Ltd [1989] BCLC 454), and any person to whom a member's shares have been transmitted by operation of law, ie the personal representatives of a deceased member and the trustee of a bankrupt member; and

2. the DTI following the submission of a report under s437 by inspectors appointed to investigate the company's affairs (and some related matters which may arise in the course of investigation): s460 (see paragraph 11.3).

The court's powers   *relief for Peter as member = arbitration*
shareholder
clause + shares being diluted

If the court is of the opinion that the company's affairs are being conducted in a manner unfairly prejudicial to the interests of some part of the members, then the court may make such order as it thinks fit for giving relief (s461(1)), for example:

1. it may be to regulate the conduct of the company's affairs in the future. In *Re H R Harmer Ltd* [1959] 1 WLR 62 the respondent was removed from his position as chairman and managing director and employed as consultant only and the court ordered that he should not interfere with the affairs of the company except in accordance with the board's decisions;
2. it may require the company to refrain from some act;
3. it may authorise proceedings to be brought in the name and on behalf of the company by some person;
4. it may require the purchase of the shares of any members of the company by other members or by the company. In *Scottish Cooperative Wholesale Society* v *Meyer* (above) the respondents were ordered to purchase the petitioner's shares. The court fixed the price with an element of compensation for the loss caused by the respondent's conduct.
5. it may order the transfer of a shareholding on condition that loans paid to the company by the shareholder be repaid by the person acquiring the interest: *Re Nuneaton Borough Association Football Club Ltd (No 2)* [1991] BCC 44.

Where an order of the court makes an addition to or alteration of the company's memorandum or articles, the company cannot make a further alteration to them inconsistent with the order, save with leave of the court: s461(3) (see paragraph 4.1 *Alteration of the objects*). An office copy of such an order must be delivered to the registrar for registration: s461(5).

The petitioner should specify in his petition the type of relief which he seeks. The court, although it has unfettered discretion, will not decide what relief is most appropriate in response to a petition for 'such relief as the court deems just': *Re Antigen Laboratories Ltd* [1951] All ER 110.

In making an order for the purchase of the petitioner's shares the court has to consider how they are to be valued in fixing the price. In a normal valuation of a minority shareholding the valuer values the company as a whole and then makes some deduction from the proportionate value of the minority holding because it does not carry control. The court has unfettered discretion in deciding whether to follow that practice. If the petitioner had been at fault, it might do so. In the more usual case where he has solid grounds for alleging unfair prejudice, the court is more likely to order valuation on a strictly proportionate ratio to the value of the whole company, without deduction for lack of control: *Re Bird Precision Bellows Ltd* [1984] Ch 419.

If there is an independent valuer the court may prefer to leave him to decide on the basis of valuation: *Re Boswell & Co (Steels) Ltd* (1989) 5 BCC 105. If purchase at a fair value has been offered to the petitioner, the court will not allow him to use disputes on the formula to exert pressure on the majority: *Re A Company* (No 0006834 of 1988) (1989) 5 BCC 218.

If the articles provide for the sale at a fair value of the shares of a director who vacates office, the court is disposed to uphold this as a pre-agreed and fair solution: *Re A Company* (No 004377 of 1986) [1987] BCLC 94.

In s459 proceedings, unless there are the most compelling circumstances proven by cogent evidence, a court is unlikely to consent to active participation and expenditure by the company. Where the petitioner seeks relief which does not require the company to do, or omit doing anything, then if the directors commit the company to participate, they may be liable for any costs incurred in the participation: *Re a Company* (No 001126 of 1992) [1993] BCC 325.

In *Supreme Travels Ltd* v *Little Olympian Each-Ways Ltd & Ors* [1994] BCC 947, the court had to decide whether or not to add a non member as a respondent to a s459 action. It was held that the wording of s459 was wide enough to encompass a non-member as a respondent, but that this would not be ordered where the likelihood of relief sought being ordered was so remote as to amount to an abuse of process. On the facts, this was such a case and the court refused to grant the application. See Chapter 15, paragraph 15.8, for further details.

Is there an effective remedy?

Almost all the cases on the reformulated statutory remedy, introduced in 1980, have related to disputes within small private companies of a quasi-partnership type. In these situations the court can apply its discretion to a clear-cut issue of personal interests and relationships. There must always be some doubt, until the case comes to court, as to how the court will view the facts of the dispute in relation to the concept of unfair prejudice. Subject to that, the petitioner with a good case will usually obtain a remedy avoiding the procedural and technical difficulties of the common law (see paragraphs 4.3 and 11.1). In particular, if he wishes to sue the directors or controlling shareholders for wrong done or loss caused to the company, he can simply ask the court in its discretion to authorise him to do so (at the company's expense).

The situation as regards mismanagement of public companies by their directors, as in the *Prudential* (see paragraph 11.1 *Expropriation of the company's property*) and *Carrington Viyella* cases (see paragraph 11.2 *Unfair prejudice*) is less satisfactory. On the authority of the *Prudential* case it must be inferred that the court will not recognise de facto control by the directors through their management powers, if they are not also controlling shareholders, which is unlikely in such cases. *Carrington*

Viyella shows that mismanagement which does not have a demonstrable effect on the value of shareholdings, will not be within the ambit of relief under s459.

11.3 Inspections and investigations

Supervision by public bodies

Before coming to investigations by or under the auspices of the DTI it is useful to consider the wider context of investor protection of which they are part.

In 1984 Professor LCB Gower's *Review of Investor Protection* (Cmnd 9125 of 1984), commissioned by the DTI, recommended bringing all forms of investor protection in financial markets into one system, with a statutory basis but still preserving the practice of 'self-regulation' under rules of autonomous bodies such as the Stock Exchange. The Financial Services Act 1986 is the legal framework of the new system.

The wide statutory powers of the DTI have been delegated to a Securities and Investments Board (SIB), whose members representing different elements of the financial system, are appointed jointly by the DTI and the Governor of the Bank of England: FSA Sch. 7 para 1. The SIB in turn gives formal recognition, and power to regulate the conduct of their own members, to a number of Self Regulating Organisations (SRO). One of the most important among the SRO is the Securities Association, formed by the Stock Exchange and the International Securities Organisation (ISRO). The SIB monitors the rules and practice of each SRO and would withdraw its recognition from any SRO which permitted abuses or unsatisfactory practices to prevail among its members by its failure to take effective disciplinary action.

The functions of the Stock Exchange in connection with listed companies have already been described in connection with those prospectus issues (see Chapter 2 para 2.3) which lead on to an official Stock Exchange listing of company securities. It is much more than a system of regulating the market in listed securities. A listed company must undertake to comply with the 'Continuing Obligations' specified, in much detail, in the Stock Exchange handbook, known colloquially as 'the Yellow Book' (see paragraph 5.2 *The control of listed securities*). If it failed to observe these requirements the company would lose its listing. Compliance requires elaborate disclosure of information and prevents or restricts a number of questionable internal management practices. In this way the market discipline imposed by the Stock Exchange produces stricter and more orderly practice within companies.

Within a company an individual shareholder, or group of shareholders, has a variety of forms of 'minority protection' (see paragraph 11.2) given by law.

The system of DTI investigation of companies, large or small, is a much older procedure, which originated in the mid-nineteenth century. It still has a role, and the relevant powers and procedures, as described below, are part of the Companies Act 1985. Its essential basis is the responsibility of the DTI for the general supervision of registered companies (the Companies Registry is part of the DTI). If serious malpractice occurs, the DTI may still exercise its statutory powers. The advantage to the shareholder, if he suspects malpractice, is that if he can get the DTI to intervene, he does not have to bear the expense and cope with the hassle of a legal struggle with company directors. Hence, it is a form of minority protection, though limited in its technical scope and by the reluctance of the DTI nowadays to take action in any but the most serious situations.

In the remainder of this section we describe the procedure of DTI investigation and finally (see paragraph 11.3 *DTI investigations – practical aspects*) attempt an assessment of its impact.

Powers of the Department of Trade

Production of documents

1. If it thinks there is good reason so to do, the Department of Trade may give directions to a company requiring it to produce, at such time and place as may be specified, or may authorise an officer or the Department or other competent person to require the company to produce to him any documents which he may specify: s447. The power extends over a person in possession of such documents (s447(4)) and may be augmented powers under search warrant issued by a justice of the peace to enter and search premises: s448. Non-compliance and destruction, mutilation and falsification of documents are punishable by fine and/or imprisonment: s450.
2. Documents must also be produced in an investigation by inspectors under ss431–433 and ss434–436.

Inspection and investigation

In certain situations, the Department of Trade can appoint an inspector to investigate and report on the affairs of a company, its ownership and its directors' share dealings.

1. Under s431, on the application of not less than 200 members or of members not holding less than one tenth of the shares issued, or upon application by the company. The application should be supported by such evidence as the Department may require for showing that the applicants have good reason for requiring the investigation.
2. Under s432(1), if the court by order declares that the company's affairs ought to be investigated, an inspector must be appointed. In *R v Board of Trade, ex parte St Martin's Preserving Co Ltd* [1965] 1 QB 603, transactions of receiver and manager were held to be 'affairs of the company'. In practice court orders are not issued to the DTI.
3. Under s432(2), if it appears to the Department of Trade that there are circumstances suggesting:
   a) that the company's business is being, is about to be, or has been conducted with intent to defraud its creditors or another person's creditors or otherwise

for a fraudulent or unlawful purpose or in a manner unfairly prejudicial to any part of its members; or

b) that persons concerned with the management of its affairs have been guilty of misconduct; or

c) that its members have not been given all the information which they might reasonably expect.

4. Under s442, where it appears to the Department of Trade that there is good reason, to investigate the membership of the company and otherwise for the purpose of determining the true persons financially interested in its success or failure or able to control or materially to influence the policy of the company.

   If those members who may apply under s431 (see (1) above) apply for an investigation under s442, the Department must appoint an inspector unless it is satisfied that it would not be reasonable (s442(3)).

   The applicants may be required to contribute up to £5,000 towards the cost of the investigation.

5. Under s446, if it appears to the Department of Trade that there are circumstances suggesting that the sections of that Act requiring notifications of interests in securities by directors have not been complied with (see paragraph 9.1 *Publicity about directors*).

In the majority of cases, even where someone other than the Department of Trade can request or require the appointment of an inspector, the power most used is that under s432(2), an approach being made to the Department to exercise its power to appoint under that section.

Additional powers

1. An inspector appointed under s431 or s432 can carry his investigation into the affairs of related companies: s433.

2. Where the Department of Trade has power to appoint an inspector under s442 but considers it unnecessary to do so, it may require information from persons it believes to be interested in the securities: s444.

3. Where information under ss442–444 is not forthcoming due to the unwillingness of the persons concerned, restrictions can be imposed on the securities (eg as to transfer, voting, etc): s445.

4. All evidence given to the inspector will be admissible in any criminal proceeding: s434(5); see, eg, *R* v *Seelig* [1991] 4 All ER 429 where the Court of Appeal decided that where testimony has been obtained by inspectors under s434, such evidence may be used in a criminal trial against the maker of the statements and the inspectors did not have to caution him before questioning began.

5. After the inspector's report, the DTI may present a petition for winding-up or a petition under s459 and the company cannot defeat this by an undertaking to reform: *Re Banford* (1977) The Times 4 May (see paragraph 13.3 *Who may petition*).

   The DTI cannot petition for winding-up if the company is already being wound up by the court but its power to petition on the just and equitable ground is unaffected by the fact that the company is being voluntarily wound up. The petition may be founded on the inspector's findings: *Re Lubin, Rosen and Associates Ltd* [1975] 1 All ER 577. The inspector's report is prima facie evidence of its subject matter and the company has to produce evidence in rebuttal: *Re Armvent Ltd* [1975] 3 All ER 441.

6. If it appears to the Department of Trade from any such report that any civil proceedings ought in the public interest to be brought by any company, the Department itself may bring such proceedings in the name and on behalf of the company: s438.

Conduct of the investigation

It was held in *Norwest Holst Ltd* v *Department of Trade* [1978] 3 All ER 280 that the appointment of an inspector under s432(2) is a preliminary stage, for the purposes of good administration, and carries no implication misconduct against the company; therefore, the rules of natural justice are inapplicable. But, although the inspector's function is investigatory and not judicial, he (or, more usually, they) must, in view of the consequences which may flow from his report, act fairly; subject to that, inspectors are masters of their own procedure and are not required to give any assurances: *Re Pergamon Press Ltd* [1970] 3 WLR 792.

They are not bound to tell a witness likely to be criticised in their report what they have in mind to say about him but they must ensure that the witness whose credibility is suspected has a fair opportunity of correcting or contradicting the substance of what other witnesses have said or are expected to say which is in conflict with his testimony: *Maxwell* v *Department of Trade* [1974] 2 WLR 338. Witnesses may be examined on oath.

When inspectors have been appointed under ss431 or 432 of the Act of 1985, no person considered by them to possess relevant information is entitled to invoke the common law privilege against self-incrimination when required to answer relevant questions: *Re London United Investments plc* [1992] BCLC 91 (affd [1992] BCLC 285) which was applied in *Re Jeffrey S Levitt Ltd* [1992] 2 All ER 509; see also *Bishopsgate Investment Management Ltd* v *Maxwell* [1992] 2 All ER 856 and *R* v *Kansal* [1992] 3 All ER 844 (no privilege in public examination of bankrupt). Again, in *Smith* v *Director of Serious Fraud Office* [1992] 3 All ER 456 the House of Lords decided that the Director's powers of investigation under s2 of the Criminal Justice Act 1987 were not subject to any implied qualification that a person charged with an offence (in this case, carrying on the business of a company with intent to defraud its creditors) could invoke the right to silence once he had been so charged. See also 13.3 *Procedure*.

Admissions made to inspectors conducting an investigation pursuant to s432 of the 1985 Act are admissible as evidence in criminal proceedings against the person making the admissions even though they might be self-incriminating: *R* v *Seelig* [1991] 4 All ER 429.

Results of investigations

The inspectors must report to the Department of Trade and may make interim reports to it: ss437, 443 & 446(5). The Department must forward a report to the company and may also cause it to be published: ss437(3)(c) and 443.

In 1989 in proceedings concerned with the inspectors' report on the take-over of the House of Fraser Ltd the DTI stated (and the court upheld its direction in such matters) that if criminal proceedings were contemplated prior publication of the report might prejudice the trial.

When the inspectors report into this take-over was eventually published, it concluded that the Fayed brothers who, through Fraser Holdings plc, had acquired House of Fraser plc (which included the famous department store Harrods), had dishonestly represented their origin, wealth, business interests, and resources. These representations were said to have been made to the Secretary of State, the board and shareholders of House of Fraser plc, the Office of Fair Trading, and their legal advisors. The report was published and widely reported in the media. Despite these findings, no criminal charges were brought and neither were disqualification proceedings initiated. The Fayed's wanted to challenge the findings and claimed that the inspectors had determined their civil rights (as to honour and reputation) in breach of article 6(1) of the European Convention on Human Rights, which requires a fair and public hearing by an independent and impartial tribunal.

In *Fayed* v *United Kingdom* (Case No 28/1993/423/502) (1994) The Times 11 November, their action failed. The court held that the function of inspectors was essentially investigative, rather than judicial. The requirement of a judicial procedure in article 6(1) did not therefore apply to investigations by inspectors. Furthermore, the inspectors report showed what information was required of them, and they were given ample opportunity to reply and furnish evidence in support. See Chapter 15, paragraph 15.8, for further details.

An aggrieved shareholder petitioning for winding-up under s122(1)(g) (just and equitable grounds) may use an inspector's report in support of his claim: *Re St Piran* [1981] 3 All ER 270.

The Department of Trade has powers to petition for a winding-up or an order under s459 or to bring civil proceedings in the company's name.

DTI investigations – practical aspects

Types

There are three possible types of investigation, which differ according to the subject investigated. They are investigation of the affairs, ie the management, of a company; of the ownership of its shares; and of default in giving notice of directors' interests in securities of the company. Only the first of these is at all common and so the others are not of much importance. In addition, the Secretary of State has power to require the production of documents. In the DTI booklet *Investigations – How They Work* (1990) the position was summarised on lines as follows:

1. Section 432 – the Secretary of State can appoint inspectors if he suspects fraud or misconduct or if the company's shareholders have not been given the information which they might reasonably expect. He must also appoint inspectors if the court tells him to do so.

2. Section 442 – here the Secretary of State generally appoints inspectors at the request of shareholders or of the companies themselves. Companies have a legal right to know who owns their shares. Normally private sector inspectors are appointed – a leading lawyer and a leading accountant – but inspectors with other professional skills are used where this is beneficial. They have very wide powers to obtain documents and to require people to give evidence. These powers are needed to get at the facts in the big and difficult cases where there is major public interest. The Secretary of State always announces the inspectors' appointments. Their reports are usually published if there is a public interest. But this may be delayed if criminal proceedings are being considered or are already under way. In some cases inspectors may be appointed under s432 on the basis that their report to the Secretary of State is not for publication. There are cases in which there is little or no interest in a published report. Investigations can take more than 12 months. The Secretary of State may ask for an interim report if the final report is likely to take a long time or if urgent action is necessary. The inspectors must tell any person they intend to criticise the substance of the evidence for what they intend to say, and give them an opportunity to respond. This too can delay a report. Where matters in an investigation by inspectors suggest that a criminal offence may have been committed, and these matters have been referred to the appropriate prosecuting authority, inspectors may be directed to take no further steps or only limited further steps.

3. Section 446 – the Secretary of State can appoint inspectors to investigate share dealings by directors or their families in their own companies or related ones. He can do this if there is reason to suspect illegal dealings in options, or if directors fail to disclose interests in the companies they control.

4. Section 447 – this enables the Secretary of State, if he considers that there is good reason, to require a company to produce its records: most investigations are of this kind. If a company refuses to cooperate or there is a risk of documents being destroyed, DTI can ask a magistrate for a warrant. The police and investigators can then search premises and seize papers. Investigators can also ask any person involved with a company, now or in the past, to explain the company's records. These investigations are normally carried out by DTI officials, but can also be carried out by any other competent person, and are much more limited than those under s432 or 442. However, a s447 investigation can lead to a wider one under ss432 or 442. Investigations under s447 allow suspicions of misconduct to be looked at without risk of harming the company. If such inquiries were publicised, the company might be unfairly damaged. Therefore DTI does not announce such investigations, and refuses to comment on whether or not a particular company is under investigation. These inquiries are usually completed within weeks. Information obtained in these inquiries is

generally confidential. It is usually a crime to reveal such information without the company's agreement. The main exceptions are in cases of suspected crime and to enable regulatory and professional authorities to take action.

5. Section 82 of the 1989 Act – the Secretary of State has wide powers to assist an overseas regulatory authority which has requested assistance in connection with enquiries being carried out by it or on its behalf. Section 82(4) mentions various matters which the Secretary of State may take into account in deciding whether to exercise these powers. DTI does not intend to announce such investigations.

Compulsory or discretionary

Unless the court orders it to do so, which in practice it does not, the DTI always has discretion whether or not to launch an investigation of a company's affairs.

It may also be compelled to investigate the ownership of shares of the company if the demand is made by at least 200 members or members holding at least 10 per cent of the issued share capital. As already stated, however, this type of investigation is a rare occurrence.

How shareholders may get a DTI investigation started

The first step is usually that a shareholder, or a group of shareholders, makes an informal application to the DTI, alleging malpractice by the management (see paragraph 11.3 *Powers of the Department of Trade, Inspection and investigation*). Applications of any other kind are infrequent. The applicants must persuade the DTI that there are solid grounds for their suspicions or allegations. If they have already tried to bring matters up at a general meeting or the financial press has begun to comment on the matter, or the Stock Exchange is already interested, it may be less difficult to persuade the DTI that it should intervene.

Follow up

As the DTI explains in its booklet (see (1) above), it can take action in many ways if an investigation finds misconduct. Some reports of investigations may be made public. But information obtained under s447 or s82 of the 1989 Act is never (or rarely) published. When the public is at risk, the Secretary of State may ask the court to stop a company trading at once by appointing a provisional liquidator and winding it up. This is the quickest action DTI can take. The court demands detailed and substantial evidence for this very serious step. DTI press notices are usually issued in these cases.

Where there is evidence of misconduct by a company's directors, DTI can also ask the courts to disqualify them. In other cases DTI may use the information it has obtained to prosecute offenders. Or it can pass the information to the Serious Fraud Office or the Crown Prosecution Service.

The DTI may take regulatory action or pass information to other regulatory bodies or professional bodies. In less serious cases, DTI may simply give a warning, and tell the directors to rectify the faults found. If necessary, it can take further action later.

Conclusions

A DTI investigation, making use of wide statutory powers, is sometimes the best means of getting to the bottom of a complicated matter. However, the DTI much prefers to use its own powers under s447 rather than launch into a protracted and very expensive investigation by inspectors.

The shareholder who is daunted by the prospect of pursuing minority remedies in the courts has an easier alternative in application to the DTI for an investigation. But he will have to collect and present a persuasive case of suspected malpractice, which itself may be difficult since he will get no help from the company, before the DTI is likely to use its powers of any kind.

The purpose of the changes made by Part III of CA 1989 is to confer more drastic and effective powers of investigation, in a field where evasion is often well-planned and spreads across international frontiers. There are new provisions for, inter alia, co-operation with regulatory authorities in foreign countries: s82 CA 1989. Part VIII of CA 1989 makes parallel changes in the regulation of markets in securities under the provisions of FSA (see paragraph 5.2).

12

Reconstruction

12.1 Financial reorganisation

12.2 Schemes of arrangement

12.3 Reorganisation in the course of liquidation

12.4 Compulsory acquisition of shares in a take-over

12.1 Financial reorganisation

Introduction

The latter part of Chapter 7 has dealt incidentally with the creditors' reaction to the possibility that insolvency of a company debtor may result in a loss to the creditor. Apart from putting in a receiver, if the creditor has security to enforce by taking assets under his control, he may decide that the only wise course is to liquidate the company.

However, both these measures can have adverse consequences. The effect may be to worsen the company's financial position, since its suppliers and customers may no longer be willing to do business with the company. If its business is closed down or even sold, there may be heavy expenses due to redundancy payments to company employees and/or payments in settlement of claims for breach of contract arising from the company's inability to complete its existing contracts. If the creditor is a bank, its action in closing down a company customer may lead to public criticism or loss of business goodwill with other customers.

A prudent creditor should always consider whether he may avoid or at least reduce loss from a bad debt by promoting the reorganisation of the company's finances in the hope that it will recover, or at least go out of business in an orderly fashion and with minimum expense.

A debt is a matter of contract and so it is always possible for a debtor company and its creditors to enter into a new contract by which the immediate financial pressure on the company is eased in the hope that it will be restored to solvency. Such a strategy obviously has its risks. The creditor may find that in the end his loss is even greater than if he had taken a drastic decision at the outset.

This section of deals with two procedures introduced by the Insolvency Act 1986 to facilitate 'rescue' operations, subject to appropriate safeguards.

12.2 Schemes of arrangement

Introduction

A scheme of arrangement under ss425–427 is a flexible and versatile method of resolving problems of variation of rights attached to shares which cannot be dealt with under s125 (see paragraph 3.1 *Variation of class rights – procedure*), compromises between a company and its debentureholders (but a 'voluntary arrangement' is now a possible alternative: see paragraph 13.1 *Voluntary arrangements with creditors*), take-over bids in which acceptance in respect of 90 per cent of the shares is difficult to obtain or will entail very heavy costs in stamp duty. The only limit on the possible use of a scheme of arrangement is that it may not used to by-pass some other specific statutory procedure, such as a reduction of share capital or a purchase by the company of its own shares or the type of reconstruction in the course of liquidation which is described later in this chapter (see paragraph 12.3).

The advantage of a scheme of arrangement is that a complicated alteration of rights or of capital structure can be implemented by a simple court order approving the scheme (see paragraph 12.2 *Scheme of arrangement – procedure*). There is no elaborate follow-up action to be taken and, in some cases, stamp duty is avoided since there are no instruments of transfer requiring to be stamped.

The disadvantage of using a scheme of arrangement is that it requires the preparation of a document setting out the scheme and of an explanatory circular, with two applications to the court, at the start and at the end of the procedural sequence. For that reason a scheme of arrangement is likely to be uneconomic unless large companies, with millions of pounds of assets, are involved.

Scheme of arrangement – procedure

Where a compromise or arrangement is proposed between a company and its creditors or any class of them or between the company and its members or any class of them the court may, on the application of the company or any creditor or member or the liquidator (in a winding-up), order a meeting of the creditors or members or of a class of either: s425(1).

The notice of the meeting must include a statement explaining the effect of the compromise or arrangement and in particular stating any material interests of the directors (whether as directors, members or creditors) or (where the scheme effects the rights of debentureholders) the trustees for debentureholders (who are both bound to give notice of such matter to the company or be fined) and stating any special effect thereon of the scheme: s426. Non-compliance by the company or any officer (including trustees and the liquidator) results in liability to a fine, and the court will not sanction a scheme where s426 has not been complied with (see paragraph 12.2 *The court's discretion*).

If a majority of three quarters in value of those entitled to attend and voting at the meeting agree to the scheme, it will, if sanctioned by the court, be binding on all of such persons and the company or, in liquidation, on the liquidator and contributories: s425(2). The court's order is ineffective until a copy is received by the registrar: a copy must be annexed to the memorandum: s425(3). The scheme may succeed even though rights contained in the memorandum are stated to be unalterable (see paragraph 4.1 *Alteration of optional clauses of the memorandum*).

If the scheme is for the purpose of or in connection with a scheme for the reconstruction of any company or companies or the amalgamation of any two or more companies, and under the scheme the whole or any part of the undertaking or the property of any company (the transferor company) concerned in the scheme is to be transferred to another (transferee company), the court may also provide for the following matters (s427):

1. the transfer to the transferee company of the whole or part of the undertaking and of the property or liabilities of any transferor company;
2. the allotting or appropriation by the transferee company of shares, debentures or like interests in that company;
3. the dissolution or winding-up of the transferor company;
4. the provisions to be made for any persons who dissent;
5. the continuation by the transferee company of legal proceedings involving the transferor.

The court's discretion

In *Re Alabama, New Orleans, Texas and Pacific Junction Railway Co* [1891] 1 Ch 213 the court said that it should exercise its discretion in deciding whether to approve a scheme of arrangement as follows:

> 'The court must look at the scheme, and see whether the Act has been complied with, whether the majority are acting bona fide, and whether they are coercing the minority in order to promote interests adverse to the class whom they purport to represent; and then see whether the scheme is a reasonable one or whether there is any reasonable objection to it, or such objection that a reasonable man might say that he could not approve it.'

When application is made to the court for an order that the meetings be convened to consider the scheme, the court is concerned with whether the scheme is within the ambit of s425 and whether the initial statutory requirements, in respect of documents, have been complied with.

The second application to the court for approval of the scheme, following its approval at meeting(s), is the moment when a dissenting minority may seek to persuade the court that there has been improper discrimination or that the scheme is such that a reasonable man would not approve it. In the light of those objections, if any, the court may look again at the formal requirements. It is not disposed to withhold approval from a scheme approved by three quarters majority vote(s), unless there are clear gounds for doing so.

The court's sanction was refused in *Re Hellenic & General Trust Ltd* [1975] 3 All ER 382; Prentice (1976) 92 LQR 13. Fifty-three per cent of the shares were held by MIT, a wholly owned subsidiary of Hambros and 47 per cent by independent shareholders. It was proposed to cancel all ordinary shares of Hellenic and to issue new ordinary shares to Hambros, of which Hellenic would thus become a wholly owned subsidiary. Hambros would pay to the existing shareholders the true net value of the shares, which was up to 25 per cent more than they would get on the open market. But NBG, the holder of 14 per cent of the shares, would be liable to a very heavy capital gains tax in Greece, and therefore objected. It was held by Templeman J that:

1. the class meeting was improperly constituted because the shareholders were really comprised of two classes (MIT, the subsidiary of the offeror, and the other shareholders) and that in a class meeting excluding MIT the offer would have been rejected; and
2. even if the class had been properly constituted, the majority could not succeed under s425 because NBG could have defeated the take-over under ss428–430 (below) having more than a 10 per cent shareholding.

The *Hellenic* case decision is more reliable in respect of proposition (1) than (2). In reaching its conclusion on 1. the court followed *Re United Provident Assurance Co Ltd* [1910] 2 Ch 477, where it was held that holders of fully paid and of similar partly paid shares were different classes, who should consider the scheme at separate meetings. It also considered *Sovereign Life Assurance Co* v *Dodd* [1892] 2 QB 573, where it was held that holders of insurance policies which had matured and become payable were in a different class (of interest as creditors) from holders of policies which had not yet matured.

On point (2) the court's decision was in conflict with *Re National Bank* [1966] 1 WLR 819, where the court declined to add to s425 words of limitation which are not in the statutory text. In his judgment in the *Hellenic* case Templeman J conceded that it was not 'necessarily fatal' to a scheme of arrangement that s428 (see paragraph 12.4) offered an alternative and more specific procedure for acquiring shares of a minority. But he added that:

> 'At its lowest there must be a very high standard of proof on the part of the petitioner to justify obtaining under [s425] what could not be obtained under [s428], especially when there is the added element that [s425] itself only works with the help of a wholly owned subsidiary of the petititoner.'

On point (2) therefore the decision is related to what was fair in relation to the particular facts, ie that the minority would have been able to block the scheme if s428 procedure had been used. It was not a decision that s425 was incapable of application to a take-over.

The most common occasion for using s425 (in cases where s428 is an available alternative) is that the court order under s427 effects an issue of shares of the acquiring company and the cancellation of the shares acquired, so that they are not actually transferred and no stamp duty is payable. In a merger of, for example, two large banks it has been used to save millions of pounds in stamp duty. If there were objections raised in such circumstances, the court would give due weight to the cost factor.

12.3 Reorganisation in the course of liquidation

Introduction

Paragraph 13.4 deals with a number of the statutory powers given to a liquidator by IA s167 and Sch. 4. These include a power to make compromises and arrangements with creditors and with members of the company. Note also that a liquidator may promote a 'voluntary arrangement' with creditors, as described above (see paragraph 13.1).

Transfer of assets in exchange for shares

This section deals with a special procedure by which a company may transfer its undertaking and assets to another company in return for shares of the transfeee company which are usually allotted direct to shareholders of the transferor company. The procedure may be used to effect an amalgamation if the transferee company already has its existing shareholders and its own business. It is also useful as a method by which the business of the transferor company, if that company has internal problems, may pass into a new company with the same shareholders. In that way the 'slate is wiped clean' to the extent that the new (transferee) company is free of the complications which beset the transferor company.

This procedure is now found in ss110–111 of the Insolvency Act 1986, which are substantially the same as earlier provisions of the various Companies Acts under which the reported cases were decided.

It will be apparent that the transferor company, after disposing of its business to another company, is likely to be wound up. It is, moreover, a pre-condition of resort to these procedures that the transferor company shall be, or about to be, in voluntary liquidation. The normal sequence is that the special resolution to approve the transfer is put to the vote at a general meeting of the transferor company. If it is passed, the meeting then passes another resolution to wind up the company. If the company goes into creditors' voluntary liquidation, the transfer also requires the sanction of the court or of the liquidation committee: IA s110(3)(b).

In this, as in other procedures for reconstruction of companies, a dissenting minority is given certain safeguards. The effect of the scheme is that each member of the transferor company will, if he does not object, be allotted shares of the transferee company in respect of his interest in the assets transferred. He may, however, if he did not vote in favour of the special resolution to approve the transfer, deliver to the company at its registered office within seven days of the passing of the resolution a notice of his dissent. The liquidator is then required either to pay to the dissenting member the cash value of his interest or to abandon the scheme: IA s111.

If there is disagreement as to the value of the member's interest, it is to be determined by an arbitrator.

If he fails to exercise his statutory right to be paid in cash but will not accept the shares of the transferee company, to which he is entitled, eg because they are partly paid, the shares may be sold and the proceeds paid to him.

It is not permissible for the company to dispose of its assets in exchange for shares (to be distributed to its members) under any other procedure nor to deprive members of their statutory rights by provisions of the articles: *Bisgood* v *Henderson's Transvaal Estates Ltd* [1908] 1 Ch 743.

The other possible obstacle to a scheme of this kind is the opposition of the creditors. As stated above, if the company goes into creditors' voluntary liquidation, the scheme requires external approval. Moreover, a creditor, if his debt is not paid, may petition the court for an order for the compulsory winding-up of the company. If such an order is made within a year of the passing of the special resolution, the resolution ceases to be valid unless sanctioned by the court.

In practice therefore a company has to plan in advance how to deal with dissenting members and creditors. If it is able to pay off all its debts, or if the creditors will agree to accept the transferee company as their debtor in place of the transferor company, the liquidator will not be troubled by creditors' objections. As regards dissenting members, the transferor or transferee company should ensure that there is cash available, from which to pay the cash value of the company's undertaking and assets to up to 25 per cent of its members. In a small company it may of course be possible to reach a preliminary agreement with members that they will vote in favour of the scheme.

Because of these obstacles this procedure is little used at the present time. A simple transfer of the assets to a newly formed company will not generate the cash from which to pay off all creditors. A transfer to an existing company which has other members will entail expense in connection with capital duty (1 per cent ad valorem) which can be a disincentive.

12.4 Compulsory acquisition of shares in a take-over

Introduction

It has long been accepted practice that a company may enlarge its business by acquiring the issued shares of another company, which becomes its subsidiary (see paragraph 1.4 *Holding and subsidiary companies*). If all the shareholders of the company whose shares are to be acquired ('the target company') agree to sell their shares, the target company becomes the wholly owned subsidiary of the acquiring company ('the take-over bidder').

Some inconvenience results if a small minority of the shareholders of the target company reject or do not respond to the offer for their shares, even though it is accepted by the large majority (as will be seen the critical figure is 90 per cent). The target company then becomes a partly owned subsidiary and in producing group accounts (see paragraph 14.1 *Parent companies and subsidiary undertakings*) the take-over bidder must distinguish the minority interest in the subsidiary. The management of the group enterprise may be impeded by this interest, if the minority disagree with its policy.

The minority, who have resisted the take-over bid, may alter their attitude, when they realise that they will be a small minority in a company under the domination of another, and may then wish to take up the bid for their shares which they previously rejected.

For these and other reasons there is a long-established procedure by which a successful take-over bidder may compulsorily acquire the outstanding minority interest. This power may also be used to acquire outstanding shares of a partly owned subsidiary, or of any company in which the bidder is already a shareholder, provided that a sufficient acceptance is achieved among the minority. Finally, the minority is given the right to compel a successful take-over bidder to acquire their shares. All this, and the relevant safeguards, are explained in more detail in this section.

The original statutory provisions (Companies Act 1948 s209) re-enacted as Companies Act 1985 ss428–430) were imprecise and did not fully reflect modern practice in these transactions. They have therefore been replaced (from 30 April 1987) by the Financial Services Act 1986 Sch. 12, which substitutes new, and much expanded, ss428–430F in the 1985 Act.

There are other regulatory procedures which may affect the conduct of a take-over bid (see paragraph 12.4 *Other regulations*). If the take-over bidder offers its own shares as the consideration (or part of it) for the shares of the target company, that offer is now subject to prospectus law. If, as is likely, the shares offered are listed on the Stock Exchange, listing particulars will be required (see paragraph 5.2 *The control of listed securities*). There is also a general control of the conduct of take-over bids (and of action by the target company or third parties to resist such a bid), exercised by the City Panel on Take-overs and Mergers. That control is made effective by non-statutory sanctions within the financial markets of the City of London. The Panel draws its members from various institutions in the City and so it has considerable authority.

The offer to be made

Any person, or two or more persons acting jointly, either an individual or a company, may (for the purposes of invoking the statutory powers) make an offer to acquire all the shares of a company which it, he or they do not already own, directly or indirectly. All shares of the target company which the bidder and its associates already own or have contracted to buy, and all shares which they may acquire outside the terms of their offer while it is in force, are not within the offer for statutory purposes. The offer may be expressed to apply to new shares, if any, issued by the target company during the period of the offer.

If the target company has more than one class of shares, eg preference as well as ordinary shares, a separate offer may be made for each class, though there is no obligation to make an offer for both. The extent of acceptance is reckoned separately for shares of each class.

If while the offer is outstanding, the offeror varies the terms of his offer, usually by increasing the offer price, this is treated as a continuation of the original offer and not as a new offer. The offer may take the form of alternatives, eg an offer of shares of the offeror company or of cash (or debentures) or some combination of both, either fixed or in such proportions as the acceptor may select. However, the same terms must be offered to all holders of shares for which the offer is made, except that if some of them reside in countries whose law restricts their acceptance of the offer made within the UK, it may be varied for those foreign holders.

The acquisition procedure

To bring the compulsory acquisition provisions into play the offer, as described above, must attract acceptances, within four months of the offer being made, from holders of at least 90 per cent of the shares for which the offer has been made ('90 per cent acceptance').

If the offeror secures 90 per cent acceptance he may then, without waiting for the expiry of the four month period, serve notice on every non-accepting holder of shares of his intention to acquire the latter's shares on the terms of the offer, including any alternative or option, eg to take cash rather than shares, which was part of the offer. This principle was first established in *Re Carlton Holdings Ltd* [1971] 2 All ER 1082; it is now statutory. The offeree has six weeks in which to decide which alternative or option (if any) he will select.

The offeror need not issue this acquisition notice, but if he does so it must be given within two months of attaining 90 per cent acceptance. The effect of the notice is that the offeror then becomes bound to complete the acquisition and the shareholder on whom the notice is served is bound to comply, unless he makes a successful application to the court to have it cancelled.

If sometimes happens that a shareholder cannot be traced or, for some other reason, does not respond in any way. In that case the transfer of his shares may be executed on his behalf and the price is held in trust until he claims it.

The right to object

On receiving the acquisition notice the shareholder may within six weeks apply to the court for a cancellation of the acquisition or a variation of its terms. Hence, the case law on the original statutory procedure (replaced in 1986) is still a guide to the attitude which the court is likely to adopt. In brief the prospects of success in any such application to the court are poor, since the court takes the view that an offer which has attracted acceptance from holders of 90 per cent of the shares is inherently reasonable.

In *Re Evertite Locknuts Ltd* [1945] Ch 220 holders of 699 shares had accepted the offer but the holder of the one other share objected, saying that he lacked information on which to decide whether the offer was fair. His application to the court failed.

However, the court will intervene if these powers are being used as a means of oppression of a minority, and will for this purpose 'lift the veil of incorporation' (see paragraph 1.3 *Company identity used to evade obligations*). The leading case here is *Re Bugle Press Ltd* [1960] 3 All ER 791. There were three shareholders: A and B each held 4,500 shares and C had 1,000 shares. A and B planned to acquire the shares of C, who did not wish to sell out. As related above (see paragraph 1.3) A and B, who as fellow shareholders with C, could not resort to compulsory acquisition of C's shares under s428, hit on the idea of interposing a new company, of which A and B were joint owners, which would offer to acquire the shares of A, B and C in Bugle Press. A and B accepted to provide the required 90 per cent acceptance and their company then served notice on C of its intention to acquire his 10 per cent. The court, however, 'lifted the veil of incorporation' and declined to treat the new company as anything other than A and B. C's objection was upheld, on the grounds that the ploy of A and B was a misuse of s428 procedure.

Bidder required to acquire minority shares

If the offeror, after obtaining 90 per cent acceptance does not serve an acquisition notice on the non-accepting shareholders to acquire their shares, he is nonetheless required, within one month, to give them notice that he has reached the 90 per cent acceptance level. On receiving that notice they may then within the ensuing three months require the bidder to acquire their shares, even though the original offer has expired, on the terms of the offer.

Other regulations

When the Financial Services Act 1986 was drafted, it provided a convenient means of including the technical revision of company law on compulsory acquisition of shares, as described above. However, the FSA does not extend to take-over procedure generally, which is left under the supervision of the Take-over Panel. If, however, a take-over is in the form of an offer of shares of the bidder (company) as consideration for the shares of the target company, there is a proposed issue of securities, ie the shares of the bidder, which is a prospectus issue, to which the FSA applies (see paragraph 5.2).

Before 1986 a take-over by share exchange was not a prospectus issue, since a prospectus as then defined in company law was an offer of securities for cash. Take-over by share exchange was a form of dealing in securities to which the Prevention of Fraud (Investments) Act 1958 applied. That Act, however, has now been repealed since it has been replaced by the more elaborate scheme of the FSA.

The City Panel on Take-overs and Mergers has issued (in several successive editions since 1967) a 'City Code', comprising general principles, rules and practice notes. As already explained the Code is enforced by non-statutory sanctions. The decisions of the Panel are however subject to judicial review, even if the petitioner has not yet exhausted his rights of appeal under Panel procedure: *R* v *Panel on Takeovers and Mergers, ex parte Guinness plc* [1989] 1 All ER 509.

The main object of the Code is to procure fair and equal treatment of all shareholders of a target company based on disclosure of information and equal opportunity for all.

If, for example, an investor (usually a company) has acquired 30 per cent of the issued capital of another public company, it is generally required by the Code to make an offer to acquire all the shares which it does not own at the highest price which it has paid in the recent past in building up its holding of 30 per cent or more. The reason for this requirement is that in a large company, with many small shareholders, one shareholder with 30 per cent or more of the votes can usually exercise effective control of the company since the other shareholders are unlikely to combine against him and many of them will not cast their votes at all at general meetings, owing to indifference or ignorance. The shareholder who has effective control is therefore required to make an offer to buy out the rest at a price related to his past purchases of the shares which he has acquired.

Much of the Code is concerned with matters which arise in the course of a take-over bid. It is normal practice in an offer of this kind to stipulate that the offer is conditional on obtaining acceptances in respect of 90 per cent of the shares of the target company, or such lesser percentage as the offeror may elect to acquire. The Code prevents him from fixing the minimum percentage, for declaring the offer unconditional, at less than 50 per cent. If the acceptances do not reach 50 per cent, the offer is withdrawn; if in the range 50 to 90 per cent, the offeror may take up the acceptance if he wishes although he will be unable to apply ss428–430 to acquire 100 per cent; if he gets 90 per cent or more he must take up the acceptances. However, if he declares his offer unconditional because he has 50 per cent or more of the shares, the Code then requires him to extend his offer for at least a fortnight, so that the non-accepting offerees may, if they wish, come in with acceptances.

There are also elaborate rules on disclosure of information, eg about dealings in the market in the shares while the offer is available. If the bidder, or the target company, makes a forecast of future profits, which is often an important factor in determining the attitude of shareholders, various safeguards are imposed to ensure, as far as possible, that the forecasts are well-founded and reasonable.

Finally, if a proposed take-over will produce a concentration of ownership in some industry, the Fair Trading Act 1973, provides means by which the effect of the merger on competition and other factors relevant to the public interest may be examined. If the Secretary of State at the DTI decides that a proposed take-over shall be referred to the Monopolies and Mergers Commission for investigation and report, it is certain that a delay of six months or more will be imposed on the proposed take-over. In those circumstances the bidder commonly withdraws his offer because he cannot assess whether it will be advantageous to him to make it, if the decision goes in his favour after the investigation. By that time the factors which he took into account in deciding to make his offer, and in fixing its terms, may be very different.

13

Liquidation

13.1 Introduction

13.2 Basic points

13.3 Compulsory liquidation

13.4 Voluntary winding-up

13.5 Assets and liabilities in liquidation

13.6 Voidable transactions and compensation

13.1 Introduction

Voluntary arrangements with creditors

We are here concerned with arrangements such as a discharge of debts on the basis of part payment in full settlement or a moratorium to give the company time to improve its position.

There are two major problems im promoting any such arrangement. First, the creditors will wish to be assured that the proposals made to them are realistic and that the company will adhere to them if accepted. Secondly, an individual creditor may exploit his nuisance value by demanding preferential treatment of his claim as the price of his necessary co-operation in the adoption of the scheme. It is also essential to take account of the priority given to secured and to preferential unsecured debts which the creditors entitled to them will not readily give up.

The provisions now found in the Insolvency Act 1986 Pt I replace earlier statutory provisions (Companies Act 1985 s601 re-enacting Companies Act 1948 s306) which for technical reasons had proved almost unworkable and had been little used. Those earlier sections have been repealed.

As 'voluntary arrangement' by a company is defined as 'a composition in satisfaction of its debts or a scheme of arrangement of its affairs': IA s1(1). It may be proposed either by the directors of a company, if it is not in liquidation or subject to an administration order (see paragraph 13.1 *Administration orders*), or by a liquidator or administrator if it is in either of those situations.

If the arrangement is proposed by directors they must find an insolvency practitioner (see paragraph 13.2 *Insolvency pratitioners*) to sponsor the scheme and he makes a preliminary report to the court: IA s2. This first step is not required where the arrangement is proposed by an insolvency practitioner already acting as liquidator or administrator.

In whatever capacity he is acting the insolvency practitioner convenes meetings of creditors and of members of the company to consider, and if they see fit, approve the arrangement, with or without modifications: IA s4.

Under the 1986 Insolvency Rules, the creditors vote according to the amount of their debts as at the date of the meeting. A majority in excess of three-quarters in value of the creditors present in person or by proxy is required to approve the arrangement (IR 1986 rr.1.17(2) and 1.19(1)).

In *Re Cranley Mansions Ltd* [1994] 1 WLR 1610 Chancery Division, the court had to decide whether a creditor was bound by a voluntary arrangement. The company was insolvent and a meeting was called to consider a proposed voluntary arrangement. S, a creditor of the company attended the meeting and she claimed the company owed her a contingent debt worth £900,000. This was entirely dependent on the outcome of litigation against the company. In accordance with the 1986 Insolvency Rules, the chairman of the meeting put a minimum value on the debt at £1, in order that S could vote at the meeting.

The figure of £1 was arrived at, without any agreement with the creditor and was therefore a unilateral decision by the chairman. At the meeting, the proposals for the voluntary arrangement were approved by the relevant majority of the other creditors. However, if the debt had been given a value in excess of £1,722, S could have prevented the approval. S appealed against the chairman's decision to give her debt a minimum value of £1. The court allowed the appeal and held that S was not bound by the voluntary arrangement as the chairman had no right to unilaterally ascribe a minimum value of £1 to her debt. The chairman had not 'agreed' within the meaning of r.1.17(3) of the Insolvency Rules 1986 to put an estimated minimum value on her debt for the purpose of ascertaining the extent of her voting rights. This was a material irregularity. See Chapter 15, paragraph 15.9, for further details.

Re Cranley Mansions Ltd was distinguished in the later case of *Re a Debtor (No 162 of 1993)* [1994] BCC 994. In this case, which did not involve a corporate voluntary arrangement but an individual one, Knox J held that what r.1.17(3) requires, is the chairman's agreement to put a minimum value on a debt, and not an agreement upon the minimum value.

The proposed arrangement may not modify the existing rights of secured or preferential creditors without their consent.

If the arrangement is approved it becomes binding on the company and on all creditors, subject to certain limited rights of challenge by appeal to the court given to creditors and to members. To sustain such an appeal the applicant must show either that there was material irregularity in connection with the meetings or that he is 'unfairly prejudiced' by the arrangement: IA s6. In particular a creditor would probably have to show some form of discrimination against himself to have any prospect of overturning an arrangement approved by a majority of creditors.

The arrangement if adopted is supervised by an insolvency practitioner, who may be but need not be the same individual as originally put forward the arrangement for approval at the meetings. If when the arrangement was proposed the company was already in liquidation or subject to an administration order, the court has power to stay those proceedings or otherwise provide for the situation.

It will be seen that this new procedure offers some solutions which may help in dealing with the difficulties experienced in the past. An insolvency practitioner is required to bring the proposals before the meetings for approval and to supervise their implementation if approved. This means that a practitioner must be found to accept responsibility for the scheme. If it were deceptive or unlikely to succeed, it would be difficult to find a practitioner willing to act in connection with it.

Secondly, a majority decision at the creditors' meeting is binding on all creditors, provided that there is no 'unfair prejudice' against a minority. There is no possibility of a creditor holding the rest to ransom simply by demanding preferential treatment. Secured and preferential creditors' existing rights are safeguarded.

Administration orders

In many respects the functions of an administrator, who must always be an insolvency practitioner, under an administration order are similar to those of a receiver (see paragraph 7.4). However, he is appointed by the court, for a specified programme in relation to the affairs of the company. His appointment can have the same effect as a liquidation in reopening recent transactions of the company (see paragraph 13.6 *Avoidance of floating charges* to *Transactions at an undervalue*). A receivership does not have that effect. The administration order provisions are designed as an alternative to liquidating the company and to facilitate the rescue and habilitation of insolvent but viable businesses.

Application may only be made to the court for an administration order for one or more of the following purposes:

1. the survival of the company, wholly or in part, as a going concern;
2. the approval of a voluntary arrangement (see paragraph 13.1 *Voluntary arrangements with creditors*);
3. the approval of a scheme of arrangement (see paragraph 12.2);
4. a more advantageous realisation of the company's assets than would be effected by a liquidation: IA s8(3) and see, eg, *Re Atlantic Computer Systems plc* [1992] 1 All ER 476 and *Barclays Mercantile Business Finance Ltd* v *Sibec Devopments Ltd* [1993] 2 All ER 195.

There are limitations on the court's power to make an administration order:
1. it must be satisfied that the company already is or is likely to become unable to pay its debts;

2. it must consider whether making an order is likely to achieve one of the above purposes: IA s8(1). 'Likely' does not require a strong degree of probability, ie a better than even chance. In the words of the Cork Committee the court should consider whether there is a 'prospect of (the company) returning to profitability or selling (its business) as a going concern': *Re Harris Simons Construction Ltd* [1989] 1 WLR 368 and *Re Primlaks (UK) Ltd* [1989] BCLC 734.

3. it may not make an order if a secured creditor has appointed a receiver, unless the creditor gives his consent: IA s9.

Application to the court for an administration order may be made by the company, or its directors, or by a creditor, including an unsecured creditor.

In the interval between the presentation of a petition for the order and the court's decision at the hearing, there is a standstill on putting the company into liquidation or taking proceedings of various kinds against it as a debtor: IA s10. These restraints continue if an order is made: IA s11. Upon the making of the order any outstanding petition for the compulsory winding-up of the company is dismissed and any receiver vacates office.

In *Barclays Mercantile Business Finance Ltd* v *Sibec Developments Ltd* [1993] BCC 148, Millet J held that the effect of an administration order being made, is that IA s11(3) imposes a moratorium on the enforcement of a creditor's legal rights but does not alter or destroy those rights. Therefore, a supplier who has leased goods to a company or supplied goods on hire purchase, is entitled to repossess the goods with leave of the court. The administrators, until their release, remain liable at the discretion of the court to pay for the use of the goods and to pay for compensation for wrongfully refusing to deliver up the goods to the suppliers. Leave to repossess the goods supplied under hire purchase agreements was refused in *Re David Meek Access Ltd* [1993] BCC 175. One of the arguments presented by the administrators was that the company's business was hiring out the equipment subject to the hire purchase agreements. Therefore, without this equipment there would be no point in the administration and no proposals to present to the meeting of creditors.

An administrator has the same statutory powers as are given to a receiver: IA s14. His working procedure is to call for a statement of affairs (see paragraph 7.4 *Action after the receiver's appointment*) and then within three months of the making of the administration order lay before a meeting of the creditors a statement of his proposals for achieving the purpose of the order: IA ss22–23. The creditors meeting may only modify the administrator's proposals to the extent that he consents. Subject to that the creditors either approve the proposals, which the administrator then seeks to implement or they reject them. The administrator reports to the court the outcome of the meeting and, if his proposals have been rejected, the court may make consequential orders: IA s24.

The creditors at their meeting, to consider the administrator's proposals, may establish a creditors' committee to work with the administrator: IA s26.

The administration order is discharged, if its purpose is completed or becomes impossible to achieve.

The administration order procedure – pros and cons

The administration order procedure offers to the unsecured creditor the opportunity to seek the appointment of an administrator, with the powers of a receiver and obligations to the general body of creditors. The drawback is that no administration order may be made if there is already a receiver in office appointed by a secured creditor, unless he consents.

Moreover, on the presentation of a petition for an administration order, notice must be given to any person who has appointed or is entitled to appoint a receiver, so that he may decide before the court reaches its decision whether to appoint a receiver. Hence, the secured creditor has an effectual veto, which he may be expected to exercise in most cases. It suits him better to appoint an insolvency practitioner of his choice to serve as receiver rather than have control taken over by a practitioner with wider responsibilities to all creditors.

From the standpoint of a secured creditor the possible advantages of submitting to the appointment of an administrator are that:

1. the appointment of an administrator imposes a standstill on moves to sue the company for debt, seize its assets or put it into liquidation. Any such action may well defeat the policy which the receiver, with the approval of the secured creditor, is seeking to implement, including carrying on the business with a view to selling it off as a going concern;
2. if an administration order is made any floating charge created by the company within the previous year (extended to two years in certain cases) is likely to be void and any preference given to a creditor or guarantor or company transaction at an undervalue within the recent past may be set aside by the court. In this way an administrator can upset previous transactions by which the directors have sought to impede or defraud its creditors; a receiver has no such power. These subjects are explained in detail in connection with liquidations (see paragraph 13.6 *Avoidance of floating charges* to *Transactions at an undervalue*).

The administration order procedure (not in identical form) has been found useful in some other countries, notably the USA. It is an untried novelty of English company insolvency, whose usefulness remains to be tested. It is generally expected however that, wherever there is a secured creditor, he will usually appoint a receiver and thus make it impossible for the court to make an administration order.

Administration is considered by many to have developed into a costly and time consuming process. One of the reasons for this is the procedure for obtaining an administration order, the cost of which can put administration beyond the reach of smaller companies. Rule 2.2 of the Insolvency Rules require that an application for an administration order may be supported by a report by an independent person that the appointment of an administrator is expedient. While such reports are not compulsory, time and custom have resulted in their being almost mandatory. This can sometimes lead to unnecessary time and expense being spent in the preparation of the report, with figures of up to £20,000 being cited.

The Chancery Division in a *Practice Note* [1994] BCC 35, has gone some way to alleviating this problem. Sir Donald Nicholls V-C reminded Insolvency Practitioners that a r.2.2 report is not always necessary and that 'Every endeavour should be made to avoid disproportionate investigation and expense' in preparing it. In the normal case the court will require a concise assessment of the company's situation. In helping the court decide what the prospects are of the administration order achieving one of the statutory purposes, it will need to be told of the availability of any finance required during the administration.

The DTI has addressed this and other barriers to the use of administration orders in a consultative document published in October 1993 called 'Company Voluntary Arrangements and Administration Orders'.

Administration and the Insolvency Act (1994)

The Insolvency Act 1994 was passed in response to the important Court of Appeal decision in *Re Paramount Airways Ltd (No 3)* [1994] BCC 172, which concerned a petition by two employees under s27 IA 1986. This provides that while the administration order is in force any creditor or member of the company may apply to the court for relief on the grounds of unfair prejudice to himself in the management of the company's affairs by the administrator.

In *Paramount*, administrators were appointed on 7 August 1989 and, in accordance with established practice, wrote to the company's employees on 14 August stating that their contracts of employment were not adopted by the administrators. The company continued to trade until 30 November 1989, when the business closed down and all the employees were dismissed. The administrators paid the employees their wages for the period of the administration, but two employees now claimed for additional sums representing (1) holiday pay accrued but unpaid prior to the administration period, (2) pay in lieu of two months notice under their contract of employment, (3) agreed loyalty bonuses, (4) pension contributions, and (5) compensation for unfair dismissal. The employees claimed entitlement to these sums under s19(5) IA 1986.

Section 19(5) IA 1986 provides for the administrators expenses to be paid out of the company's property. Under s19(4), this is said to be the uncharged assets of the company and the assets subject to a floating charge. Section 19 also provides for the payment of sums incurred by the administrators under contracts of employment 'adopted' by the them. The Court of Appeal had to decide whether the employees contracts of employment had been 'adopted' by the administrators, and, if they had, the extent to which the administrators had 'incurred' liability to pay them the sums claimed. The administrators denied the contracts had been adopted, and said that their only liability was for sums 'incurred' during the period of administration and not for sums incurred before the administration commenced.

The Court of Appeal held that the contracts had been adopted by the administrators. This was despite the administrators' letter of 14 August. On this point Dillon said:

'And the mere assertion by an administrator or receiver that he is not adopting the contract is mere wind with no legal effect, because adoption is a matter not merely of words but of fact. Here all the facts point to the administrators having adopted the contracts.'

It was also held that liability under s19(5) extended to sums incurred under contracts of employment prior to the administration period. The employees were able to claim, therefore, their accrued holiday pay, pay in lieu of notice and the pension contributions. The claim for the loyalty bonus failed as did the claim for an unfair dismissal payment as this arose under statute, rather than their contracts of employment.

The effect of this decision is far reaching, for it means that where the administrators adopt the employees contracts of employment they will have to pay out accrued sums due, such as accrued holiday pay etc, in priority to their own remuneration. As one commentator has observed, as the claims are contractual the normal six-year limitation period applies and initial estimates have put the value of potential claims at anything between £500 million to £1 billion. See Barham [1994] ICCLR 155.

As pointed out earlier, the government responded to the *Paramount* decision by passing the Insolvency Act 1994, which effects contracts of employment adopted on or after 15 March 1994. This short Act amends the wording to s19(5) of the IA 1986 and inserts new subsections (6) to (10). The result is that sums payable under contracts of employment adopted by the administrator will now only be paid out of the company's property if they amount to 'qualifying liabilities': s19(6). Qualifying liabilities are then defined under the new subsections s19(7) to (10). Payments incurred before the adoption of the contract are now specifically excluded. Provided they are incurred after the adoption of the contract of employment by the administrator, qualifying liabilities cover pay, sick pay, holiday pay and pension contributions. The Act does not deal with the meaning of adoption within s19(5) IA 1986, and in this respect the decision in *Re Paramount* remains unaffected.

13.2 Basic points

Statutes

The Insolvency Act 1986 consolidates the provisions of the Companies Act 1985 on company liquidation, including those which relate to liquidation of solvent companies, with the sections of the Insolvency Act 1985 on those topics. The latter Act, which was a major measure of law reform, has been repealed, since it is re-enacted in the 1986 Act. The 1986 Act is therefore a comprehensive statutory code on company liquidation (and also on individual bankruptcy) and it is unnecessary to go back to either of the two 1985 statutes referred to above in connection with liquidation.

As before the main Act is supplemented by lengthy regulations (the Insolvency Rules 1986) which contain much of the details of procedure. However, for examination purposes it is unnecessary to study those details.

The Company Directors Disqualification Act 1986 contains the provisions for disqualification of individuals from acting as directors and from being concerned in the promotion or management of companies (see paragraph 9.9 *Disqualification of directors*). The same Act also provides for disqualification from acting as a receiver, administrator or liquidator of a company (see paragraph 13.2 *Insolvency practitioners*).

Dissolution of companies

A company as an artificial person comes into existence when the registrar enters its name on the register of companies and issues a certificate of incorporation (see paragraph 2.1 *Registration*). Its existence ends three months after the registrar removes its name from the register of active companies: IA s205. This is called 'dissolution'.

Before a company can conveniently be dissolved it must usually be wound up (or 'liquidated' – the two terms are used interchangeably). Liquidation entails collecting the company's assets and converting them into money, using the money to pay its debts, and if anything then remains, distributing the surplus to the members in accordance with their entitlement.

The first step toward dissolution is therefore to put the company into liquidation and appoint a liquidator (or joint liquidators). When the liquidation is completed the liquidator gives notice of it to the registrar: IA s205. There are procedures for suspending or reversing the dissolution of a company in appropriate cases.

In compulsory liquidation the Official Receiver, if he is the liquidator and he concludes that the assets of the company will not suffice to cover the expenses of liquidation and that its affairs do not require further investigation, may apply to the registrar for 'early dissolution', so that dissolution ensues without further work or expense: IA s202.

There is also a procedure under which the registrar may, without a liquidation, proceed to the dissolution of a company which does not appear to be carrying on business: s652. This procedure is used if a company fails to submit annual returns etc and the registrar's formal enquiries elicit no response. It is also possible, by arrangement with the registrar, to have an inactive company dissolved under these powers without the expense of a useless liquidation. But in this case the registrar will have to be satisfied that the company has no outstanding liabilities, particularly unpaid taxes.

Types of liquidation

There are now three types of liquidation:

1. Compulsory liquidation by order of the court: IA s117. The High Court, or, if the company's paid up share capital does not exceed £120,000, in some instances the local county court has jurisdiction to order compulsory liquidation.

2. Voluntary liquidation which may be either:
   a) members' voluntary liquidation; or
   b) creditors' voluntary liquidation.
3. The characteristic of a voluntary liquidation of either type is that it is begun by passing a resolution in general meeting, so that the decision is taken, however reluctantly, by the members.

These three types of liquidation are described in paragraphs 13.3 and 13.4.

Liquidation under the supervision of the court had become obsolete and was abolished in the course of the reforms of 1985–86.

Insolvency practitioners

Only an authorised insolvency practitioner may act as a liquidator (or as a receiver, administrator, supervisor of a voluntary arrangement etc: see paragraph 13.1 *Voluntary arrangements with creditors*).

He must be an individual. If he is an undischarged bankrupt he may not act in this capacity except by leave of the court: IA s390.

To obtain authorisation the applicant must satisfy either a professional body to which the DTI has delegated its powers of authorisation in respect of its own members, or a competent authority (tribunal) appointed by the DTI that he is:

1. a fit and proper person; and
2. satisfies prescribed requirements in respect of education, practical training and experience.

The intention and effect of this system is to confine the position of insolvency practitioner to members of certain prominent professional bodies, mainly accountants, and among members of those bodies to authorise only those of their members who have specialised in insolvency work. It is said that applicants are generally required to show that over the previous three years they have had at least 200 hours annually of insolvency work charged to clients. It is contemplated that in due course new applicants will be required to pass an examination in insolvency practice.

The system, which was recommended by the Cork Committee in 1982, is designed to exclude a minority of unqualified persons of dubious character from continuing to act as insolvency practitioners.

An authorised insolvency practitioner is required to obtain renewed authorisation at intervals, when his record will be taken into account.

The Company Directors Disqualification Act 1986 s7 contains 'reporting provisions' by which an insolvency practitioner who is acting in any of the capacities mentioned above in connection with a company will report to the DTI on certain aspects of the past performance of the directors. Indirectly therefore the restriction of insolvency work to authorised practitioners is a means of introducing much closer examination of the record of directors of companies which have become insolvent, possibly owing to the neglect of those directors (see paragraph 9.1 *Directors and company insolvency*).

In the years before 1986, when there was no effective restriction on the choice of a liquidator, directors might select (and recommend to their shareholders for appointment) someone who would not examine the directors' performance nor reopen their transactions. At its worst, in a minority of cases, there was collusion between directors and the liquidator to facilitate operations intended to defraud creditors by the sale of the business of an insolvent company to a new company, with a similar name and under the same management ('the phoenix syndrome'). As will be seen (paragraph 13.4 *Creditors' voluntary winding-up*) obstacles have now been put in the way of such practice.

However, the system of authorised insolvency practitioners is intended to go much further than restraining malpractice. Its purpose is to promote a stringent review by competent experts of the management of companies, which have become insolvent, with some pressure on them to be thorough in their investigations.

The liquidation of solvent companies

Even if the company is believed to be able to pay its debts in full, its liquidator must be an insolvency practitioner. It will be seen, however, that a members' voluntary liquidation is not under the control of creditors and it usually proceeds in a rather more relaxed manner.

Contributions

Any person who may be liable to contribute to the assets of a company in liquidation is a 'contributory': IA s79. Even if they do not in fact have any actual liability all past and present members of a company, and also the personal representatives of a deceased member and the trustee in bankruptcy of a bankrupt member are declared to be contributories: IA ss74, 81–82. The purpose of this wide definition is presumably to enable those who are classed as contributories to exercise the rights attached to that status, even though by reason of holding fully paid shares, they have no actual liability: *Re Anglesea Colliery Co* (1886) 1 Ch App 555.

A person who has been ordered to contribute to the company's assets on account of his part in its fraudulent or wrongful trading (see paragraph 13.6 *Fraudulent trading* and *Wrongful trading*) is not, however, a contributory in the above sense: IA s79(2).

After casting the net wide to categorise all past and present members (and their representatives) as contributories, the Act (IA s74) then lays down a sequence of exclusions from liability as follows:

1. A past member has no liability if he ceased to be a member at least a year before the commencement of winding up. This is qualified, however, in the case of a person who was a member of an unlimited company at the time of its re-registration as limited (see paragraph 1.4 *Public and private companies*). He remains liable if the company goes into liquidation within three years of its re-registration as limited: IA s77(2).

This is a device to prevent members of unlimited companies from seeking to avoid liability for its debts by re-registering it as limited when the unavoidable insolvency can be foreseen.

2. A past member is only liable in respect of outstanding debts of the company incurred while he was still a member.

3. A past member is only liable if the existing members are unable to meet their obligations to the company.

4. If the company is limited by shares no member is required to pay more than the amount, if any, unpaid on his shares (or the shares which he previously held if he is a past member). If the company is limited by guarantee his liability is limited to the amount specified in the memorandum (see paragraph 1.4 *A company limited by guarantee*).

In practice therefore a contributory rarely has to contribute to the company's assets unless he holds, or held within the past year, partly paid shares, or it is a guarantee company. A past member, even within the previous year, will only be liable if the transferee to whom his shares passed, is insolvent, or if he has been involved in a scramble to escape liability as member of an unlimited company (see (1) above). It will be seen that a member of a company which is unlimited, at the time of liquidation, will be liable without limit if the company is then insolvent but only in respect of its debts incurred up to the time when he ceased to be a member (if he is no longer a member).

Commencement of liquidation

The date of commencement of liquidation is often significant in its effect on halting legal action by creditors, avoidance of transactions, etc.

1. In a compulsory liquidation the date of presentation of a petition to the court for an order is the normal date of commencement. But if the company was at the date of the petition then in voluntary liquidation, the date on which voluntary liquidation began is the critical date: IA s129. In either case an order for compulsory liquidation has retrospective effect. To put the matter another way the presentation of a petition may prove to be the commencement date of liquidation and so the company has to manage its affairs, over a period of weeks or months, without any certainty as to whether various restrictions will be retrospectively applied to it.

2. Voluntary liquidation commences on the date of passing the resolution to wind up: IA s86.

13.3 Compulsory liquidation

Introduction

The majority of company liquidations are voluntary, initiated by a resolution passed in general meeting. Even if the company is insolvent and under pressure from its creditors, it usually suits both the directors and the creditors to promote a creditors' voluntary liquidation which is a less expensive and formal procedure.

However, compulsory liquidation is the possible remedy of last resort for the creditor or member (and some public agencies: see paragraph 13.3 *Who may petition*) if a company obdurately refuses to satisfy their legitimate demands or is simply unresponsive, usually because it has been abandoned by the directors. However, in every case a petition to the court for compulsory liquidation must state, and be supported by evidence of, certain specified grounds upon which the court in its discretion may order compulsory liquidation.

Grounds for compulsory liquidation

A company may be wound up by the court on the following grounds specified in IA s122(1):

1. the company has so resolved by special resolution;
2. default is made in delivering the statutory declaration of capital etc in order to obtain the registrar's certificate that a public company may commence business: s117;
3. the company does not commence its business within a year from its incorporation or suspends its business for a whole year;
4. the number of members is reduced below the statutory minimum (two, for private and public companies);
5. the company is unable to pay its debts;
6. the court is of the opinion that it is just and equitable that the company should be wound up.

(A seventh ground incidental to re-registration of public companies under CA 1980 is no longer significant.)

Inability to pay debts: IA s123

A company is deemed to be unable to pay its debts if it defaults for three weeks or more in meeting a demand for a debt exceeding £750 (or such other limit as the Secretary of State may fix under IA s416), or if it fails to satisfy a judgment debt, or the court is satisfied that it is unable to pay its debts (in which case it can take account of the company's contingent and prospective liabilities). The demands of two or more creditors may be aggregated.

The fact that, for the time being, the company has insufficient liquid assets to pay its present debts where payment of those debts has not been demanded, is insufficient: *Re Capital Annuities Ltd* [1978] 3 All ER 704.

Just and equitable ground

The wording of this ground is wide. In *Re German Date Coffee Co* (1882) 20 Ch D 169, this was the ground for winding up a company whose substratum had disappeared.

Provided a member has sufficient grounds for presenting a petition for winding up, the size of his shareholding and his motives in petitioning are irrelevant: *Bryanston Finance Ltd* v *de Vries* (No 2) [1976] 1 All ER 25. But, in the absence of mala fides, the mere exercise of their majority strength by the majority shareholders will not per se entitle the petitioner(s) to succeed.

The shareholder is not necessarily restricted to grounds for complaint which affect him solely in his position as shareholder. The section enables the court to subject the exercise of legal rights to equitable considerations of a personal character and a shareholder is not confined to grounds which affect him as such: *Ebrahimi* v *Westbourne Galleries Ltd* [1973] AC 360.

Those equitable considerations will not arise merely because the company is a small one: *Re A Company* (No 002567 of 1982) [1983] 1 WLR 927. However, in such a case it will obviously be more appropriate, even essential, to take account of personal relationships involving mutual trust and confidence and of an understanding that all shareholders will participate in the business. In the case of what amounts to an incorporated partnership the court may rely on grounds suitable for dissolution of partnerships on the just and equitable ground (*Re Yenidje Tobacco Co* [1916] 2 Ch 426) but it is still a company subject to company law.

An order may be made where the majority shareholders deprive the minority of their legal right to appoint and remove their own director in furtherance of their right to participate in management: *Re A & BC Chewing Gum Ltd* [1975] 1 All ER 1017.

The alternative remedy

If a petition is presented by members of the company as contributories on the just and equitable ground the court is required by IA s125(2) to consider whether the petitioners have some other remedy and are acting unreasonably in seeking to have the company wound up. If that is the position the remedy of compulsory liquidation is likely to be refused.

This limitation has become much more important since the reformulation (now ss459–461) of the statutory right of a minority to apply to the court for appropriate relief on grounds of unfair prejudice. The abundant recent case law on this subject is considered in an earlier lesson (see paragraph 13.2 *Who may petition*). It has become common practice therefore, though it is not obligatory, to present simultaneous petitions under IA s122(1)(g) for compulsory liquidation and under s459 for minority relief. If the court is not satisfied that there has been unfair prejudice, it may grant the former remedy and refuse the latter. This outcome is particularly likely where faults on both sides have led to deadlock in the company: *Re R A Noble (Clothing) Ltd* [1983] BCLC 273 (facts in paragraph 11.2 *Unfair prejudice*) is an example. If on the other hand the court concludes that there has been unfair prejudice, it is almost bound to refuse an order for compulsory liquidation but may grant the petitioner relief on his petition under s459, eg by sale of his shares at a fair price.

In *Jesner* v *Jarrad Properties Ltd* [1992] BCC 807 the Court of Session affirmed that a minority shareholder was entitled to an order that a company be wound up on the ground that it was just and equitable to do so in terms of s122(1)(g) of the 1986 Act notwithstanding that he was not entitled to a share purchase order on the ground of unfair prejudice in terms of s459 of the 1985 Act. An application for a winding-up order should only be included as an alternative to an order under s459 if it is the preferred relief or the only relief to which the petitioner may be entitled: *Practice Direction* [1990] 1 All ER 1056.

An 'alternative remedy' may be found in some other form and not necessarily under s459. In *Re A Company* (No 002567 of 1982) [1983] 1 WLR 927 (see paragraph 13.3 *Just and equitable ground*) the petitioner had offered, following his exclusion from the board, to sell his shares to the other directors and they had proposed that the price should be fixed on the basis of fair market value by an independent valuer. His conduct in persisting with a petition for compulsory winding-up was therefore unreasonable. The court did not dismiss the petition but adjourned the hearing so that the fixing of the price and sale of the shares might proceed. If the articles provide for the situation which has emerged, it is unliked that it will afford grounds for compulsory liquidation: *Re K/9 Meat Supplies Guildford Ltd* [1966] 3 All ER 320 (transfer of shares of a bankrupt to his trustee in bankruptcy the available solution).

Who may petition?

The above description of the more usual grounds for a petition incidentally indicates that most petitions are presented either by one or more creditors on the ground that the company is unable to pay its debts in excess of £750, or by one or more contributories on the basis that deadlock or oppressive conduct in the management or other grounds make it just and equitable to wind-up the company. However, the full list of those who may present a petition in appropriate cases is rather longer:

1. The company: IA s124.
2. Any creditor or creditors who establish a prima facie case: IA s124.

   In *Re Dollar Land Holdings plc* [1993] BCC 823, W gave a bank security, on behalf of the company, so that the bank would guarantee the company's liabilities to another bank. W agreed with the company that he would provide the security in return for a 25 per cent stake in a property which was been acquired by one of the company's subsidiaries. The guarantee was drawn on to the sum of £422,00, but the property was never acquired. On discovering this W demanded that the company release him from his guarantee and issued a winding up petition against the company. One of the company's arguments was that he had no standing as a creditor. It was held that W was a contingent or prospective creditor under IA s124.

Where a director deposits money with a bank as security for the company's indebtedness to the bank, then these deposits can be set off against the total indebtedness of the company to the bank in the bank's liquidation. The bank cannot in these circumstances require full payment of the indebtedness leaving the directors to claim as unsecured creditors for the amount of the deposits: *MS Fashions Ltd and Others* v *Bank of Credit and Commerce International SA (In liquidation)* [1993] 3 WLR 220. See also *Re Bank of Credit and Commerce International SA (No 3)* [1994] BCC 462.

Generally the court ought not to deprive a petitioning creditor of his prima facie right to a winding-up order unless his petition is opposed by creditors with the majority in the value of their debts. Where the petitioning and supporting creditors belong to the same group of companies as the company in liquidation, the court should have regard to the nature of their debts (eg that they were 'domestic' (intra-group) debts owed to a member company). Where the petitioning creditor was the parent company, it could control the activities of the company in liquidation: *Re Southard & Co Ltd* [1979] 1 All ER 582.

The court can and will restrain a petition which is an abuse of process. In *Re A Company* (No 001573 of 1983) (1983) The Times 12 May, it was held an abuse to petition for winding-up on the same day that an order for costs was made against the company and the petitioner doubted its ability to pay.

If a debt is genuinely disputed, the court may restrain a winding-up petition. But the court will take due heed of potential difficulties in establishing a debt against, for example, a foreign company: *In Re Russian and English Bank* [1932] 1 Ch 663. However, this is a rule of practice and the court will always consider whether there appears to be a substantial dispute: *Re Claybridge Shipping Co SA* [1981] Com LR 107.

In *Re A Company* (No 0012209 of 1991) [1992] 2 All ER 797 Hoffman J granted an injunction to restrain the presentation of a winding-up petition by a creditor as the company was solvent and it appeared that its defence to the creditor's claim had a prospect of success. The creditor was ordered to pay the company's costs on an indemnity basis. His Lordship added, however, 'that if the court comes to the conclusion that a solvent company is not putting forward any defence in good faith and is merely seeking to take for itself credit which it is not allowed under the contract, then the court would not be inclined to restrain presentation of the petition.'

3. A contributory or contributories, when the number of members has fallen below the statutory minimum or if the contributory is an original allottee or held shares for six months in the 18 months preceding the winding up or received them through devolution from a former member: IA s124(2).

He will generally have to show that there will be a surplus available for distribution to the members after the winding up: *Re Rica Gold Washing Co* (1879) 11 Ch D 36. A petitioner is without locus standi unless he would derive an advantage from winding up qua member: *Re Chesterfield Catering Co Ltd* [1976] 3 All ER 294.

A contributory has been able to rely on a report of inspectors, appointed by the Secretary of State for Trade on the ground (inter alia) of the withholding of information from shareholders, in support of a winding-up petition in *Re St Piran* [1981] 1 WLR 1300 (see paragraph 11.3 *Results of investigations*).

4. The DTI after an investigation (s440 and IA s124(4)) and on certain other grounds. The court may use a report of the inspectors as prima facie grounds for ordering a winding up: *Re Armvent Ltd* [1975] 3 All ER 441.

5. The Official Receiver, where a voluntary winding up cannot be continued with due regard to the interests of creditors or contributories: IA s124(5). The power of the Secretary of State (4) is not so limited: *Re Lubin, Rosen and Associates Ltd* [1975] 1 All ER 577.

6. In the case of an English charitable company, the Attorney-General or any other person authorised by the Insolvency Act 1986: s30 of the Charities Act 1960, as substituted. In certain circumstances it is also possible for the Charity Commissioners to present a petition: s30(2)–(6) of the 1960 Act as added by s10 of the 1992 Act, s30 of the 1960 Act having become s30(1). It should be noted, too, that ss8 and 9 of the 1992 Act confer on the Commissioners power, inter alia, to appoint a receiver and manager in respect of the property and affairs of a charity.

The court may have regard to the wishes of creditors and contributories when hearing a petition and may order meetings to ascertain those wishes: IA s195.

Procedure

The petitioner(s) present(s) a petition supported by affidavit vertifying the facts stated therein. Unless the petition is presented by the company itself (see paragraph 13.3 *Who may petition*), a copy is supplied for service on the company, which is entitled to appear and oppose the petition at the hearing.

The petition is advertised in the *London Gazette* at least seven business days in advance of the date fixed for the hearing. This is to enable creditors of the company, and other interested parties, to have notice in time to be represented at the hearing if they wish.

The petition is heard in open court: at present it is the practice of the High Court to set aside Mondays for this purpose. On hearing the petition the court may: (1) dismiss it; (2) adjourn the hearing; (3) make an interim order; (4) make any other order it thinks fit; and (5) make an order for compulsory winding up: IA s125. The court is not to refuse to make a winding-up order merely because all the company's assets have been mortgaged for an amount equal to or more than the assets or that the company has no assets.

At any time after the presentation of the petition the court may appoint a provisional liquidator, usually to safeguard the assets of the company pending the outcome of the hearing of the petition: IA s135. It is not normally necessary to take this precaution, however, as the order, if made, is retrospective to the date of presentation of the petition (see paragraph 13.2 *Commencement of liquidation*) and disposition of assets after that date are made void by the winding-up order (see paragraph 13.3 *The effect of the winding-up order*).

The order when made leads to an investigation by the Official Receiver as provisional liquidator into the causes of the company's failure and the general record of its management: IA s132. The Official Receiver, like an administrative receiver (paragraph 13.1 *Administration orders*), may call for a statement of affairs from company officers: IA s131. He reports to the court and he may apply to the court for the public examination of officers in open court: IA s133. Such an examination of a director of a company in compulsory liquidation may be ordered irrespective of his nationality and notwithstanding that he is resident abroad: *Re Seagull Manufacturing Co Ltd (No 2)* [1993] BCC 833.

A director of a company is not entitled to rely on the privilege against self-incrimination to refuse to answer questions put to him by provisional liquidators under ss235 and 236 of the 1986 Act, but such privilege is available to a fiduciary from whom the principal is seeking information about dealings with trust money under the general law: *Bishopsgate Investment Management Ltd* v *Maxwell* [1992] 2 All ER 856. The restrictions imposed by s2(8) of the Criminal Justice Act 1987 on the use of statements obtained under that section (investigation powers of the Director of the Serious Fraud Office) do not apply to documents obtained in an examination under s236 IA 1986.

The liquidator must hand over the transcripts of interviews conducted under s236 of the IA 1986 to the Serious Fraud Office, even if the person has not yet been charged with a criminal offence: *Re Advisor (188) Ltd & Anor, ex parte Trachtenberg* [1993] BCC 492

A defendant in criminal proceedings has no right to ask that the liquidator supplies him with copies of the transcripts of interviews conducted under s236 IA 1986 at the same time that they are supplied to the Serious Fraud Office: *Re Headington Investments Ltd* [1993] BCC 500.

In *Morris* v *Director of Serious Fraud Office* [1993] 1 All ER 788 Sir Donald Nicholls V-C said that, in the ordinary way when an application is made or is proposed to be made against the Serious Fraud Office for an order under s236 requiring disclosure of documents acquired by the office under its compulsory powers, a third party who might be affected by the disclosure ought to be notified of the application and the Serious Fraud Office's attitude to disclosure, and asked whether he objects to an order being made. If his assent is not forthcoming, he should be joined as a respondent to the application. However, in exceptional cases, if it is just to do so, the court may make an order under s236 in the exercise of its discretion even though the third party has not been notified.

In *Re Arrows Ltd (No 4)* [1994] BCC 641 House of Lords, N was a director and principal shareholder in the company when it went into liquidation. He was examined by the liquidators under s236 IA 1986 and the Serious Fraud Office, ('SFO') under s2(3) of the Criminal Justice Act 1987, asked the liquidators to hand over the transcripts of the examination. The SFO wanted to consider them in order that they might be used in criminal proceedings against N. The trial judge ordered that they should not be handed over, unless the SFO give an undertaking that they would not be used in evidence in criminal proceedings. This decision was reversed by the Court of Appeal and N appealed to the House of Lords. It was held that N's appeal should be dismissed. Although the judge at first instance, in the companies court, had a discretion to require the SFO to give an undertaking that the transcripts would not be used in later criminal proceedings, he exercised the discretion improperly. It was for the judge in the criminal proceedings to decide whether the admission of the transcripts would prejudice a fair criminal trial. The trial judge will have all the circumstances of the case known to him, which the judge in the Companies Court did not have. See Chapter 15, paragraph 15.9, for further details.

The conduct of the liquidation

The Official Receiver is automatically appointed provisional liquidator on the making of the order: IA s136(2), so that there is from the outset a liquidator in office. The Official Receiver resumes the office of liquidator if it latter falls vacant.

He has 12 weeks in which to decide whether to convene meetings of creditors and contributories with a view to appointing someone else (who must be an authorised insolvency practitioner: see paragraph 13.2 *Insolvency practitioners*) in his place. He must call these meetings on the demand of one quarter, in value, of the creditor: IA s136. If he does not call meetings, he gives notice to the court, to the creditors and to the contributories of his decision.

The purpose of this discretionary procedure, which differs from the pre-1986 system in which holding the meetings was obligatory, is to avoid the useless formality of holding meetings at which the creditors are unlikely to propose a substitute liquidator to replace the Official Receiver. Any candidate whom they might propose would probably look to them to guarantee the payment of his fees, if few assets remain, and they may well decide that it is not worthwhile to do so.

If meetings are held, each meeting may nominate a liquidator but the nominee of the creditors automatically takes office, subject to a right of objection to the court, given to all creditors and contributories, to be exercised, if at all, within seven days: IA s139.

The same meetings, or subsequent meetings, may resolve to establish a liquidation committee, including representatives of creditors and of contributories, to work with the liquidator, who may obtain the sanction which he needs from a liquidation committee for the exercise of those of his statutory powers for which sanction is required: IA s141. If there is no liquidation committee its functions are vested in the DTI.

As the liquidation progresses, the liquidator calls meetings as necessary, and in the end a final meeting of creditors and of contributories, as the first step to completing the liquidation and seeking the dissolution of the company: IA ss146 and 205 (see paragraph 13.2 *Dissolution of companies*).

The effect of the winding-up order

The winding-up is deemed to have begun at the time of presenting the petition (or the commencement of voluntary liquidation if that preceded compulsory liquidation) and the Official Receiver becomes provisional liquidator, unless already appointed as such at an earlier stage (see paragraph 13.3 *Procedure*): IA s136(2).

In addition a standstill is imposed on the company's transactions with retrospective effect to the commencement of the winding-up as follows:

1. any disposition of property of the company is void unless sanctioned by the court: IA s127. In *Re Barn Crown Ltd* [1995] 1 WLR 147, it was held that there is no disposition of property within IA 127 where a bank collects third party cheques, which it then credits to the company's account at the bank. An order that the bank pay the sums collected to the liquidator was therefore refused. See Chapter 15, paragraph 15.9, for further details;
2. any transfer of shares or alteration of status of members is similarly void: s127;
3. any attachment etc of assets of the company is void: IA s128;
4. no legal proceedings against the company may be commenced or continued except by leave of the court: IA s130;
5. the employees of the company are dismissed but the liquidator may by mutual agreement retain them in the service of the company;
6. the management of the company and the control of its business and property is in the hands of the liquidator, who has wide statutory powers (IA Sch. 4) but requires sanction for the exercise of the more important powers. He may also apply to the court for an order vesting assets in him: IA s145;
7. charges on company property and dispositions of that property may become void (see paragraph 13.6 *Avoidance of floating charges* to *Transactions at an undervalue*).

If an order for winding up a company is made by mistake in respect of the wrong company, the court may cancel it and direct the registrar to remove all record of it from the register: *Re Calmex Ltd* [1989] 1 All ER 485.

Where a company has been dissolved, the court has a discretionary power to make an order restoring the company to the register for the purpose of enabling an action to be brought against the company to recover damages for, inter alia, personal injury or death: s651(5) of the Companies Act 1985 as inserted by s141(3) of the Companies Act 1989. This discretion may be exercised at any time provided the court does not think that an action brought as the result of a successful application for restoration will fail. As to the relationship between such a restoration and a limitation period, see *Re Workvale Ltd (in dissolution)* [1992] 1 WLR 416.

13.4 Voluntary winding–up

Type of resolution required

Every kind of voluntary winding-up is commenced by passing a resolution in general meeting. The type of resolution required varies according to the circumstances:

1. If the articles fix the period of duration of the company or provide that upon the happening of an event it shall be dissolved and the period has expired or the event has occurred, it suffices to pass an ordinary resolution, referring to the articles, and resolving that the company be wound up accordingly. In practice articles rarely include any such automatic winding up provisions.
2. The company may resolve to wind-up by special resolution (which states no reasons). This is the normal method of winding-up a solvent company.
3. The company may by extraordinary resolution resolve that by reason of its liabilities the company is unable to continue its business and that it is advisable to wind-up: IA s84(1).

Any such resolution must be advertised in the *London Gazette* within 14 days of the meeting: IA s85(1). A copy of it must also be delivered to the registrar within 14 days: IA s84(3).

Members' voluntary winding–up

Any voluntary winding-up is a creditors' voluntary winding-up unless the directors have made and delivered to the registrar a declaration of solvency: IA s90. It is not a question of whether the company is solvent, which may be uncertain when it goes into liquidation. It must be assumed to be insolvent unless the directors accept personal responsibility for stating that they believe it is solvent.

The declaration, if made, is on a form which incorporates a statement of estimated assets and liabilities up to the latest practicable date. The directors state that after making full inquiry they are of opinion that the company will be able to pay its debts in full within a specified period which may not exceed 12 months. If the number of directors does not exceed two, they must all join in making the declaration. If there are more than two a majority suffices.

The declaration must be made not more than five weeks before nor any later than the passing of the resolution to wind-up and it must be delivered to the registrar within 15 days of passing the resolution.

If in the event the company is unable to pay its debts in full within the 12 month period, the directors are presumed to have made their declaration without having reasonable grounds for it, which is a criminal offence. The burden of showing that they did have reasonable grounds, as a defence, rests on them.

If a declaration has been made and filed, the company resolves to wind-up and it appoints an insolvency practitioner to be liquidator. The creditors have no part in the liquidation because it is expected that they will be paid in full and they have no right to interfere with the company's conduct of its affairs.

If in the course of the liquidation the liquidator concludes that the company will after all be unable to pay its debts in full within the specified period, within 28 days he must call a meeting of creditors on seven days' notice, which is advertised in the *London Gazette* and in two local newspapers. Before the meeting the creditors may demand information about the company's affairs. At the meeting the liquidator lays before the creditors a statement of affairs. Thereafter the liquidation proceeds as a creditors' voluntary winding-up, as if the declaration of solvency had not been made: IA ss95–96. The consequences for the directors who made the declaration have been stated above.

At the end of each year of the liquidation, and within three months of the anniversary date, the liquidator holds a general meeting of the company and lays before it a statement of his acts and dealings: IA s93. When the liquidation has been completed the liquidator calls a final meeting, by advertisement in the *London Gazette*. He lays before the meeting accounts of his dealings with the company's property. Within the week after the meeting the liquidator sends to the registrar a copy of his accounts and a return that the meeting has been held (or if there was no meeting due to lack of a quorum a return that it was duly summoned). This leads on to the dissolution of the company: IA s94 (see paragraph 13.2 *Dissolution of companies*).

Creditors' voluntary winding-up

There is no declaration of solvency and instead the company is required to call a meeting of its creditors not later than the fourteenth day after it holds its own meeting to resolve to wind-up. The meeting of creditors is called on seven days' notice and this is advertised in the *London Gazette*. The notice must either give the name and address of an insolvency practitioner from whom creditors may obtain information in advance or it must specify a place where, in the final two business days before the meeting creditors may obtain a list of all the creditors. No charge is to be made for these services: IA s98.

At the creditors' meeting one of the directors presides and lays before the meeting a statement of the company's financial affairs: IA s99.

The members and the creditors at their respective meetings may nominate an insolvency practitioner to be liquidator. If different persons are nominated, the creditors' nominee takes office, subject to a right of appeal to the court, given to directors, members and creditors, to be exercised within seven days: IA s100.

As there may be an interval between the meeting of members and the meeting of creditors, any liquidator appointed by the members takes office until, if ever, a different person is appointed by the creditors. However, a liquidator appointed by the members has no power to dispose of the company's assets, except those which are perishable etc and such as the court may sanction, until the meeting of creditors is held: IA s166.

Then if the creditors do not appoint a different liquidator the members' nominee has a liquidator's normal powers of disposal.

This rather involved provision is intended to resolve two problems. First, until the law was changed in 1985 a liquidator appointed by the members had full powers from the outset which he might use to dispose of the company's major assets before the creditors' nominee took office in his place. This possibility was exploited to arrange transfer of the insolvent company's business to a successor company on advantageous terms to the latter. This practice was colloquially called 'centrebinding' because the transactions of the first liquidator were held to be valid in *Re Centrebind Ltd* [1966] 3 All ER 889.

The second potential problem is that the creditors, when they hold their meeting, may not appoint any liquidator, if they consider that the state of the company makes it unprofitable to incur the expense. Yet, if the company itself wishes to proceed with an insolvent liquidation, it should be allowed to do so. In brief s166 imposes a standstill on major disposal of assets until the creditors have had their opportunity of putting in a liquidator of their choice. There is a similar restriction on disposal by the directors if the company goes into a creditors' voluntary liquidation without appointing any liquidator at all: IA s114.

It is relevant at this point to mention another provision intended to restrain this type of malpractice by directors of insolvent companies. If a company goes into insolvent liquidation any person who was a director within the period of 12 months before liquidation is prohibited from being a director or otherwise concerned with the management of any other company which has the same or a similar name (see paragraph 2.2 *Misleading names*). This prohibition, which is automatic, lasts for five years though the court may grant exemption from it in deserving cases: IA s216. This restriction is to prevent the same dishonest management continuing to operate through a sequence of companies, carrying on the same fraudulent business under substantially the same name ('the phoenix syndrome') (see paragraph 13.2 *Insolvency practitioners*).

The creditors may resolve at their meeting to establish a liquidation committee with up to five representatives of the creditors and five of the members: IA s101. The function of such a committee, if established, is to work with the liquidator who may seek its sanction for the exercise of certain of his statutory powers.

If the liquidation continues for more than a year, the liquidator calls separate meetings of creditors as well as of members within three months of each year's end: IA s105. He also calls a final meeting of creditors, as well as of members, at the completion of the liquidation: IA s106.

The effect of going into voluntary liquidation

The decision to liquidate is effective from the day on which the resolution is passed in general meeting: IA s86.

The directors remain in office but their powers cease except insofar as they may be authorised by the competent authority to continue: IA ss91(2) and 103.

The company's property must be applied in payment of its debts and any surplus may then be distributed to its members: IA s107. The company, through the liquidator, may carry on its business but only for purposes of beneficial winding up, ie ultimate sale or closure: IA s87.

The employees' contracts of service with the company continue until determined by the liquidator. On a sale of the business as a going concern, they are transferred to the service of the purchaser, unless action is taken to dismiss them: Transfer of Undertakings (Protection of Employment) Regulations 1982.

No transfer of shares or alteration of members' status may be made unless the liquidator sanctions it: IA s88. There is no automatic restraint on legal action against the company or its property. However, the liquidator may apply to the court for an order to halt any action of that kind by a creditor: IA s112.

13.5 Assets and liabilities in liquidation

Introduction

The liquidator's duty is to get in the company's assets, convert them into money and apply them in payment of the company's debts before distributing what remains, if anything, to the shareholders: cf *Mettoy Pension Trustees Ltd* v *Evans* [1991] 2 All ER 513.

In the course of this programme the liquidator may take action to set aside company transactions of the recent past or to recover contributions or compensation from company officers. That subject is dealt with in the final section (paragraph 13.6) of this chapter.

In the distribution of surplus assets to shareholders, the liquidator must conform to their respective rights. In principle they all participate equally, but if the company has issued preference shares the holders of those shares usually (1) have a priority entitlement to repayment of capital but (2) have no right to participate in distribution of any surplus assets remaining after the repayment of capital on ordinary shares. If there are arrears of unpaid preference dividends, they lapse unless it is expressly provided that they shall be paid off (as capital) in liquidation. This has been described in paragraph 6.3 *Class rights – preference shares*

In dealing with the assets the liquidator may have to take action against creditors (see paragraph 13.5 *Assets in the hands of creditors*) or to disclaim burdensome assets which entail more outlay than they are worth (see paragraph 13.5 *Disclaimer of assets*).

Apart from considering the order of priority of debts of different kinds the liquidator must ensure that only legally enforceable claims are recognised. If, for example, a debt is statute-barred, he should refuse to pay it: *Re Art Production Co Ltd* [1952] Ch 89. He may reject claims arising from transactions in which the directors have exceeded their powers (paragraph 2.3 *Validity of transactions*).

It may also happen that the same person is both a creditor and a debtor of the company. For example, the company may have more than one bank account with a debit balance on one and a credit on another. As a general rule this situation is adjusted by set-off so that a net figure is calculated.

The accounting records of insolvent companies are often in disorder. In any case it is the liquidator's duty to satisfy himself that a creditor has a valid claim and that the amount demanded is correct. There is a formal procedure for 'proof of debts' in compulsory liquidation. However, the liquidator would as a matter of course write to every creditor of whom there is a record in the books and invite him to give notice of the amount due to him, with supporting papers.

The liquidator has statutory power to pay any class of creditors in full and also to negotiate a compromise or arrangement, eg with debentureholders. However, these are powers which he may only exercise with the prescribed sanction, eg of the liquidation committee: IA Sch. 4 Pt I.

After dealing with these and any other problems the liquidator should follow the proper 'order of application of assets' (see paragraph 13.5 *Order of application of assets*) according to the priority of the company's debts. If he fails to pay a creditor out of assets available, in accordance with the proper order, the creditor may sue the liquidator: *Pulsford* v *Devenish* [1903] 2 Ch 625.

Assets in the hands of creditors

A creditor who has obtained judgment against the company for a debt which the company still does not pay, may then issue execution to attach property of the company. However, unless he has completed this action before liquidation commences, he must hand back to the liquidator the property which he has attached.

Execution is completed by seizure and sale, the appointment of a receiver or obtaining a charging order under the Charging Orders Act 1979: IA s183. The method varies according to the type of property which is affected.

Although voluntary liquidation commences on the passing of the resolution to wind up, a creditor who has notice that a meeting has been called for this purpose is affected by that notice as if it were the commencement: IA s183(2).

In the course of execution the sheriff (a county court officer) may have seized goods of the company with a view to sale. If before he has sold them, the sheriff has notice of an order for compulsory liquidation or of the passing of a resolution for winding up, he must return the goods to the liquidator. Moreover, if the judgment debt exceeds £500, he must after sale retain the proceeds (less expenses) for 14 days and account for the money to the liquidator, if within that period he has notice of an order for compulsory liquidation or of the issue of a notice to convene a meeting to wind-up voluntarily: IA s184.

If, however, the company pays its debt to the sheriff, after he has seized its goods, to avoid sale of the goods, this is not money paid in the course of execution and the creditor is entitled to retain it: *Re Walkden Sheet Metal Co Ltd* [1960] Ch 170.

In compulsory liquidation execution or distress by a creditor or landlord after the presentation of the petition is void: IA s128. In voluntary liquidation the liquidator may apply to the court for an order to avoid execution or distress effected after the passing of the resolution to wind up: IA s112. The order would be made unless the company had deceived the creditor in order to delay his action against its goods.

Disclaimer of assets

The liquidator has a statutory power to disclaim 'onerous property' of the company. As a result of changes made in 1985 he is no longer required to obtain leave of the court for a disclaimer. Onerous property is defined to include unprofitable contracts and other property which it would be difficult to sell: IA s178(3). A typical example would be an empty factory in an area of high unemployment held by the company under a lease at a full economic rent.

The effect of disclaimer is that the company's entire interest in the property ceases but any person who thereby suffers loss becomes a creditor of the company for the amount of his loss. There are special provisions for the disclaimer of leases, to safeguard the position of an underlessee or a mortgagee: IA s179.

A liquidator may disclaim property although he has taken possession, exercised rights of ownership over it or tried to sell it. However, the other party who would be affected by a disclaimer may bring the liquidator to an immediate decision by serving on him a notice, requiring the liquidator to state whether or not he intends to disclaim. Unless he then within 28 days gives notice of disclaimer, he loses the right to do so.

Secured creditors

A secured creditor has a dual relationship with the company. Like any other creditor he may claim from the company as its debtor payment of the amount due to him and pursue the normal means to enforce payment. In addition he is in the position of, or analogous to, a mortgagee with a limited interest in the property of the company which is his security. He may enforce those proprietary rights, usually by appointing a receiver (see paragraph 7.4 *The role of a receiver*).

However, against a company in liquidation the secured creditor must opt for one remedy or the other. If he elects to prove his debt by notice to the liquidator, he is deemed to have surrendered his security. More typically he enforces his security and recovers his debt by that means without making a claim against the liquidator.

It may be of course that the property which is the security now has a realisable value which is less than the secured debt. If the creditor sells the property charged to him, he may claim as an unsecured creditor for the amount by which the net proceeds of realisation fall short of the debt. If the creditor merely values his security, ie puts an estimated value on it, and claims the balance as an unsecured debt, the liquidator may redeem it at that value or have it sold.

If the security yields a surplus over the debt and expenses, the creditor accounts for the surplus to the liquidator.

Preferential unsecured debts

It is often convenient to refer to 'preferential creditors' but strictly it is only the debt which can be preferential. It may happen, for example, that part of the same debt is preferential and the rest is not.

The categories of preferential debts were reduced by the insolvency legislation of 1985–86. In particular neither arrears of corporation tax on company profits nor unpaid rates owing to a local authority are now preferential. The current categories of preferential debts are defined in IA Sch. 6 to include:

1. income tax deducted by the company as employer from the taxable pay of employees under the PAYE system during the 12 months prior to the relevant date (see paragraph 13.5 *The relevant date for preferential debts*) and not yet paid over to the Inland Revenue;
2. value added tax owed by the company in respect of the period of six months up to that date;
3. salaries or wages of company employees in respect of the period of four months ended on that date, subject to a maximum of £800 for each employee;
4. holiday pay and employer's contributions to occupational pension schemes.

In addition some other unpaid taxes such as vehicle licence duty, taxes on gaming and betting, and social security contributions in respect of the 12 months before the relevant date are preferential.

The relevant date for preferential debts

The relevant date for a company in liquidation is normally:

1. the date of the winding-up order in compulsory liquidation but it will be the earlier date of appointment of a provisional liquidator or the date of making the administration order (see paragraph 13.1 *Administration orders*) discharged when the company went into liquidation, if either of those events preceded the winding-up order;
2. the date of passing of the resolution to wind-up in a voluntary liquidation: IA s387.

It will be remembered that an administrative receiver (see paragraph 7.4 *The receiver's status within the company*) and an administrator (see paragraph 13.1 *Administration orders*) have the same duty as a liquidator to pay preferential debts before non-preferential debts. For a receiver the relevant date is the date of his appointment and for an administrator the date of the administration order: IA s387(2) and (4).

To sum up the relevant date is fixed, in different circumstances, by reference to the initial onset of insolvency.

Employees' unpaid wages as preferential debts

In the reduced list of preferential debts employees' pay is often the largest item to be met. Two points deserve mention:

1. Loans to pay wages are preferential debts to the extent that the loan money, often lent by a bank, has been used to pay wages etc which if unpaid would have been preferential.
2. The Department of Employment has statutory power, within certain limits, to pay the wages of employees (otherwise unpaid) of an insolvent employer. If it does so, it becomes a creditor of the company for the amount it has paid out, and has the same preferential claims as the employees would have had.

In connection with (1) it is always a question of fact whether the loan creditor has provided money used to pay wages, which would otherwise be preferential debts. The banks usually insist that money advanced for this purpose shall be paid from a separate wages account. However, where the company borrowed from the bank through its main account and made transfers from that account to a wages account, which was not overdrawn at the commencement of liquidation, the bank was treated as a lender (through the overdraft on the main company account) of money paid out in wages: *Re James R Rutherford & Sons Ltd* [1964] 3 All ER 137.

A director of a company is not as such an employee, so that his fees due under the articles cannot be a preferential debt. However, if he is also a working director, his arrears of unpaid salary as a manager are preferential within the usual limits indicated above.

The status of a company secretary depends on his working arrangements. If he works full-time for the company his unpaid salary can be a preferential debt. If on the other hand he is an outsider who only gives part of his time to his duties as secretary, his fees are not a preferential debt: *Cairney* v *Black* [1906] 2 KB 746.

The priority of preferential debts

A liquidator (and also a receiver or an administrator) is required to pay preferential debts, rateably between all debts in that category, in priority to:

1. debts secured by a floating charge on the company's assets; and
2. unsecured non-preferential debts: IA s175.

If a landlord of the company has levied distress on its property for arrears of rent within three months before the making of an order for compulsory liquidation, the preferential debts of the company, unless they can be paid out of other company assets, must be paid out of the proceeds of the landlord's distress. However, if that happens, the landlord is then a preferential creditor for the amount taken from him: IA s176.

If a secured creditor has more than one debt owing to him by the company, and covered by his security, and some are preferential and others are not, he is not required on realising his security to apply the money evenly in part payment of all the debts. Instead he may, since it improves his position, apply the money first to repayment of his non-preferential debts, so that he preserves the maximum entitlement as a creditor for preferential debts: *Re William Hall (Contractors) Ltd* [1967] 2 All ER 1150.

Ordinary and deferred debts

After the preferential debts have been paid in full, the non-preferential ordinary unsecured debts come next. Typically these are sums owed to trade creditors for goods or services supplied to the company.

However, a secured creditor whose security has proved to be insufficient to discharge his debt in full (see paragraph 13.5 *Secured creditors*) and a creditor for a preferential debt in excess of the limits (see paragraph 13.5 *Preferential unsecured debts*) may claim the balance as an ordinary debt.

A sum owed to a member of the company in his character of member is a deferred debt which may only be paid after ordinary debts have been paid in full: IA s74(2)(f).

The most common instance of a deferred debt is a dividend which has been declared and become due for payment, so that it becomes a debt (see paragraph 6.5 *The right to dividends*). Generally companies do not declare dividends and then default in paying them soon afterwards. However, large public companies often have unclaimed dividends due to members of whose current whereabouts the company has no information. The members may, subject to the law of limitation and the provisions of the articles, claim their dividends later. However, it is not a duty of the liquidator to set aside money to cover unpaid dividends of past years for which no claim has been made: *Re Compania de Electricidad de la Provincia de Buenos Aires Ltd* [1980] Ch 146 (see paragraph 6.5 *The right to dividends*).

Another instance of a deferred debt is where a company agrees to purchase its own shares but goes into liquidation without paying for them: s178(6) (see paragraph 6.4 *Purchase by a company of its own shares*).

Voluntary payments to employees

As the word 'voluntary' indicates these are not debts at all. but it is convenient to deal with them here since they are payments which the liquidator may be authorised and bound to make, after payment of all debts, before distributing what remains to shareholders.

These are payments to employees of the company who have been made redundant by reason of the closure or sale of the company's business. A company has statutory power (s719) to make such gifts subject to compliance with the proper internal procedure for authorisation (see paragraph 2.3 *Gifts by companies*). From the liquidator's standpoint, he must ensure (1) that he has paid all debts of the company; and (2) that he has authority to make the payments: IA s187.

Order of application of assets

As already explained (see paragraph 13.5 *Secured creditors*) secured creditors normally recover their debts from the realisation of their security. Only if there is a surplus resulting from the security will any part of its value go to the fund from which unsecured creditors are paid. To that extent the secured creditors have an automatic priority over unsecured creditors, except that preferential unsecured debts are paid out of property subject to a floating charge (see paragraph 13.5 *The priorities of preferential debts*).

The order of application of assets in the hands of the liquidator is (in descending order of priority):

1. *liquidation expenses*, including the cost of selling, preserving, collecting in assets etc, the liquidator's remuneration and the incidental expenses of the liquidation, such as the costs of a petition for compulsory liquidation if the court awards costs to the petitioner: IA s115;
2. *preferential unsecured debts* (and the balance remaining is then used to pay the debt owing to the holder of a floating charge);
3. *ordinary unsecured debts* (including the claims of secured and preferential creditors for deficiencies remaining after they have taken their priority entitlement higher up the scale);
4. *deferred debts;*
5. *repayment of members' capital*, ie first, capital paid up on their shares and then any surplus remaining to members according to their entitlement (usually it goes to the ordinary shareholders alone): IA s107.

In *Re Christonette International Ltd* [1982] 3 All ER 225 it was held that if a floating charge had crystallised before an order was made or resolution passed to initiate a liquidation, the expenses of liquidation did not take priority over the floating charge. However, the definition of 'floating charge' (in IA s251) raises some doubt as to whether that is still the position.

13.6 Voidable transactions and compensation

Introduction

Liquidation, and also an administration order, affect certain transactions of the company in the recent past, either automatically or by permitting the liquidator (or administrator) in a proper case to apply to the court for an order to avoid a transaction.

The other main subject covered in this section is the claims for compensation etc which a liquidator may initiate, mainly against directors who have mismanaged the company.

Avoidance of floating charges

The basic rule is that commencement of liquidation or the making of an administration order (see paragraph 13.1 *Administration orders*) automatically renders void a floating charge on the company's property if created within the previous 12 months: IA s245. There are, however, certain limitations or exceptions.

Unless the charge was created in favour of a person connected with the company, the charge is not void if:

1. the company was solvent at the time of creation of the charge; or
2. the charge was created more than 12 months before the liquidation or the presentation of the petition for the administration order.

If, however, the charge was created in favour of a connected person, the solvency of the company at the time is immaterial and the period over which s245 has retrospective effect is enlarged from 12 months to two years.

Secondly, where the charge is within the limits set out above, it is still valid insofar as it is security for consideration given at the time or after the creation of the charge. The charge is therefore void only to the extent that it is to secure liabilities which existed before the charge was created. The subsequent consideration, for which the charge would be valid, may be money, goods or services supplied to the company or a reduction of its indebtedness, plus interest at the agreed rate (if any) on that consideration.

Connected person is elaborately defined by IA ss249 and 435. In a typical, but by no means the only, case a connected person is a director or a shareholder who has control (alone or jointly with others).

The period of 12 months, or two years, prior to the petition for an administration order is also extended forward to cover the period between the petition and the making of the order, so that a charge created after the petition has been presented becomes void if an administration order is later made on it.

Although there are differences of detail s245 is a reformulation of earlier provisions of the same kind (Companies Act 1985 s617) and some cases decided on those earlier rules continue to afford guidance. A loan to the company made after it had created a floating charge, but for the purpose of enabling the company to repay an existing loan from the same lender obtained before the charge, is a transparent evasion of the requirement that, to be valid, the loan must follow the charge and so the charge is not a valid security for the second (or the first) loan: *Re Destone Fabrics Ltd* [1941] Ch 319.

For many years it had been thought, relying on the decision in *Re F & F Stanton Ltd* [1929] 1 Ch 180, that if the loan is granted on the understanding that a floating charge will be created as security for it, the charge may be security for the loan even though it follows the loan in strict time sequence. The Court of Appeal, however, has held that there should be no interval between the advance of money and the creation of the charge unless it is so short that it can be regarded as de minimis. Hoffmann LJ gave as an example, 'a coffee break': *Power* v *Sharp Investments Ltd & Anor* [1993] BCC 609. The significance of this decision is that as a matter of good practice, lenders should not advance any money until the charge has actually been executed.

The banks rely on the decision in *Re Yeovil Glove Co Ltd* [1965] Ch 148 in taking a floating charge as security for a running account. In the *Yeovil Glove* case the essential facts were that the company had a bank overdraft at the time when the charge was created and an overdraft of approximately the same amount at the commencement of liquidation. However, in the interval credits to the account exceeded the amount of the overdraft at the time of the charge. It was held that these credits (under the rule in *Clayton's Case*, *Devaynes* v *Noble* (1816) 1 Mer 572) should be treated as repayment of the earlier debt and the subsequent drawings on the account were new loans subsequent to the charge, which was therefore a valid security for the overdraft resulting from them.

Voidable preferences

In this case also the current rule (IA s239) is a revised version of earlier law (Companies Act 1985 s615) on what was then called 'fraudulent preference'. The basic rule is that the court, on the application of a liquidator or administrator of a company, may in defined circumstances make an order to set aside a preference given by a company to one of its creditors, or to a guarantor of its debts, at a time when the company was already (or became by reason of the preference) unable to pay its debts.

A preference for this purpose is anything by which the person who benefits from it is put in a better position, if the company went into insolvent liquidation, than he would otherwise have been. An obvious case is where the company reduces its bank overdraft, by suspending drawings to make payment of its debts to trade creditors, in order to reduce the liability of one of its directors as guarantor of the overdraft: *Re M Kushler Ltd* [1943] 2 All ER 22. The creation of a fixed charge, which would not be invalidated by IA s245 (see paragraph 13.6 *Avoidance of floating charges*), to secure an existing debt would be another instance.

However, in addition to demonstrating the advantage which the preference yields, it must be shown either that the person preferred was a connected person (as explained in paragraph 13.6 *Avoidance of floating charges*) or that in granting the preference the company was 'influenced ... by a desire to produce' such a preference, ie it must be intentional. This is in accord with case law on the previous statutory provision (on 'fraudulent preference'), where the act was valid if it appeared that it was done for good commercial reasons and not in order to grant preference: *Re Paraguassu Steam Tramway Co*, *Adamson's Case* (1874) LR 18 Eq 670; see also *Re Beacon Leisure Ltd* [1990] BCC 213.

If the person preferred is a connected person, he may still be able to resist an order to reverse the preference shown to him if he is a connected person solely by reason of being an employee of the company, or if he can show, ie the burden of proof is on him, that the company was not 'influenced by a desire' to prefer him.

The statutory formula (in s239) 'influenced by a desire' is new and the test was applied in *Re DKG Contractors Ltd* [1900] BCC 903.

The other major limitation is that the preference must have occurred within 'the relevant time': see, eg, *Re DKG Contractors Ltd*, above. The standard period is six months before the commencement of liquidation or the date of the petition for an administration order (plus the subsequent interval between petition and making the order). But the period is two years if the person preferred is connected with the company, otherwise than merely as an employee.

If the case is made out the court is required ('the court shall ...') to make whatever order it thinks fit to restore the position to what it would have been if there had been no preference.

Transactions at an undervalue

The court has a similar power under IA s238 to make an order to neutralise a transaction at an undervalue, into which the company entered at a time when it was unable to pay its debts. The application to the court may only be made by a liquidator or an administrator and certain limiting conditions restrict the court's powers.

A transaction is at an undervalue if it is an outright gift or is for significantly less in consideration received by the company than the value of the consideration which it gave. However, such a transaction may not be set aside if:

1. the company entered into it in good faith and for the purpose of carrying on its business (see, eg, *Re Welfab Engineers* [1990] BCC 600); and
2. there were at the time reasonable grounds for believing that it would benefit the company.

The effect of this stipulation is substantially to confine the scope of the avoidance power to artificial transactions. These criteria have something in common with those which are applied in determining what powers, if not expressed in the objects clause, may be implied (see paragraph 2.3 *The ultra vires principle and CA 1989*). The cases on that issue might be relevant to the meaning of this statutory formula.

A transaction at an undervalue may only be set aside under s238 if it occurred within the period of two years before the commencement of liquidation or of the petition for an administration order (with an extension forward to take in the interval between the petition and the making of the order). While s238 has unrestricted extra-territorial effect and allows service of process on a foreign bank not carrying on business in England, the court has an overall discretion not to make an order under the section, in particular if it is not satisfied that the foreign defendant is sufficiently connected with England for it to be just and proper to grant the relief sought: *Re Paramount Airways Ltd* [1992] 3 All ER 1.

Measures against debt-avoidance

In contrast to the three topics so far considered this is an innovation in company law, which is derived from the former law on attempts by individuals to defraud their creditors.

It will be noted that the safeguards above (see paragraph 13.6 *Avoidance of floating charges* and *Voidable preferences*) are limited to transactions at a time when the company is insolvent; they require that the company shall have gone into liquidation or become subject to an administration order; and they are subject to time limits on their retrospective effect. Section 423 is not subject to these limitations.

Insolvency Act s423 relates to a transaction at an undervalue of any person, either a corporate body or an individual. If a company is in liquidation, or is subject to an administration order or to a voluntary arrangement (see paragraph 13.1 *Voluntary arrangements with creditors*), its liquidator, administrator or supervisor, as the case may be, is entitled to seek relief. In addition, and where none of those situations exist, 'the victim of the transaction' who could be the company or somebody interested in it, may apply to the court.

In dealing with any such application the court is required to satisfy itself that this transaction at an undervalue was entered into for the purpose of putting assets beyond the reach of the person making the claim or otherwise prejudicing his interests in relation to his claim. As long as the dominant purpose of a debtor in entering into a transaction at an undervalue is for the purpose of putting assets beyond the reach of a creditor, the transaction is caught by s423 of the 1986 Act, despite the existence of other possible motives for the transaction: *Chohan* v *Saggar* [1994] BCC 134. However, there is no time limit and no requirement that the company shall be insolvent. In this respect s423 follows the model of the Law of Property Act 1925 s172 (transactions in fraud of creditors) which it replaces. The case law on the old s172 (now repealed) relates only to the transactions of individual debtors, since it did not apply to corporate bodies. However, that case law indicates that the provision is likely to catch schemes by which assets are put beyond the reach of a take-over bidder who is expected to gain control of the company or to frustrate its creditors, if it should become insolvent. One such type of scheme involves the grant of a lease, possibly with stringent limitations on the use of land or buildings, to preserve the existing occupation and/or use: *Lloyds Bank Ltd* v *Marcan* [1973] 3 All ER 754.

Under s423 the court has discretion as to whether it will make an order. If it does make an order, it should restore the position to what it would have been without the transaction and protect the interests of those who are the victims of the transaction.

A claim by a creditor based on s423 failed in *Menzies* v *National Bank of Kuwait SAK* [1994] BCC 119, where it was argued that a letter given by a company to the bank amounted to a transaction at an undervalue. The letter contained instructions given to the bank as to which creditors should be paid off from money earned from lucrative contracts to fit and furnish prestigious buildings. The Court of Appeal held that the real basis of the complaint was that the letter amounted to a preference within IA s239, which can only be challenged by a liquidator.

Fraudulent trading

This is a legacy from the previous law, which has lost much of its importance by reason of new provisions.

If in the course of liquidation of a company it appears to the court that its business has been carried on with intent to defraud its creditors or the creditors of any other person, or for a fraudulent purpose, the court may on the application of the liquidator declare that any persons who were knowingly parties to carrying on the business in this way shall make such contribution to the company's assets as the court may determine: IA s213.

Two prescribed points in s213 should be noted. First, only the liquidator can now seek this remedy. It is no longer possible for a creditor to ask for an order for payment to be made to him, as occurred in *Re Cyona Distributors Ltd* [1967] Ch 889. Secondly, the court has discretion as to the amount of the contribution which it may order. It is not a question of ordering payment of specific debts. See, eg, *Re A Company* (No 001418 of 1988) [1990] BCC 526 where it was decided that the amount ordered to be paid would include a punitive element.

Fraudulent trading is also a criminal offence and in this instance it is not required that the company shall have gone into liquidation: s458; see also paragraph 11.3 *Conduct of the investigation.*

The Cork Committee on Insolvency (Cmnd 8558 of 1982, Chapter 44) discussed this subject at length. The normal grounds for invoking the sanctions against fraudulent trading are that the directors have failed to take proper steps to avoid or to minimise the consequences of impending insolvency. Usually they permitted the company to continue to trade at a time when there was no prospect that the company would be able to pay the debts incurred in the course of this trading.

A single transaction can constitute carrying on the business: *Re Gerald Cooper Chemicals Ltd* [1978] 2 All ER 49. Payment of some debts but not all may also amount to carrying on business: *Re Sarflax Ltd* [1979] 1 All ER 49. Section 458 is designed to include those who exercise a managerial function or are 'running the business': *R v Miles* [1992] Crim LR 657.

However, proceedings against directors under what was Companies Act 1948 s320 (now IA s213) have rarely been successful because it is necessary to prove fraud on their part. As fraudulent trading is also a criminal offence, the standard of proof required, even in civil actions, is demanding. Yet it is rarely possible to prove actual dishonest intent. It was once held that this intent would be inferred from the directors' decision to incur debts without any reasonable prospect that the company would be able to pay them: *Re William C Leitch Bros (No 1)* [1932] 2 Ch 71. However, the same judge in another case said that is was necessary to show 'real dishonesty ... involving moral blame': *Re Patrick & Lyon Ltd* [1933] All ER 590. Evidence of that is not easy to get.

The Cork Committee therefore recommended a new basis of civil liability ('wrongful trading' as described in paragraph 13.6 *Wrongful trading*), which should impose an objective test. However, it proposed that civil and criminal liability for fraudulent trading, despite the inherent problems of evidence, should be left on the statute book (as it has been) as a deterrent and sanction for extreme cases.

One should also take account of the much stricter tests of unfitness to act as a director, leading to disqualification under the Company Directors Disqualification Act 1986 (see paragraph 9.1 *Disqualification of directors*), which is another key element in the Cork Committee's programme for inducing greater responsibility, as well as honesty, among directors who might otherwise be lax if not dishonest. A director may be disqualified for wrongful trading: CDDA s10 (see paragraph 9.1 *Directors and company insolvency*).

Wrongful trading

The'Cork Committee's proposal for civil (only) liability for wrongful trading, with a less demanding standard of proof, has been adopted: IA s214. But the basis of liability is defined in a different manner from that proposed by the Cork Committee.
The Committee (para 1781) wrote:

> 'We propose that a company shall be trading wrongfully if, being insolvent or unable to pay its debts as they fall due, it incurs liabilities to other persons without any reasonable prospect of meeting them in full; and that a person who was a party to the carrying on of the company's trading may be made personally liable for the debts if he knew or, as an officer, ought to have known that the trading was wrongful.'

In framing what is now IA s214 the DTI decided that a wider test was desirable. The Cork formula would not, for example, apply to directors who did not let the company incur additional unpaid debts but who failed to take action, eg to sell off assets or retrench expenditure, which was a necessary remedial measure to avoid the likelihood of insolvency.

The substantive content of s214 has been heavily criticised both in parliamentary debate and among bodies representative of business managers and the professions. It provides that liability for wrongful trading shall exist if the following conditions are satisfied:

1. the person to be made liable must be or have been a director of a company which has gone into insolvent liquidation (see, eg, *Re DKG Contractors Ltd* [1990] BCC 903); and

2. at some time before the commencement of liquidation, he actually knew or 'ought to have concluded' that there was no reasonable prospect that the company would avoid going into insolvent liquidation (see, eg, *Re Purpoint Ltd* [1991] BCC 121); and

3. on reaching stage (2) he did not in the court's view 'take every step' which he ought to have taken 'with a view to minimising the potential loss to the

company's creditors'. That he did take such steps is the defence open to him in any proceedings against him under s214.

In considering the conduct of a defendant director, he is to be judged by the standard of 'general knowledge, skill and experience' which might reasonably be expected of both (1) any person in his position; and (2) of this individual in particular. The latter point means that the director's personal qualifications and experience, eg as an accountant, are to be taken into consideration as well as more general criteria, in deciding whether he acted correctly: see, eg, *Norman* v *Theodore Goddard* [1992] BCC 14 (director absolved as he had taken expert professional advice).

Much of the argument about this involved formula relates to the words 'ought to have concluded'. The critics object that it tests the actual performance of an individual by reference to matters of which he may have been ignorant. The DTI argued that it imposed on directors, at all times, a duty to keep themselves informed of the financial position of the company, eg by insisting that management accounts of some sort should be laid before each board meeting. The latter requirement was at one stage proposed for inclusion in express terms in the formula. However, it was abandoned on the grounds that no satisfactory statutory definition of the content of unaudited management accounts could be devised.

The other main criticism is of the words 'every step' which are deliberately very vague. The Cork Committee's recommendation, relating to debts which might not be paid, is more precise and on that account less comprehensive.

A particular criticism is that these wide and uncertain provisions may make it difficult for major creditors of companies, such as banks, to arrange with a company customer that some experienced 'company doctor' shall join the board to improve its financial expertise in time of need.

In *Re Purpoint Ltd* [1991] BCC 121 Vinelott J explained the position as follows:

'The court, in making an order under s214, is concerned to ensure that any depletion in the assets of the company attributable to the period after the moment when the directors knew or ought to have known that there was no reasonable prospect of avoiding an insolvent winding up – in effect, while the company's business was being carried on at the risk of creditors – is made good: see *Re Produce Marketing Consortium Ltd (No 2)* [1989] BCLC 520 at 553 per Knox J. The purpose is to recoup the loss to the company so as to benefit the creditors as a whole. The court has no jurisdiction to direct payment to creditors or to direct that moneys paid to the company should be applied in payment of one class of creditors in preference to another.'

Directors who seek to justify themselves must relate their defence to s214. They will not be able to obtain relief under s727 (paragraph 9.4 *Relief from liability*) merely on the general grounds that they claim to have acted reasonably and ought fairly to be excused: *Re Produce Marketing Consortium Ltd* [1989] 1 WLR 745; see also *Re DKG Contractors Ltd*, above.

The most recent case on wrongful trading is *Re Sherborne Associates Ltd* [1995] BCC 40, which involved three non-executive directors, of whom two had extensive experience of managing large companies. After deciding that a claim for wrongful trading survived the death of one of the directors, so that it could be pursued against his personal representatives, His Honour Judge Jack QC, declined to make an order that they make a contribution to the assets of the company under s214 IA 1986. The liquidator had selected the dates of two board meetings which he relied on as being the time when the directors ought to have realised that there was no reasonable prospect of the company avoiding liquidation. The judge, however, felt that sales forecasts presented to them at the meetings by three executive directors were such that the company could achieve a turnaround and make a profit. This prospect, he said, was a 'reasonable' and not a 'fanciful' one. It was further held that it was not open for the liquidator or the court to make a finding of wrongful trading on alternative dates, which were not specifically pleaded. See Chapter 15, paragraph 15.9, for further details.

Other bases of liability

What used to be called 'misfeasance' reappears, with slight modifications of definition, in IA s212 – summary remedy against delinquent directors, liquidators etc. For an example of this remedy see: *Re D'Jan of London Ltd* [1993] BCC 646.

It permits the liquidator, or a creditor, of a company in liquidation to apply to the court to examine the conduct of any officer of the company on the grounds that he has misapplied company property or been guilty of breach of fiduciary or other duty in relation to the company. If the court sees fit it may order the delinquent officer to return company property or to pay compensation. The proceedings are civil not criminal.

Misfeasance is a flexible, though rather uncertain, means of bringing to account officers of a company, notably its directors, if they have misused their position or failed seriously in their duties.

In addition there is a long list of specific offences for which officers of companies may be brought to account in the course of liquidation: IA Pt IV Chapter X. There are also more general sanctions against dishonesty under general criminal law. Lastly, the DTI has power to appoint inspectors to conduct investigations (see paragraph 11.3 *Conduct of the investigation*), the Official Receiver may apply to the court for public examination of company officers (see paragraph 13.3 *Procedure*) and there is the elaborate system for review of the conduct of directors of companies with a view to their disqualification (see paragraph 9.1 *Disqualification of directors*) on various grounds which include participation in wrongful trading: CDDA s10.

14

Accounts

14.1 Accounts

14.2 Auditors

14.3 Accounts and audit and the Cadbury Committee

14.1 Accounts

Introduction

English law is less concerned with providing a system of control of companies than with attempts to ensure that the means of control are made available. So far as information concerning the affairs of the company is concerned, the companies' legislation requires disclosure and publication of certain information, the accuracy of some of which must be verified by qualified auditors (see below). There is nothing to prevent the company's officers making more information available than the law requires (subject to complying with their duties of confidentiality as to company affairs) and certainly there is little to prevent their being able to present it in more readily intelligible form than the Acts require. But the legal requirements provide a good base.

The problem is whether that is sufficient. Large investors and creditors can obtain professional advice as to the significance of the published details. Major items of comment may receive wider publicity in the press. Against this it can be said that the smaller investor may not understand the details or read the press comments, and potential creditors may not look them up. Have they only themselves to blame? Should the law do more or does the law do all that can reasonably be expected of it?

The Companies Act 1981 introduced into English law the accounting principles and practice set out in the EC Fourth Directive and these appeared as Part VII of CA 1985. Part I CA 1989 repeals and replaces the whole of this material with revised sections, whose main purpose is to bring English law into conformity with the EC Seventh Directive on consolidated accounts of groups of companies. This part of the EC harmonisation process had been held up by lengthy discussion of the definition of the relationship of companies which would require them to produce consolidated accounts as a single enterprise. The nature of the agreed definition appears in paragraph 14.1 *Parent companies and subsidiary undertakings.*

All companies must produce for their members accounts which comply with those requirements. However, while public companies must within seven months and private companies within ten months of the relevant general meeting file with the registrar all documents required to be laid before the company, small and medium-sized companies may file shorter 'modified' accounts which must identify themselves as such: ss247–250 (see paragraph 1.4 *Other types of company*).

Duties with respect to accounts

1. Every company must cause accounting records to be kept in accordance with the provisions of ss221–222:
   a) they must be sufficient to show and explain the company's transactions;
   b) they must be such as to disclose with reasonable accuracy the financial position of the company at any time;
   c) they must contain entries from day to day of sums of money received and expended, a record of the company's assets and liabilities and statements of stocktaking and stock held at the end of each financial year;
   d) they must be kept at the company's registered office or other designated place and open to inspection by officers of the company for the purposes of their duties: *Conway* v *Petronius Clothing Co Ltd* [1978] 1 All ER 185.
2. The directors must, for each accounting reference period (usually the company's financial year: s226) cause to be prepared, sign where required and lay before the company in general meeting financial statements comprising:
   a) a balance sheet; and
   b) a profit and loss account;
   together with notes thereto, which may conveniently appear on the face of the accounts and a directors' report and an auditors' report: s241.

   A private company may by elective resolution dispense with the laying of accounts before a general meeting (paragraph 8.1 *Proceedings at meetings, Elective resolutions*).
3. If the company wishes to change its accounting reference period, for example to bring it into line with other companies within a group, the period may be altered (s225) but the changeover period must not exceed 18 months between accounting year ends.
4. Together with the notes, every balance sheet must give a true and fair view of the financial position of the company at the end of the given period and every profit and loss account must give a true and fair view of the profit and loss for that period: s226(2).
5. The balance sheet and profit and loss account must so far as possible comply with the requirements of Sch. 4: s228. If adhering strictly to the prescribed

format would not result in a true and fair view, the notes must explain any departure made in order to provide a true and fair view. The notes form a very important part of the financial statements and have to contain matter which used to be set out in the directors' report.

6. Depending on the circumstances and size of the company its directors' report must contain information inter alia on the following subjects (s234 and Schedule 7, as amended by the Companies Act 1985 (Accounts of Small and Medium Sized Enterprises and Publication of Accounts in ECUs) Regulations 1992):
   a) a fair review of the development of the company and its subsidiary undertakings;
   b) a summary of the activities of the company and changes over the year;
   c) details of the company's likely future development;
   d) research and development activities and proposals;
   e) details of important post-balance sheet events;
   f) the amounts (if any) recommended as dividend distributions and for transfer to reserves;
   g) the amount recommended to be paid by way of dividends;
   h) directors' names, details of their interests and (if over £60,000 in aggregate) remuneration;
   i) significant changes in fixed assets of the company and its subsidiary undertakings;
   j) the company's purchases of its own shares and loans for such purchases by others;
   k) details of employees and their remuneration, including provisions for disabled employees;
   l) progress towards better employee information and participation; and
   m) securing the health, safety and welfare at work of employees.

7. Although the legal duty of producing the accounts is placed upon the directors, the auditors (see paragraph 14.2 *Duties of auditors*) report on their accuracy and a number of related matters, such as the company's eligibility (if any) for some exemptions (see paragraph 14.1 *Exemptions from statutory requirements*). In practice, although the law does not require it, the auditors are involved, as expert advisers, in the preparation of the accounts, so that much of their duty of satisfying themselves is done as the work progresses rather than by formal investigation when the accounts are complete.

8. Since the company structure of most large enterprises is a parent company with subsidiary undertakings (see paragraph 14.1 *Parent companies and subsidiary undertakings*) there are elaborate requirements for disclosure of the identity of the parent by the subsidiary undertakings, as well as by the parent of its interests in subsidiary undertakings and also in joint ventures, associated undertakings and other related companies in which it has a sufficient interest, such as one tenth of its issued share capital: s231 and Sch 5.

9. Section 19 CA 1989 gives statutory support to the statements of standard accounting practice ('accounting standards') which the leading professional

accounting bodies issue for the guidance of their members, both as accountants and in their work as auditors.

The object of large public companies is to produce annual accounts upon which their auditors give an 'unqualified' report. Some qualifications by auditors relate to purely technical matters but a substantial qualification, as to whether the accounts give 'a true and fair view' is a very serious matter, which gives to the auditors considerable influence over the manner in which the accounts are prepared.

Parent companies and subsidiary undertakings

It has already been explained (paragraph 1.4 *Holding and subsidiary companies*) that to accommodate the new and more comprehensive requirements for the preparation of consolidated accounts, there are separate definitions of 'holding' and 'subsidiary' company, for general purposes of company law and also of 'parent company' and 'subsidiary undertaking' for accounting purposes. This paragraph deals with the latter.

By s258 a company is a parent (P) and the other company is a subsidiary undertaking (SU) in any of the following situations:

1. P holds a majority of the voting rights in SU exercisable on all or substantially all matters;
2. P is a member of SU and has the right, without obtaining the consent of another person, to appoint or remove directors of SU, being directors who have a majority of voting rights at board meetings on all or substantially all matters;
3. P has the right to exercise a dominant influence over SU by virtue of either (1) the memorandum or articles of SU or (2) a control contract authorised by those documents. A dominant influence exists where P has the right to give directions with respect to the operating and financial policies of SU and the directors of SU must comply with those directions whether or not they are for the benefit of SU;
4. P is a member of SU and controls, either alone or under an agreement with other members of SU a majority of voting rights at general meetings of SU;
5. P has a participating interest, which is normally at least 20 per cent of the shares of SU, in SU and exercises dominant influence over SU or P and SU are managed on a unified basis.

In determining whether P is a member of SU any shares of SU held by another subsidiary undertaking of P or by its agent or trustee are attributed to P, as are rights, where relevant, held for P in that fashion: ss259–260 and Sch 10A.

The directors of a parent company have a duty to prepare group accounts (in addition to separate accounts of that company). Group accounts are consolidated accounts in which the balance sheet and profit and loss account relate to the parent and its subsidiary undertakings as if they were a single undertaking: s227. Subject to that requirement the same general accounting principles and procedures apply to consolidated as to individual company accounts.

A parent which is itself the wholly-owned subsidiary of another parent company (established in a member state of the European Community) need not prepare group accounts in respect of itself and its subsidiary undertakings. The exemption also applies, subject to a right of a specified proportion of shareholders to require that group accounts be prepared, where the ultimate parent company has no more than 50 per cent of the shares of the intermediate parent company: s228(1).

A subsidiary undertaking may also be excluded from consolidated accounts on various grounds, such as that it is not material, or there are specified obstacles, or the parent company acquired its interest merely as a short-term investment with a view to re-sale: s229.

Laying and delivering accounts

The directors have two basic duties with respect to the accounts of each financial year:

1. they must lay the accounts, with the reports of the directors and auditors, and any group accounts of the company and its subsidiary undertakings, before the company in general meeting: s241(1). On elective resolutions to dispense with this procedure see paragraph 14.1 *Exemptions from statutory requirements*;
2. they must deliver to the registrar a signed copy of the accounts, with the supporting reports etc: s242(1).

The directors have a period of ten months (for private accounts) or seven months (for a public company) in which to comply with these obligations. The period runs from the terminal date to which the accounts are made up: s241(1). For a newly formed company there is a different period for its first annual accounts. Companies which have overseas interests may claim an extension of three months to the standard period by notice to the registrar: s244(2) and (3).

A copy of the accounts should be sent to every member and debentureholder of the company not less than 21 days before the general meeting at which the accounts are to be considered. A member is also entitled to be supplied, on demand and without charge, with a copy of the accounts: ss238–239.

If the directors are in default over these obligations they are liable to a fine and the company is liable to a civil penalty, which increases with the length of the period of default: ss242–242A. Late filing penalties are distinct from fines which are payable for non-submission of accounts and both a penalty and a fine could be payable in respect of the same set of accounts filed late.

If it is later found that the accounts produced do not comply with statutory requirements, the directors, of their own initiative or in compliance with notice from the DTI or a court order, must take action to correct the accounts already distributed: ss245–245C.

The amounts set out in a company's annual accounts may also be shown in the same accounts translated into the European Monetary System's ECUs and, when complying with s242 of the 1985 Act, a company may deliver an additional copy of its accounts, so translated: s242B of the 1985 Act, as inserted by the Companies Act 1985 (Accounts of Small and Medium-Sized Enterprises and Publication of Accounts in ECUs) Regulations 1992.

Exemptions from statutory requirements

A listed public company (see paragraph 1.4 *Other types of company*) may, subject to regulations made by the DTI, send to members who do not require a copy of the full accounts, a summary financial statement instead: s251. It is contended that many small investors would find a summary easier to understand than the very elaborate statutory accounts of a large parent company; incidentally this alternative would save the company much expense.

Private companies, subject to certain limiting conditions, may qualify either as medium-sized or as small companies, which are entitled to deliver to the registry modified accounts which do not contain all the information prescribed for inclusion in standard company accounts: s246(1)(b) and Sch 8, as amended by the Companies Act 1985 (Accounts of Small and Medium-Sized Enterprises and Publication of Accounts in ECUs) Regulations 1992. Three criteria of turnover, balance sheet total and number of employees are applied. To qualify for remission under this procedure a company must satisfy at least two of the three criteria: s247, as amended by the 1992 Regulations. In claiming exemption the directors must obtain a report from the auditors to support their figures.

A dormant company, as defined by s250, may by special resolution decide not to appoint auditors, with the result that there is no auditors report to attach to the accounts which it lays and delivers, as described above: s250(4).

A private company may by elective resolution (paragraph 8.1 *Proceedings at meetings, Elective resolutions*) dispense with the laying of accounts before a general meeting: s252. In such a case however a copy of the accounts must be sent to each member at least 28 days before the expiry of the statutory time limit for laying the accounts before a general meeting. With the accounts the company sends a notice to inform each member that he has a right, as has the auditor, to override the elective resolution and require the company to lay the accounts before a general meeting: s253.

An unlimited company, subject to certain conditions (see paragraph 1.4 *Unlimited companies*) is not required to deliver a copy of its accounts to the registrar: s254.

Banking and insurance companies are subject to modified statutory requirements in respect of the information to be given in their accounts: ss255–255D; see also the Companies Act 1985 (Bank Accounts) Regulations 1991 which amend some of these provisions.

The DTI may by regulation alter the statutory requirements and procedures on company accounts: s257. This power is most likely to be used when the DTI is advised by professional accountancy bodies that an alternation is desirable without waiting for the next Companies Act. It has, for example, been exercised to permit Welsh private companies to furnish their directors' reports, etc, in Welsh.

The requirement to have the accounts audited has recently been relaxed in the case of some private companies (see paragraph 14.2 *Relaxation of the audit requirement for private companies*).

Supplementary information

When the registrar receives a copy of the annual accounts of a company he gives notice of that fact in the *London Gazette*: s711(1)(k).

Public companies often supplement their formal reports and accounts, required by statute, with additional information in a form which the non-professional shareholder may find easier to read and understand. It is also a useful form of 'public relations' to enhance the company's public image.

These additional documents take the form of a 'Chairman's Statement' or directors' 'Review of the Year's Operations' etc. This material may be illustrated with colour photographs of the company's installations and activities.

Statute neither requires nor recognises material of this kind, though the information which it gives would presumably be taken into account in considering how far the directors have gone in providing information to their shareholders.

Whether or not the formal documents for an annual general meeting of a large public company are supplemented in this way, it is usual to print them and issue them in the form of a single booklet of 20–30 pages. The accounts must of course be distributed (in this format) to all members and debentureholders. But the latter, and possibly some shareholders if they hold only preference shares, are not entitled to attend the meeting. Hence, the booklet includes a note that the AGM notice (in the booklet) is sent for information only to those recipients not entitled to attend the meeting.

14.2 Auditors

Appointment

In the normal course at each general meeting before which annual accounts are laid the meeting appoints auditor(s) to hold office until the next such meeting in a year's time. The first auditors of a new company are appointed by the directors, or if they fail to do so, by a general meeting: s385. In any case of failure to appoint or reappoint auditors the company must within seven days give notice to the DTI which has a residuary power of appointment: s387.

A private company which has elected not to lay accounts before a general meeting is required (unless exempt under s386) to appoint auditors within the period of 28 days from the date on which copies of the accounts are sent to members (paragraph 14.1 *Exemptions from statutory requirements*): s385A.

A private company may also elect to dispense with the annual appointment of auditors, with the result that they are deemed to be re-appointed each year: s386. This provision of course neatly supplements s385A above, so that the preparation and auditing of the accounts goes on each year without the formality of holding a general meeting to consider the accounts and incidentally to reappoint the auditors. The members receive their copies of the audited accounts and so does the registrar.

The first auditors of the company may be appointed by the directors or, failing that, the general meeting: s384(2)–(3). Casual vacancies may similarly be filled: s384(4).

Sections 388(3) and 391A provide that special notice (see paragraph 8.1 *Notice of meetings*) is required for a resolution at a general meeting:

1. appointing a person other than a retiring auditor; or
2. filling a casual vacancy; or
3. re-appointing a retiring auditor who was appointed by the directors to fill a casual vacancy; or
4. removing an auditor before the expiration of his term of office.

On receipt of notice of such an intended resolution the company must send a copy:

1. to the person to be appointed or removed;
2. to a retiring auditor who is to be replaced; and
3. to a resigning auditor whose place is to be filled by another.

Remuneration of auditors is determined by the person appointing them, whether the company in general meeting or the Secretary of State (s390A) and must be shown separately in the profit and loss account: s390A. In practice the general meeting usually appoints the auditors and authorises the directors to fix their remuneration.

A dormant, ie inactive, private company (with some limiting exclusions), may by special resolution decide not to appoint auditors: s250. It loses its exemption if it later has any significant accounting transaction. However, while exempt, it may deliver to the registrar unaudited accounts without of course any auditors' report: s388A.

Qualifications

To implement the EC Eighth Directive there is a completely new set of rules on the qualification of auditors, enacted by Part II CA 1989. However these are mainly changes of form and procedure which will not significantly alter the existing system by which company auditors are drawn from the members of a select group of leading accountancy bodies.

The basis of the new system, as of the previous one, is that recognition is given to these professional bodies, but they must now in turn determine under their internal rules which of their members are suitably qualified as individuals to be company auditors: s25 CA 1989. There are supplementary and transitional provisions whereby individuals who were qualified under the previous system or who hold suitable overseas qualifications may be approved under the new system.

The new system recognises that company auditors are more often partners of professional firms than sole practitioners: s25(2) CA 1989. A company may appoint a partnership firm by name to be its auditors. The effect then is that the partners for the time being of the firm or its successor firm, if qualified as individuals, are the auditors of the company for the period of the appointment: s26 CA 1989.

As under the previous system an auditor, in addition to having professional qualifications, must also be independent of the company. Any officer or employee of the company, or a partner or employee of such a person (or a partnership of which any such person is a partner) is ineligible to be the auditor of the company. A person who is ineligible to be the auditor of one company of a group will, under regulations to be made by the DTI, be ineligible to be auditor of any company in the group: s27(2) CA 1989.

If an auditor becomes ineligible while in office, he must immediately vacate office and give notice to the company of his reason for so doing: s28 CA 1989. If it is found that an audit has been conducted by an ineligible person, the DTI may require the company to appoint an eligible auditor to conduct a second audit: s29 CA 1989.

Names of persons who are qualified to be auditors of companies will be entered in a register. Only those persons may describe themselves as 'registered auditors': s35 CA 1989. This will serve to distinguish company auditors from other accountants, many of them members of professional bodies, who audit the accounts of sole traders and of partnerships etc but are not deemed qualified to be company auditors.

Vacation of office

There are various ways in which an auditor may cease to act as such:

Retirement
An auditor is appointed (or automatically reappointed under s386) to hold office for a term of approximately a year at a time. If he retires special notice must be given of the proposal to appoint another auditor in his place: s391A(1). The auditor who does not seek reappointment must give notice as if he had resigned (see Resignation below).

Removal
A company may by ordinary resolution of which special notice has been given (see paragraph 8.1 *Notice of meetings*) remove an auditor before the expiration of his term of office, not withstanding anything in the agreement between it and him; if this happens, the company must notify the registrar: s391(1). This does not deprive a person so removed of a right to compensation or damages payable in respect of the termination of his appointment as auditor or of any appointment terminating with that of auditor: s391(3).

An auditor who has been removed is entitled to attend:

1. the general meeting at which his term of office would have otherwise expired;
2. any general meeting at which it is proposed to fill the vacancy caused by his removal and to receive notices and to be heard on matters concerning his removal: s391(4).

Resignation

An auditor may resign by depositing notice to that effect at the company's registered office: s392(1).

The notice is ineffective unless it contains either:

1. a statement that there are no circumstances connected with the resignation which he considers should be brought to the notice of the members or creditors; the company sends a copy to the registrar only; or
2. a statement of the circumstances: s394(1). The company must then either send a copy of the auditor's statement to every person who is entitled to receive a copy of the accounts (mainly members and debentureholders) or it may apply to the court for an order relieving it of the duty to distribute the statement, on the grounds that the auditor is seeking to secure needless publicity for defamatory matter. In so doing the company also gives notice of its application to the auditor. Unless the auditor receives notice of the company's application to the court (within 21 days of delivering his statement to the company) he then sends a copy of his statement to the registrar: s394.
3. Where the notice contains a statement of circumstances which should be brought to the notice of members or creditors, the auditor may requisition an extraordinary general meeting to receive and consider his explanations: s392A (see paragraph 8.1 *Persons able to convene meetings*).

He may require the circulation in writing of the circumstances (s392A(3)) and may attend and be heard at the meeting: s392(8).

Powers of auditors

Every auditor has a right of access to the company's books and accounts and is entitled to require from the officers such information and explanation as he thinks necessary for the performance of his duties. The supplier of false or misleading information may be punished: s389A.

He may attend every general meeting, receive communications relating thereto and be heard thereat: s390(1).

An auditor may require from a subsidiary company information necessary to enable him to carry out his duties: s389A(3).

Duties of auditors

The auditors must report to the members on the accounts examined by them, and on every balance sheet, every profit and loss account and all group accounts, of which a copy is laid before the general meeting: s235.

The auditors must state in the report whether in their opinion the company's balance sheet and profit and loss account and (if a holding company submitting group accounts) the group accounts have been properly prepared and whether a true and fair view is given of the matters stated therein: s235(2).

In preparing their report, the auditors must carry out such investigations as will enable them to form an opinion as to:

1. whether proper accounting records have been kept by the company and proper returns adequate for their audit have been received from branches not visited by them; and
2. whether the company's balance sheet and profit and loss account are in agreement with the accounting records and returns.

If not, they must state that in their report: s237(2).

After having signed their report, the auditors must forward it to the secretary, leaving it to the company's officers to convene a meeting to consider it; they are not required to make their report direct to every member of the company: *Re Allen, Craig & Co (London) Ltd* [1934] Ch 483.

An auditor must exercise the duties of reasonable care and skill which he owes to the company.

1. He must bring to bear that skill, care and caution which a reasonably competent, careful and cautious auditor would use; this depends on the circumstances: *Re City Equitable Fire Insurance Co* [1925] Ch 407 and on the accepted and recommended practice of auditors generally.
2. He is not required to act as a detective and is generally entitled to rely on the honesty of the company's officers or responsible employees: *Re Kingston Cotton Mill (No 2)* [1896] 2 Ch 279.

   But he should do some sample checks to verify the accuracy of his information and should take further professional advice if necessary: *Fomento (Sterling Area) Ltd v Selsdon Fountain Pen Co Ltd* [1958] 1 WLR 45.

   And certainly he should only certify what he believes to be true: *Re London & General Bank (No 2)* [1895] 2 Ch 673; see also *Shorrock Ltd v Meggitt plc* [1991] BCC 471 where the Court of Appeal held that the duty of auditors to give a certificate of a company's net deficit was not discharged when, having arrived at a figure for the deficit, they proceeded to state that a component of that figure could not be determined.
3. He should adopt an enquiring, although not a suspicious, approach and, once put on enquiry, should make a thorough investigation: *Re Thomas Gerrard & Sons Ltd* [1968] Ch 455.

The auditor is appointed by the company to perform a statutory duty of reporting to members on the annual accounts. The question which has been examined in a number of cases is whether, in performing a statutory duty in a position to which he is appointed by the company, the auditor owes to individual members of the company, and perhaps also to those who may later invest in the company or make a loan to it, the common law duty of care, derived from *Hedley Byrne & Co Ltd* v *Heller & Partners Ltd* [1964] AC 465. If there is such a duty, persons who suffer loss by reason of errors in the accounts which remained undetected through negligence on the part of the auditors, could base a claim for damages upon the breach of duty to show proper care and skill.

If there is such a duty and the auditors have failed in it, the person who claims damages for his loss will also have to show that he relied upon the audited accounts in the transaction which led to his loss, such as a takeover of the company in *JEB Fasteners Ltd* v *Marks Bloom & Co* [1983] 1 All ER 583. There are also other limiting factors such as the standard practice of making preliminary enquiries and obtaining warranties and indemnities from vendors of shares: *Lloyd Cheynham & Co* v *Littlejohn & Co* [1986] PCC 389 (DC).

Caparo Industries plc v *Dickman* [1990] 2 WLR 358 (reporting the decision of the House of Lords) has produced an authoritative analysis of this difficult question.

In the Court of Appeal Bingham LJ applied tests of: (1) foreseeable loss; (2) proximity; and (3) what is just and reasonable. By a majority the court held that the auditors did have a degree of 'proximity' to existing members of the company which imposed on them a duty of care to the members individually, in respect of sale or purchase of their shares. However the court declined to extend the duty (as the High Court appeared to have done in the *JEB Fasteners* case) to prospective investors, such as a takeover bidder, of whose interest and intentions the auditors had no notice at the time of auditing the accounts.

The House of Lords however has reversed the finding of the Court of Appeal on the auditors' duty of care to members, holding that in such situations the auditors have no duty of care a breach of which makes them liable to anyone for economic loss. Lord Bridge took the view that the statutory duty of the auditors to report on the accounts to the members of the company was a procedural provision not intended to give even to existing members a protection, at the auditors' expense, against economic loss. The House of Lords' decision was applied in *Al-Nakib Investments (Jersey) Ltd* v *Longcroft* [1990] 1 WLR 1390

In *James McNaughton Paper Group Ltd* v *Hicks Anderson & Co* [1991] 1 All ER 134 the Court of Appeal decided that a company's accountants had not owed a duty of care to a prospective takeover bidder in preparing the company's draft accounts. Neill LJ said that the natural starting point had been *Hedley Byrne & Co Ltd* v *Heller & Partners Ltd*, above, and he recalled Lord Oliver of Aylmerton's statement as to the guidance which could be obtained from that case in *Caparo Industries plc* v *Dickman*, above. His Lordship had also considered the more recent authorities, in particular in *Smith* v *Eric S Bush* [1989] 2 WLR 790 and in *Caparo* itself.

However, in *Morgan Crucible Co plc* v *Hill Samuel Bank Ltd* [1991] 1 All ER 148 the Court of Appeal accepted, distinguishing *Caparo*, that if, during the course of a contested takeover bid, the directors and financial advisers of the target company made express representations after an identified bidder had emerged, intending that the bidder would rely on those representations, they owed the bidder a duty of care not to be negligent in making representations which might mislead him.

In addition to the issue of proximity between the auditors and those relying on their statements, it is also necessary to consider causation. In particular, the question to be addressed is, did the auditors cause the loss or did they merely allow the opportunity for such losses to occur? See *Galoo Ltd* v *Bright Grahame Murray* [1994] 1 WLR 1360 (Chapter 15, paragraph 15.10, for further details).

Auditors as valuers of shares

The articles of association of private companies may give to members a right of first refusal of any shares which another member may wish to transfer (see paragraph 6.7 *Pre-emption rights over transfers*). In such cases the articles provide either (1) that the auditors shall fix a fair value as the basis of the offer price; or (2) that any dispute over the price demand shall be submitted to the auditors for adjudication of a fair value.

In case (1) the auditor is simply a valuer who owes a duty of care to both parties. If he is negligent, the party who suffers loss may recover damages from him: *Arenson* v *Casson, Beckman, Rutley & Co* [1977] AC 405. In case (2) only is the auditor given the normal judicial immunity of an arbitrator.

The auditor is of course only liable if the party aggrieved has to complete the transaction at an incorrect value (see paragraph 6.7 *Pre-emption rights over transfers*).

Relaxation of the audit requirement for private companies

As part of the government's aim to facilitate the deregulation of private companies whenever possible, new provisions have been recently introduced to relax the audit requirement for small private companies. The Companies Act 1985 (Audit Exemption) Regulations 1994 (SI 1994/1935) inserts a new s249A–E into the Companies Act 1985 which came into force on 11 August 1994.

Total exemption from the audit requirement is available under s249A(3), provided the following conditions are met by the company:

1. it qualifies as a small company under s246;
2. its turnover is not more than £90,000; and
3. its balance sheet total is not more than £1.4 million.

An additional way of obtaining total exemption is for the company to prepare a 'compilation' report in accordance with s249C. (The term 'compilation report', although well known, is not used in the legislation. It is, however, mentioned in the draft regulations and also in the DTI Consultative Document preceding the regulations.) This method of obtaining exemption will only be available, and thus a report will be required, if the company:

1. qualifies as a small company under s246;
2. its turnover is more than £90,000, but not more than £350,000; and
3. its balance sheet total is not more than £1.4 million.

The report must be prepared by the 'reporting accountant' who must, under the rules of the various accountancy bodies listed in s249D(3), be eligible to be the company's accountant or auditor. The report must state that the accounts are in agreement with the accounting records kept by the company and that the accounts have been prepared in accordance with various provisions of the Companies Act, for example the provisions relating to the form and content of the balance sheet and profit and loss account. The reporting accountant must also state that the company qualifies for the audit exemption and is not one of the companies which are specifically excluded from the exemptions under s249B.

Section 249B lists the companies who cannot take advantage of the audit exemption. By way of illustration, public companies, banking or insurance companies, and parent and subsidiary companies are not included in the relaxation rules. Section 249B also gives members holding at least 10 per cent of the nominal value of the company's issued share capital the right to require the company to have its accounts audited. To invoke this right, the members must give written notice of their wishes, which must be deposited at the company's registered office, not later than one month before the end of its financial year. By virtue of s249B(4), the balance sheet must contain a statement by the directors that:

1. the company is entitled to the audit exemption;
2. no notice has been delivered by 10 per cent of the members requiring an audit; and
3. the directors recognise their responsibilities to keep accounting records and prepare accounts which give a true and fair view of the state of the company.

Special rules have been included for charities, but these are beyond the scope of this book.

It may be that the new audit exemptions, significant though they are, will not, for many companies, produce the benefits hoped for. The reason for this is that banks, and other lending institutions, will probably make it a condition of lending that companies continue to have fully audited accounts.

14.3 Accounts and audit and the Cadbury Committee

The Cadbury Committee (see paragraph 9.1 *The Cadbury Committee*) on the Financial Aspects of Corporate Governance considered, as part of its terms of reference:

'ii the case for audit committees of the board, including their composition and role;
iii the principal responsibilities of auditors and the extent and value of the audit;
iv the links between shareholders, boards and auditors;'

The objective of the Committee was to help raise standards of corporate governance and the level of confidence in financial reporting and auditing.

With this in mind it is now provided for in the Code of Best Practice, which was the main product of the committee's report, that:

1. That the board of directors have a duty to 'present a balanced and under-standable assessment of the company's position' (paragraph 4.1). This is strengthened in Note 10 of the Code, which requires the directors report and the accounts to contain an explanation of the company's performance and prospects. This should be supported by the figures and should include references to setback's as well as successes. In this context, words are expressed to be as important as figures.

2. In addition to ensuring that an 'objective and professional relationship is maintained with the auditors', the board should establish an audit committee (paragraphs 4.2 and 4.3). The Committee was impressed with the evidence presented to it that around two-thirds of the top UK listed companies had already established an audit committee, and that the majority of these companies were enthusiastic about their value. The audit committee should consist of at least three non-executive directors, who should have written terms of reference. (paragraph 4.3 and Note 11).

    The full report of the Committee contains specimen terms of reference for an audit committee which lists, among other things, what the duties of the audit committee are. Included in the list of duties are the duty to consider the appointment, resignation, dismissal and fee of external auditor, to discuss the nature and scope of the external audit with the external auditor, to review the internal audit programme, and to review the half yearly and yearly accounts. The main benefits of an audit committee were seen to be, for example, providing a forum for the finance director and external auditor in which they can raise issues of concern, provide a framework within which the external auditor can assert his independence in the event of a dispute with management, and help increase public confidence in the credibility and objectivity of financial statements.

3. The directors should explain in a statement their responsibility for preparing the accounts, report on the effectiveness of the company's internal financial control, and also report that the business is a going concern (paragraphs 4.4, 4.5, and 4.6).

Finally, it should be remembered that Code only applies to UK listed companies, but that as many companies as possible are encouraged to adopt it.

15

Recent Cases

15.1 Introduction and corporate personality

Mephistopheles Debt Collection Service (A Firm) v *Lotay* (1994) The Times 17 May Court of Appeal (Nourse LJ and Wall J)

Limited partnership – corporate status

Facts
The plaintiffs were a limited partnership registered under the Limited Partnership Act 1907. A debt, owed by the defendant to a builder, was assigned by the builder to the partnership. After the assignment, an order was made substituting the partners as the plaintiffs in the action. G, one of the partners, was the subject of a civil proceedings order under s42 of the Supreme Court Act 1981, in which he was judged to be a vexatious litigant. As such, he was not allowed to make any application, in any civil proceedings instituted in any court, by any person, without leave of the court. A district judge had already stayed the proceedings and the

question was whether an appeal to a judge against the district judge's order staying the proceedings was an application 'made by' G for the purposes of s42 of the Act.

Held

It was an application 'made by' G.

Nourse LJ said that it was important to remember that the plaintiffs were the three individual partners. Their entitlement, under the Rules of the Supreme Court to sue in the name of the firm, was procedural only. It does not confer corporate status on a partnership. It followed therefore that the application was made by G. His Lordship also held that it was not possible for the application to be made by two of the partners, without the third as well.

Wall J said that it was not in the interests of justice for a person subject to a civil proceedings order to be able to side-step the order simply by forming a limited partnership and then instituting proceedings with other partners.

Commentary

This case illustrates that it is only a company that enjoys a separate legal personality that can sue and be sued in its own name. A partnership does not have this characteristic, even though the Rules of the Supreme Court and the County Court Rules allow litigation in the name of a firm. It is a procedural rule only and is based on administrative convenience in that it saves having to name each individual partner on the front of the writ.

Seaboard Offshore Ltd v *Secretary of State for Transport* [1994] 1 WLR 541 House of Lords (Lords Keith, Bridge, Jauncey, Browne-Wilkinson and Nolan)

A company was not vicariously liable for the acts of all its employees

Facts

Seaboard Offshore Ltd were the charterers and managers of the mv *Safe Carrier*, which set sail from the River Tyne bound for Aberdeen. The vessel broke down three times within a period of 24 hours, leaving her drifting at sea. The chief engineer, who was responsible for the mechanical running of the ship, boarded the vessel only 2 hours and 50 minutes before she put to sea. The minimum time needed to familiarise himself with the vessel was in fact three days. The company was charged with failing 'to take all reasonable steps to secure that the ship was operated in a safe manner', pursuant to s31 of the Marine Shipping Act 1988.

The issue that the House of Lords had to decide was whether s31 imposed vicarious liability on the company for the acts of all its employees.

Held

The appeal was dismissed.

Section 31 imposed a personal duty on the owner, charterer or manager of a ship to take all reasonable steps to secure that the ship was operated in a safe manner. Construed properly, Parliament could not have intended that s31 made the owner of a ship always liable for any act or omission by any officer of the company or member of the crew, which led to the unsafe operation of the ship.

Lord Keith of Kinkel:

'... As Staughton LJ observed in the course of his judgment in the Divisional Court, it would be surprising if by the language used in s31 Parliament intended that the owner of a ship should be criminally liable for any act or omission by any officer of the company or member of the crew which resulted in unsafe operation of the ship, ranging from a failure by the managing director to arrange repairs to a failure by the bosun or cabin steward to close portholes (see [1993] 3 All ER 25 at 33, [1993] 1 WLR 1025 at 1033). Of particular relevance in this context are the concluding words of s31(4), referring to the taking of all such steps as are reasonable for *him* (my emphasis) to take, ie the owner, charterer or manager. The steps to be taken are to be such as will secure that the ship is operated in a safe manner. That conveys to me the idea of laying down a safe manner of operating the ship by those involved in the actual operation of it and taking appropriate measures to bring it about that such safe manner of operation is adhered to. Where the owner, charterer or manager is a corporation which can act only through natural persons, the natural persons who are to be treated in law as being the corporation for the purpose of acts done in the course of its business are those who by virtue of its constitution or otherwise are entrusted with the exercise of the powers of the corporation: see per Lord Diplock in *Tesco Supermarkets Ltd* v *Nattrass* [1971] 2 All ER 127 at 155, [1972] AC 153 at 199–200.

In the judgment of the Divisional Court there is some discussion as to whether or not the offence provided for by s31 is one of strict liability, involving no necessary element of mens rea. It is not, however, helpful to seek to categorise the offence as either being or not being one of strict liability. It consists simply in failure to take steps which by an objective standard are held to be reasonable steps to take in the interests of the safe operation of a ship, and the duty which it places on the owner, charterer or manager is a personal one. The owner, charterer or manager is criminally liable if he fails personally in the duty, but is not criminally liable for the acts or omissions of his subordinate employees if he has himself taken all such reasonable steps.

My Lords, for these reasons I would dismiss the appeal.'

Commentary

The Secretary of State also argued that there had been a breach of s31 of the Marine Shipping Act 1988 in that there was no established system to ensure that the chief engineer had had sufficient opportunity to familiarise himself with the ship's equipment and machinery. It was argued that this was the responsibility of those whom the company had entrusted with the exercise of its powers. This was rejected by their Lordships because the case was not originally argued on this basis before the justices. Therefore, they did not consider it and it could not now be the basis for an appeal. This case illustrates that where criminal responsibility of a company is based on vicarious liability, the company may not be liable for all of the acts of all of its employees.

15.2 Memorandum of association

New Zealand Guardian Trust Co Ltd v *Keneth Stewart Brooks and Others* [1995] 1 WLR 96 Privy Council (Lords Keith of Kinkel, Oliver of Aylmerton, Mustill, Lloyd of Berwick and Nicholls of Birkenhead)

Whether company vicariously liable for directors' negligence.

Facts

A company (Budget) borrowed money from a consortium of financiers which was secured by a debenture trust deed. The deed required the company to provide the trustee with quarterly reporting certificates which required, among other things, the directors to state whether any matters had arisen which would adversely affect the lenders position. The certificates were prepared and signed by the company's directors. When the company was unable to pay back the monies advanced, two of the debenture holders accepted a sum less than the amount owed in full and final settlement of the loan. The two debenture holders then sued the trustee for the shortfall, amounting to £2,712,000. They alleged breaches of duties owed to them by the trustee under the trust deed. The trustee, NZGT Ltd, joined Budget's directors as third parties, alleging that the quarterly reporting certificates were prepared negligently. NZGT Ltd had previously released Budget from all liabilities towards it, but the release did not cover the directors of Budget.

Held

The directors of Budget were joint tortfeasors with Budget in negligently preparing the certificates. The release of Budget's liability also released the directors from further liability. The directors were properly struck out as third parties to the proceedings.

Lord Keith of Kinkel:

> 'The directors of Budget were its agents, and the question is whether or not they were acting in the course of their agency when they prepared the certificates. There can be no doubt that they were acting in their capacity as directors when they did so, and indeed this was conceded by counsel for the NZGT. Further, they were acting within the scope of their agency. They could not have prepared the certificates if they had not been authorised by Budget to do so, and their doing so was for the benefit of Budget because the rendering of the certificates was necessary to the maintenance of the loans to it. It is to be accepted that the directors assumed a personal responsibility towards NZGT to see that the certificates complied with the requirements of the trust deed and to exercise reasonable care in their preparation, but in most if not all cases where the acts of an employee or agent render the employer or principal vicariously liable it is because the employee or agent was in breach of a duty which he personally owed to the injured party.'

After referring to *Cassidy* v *Ministry of Health* [1951] 2 KB 343 and *Kuwait Asia Bank EC* v *National Mutual Life Nominees Ltd* [1991] 1 AC 187, his Lordship concluded:

'In their Lordships' opinion Budget was vicariously liable for the negligence of its directors in the preparation of the certificates and was accordingly a joint tortfeasor with them. The release of Budget therefore had the effect of releasing also the directors.'

15.3 Articles of association

Northern Engineering Industries plc, Re [1994] BCC 618 Court of Appeal (Neill, Leggatt and Millett LJJ)

Whether a reduction of capital amounted to a variation of class rights – variation and relationship with the articles

Facts

The company was seeking the court's approval of a reduction of capital, which involved paying off all of the preference shares and cancelling them. The reduction was opposed to by a preference shareholder.

The company's articles provided in article 7(B) that 'rights attached to any shares shall be deemed to be varied by a reduction of capital paid up on such shares'. Article 6 required such variation to be consented to by the preference shareholders or by an extraordinary resolution passed at a separate meeting of the preference shareholders.

The preference shareholders argued that in the absence of consent or an extraordinary resolution, the court should not confirm the capital reduction. The company argued that article 7(B) only applied where there was a reduction of capital paid up on particular shares to a figure which exceeded zero. In other words, 'reduction' means something different from 'cancellation' or 'extinction'.

Held

The court declined to confirm the reduction. Article 7(B) had the effect that the proposed cancellation of the preference shares was a variation of rights attached to the preference shares and a class meeting was therefore required by article 6. As no such meeting had been held, the reduction of capital had not been carried out in accordance with the company's articles.

Millet LJ (considered s135 of the Companies Act 1985 and the authority of *Re Anglo-American Insurance Co Ltd* [1991] BCC 208, and continued):

'More compelling, in my judgment, is the particular context provided by article 7(B) itself. The 'reduction' of the capital paid up on shares of a particular class is made to require the consent of the holders of the class affected. That is obviously intended to be a protection for those shareholders. It is idle to speculate whether it was included in the articles at the insistence of those who applied to be issued with preference shares or at the instigation of the ordinary shareholders as an inducement to investors to apply for preference shares. That it was intended to protect them from some risk is undeniable. The question is: what was the risk against which the preference shareholders were to be protected? In my judgment, the conclusion is inescapable: it was to protect them from the risk which was identified by Lord Greene MR [in *Re Chatterley-Whitfield Collieries Ltd* [1948] 2 All ER 593 at p596E], that of being subjected, without their consent, to a premature repayment of their investment, in whole or in part, a risk which, absent such an article, is inherent in the shares themselves. The company's argument that, without their consent, it cannot reduce the capital paid up on their shares from £1 to 99 pence, or from £1 to one penny, but that it does not need their consent to reduce it to nothing, in my view makes a nonsense of the protection which has been afforded them. It would protect the preference shareholders from a partial repayment which would leave them with something, however large and however small, but not from a complete repayment which would leave them with nothing. Yet this is a fortiori. The suggestion that the preference shareholders were to be protected merely from the piecemeal repayment of their investment and not from its complete repayment outright appears to me to be fanciful.'

Commentary
This confirms the earlier decision of Ferris J in [1993] BCC 267.

15.4 Capital

Acatos and Hutchinson plc v *Watson* (1994) The Times 30 December Chancery Division (Lightman J)

Section 143 Companies Act 1985 – whether a company had purchased its own shares.

Facts
Acatos and Hutchinson plc (AH), wanted to purchase the entire issued share capital of Acatos Ltd (A). A's sole asset was a substantial shareholding in AH. The agreement had been negotiated at arm's length and the independent directors of AH had been separately advised, by solicitors and accountants, that the transaction was in the best interests of AH and its shareholders. The question that the court had to decide was whether the transaction was in breach of the rule in *Trevor* v *Whitworth* (1877) 12 AC 409 and s143 Companies Act 1985, which prohibits a company from acquiring its own shares.

Held
The rule in *Trevor* v *Whitworth* and s143 Companies Act 1985 did not prevent AH from purchasing the entire share capital of A.

Lightman J observed that under the rule in *Trevor* v *Whitworth*, AH could not have purchased the shareholding in AH held by A. The issue was whether the rule could be side-stepped by purchasing instead the issued share capital of A, which would have the same economic consequences. The defendant argued that the veil of incorporation should be lifted to treat AH as acquiring its own shares, and this would prevent the rule and s143 being circumvented.

After referring to three Australian authorities which supported the plaintiff's case, Lightman J decided that the transaction was valid. If a takeover of a target company was prohibited when it held shares in the bidding company, this would provide the target company with a good defence. Lightman J said that it was plain that the rule did not have this remarkable and far-reaching effect. Section 23 of the Companies Act 1985 put the matter beyond question, for this expressly allowed A, after the acquisition, to keep its shareholding in AH. (Under s23, A's voting rights are suspended during the ownership.) Finally, his Lordship added that due to the potential for abuse, the court would look carefully at the transaction to see if the directors of the acquiring company had fulfilled their fiduciary duties to safeguard the interests of shareholders and creditors.

Smith New Court Securities Ltd v *Scrimgeour Vickers (Asset Management) Ltd and Another* [1994] 1 WLR 1271 Court of Appeal (Nourse, Rose and Hoffmann LJJ)

Misrepresentation – sale of shares – measure of damages

Facts

The plaintiff, Smith New Court Securities Ltd (SNC), purchased 28,141,424 shares in a public company at 82.25p. SNC claimed it was induced to make the purchase by fraudulent misrepresentations made by Roberts, an employee of Citibank NA (Citibank). The representations were that SNC was in competition with other bidders for the shares, which was not true. The shares had been charged to Citibank as a form of security by an American company and they were sold to SNC by Scrimgeour Vickers (Asset Management) Ltd (SVAM), who were acting as broker for Citibank. Roberts was also an executive director of SVAM.

Chadwick J, the judge at first instance, held that SNC were entitled to recover damages because of the misrepresentation. He measured the damages on the difference between the price paid and the true value of the shares on date of purchase, which was 21 July 1989. He then went on to find that due to another fraud, which was unconnected and then undiscovered, the value of each share at that date was 44p. The difference between the purchase price (£23,146,321) and the value of the shares at 44p each (£12,382,226) was £10,764,005, and judgment was awarded for this amount.

Citibank appealed against this judgment.

Held

The appeal was successful. The correct measure of damages was the difference between the price paid (82.25p per share, amounting to £23,146,321) and the price which the shares would have fetched on the open market, in the absence of the misrepresentation, on 21 July 1989 (78p a share, amounting to £21,950,311). The damages were accordingly reduced to £1,196,010.

Nourse LJ:

> 'In our judgment, therefore, the correct measure of damages was the difference between 82.25p and the price which, absent the misrepresentation, the parcel of shares would have fetched on the open market on 21 July 1989. Mr Sumption submitted that, on the evidence accepted by the judge, that price was 82.25p a share. That was the price which SNC decided to bid before any representation had been made. But that submission is undermined by our finding that the 9.43 am representation was made and that the pricing meeting acted upon it. The judge found that, in the absence of a representation, SNC would have offered 78p for a bought deal. He thought that Citibank would not have accepted this price: it would have preferred to deal in-house with CSV. But there was no evidence that CSV would have offered a higher price. It too was wanting a bought deal. It follows that, in our view, 78p was the market price on the date in question. The loss flowing from the misrepresentation was therefore 4.25p a share and the damages must be reduced from £10,764,005 to £1,196,010, being the difference between the price (£23,146,321) and the value of the shares at 78p each (£21,950,311).'

Commentary

The measure of damages for fraudulent misrepresentation in this case was assessed by the difference between the price paid and the price the shares would have fetched had the market *not* known about the fraud. An argument was put forward that damages should be assessed on the basis of omniscience, ie that the market knew everything including the unconnected fraud. This was rejected by the Court of Appeal, however, on the basis that omniscience is an 'arbitrary and irrational assumption'.

Thundercrest Ltd, Re [1994] BCC 857 Chancery Division (His Honour Judge Paul Baker QC)

Allotment of shares

Facts

The company needed additional funds to carry on litigation, in which it hoped to recover outstanding claims amounting to some £360,000. The plan was for each of the three shareholders K, C and M to put in £10,000 each to establish a litigation fund. In return they were to be allotted 10,000 £1 shares each. A letter of provisional allotment together with an acceptance form was sent to M's home but, on receiving no reply, the postman marked this fact on the letter and it was eventually returned to the company. The allotment went ahead with the other two shareholders each taking their 10,000 shares and also allotting themselves an additional 5,000 shares, representing M's entitlement.

The plaintiff sought rectification of the company's share register, by cancelling the additional allotment of 5,000 to K and C. The plaintiff argued that (1) the letter of provisional allotment did not allow at least 21 days in which acceptance could take place as provided for by s90(6) Companies Act 1985 and (2) that the letter was not properly served, despite a provision in the articles which provided that a pre-paid, properly addressed letter was deemed to have been served on the recipient.

Held

Rectification was allowed as the provisional letter of allotment did not contain a sufficient notice period of 21 days in which to accept the allotment. Further, the deeming provisions in the articles did not apply when it was obvious that the letter had not been posted, after it had been returned by the Post Office to the company before the allotment of shares had been made.

His Honour Judge Paul Baker QC:

> '... The time-limit has to be specified but that time must not be less than 21 days. It is sensible that, in a case of an allotment where large sums may be involved and have to be found to pay the call, some reasonable time should be allowed. It seems to me that the notice which was given in this case was defective in specifying less than 21 days.'

On the other point, as to service, the judge again decided in favour of the plaintiff.

> 'Here not only have we the sworn evidence of the plaintiff and his wife that the letter was not received, but it was manifest that the letter had not been delivered because it was returned by the Post Office to the defendants before the allotment of these shares was made. The purpose of deeming provisions in the case of management of companies is clear. In the case of uncertainty as to whether a document has been delivered, with large numbers of shareholders and so forth, there has to be some rule under which those in charge of the management can carry on the business without having to investigate every case where some shareholder comes along and says he has not got the document. The directors have to proceed and transact the company's business on the basis of deeming provisions. But, in my judgment, all that falls away when you find it is established without any possibility of challenge that the document has not been delivered.'

Commentary

The procedure for allotting shares must be strictly complied with. This case suggests that where a company's articles provide that acceptance of an offer of allotment of shares must be given within 21 days, this will be in conflict with s90(6) Companies Act 1985, which states that *at least* 21 days must be given in which to accept the allotment.

15.5 Debentures

Cimex Tissues Ltd, Re [1994] BCC 626 Chancery Division (Mr S J Burnton QC sitting as a deputy High Court judge)

Whether a charge over plant and machinery was fixed

Facts

The company's business was that of manufacturing toilet rolls. A debenture charged, 'by way of fixed charge', plant and machinery specified in a valuation annexed to the debenture. The machinery was used in the manufacturing process and was not of a type to be sold or replaced very often. The liquidator sought a determination whether the charge over the machinery was fixed or floating. The preferential creditors were claiming that it was a floating charge, in which case they would be paid off first out of the proceeds of the sale. The debenture-holder claimed that it was fixed, in which case he would be entitled to the proceeds at the expense of the preferential creditors.

Clause 3.2 of the debenture provided that the company would not 'without the previous consent in writing of the lender ... sell, mortgage or otherwise deal with the charged property otherwise than for the purpose of getting in and realising them in the ordinary course of, and for the purpose of, carrying on its trading business'. This, according to the preferential creditors, made the charge a floating charge, for it gave the company liberty to deal with the charged assets in the ordinary course of business, without obtaining the prior consent of the lender. Such a liberty is inconsistent with a fixed charge. The debenture-holder rejected this interpretation, but said that even if the charge did give such a liberty, it was not necessarily inconsistent with the creation of fixed charge.

Held

On its true construction, the debenture created a fixed charge.

1. The words 'getting in and realising' in clause 3.2 were inappropriate and inapplicable to the charged property due to its nature. The words were more appropriate to book debts. They were thought to be wholly inappropriate to the manufacturing equipment of a company. The clause did not therefore give the company power to deal with the charged property.
2. The words 'trading business' in clause 3.2 were construed as referring to the sale of stock and this was to be contrasted with the manufacturing business of the company. The clause gave no relevant power to the company, as the sale of capital manufacturing equipment could not be said to be 'in the ordinary course of its trading business'.
3. Where the chargor is given a licence to deal with the property this does not, in itself, lead to the conclusion that the charge is floating; however it would be if the licence to deal was extensive. On the facts, if clause 3.2 was construed as giving the chargor the right to sell the property without the lender's consent, the charge over the machinery was still a fixed one.

The decision of the case rests entirely upon the construction of the charge. The following extract concerns the difficult question of whether a liberty to sell in the ordinary course of business is necessarily inconsistent with a fixed charge.

Mr S J Burnton QC:

'The authorities on floating charges to which I have been referred do not lead me to conclude that, in the case of a charge over specific manufacturing machinery, a liberty for the chargor to deal to some extent with that machinery without the consent of the chargee is necessarily inconsistent with the creation of a fixed charge. I see no reason why, if the facts of *Holroyd* v *Marshall* were to recur today, in the case of a company, it could not be held that the charge created was a fixed charge.

In the present case, on any basis the company was prohibited from creating any charge over the secured property by virtue of cl 3.5 of the debenture. At most, the licence conferred implicitly by cl 3.2:1.2 entitled it to sell parts of the charged machinery "in the ordinary course of, and for the purpose of carrying on its trading business". If I assume that "trading" adds nothing to "business", this licence is scarcely different from that of the chargor in *Holroyd* v *Marshall*, except that in that case, substitute machinery had to be brought within the scope of the charge. I do not consider that that difference is sufficient to require me to find that the charge created by the debenture in the present case was, contrary to its description, and notwithstanding that only specific assets were charged, a floating charge. The difference relates to the commercial sense of the transaction from the point of view of the chargee, rather than the legal classification of the charge created. In this connection, I must say that I should be reluctant to be compelled to conclude, in the case of a charge on specific manufacturing equipment of a manufacturing company, that the unequivocal words of cl 2.1, explicitly referring to a fixed charge, could be overridden by what is in the present debenture a highly ambiguous and uncertain provision for sale in cl 3.2.

It follows that if I had concluded that cl 3.2:1.2 of the debenture had conferred a licence on the company without the subsequent consent of the chargee to sell parts of the specific manufacturing machinery constituting the charged property "in the ordinary course of, and for the purpose of carrying on its business", I should nonetheless have found that the charge created was a fixed charge.'

Commentary

This case is also interesting for it highlights the importance of having a well drafted debenture and one which is appropriate to the borrower's type of business. The debenture in this case was criticised as being 'defective', and the judge identified the debenture as deriving from the precedent at p145 of the *Encyclopaedia of Forms and Precedents* (5th edn). This contained a precedent for a debenture to secure bank lending. It was wholly inappropriate as the business of the company was that of a toilet roll manufacturer!

ELS Ltd, Re [1994] 3 WLR 616 Chancery Division (Ferris J)

Crystallisation of floating charge – whether this prevented a local authority from levying distress to recover business rates

Facts

ELS Ltd carried on the business of retailing furniture from premises within the areas of two local authorities, which were responsible for collecting non-domestic rates. On 15 October 1990, the company granted the National Westminster Bank Ltd a debenture, secured by a floating charge. Pursuant to the terms of the debenture, on 14 February 1992 the bank appointed joint administrators which had the effect of crystallising the floating charge. The question the court had to decide was whether a local authority having a power of distress, in order to recover business rates, can exercise that power over the goods of a company which are subject to a floating charge after that charge has crystallised.

Held

The crystallisation of the bank's floating charge over the company's property completed the assignment of that property to the bank. The result was that the goods of the company could no longer be considered as the property of the company. The two local authorities could not therefore exercise their right under statute (reg 14 of the Non-Domestic Rating (Collection and Enforcement) (Local Lists) Regulations 1989) to levy distress over the goods of the company, by appointing bailiffs to seize the goods. They were not the company's goods to seize.

Ferris J:

> 'I therefore answer the question posed by paragraph 1 of the originating summons by declaring that the crystallisation of the bank's floating charge in this case completed the assignment of the goods of ELS effected by the floating charge contained in the debenture dated 15 October 1990, with the consequence that such goods were thereafter no longer the goods of ELS for the purpose of regulation 14 of the Regulations of 1989. So expressed the declaration relates to this particular case rather than following the generalised proposition put forward in the originating summons, but, in my view, that is as far as I ought to go.'

Griffiths v *Yorkshire Bank plc* [1994] 1 WLR 1427 Chancery Division (Morritt J)

Priority of fixed and floating charges

Facts

Skainmead Ltd ('the company') granted the Yorkshire Bank plc ('the bank') a debenture secured by a fixed and floating charge on 13 January 1977.

A second debenture of 12 August 1985 was granted by the company to APH Industries Ltd (APH) to secure a loan made to the company. This was also secured by a fixed and floating charge.

On 23 June 1986 APH demanded sums due to it under the 1985 debenture, amounting to £64,000. At the same time it also served a notice on the company under clause 5(1) of the debenture. This provided that:

> 'The lender may at any time by notice in writing to the company convert the said floating charge into a specific charge as regards any assets specified in the notice which the lender shall consider to be in danger of being seized or sold under any form of distress execution diligence or other process levied or threatened and may appoint a receiver thereof.'

In its notice, the company specified all stock in trade and book debts as being converted to a specific fixed charge.

Earlier that same day, on 23 June, the bank had demanded £91,500 owed to it by the company and on 24 June appointed receivers. The company continued to trade under the control of the receivers until 9 July 1986.

The assets subject to the 1977 floating charge realised £99,500. The question for the court to decide was whether the notice served by APH under the 1985 debenture converting the floating charge to a fixed charge gave priority to APH. If it did then APH would receive its £64,000 in full, the remaining £35,500 would be paid to the preferential creditors and the bank would get nothing. If APH did not get priority, then the preferential creditors would be paid off in full, the bank would receive the balance in part payment of its debt, and APH would get nothing.

Held
APH did obtain priority and they were therefore entitled to be paid first out of the £99,500 realised from the assets subject to the 1977 floating charge.

Morritt J:

'I can express my conclusions in accordance with what I understand to be the basic principles applicable to questions concerning the priorities of fixed and floating charges relatively shortly. (1) It was inherent in the floating charge granted by the 1977 debenture that the company might subsequently confer proprietary interests on others in assets subject to the floating charge to rank prior to the bank's. A subsequent charge would constitute a breach of contract but would not be invalid. (2) The floating charge granted by the 1985 debenture was inherently capable of being converted into a fixed charge by service of the notice prescribed by clause 5(1). (3) By service of the notice on 23 June 1986 APH crystallised its floating charge over stock and book debts into a fixed charge having priority over the floating charge contained in the 1977 debenture. (4) Such priority was not lost when, the following day, the floating charge in the 1977 debenture crystallised on the appointment of the receivers for there was no agreement as to priority requiring that result. (5) APH as the first (and by then the fixed chargee) was entitled to the stock and book debts as security for its debt. (6) Section 196(2) of the Companies Act 1985 did not on its true construction apply to the 1985 debenture or require APH to pay the preferential creditors. (7) In the circumstances that APH, not the bank, was entitled to the proceeds of realisation, the fact that the receivers realised the book debts and stock, rather than leaving it to APH, is immaterial because the plaintiffs were not entitled to do so as receivers appointed under the 1977 debenture. Consequently section 196(2) imposed no duty on them.'

Commentary
Re Portbase Clothing Ltd [1933] Ch 388 distinguished.

15.6 Meetings

Harman & Anor v *BML Group Ltd* [1994] 1 WLR 893 Court of Appeal (Dillon, Leggatt and Henry LJJ)

Section 371 Companies Act 1985 – power of the court to order meeting.

Facts

The share structure of BML Group Ltd consisted of A and B ordinary shares. H and M held between them 260,000 A shares. The other three members of the company were B and L, who each owned 25,000 A shares and SB who owned 190,00 B shares. There was a shareholders' agreement between them that a shareholders' meeting would not have a quorum unless a B shareholder was present. At a shareholders' meeting on 3 August 1993 B. L and SB voted to remove H and M as directors. Accountants were also instructed to investigate allegations of financial irregularities against them. H and M then applied to the court under s371 Companies Act 1985 for an order that a meeting be held so that B and L could be removed as directors.

Held

The court would not exercise its powers under s371 where this would override the class rights of the B shareholder. Dillon LJ said that B could use his rights not only to protect himself but also his allies on the board of directors. It was not right to use s371 to bypass those rights. The court refused to order that a meeting be called.

Dillon LJ:

> 'For present purposes I do not regard it as the function of the court to intervene in these sort of proceedings by requiring various cross undertakings to achieve the conduct of the business of the company on sensible terms. That is for the parties' advisers to achieve. It is not for the court to make a new shareholders' agreement between the parties and impose it on them. Beyond that, however, I am of the view that the judge has not given sufficient weight to the situation of the s459 petition and the allegations there. He has misdirected himself. Much more, it is not right, in my view, to invoke s371 to override class rights attached to a class of shares which have been deliberately – in this case by the shareholders' agreement – imposed for the protection of the holders of those shares, although they are a minority. It is not the case that the overriding position is that the majority shareholders must prevail on everything. Class rights have to be respected and I regard the right of Mr Blumenthal, as the holder of the B shares, to be present in the quorum as a class right for his protection which is not to be overridden by this machinery. I would therefore allow this appeal.'

Commentary

Re El Sombrero Ltd [1958] 3 WLR 349 distinguished.

15.7 Directors

Duckwari plc* v *Offerventure Ltd [1995] BCC 89 Court of Appeal (Neill, Beldam and Millet LJJ)

Substantial property transaction within ss320 and 322 CA 1985

Facts

C was a director of both D plc and O Ltd. C and his wife were the only shareholders of O Ltd, which agreed to purchase a freehold property worth £495,000. C then wrote to a fellow director of D plc and offered to let D plc take over the benefit of the contract from O Ltd, so that D plc would purchase the property. The contract was later completed with D plc paying the £495,000 purchase price to the vendor and reimbursing the deposit of £49,500 to O Ltd. After completion, D plc alleged that the property was worth substantially less than this amount and argued that the arrangement was a substantial property transaction within s320 CA 1985 and sought to avoid the transaction.

Held

The court of Appeal agreed with D plc, that the arrangement was a substantial property transaction. D plc had acquired a non-cash asset from C, via his company, O Ltd. It was accepted that O Ltd was connected with C for the purposes of the substantial property transaction provisions in ss320 and 322 CA 1985.

Millet LJ:

'It remains necessary only to consider an argument which was advanced and rejected by the judge below and which has been repeated before us on behalf of Duckwari, namely, that the value of the non-cash asset acquired by Duckwari from Offerventure was £495,000. It was submitted that the reality of the matter was that it was acquiring the property or the right to buy the property and that the purchase price of £495,000 was payable in its entirety to or to the direction of Offerventure, so that even the £445,500 which was paid to the vendor was only paid to the vendor because Offerventure so directed. That is true, but we are concerned with the identification and valuation of the asset which moved in the other direction; and the problem is that, although it is true that the property itself passed from the vendor to Duckwari only because Offerventure directed the vendor to transfer the property to Duckwari and therefore moved from the vendor through Offerventure to the purchaser, the fact remains that the vendor had his own independent valuable proprietary right in the property, namely the unpaid vendor's lien. That had to be discharged by Duckwari by payment direct to the vendor (that was worth £445,500) and that figure must be deducted from the value of the property acquired from Offerventure. In my judgment, there were two assets being acquired by Duckwari. One was the asset acquired from Offerventure, viz the right to call on completion for the conveyance on discharging Offerventure's obligations to the vendor and paying Offerventure £49,500; and the other was the extinction of the vendors' unpaid lien by discharging Offerventure's obligation to pay the balance of the purchase money due to the vendor.

Duckwari has pointed to the capricious results which appear to follow from this analysis because it makes the question whether a transaction needs to be approved by the company in general meeting depend upon the amount, if any, of the deposit rather than the value of the property being acquired by the company.

If this is an anomaly it results from a combination of the facts (1) that cash assets and liabilities are excluded from the computation and (2) that Parliament has seen fit, for obvious reasons, to exclude the operation of the section where the transaction is not of substantial value. I do not think that it is possible in isolation to consider whether this analysis does lead to capricious results without considering the consequences of an infringement of the section.

These proceedings have been brought by Duckwari in order to enforce the indemnity provided for s322(3). Duckwari's object is to seek to recover from the appellants the amount of the loss which has resulted from the fall in market values since the date of the transaction. Whether Duckwari would succeed in that endeavour will depend upon the question whether the loss or damage resulting from the arrangement or transaction referred to in s322(3)(b) is to be measured by the difference between the value of the property at the date of the transaction and the purchase price (which in this case was nil) or is to be measured by the purchase price and the value of the property at some other and later date. That is a question which still remains for decision, and I express no opinion at all upon it. But it must not be assumed from anything that I have said in the course of this judgment that I take any view on that one way or the other.'

Gibson Davies Ltd, Re [1995] BCC 11 Chancery Division (Companies Court) (Sir Mervyn Davies)

Company Directors Disqualification Act 1986 s17 – whether the appellant could be given leave to act as a director

Facts

The director was disqualified in his absence on 22 March 1993 for a period of five years. His conduct while a director of Gibson Davies & Co Ltd (GDC) amounted to unfitness. The conduct relied on involved:

1. the granting of a preference contrary to s239 Insolvency Act 1986;
2. continuing to trade after distraint had been levied by the Inland Revenue, thereby eroding the position of creditors;
3. the raising of misleading invoices;
4. paying undue remuneration at a time when the company's losses were increasing; and
5. failure to file audited accounts.

The director then applied, pursuant to s17 CDDA 1986, to be allowed to act as a director of a company called Congratulations Franchising Ltd (CFL), whose main business was the selling of wedding presents contained in the company's catalogue. The appellant had set up a similar business, called Congratulations Ltd, in Ireland which was successful. He now wanted to carry on the same business in England through CFL, and be a director of the company. His application was a dismissed and he now appealed against that decision.

Held

The appeal was successful and leave to allow the appellant to act as a director was granted. Sir Mervyn Davies was satisfied that there was a need to make such an order and that the public would remain adequately protected, by virtue of the safeguards offered by the appellant.

Sir Mervyn Davies:

'Since I am of the view that there is need for the making of an order, one goes on to consider whether, if an order is made, there will be adequate protection for the public. The appellant offered the following safeguards:

(1) no cheque or financial agreement on behalf of the company be signed or executed by the appellant alone;

(2) any director's loan owed by the company to the appellant shall not be repaid unless all creditors of the company are paid first;

(3) the appellant shall not be granted or accept any security over the company assets;

(4) the appellant's total emoluments from the company shall not exceed £380 per week or such greater sum as shall hereafter be agreed in writing by the Secretary of State, such consent not to be unreasonably refused;

(5) the appellant shall procure the company to file annual returns and accounts at Companies House within the time limits set out in the *Companies Act* 1985;

(6) the appellant will procure the company to complete the implementation of the accounting controls as set out by Mr Heer of Robson Rhodes [the company's chartered accountants] in his affidavit sworn on 3 February 1994;

(7) the appellant will procure the company to prepare monthly management accounts and submit the said accounts to Robson Rhodes or to the company's auditors for the time being;

(8) Robson Rhodes, or the company's auditors for the time being, shall be instructed to report to the board of directors in writing any matters of concern relating to the management or financial control of the company and in default of prompt and appropriate action by the directors of the company will bring these matters to the attention of the Secretary of State's solicitors;

(9) in the event that the company seeks to change the identity of its auditors the appellant will procure the company only to instruct auditors who are willing to accept and act upon the obligations set out above;

(10) the appellant will take no step as a shareholder or director of Congratulations Ltd (ie the Irish company) which would in any way impede, direct or control the activities of the company.

The first nine of those safeguards were offered before Judge Gosling [the judge at first instance] in written form. The tenth safeguard was discussed but never precisely formulated. The accounting controls referred to in item (6) are: (a) all cheques over £2,500 to be signed by more than one director; (b) all cheques below £2,500 to be signed by both Mr Davies [the appellant director] and the company's financial controller, Mrs Richards; (c) monthly management accounts to be reviewed by Robson Rhodes; (d) the company to complete the implementation of the internal accounting control recommended by Robson Rhodes; (e) Robson Rhodes to accept an obligation to bring to the attention of the directors in writing any matters of concern relating to the management or financial control of the company and in default of prompt and appropriate action by the directors to bring these matters to the attention of the applicant's solicitors.

I am of the opinion that the appellant ought to be allowed to act as a director of Franchising by an order which incorporates the safeguards set out above. Accordingly, I allow the appeal and make such an order as I have mentioned.'

Commentary

This is the first case based on an appeal under s17 CDDA 1986.

Moorgate Metals Ltd, Re [1995] BCC 143 Chancery Division (Warner J)

Whether respondent was a de facto or shadow director

Facts

The case concerned disqualification proceedings against two directors, R and H. The company's business was that of a metal merchant, reselling container loads of scrap metal. One issue in the case was whether R was a de facto director. He was not formally appointed as a director as he was an undischarged bankrupt. However, R controlled the company's entire trading operation.

Held

R was a de facto director.

Warner J:

> **'The case against Mr Rawlinson**
>
> As regards Mr Rawlinson the first question is whether he was a director of Moorgate within the meaning of that expression in s6(1) of the Act. In his affidavit Mr Rawlinson contended that he was not. He pointed to the absence from the Act of any express mention of a de facto director and he referred to the definition of a shadow director in s22(5) of the Act. He said that his position was that of metal trader of the company; that every trading company on the Metal Exchange employed a metal trading expert like himself; and that the majority of such employees were not directors. He accepted that he 'controlled the company's entire trading operation', but said that that was because of his professional expertise.
>
> Mr Davis-White referred me to a number of authorities on the matter, namely *Re Lo-Line Electric Motors Ltd* (1988) 4 BCC 415, *Re Tasbian Ltd (No 3)* [1991] BCC 435 and [1992] BCC 358, *Re Cargo Agency Ltd* [1992] BCC 388, and *Re Hydrodan (Corby) Ltd* [1994] BCC 161. It appears to me clear from those authorities:
>
> (1) that the word 'director' in s6(1) includes a 'de facto director'; and
> (2) that for this purpose a de facto director is a person who in fact acts as a director, though not appointed as such.
>
> Some of the expressions used by Millett J in the *Hydrodan* case could be construed as meaning that, for a person to be held to have been a de facto director, the label 'director' must have been attached to him. But I am sure that Millett J did not mean that. He was concerned to distinguish between a de facto director and a shadow director, the latter being a person in accordance with whose directions or instructions the directors of a company (whether de jure or de facto) are accustomed to act.
>
> I have come to the conclusion that Mr Rawlinson was a de factor director of Moorgate. I have already mentioned many of the facts that have led me to that conclusion: the fact that Moorgate came into existence as a result of Mr Rawlinson inviting Mr Huhtala to join him in a business that he was minded to set up; the fact that Mr Rawlinson and Mr Huhtala shared the responsibilities of managing the company and that Mr Rawlinson was in sole charge of the company's trading with no limit on the extent of the commitments that he could enter into on behalf of the company; and the fact that Mr Rawlinson and Mr Huhtala received equal remuneration. (Mr Huhtala had the additional benefit of motor cars but the purchase of company cars for both Mr Huhtala and Mr Rawlinson was authorised at the board meeting on 4 July 1989. I was not told why none was in fact

purchased for Mr Rawlinson.) Other factors support the conclusion. Mr Huhtala told me that he consulted Mr Rawlinson on all important decisions, including the appointment of bankers, the appointment of solicitors, the appointment of Mr Robertson's firm as accountants and the investment in CIP. Indeed it is clear (as I have mentioned) that Mr Robertson thought Mr Rawlinson was acting as if he were a director of the company and in his letter to the official receiver of 11 December 1989 Mr Robertson said "We were instructed by both Mr Huhtala and Mr Rawlinson ..." When the company's main bank account was moved from Barclays Bank to Commerzbank, although Mr Huhtala was named in the mandate as the sole signatory on the account, Commerzbank were informed that both Mr Rawlinson (who was described as "chief executive") and Mr Huhtala (who was named second and described as "managing director") had authority to give instructions over the telephone to effect payment orders. Lastly, there is in evidence a promotional brochure published by Moorgate which repeatedly refers to Mr Rawlinson (there described as "senior trader") and Mr Huhtala (described as "managing director") as "partners". Again Mr Rawlinson is named first. The overall picture conveyed by the evidence is of Mr Huhtala and Mr Rawlinson as equals, running the company between them, and not of Mr Rawlinson being Mr Huhtala's subordinate in any way. In my view Mr Rawlinson was a director in all but name.

Having reached that conclusion I need not advert to the question whether Mr Rawlinson could be regarded as having been a shadow director of Moorgate.'

Commentary

Whether or not a person is fulfilling the functions of a director can be a difficult question to answer. The judgement of Warner J contains a number of useful factors which his Lordship relied on to decide that the overall picture was that R was a director. Once again the court stressed that the label attached to a director is not conclusive. Simply calling someone a director, or vice versa, will not necessarily decide the issue.

Pamstock Ltd, Re [1994] BCC 264 Chancery Division (Vinelott J)

Company Directors Disqualification Act 1986 s6 – whether director who was the provider of venture capital was unfit

Facts

The respondent director, I, specialised in assisting small, and often newly formed, companies by providing financial advice and obtaining outside finance. The new companies were often formed under the Business Enterprise Scheme and I, as the provider of venture capital, was often required to accept a directorship. The official receiver complained about the conduct of I in relation to ten companies over a 15-year period. In relation to Pamstock Ltd, the allegations by the official receiver against I were that:

1. He had allowed the company to trade whilst insolvent.
2. He failed to give sufficient attention to the financial affairs of the company, in particular, by allowing cheques to be tendered in the knowledge that they would not be met.

3. He failed to ensure the proper filing of annual accounts and returns.

Pamstock Ltd was undercapitalised and was reliant on bank borrowing and borrowing from the participators to finance its trade. As well as making losses in every year, Crown debts, such as unpaid VAT and PAYE deductions, increased each year and by the end of its life, these debts financed the company to a large extent.

Held

I's conduct as a director of Pamstock Ltd amounted to unfitness and he was disqualified for a period of two years. I was not found to be unfit in relation to the other companies, despite allegations of trading whilst insolvent and failing to submit annual returns. Despite the fact that he had not been concerned in the affairs of any company that had become insolvent since 1987–88, the court had to take into account past conduct, even if it was now satisfied that the director was now behaving responsibly.

Vinelott J:

'I accept that this is not the case of a director who has taken large remuneration or who has obtained other benefits from a company at the expense of creditors. The respondent obtained no benefit beyond the use of a flat for the purposes of the company's business and of course he suffered financially to a greater extent than the creditors even if taken as a whole. However the question is not whether there was culpable misconduct in the sense that he benefited himself at the expense of the creditors. The failure of Pamstock with substantial debts which could only be met if and to the extent that the respondent personally honoured them came about in part because he failed to put into place an adequate system of management and, when the company was clearly running into difficulty, allowed it to continue to trade beyond the point at which trading should have ceased. To that extent the respondent in my judgment fell short of the standard of conduct which is today expected of a director of a company which enjoys the privilege of limited liability. In this context the failure to file accounts and returns promptly is also a serious default. Creditors (including, in this case, the Crown) may be prejudiced if accounts which would have shown that a company's assets exceed its liabilities and that it is continuing to trade at a loss and is dependent upon the continued support of its participators are not filed.

I reach this conclusion with regret. I have had the advantage of seeing the respondent give oral evidence when he was skillfully cross-examined by Mr Chivers. There is no evidence that the respondent has been involved in the affairs of any company which has ended in an insolvent winding-up since 1987–88. He told me and I accept that in recent years he has made a practice of ensuring that a chartered accountant is appointed secretary of all companies with which he is concerned and is instructed to ensure that annual accounts and returns are promptly filed. The respondent seemed to me (so far as I can judge from the evidence before me) to be a man who today is capable of discharging his duties as a director, honestly and diligently. His failures in relation to Pamstock came at a time when his time was fully occupied with the affairs of other companies and when he was under considerable financial pressure. However, I cannot, I think, be sure that these difficulties wholly excuse the respondent's serious misconduct in relation to Pamstock.

Nor can it be said that his subsequent conduct justifies the conclusion that his past misconduct should be overlooked upon the ground that there is no reason today for saying that a disqualification order is needed for the protection of the public. A disqualification order must to some extent express the view of the court as to the seriousness of past misconduct. As I observed at the beginning of this judgment, a disqualification order is likely to have a disproportionately severe effect on him. Apart from the stigma of a disqualification order it will be difficult and may be impossible for him to continue in his career as the provider of venture capital and as a professional non-executive director if he must seek leave before accepting any appointment. However, as Mr Collings expressed it, under the legislation as it now stands, I am required to have tunnel vision and to consider whether in relation to Pamstock the respondent's conduct fell short of the minimum standard which the court today requires to be observed by the director of a company which enjoys the privilege of limited liability, and if it does, to impose a disqualification order for a minimum of two years. I have reached the conclusion after anxious consideration and some hesitation that in the circumstances I am bound to make a disqualification order. In the circumstances of this case I think I am justified for making the order for the minimum period of two years.'

Commentary

Vinelott J took the opportunity in this case to question whether it was right that a director should have to face a mandatory disqualification order under s6, where the conduct complained of was some years ago and where the court was now satisfied that the director was behaving responsibly. He urged those currently reviewing the operation of the Company Directors Disqualification Act 1986 to consider whether this is necessary. His Lordship also criticised the practice of the official receiver to include in the evidence every matter which could be the possible subject of complaint. Some matters, which do not amount to serious failures, would be better put before the court in the form of a schedule.

Rex Williams Leisure plc (In Administration), Re [1994] 3 WLR 745
Court of Appeal (Russell, Staughton and Hoffmann LJJ)

Company Directors Disqualification Act 1986 s8 – disqualification after investigation of a company – procedural points

Facts

The respondent directors were the boxing promoter, Mr Frank Warren, and a solicitor, Mr Peter Sealey. They were both directors of the company whose principal business was the supply of business machines. The company agreed to buy from Mr Warren shares which he owned in another company for £2m. The purchase did not go ahead, but £200,000 was paid to him by the company, which Mr Sealey authorised. The money was not repaid at the time Rex Williams Leisure plc went into administration in April 1990.

An investigation of the company took place under s447 Companies Act 1985 and the inspectors concluded that the money had simply been extracted from the company in breach of the directors' fiduciary duties. The result was that the Secretary of State applied for a disqualification order under s8 Company Directors

Disqualification Act 1986. He then filed his affidavit evidence against the directors in accordance with the Insolvent Companies (Disqualification of Unfit Directors) Proceedings Rules 1987 (SI 1987 No 2023). The next step would have been for the directors to file their affidavit evidence in reply. However, at this stage they sought the following relief:

1. An order striking out the summons seeking the disqualification orders on the ground that it was an abuse of process to hear the application while civil proceedings to recover the £200,000 were still pending.
2. A declaration that the directors were entitled to give evidence or call witnesses at the hearing, without first having filed affidavit evidence.
3. An order striking out those parts of the affidavit evidence filed on behalf of the Secretary of State, which included statements made by persons other than the directors themselves. Such statements, they argued, amounted to hearsay.

The judge refused the relief sought and the defendants appealed.

Held

The appeal was dismissed. The relief in (1) was dismissed as it was felt that it would be absurd to hold up the Secretary of State's application to disqualify directors indefinitely by other proceedings over which he has no control. The relief in (2) was dismissed on the ground that the words in the 1987 Rules were to be interpreted as meaning that the evidence that the director wishes the court to take into account *must* first be filed on affidavit. The hearsay relief sought in (3) was also dismissed on the basis that it was impliedly admissible in proceedings under the Company Directors Disqualification Act 1986.

Staughton LJ:

'I agree that this appeal should be dismissed. Of the two points which seem to me to be most significant, the first is whether the Insolvent Companies (Disqualification of Unfit Directors) Proceedings Rules 1987 are ultra vires. It is said that they are, if and to the extent that they do not allow a respondent to call evidence unless he has filed an affidavit of the proposed witness. That is said to conflict with s16(1) of the Company Directors Disqualification Act 1986, which provides that the person against whom an order is sought "may appear and himself give evidence or call witnesses".

The Act of 1986 contemplates in s21, although somewhat indirectly, that rules may be made. In my judgment, it enables rules to deal with how evidence shall be given and witnesses called; and in particular it permits a requirement that affidavits shall first be filed. This is essentially a rule as to how the right conferred by s16(1) shall be exercised, and not a derogation from that right.

The second point that has troubled me concerns hearsay evidence. RSC O.41, r.5 provides that, subject to a number of exceptions which do not apply in the present case, "an affidavit may contain only such facts as the deponent is able of his own knowledge to prove".

How then can the Secretary of State be entitled to use affidavits of information and belief in disqualification proceedings? As Hoffmann LJ has shown, this stems from an implied statutory provision as to the use of hearsay as evidence, or at any rate as provisional evidence until it is challenged. That doctrine is now of respectable antiquity, having been established between 1967 and 1975. I would for my part have hesitated to accept it when first propounded. But as it has existed for a substantial period of time, during which relevant statutory provisions have been replaced and re-enacted or amended, I would not now alter it.'

Secretary of State for Trade and Industry v *Gray and Another* (1994) The Times 24 November Court of Appeal (Neill, Hoffmann and Henry LJJ)

Company Directors Disqualification Act s6 – whether unfitness had to exist at the time of the hearing

Facts

In disqualification proceedings under s6 Company Directors Disqualification Act 1986, the judge made various findings of fact against two directors, namely, that they:

1. had made preferences contrary to s239 Insolvency Act 1986;
2. traded at a time when they knew the company was unable to pay its debts;
3. failed to keep proper accounting records;
4. failed to file the 1987 accounts on time.

The judge ruled that the directors were not unfit, and the Secretary of State appealed.

Held

The appeal was allowed.

This was the first case in which the Secretary of State had appealed against a refusal to make a disqualification order. The Secretary of State argued that after the judge had made her findings of fact, she should have disqualified the two directors as the condition in s6(1)(b) of the Company Directors Disqualification Act 1986 had been satisfied: that is, their conduct as directors made them unfit to be concerned in the management of a company.

Hoffmann LJ held that it was not necessary for the court to be satisfied that the director was unfit at the time of the hearing. If this was the position his Lordship explained that there would be no need to make disqualification under s6 mandatory. Further, the judge was wrong to allow, in mitigation, the fact that the remedy for making preferences lies with the liquidator pursuing a claim on behalf of the creditors. To allow this would be to deny the specific reference to preferences in Schedule 1 of the Company Directors Disqualification Act (which deals with matters that the court is to take into account when making a disqualification order) any effect. Hoffmann LJ was undecided whether the judge had considered the allegations against the directors cumulatively, which would have been more likely to lead to a disqualification order, or separately, as the Secretary of State had argued. In any event, taking into account the preferences that the judge improperly discounted, his Lordship felt that the directors were unfit and should have been disqualified.

Wimbledon Village Restaurant Ltd, Re; Secretary of State for Trade and Industry v *Thomson and Others* [1994] BCC 753 Chancery Division (Michael Hart QC sitting as a deputy High Court judge)

Company Directors Disqualification Act s6 – court refused to find that two executive directors and one non-executive director were unfit

Facts

The business of Wimbledon Village Restaurant Ltd (WVR) was that of a restaurant proprietor. It carried on business from March 1985 to late September 1989. It went into creditors' voluntary liquidation in November 1989 with debts of £327,356. The respondent directors were Mrs Woods ('W') and two brothers, Graham and Ian Thomson ('G' and 'I'). The management of the company was left to G and I. W was a non-executive director and held her directorship to protect her position as the unlimited guarantor of the company's overdraft. The allegations made against the directors, by the Secretary of State for Trade and Industry, were that:

1. Since February 1989 the directors knew or ought to have known that the company was trading whilst insolvent.
2. They had improperly used the company's bank account by issuing cheques which they knew or ought to have known would not be honoured.
3. They had failed to co-operate in the liquidation.
4. They failed to file annual accounts for the year ending 31 March 1988.
5. On one occasion there was a failure to file an annual return.

Held

In relation to allegation (1), the judge felt that I and G had not paid sufficient regard to the interests of creditors. Allegations (2) and (3) were not proved, while (4) and (5) were proved. Bearing in mind some special factors of the case, all three directors were found not to be unfit. The special factors referred to were:

1. With hindsight, the then economic climate was encouraging a degree of false optimism within the business community. It was also a climate which suffered from unpredictable instabilities, such as a rise in minimum lending rates from 7.55 per cent in May 1988 to 14 per cent in May 1989.
2. The brothers believed that if the matters came to a head, they could sell the lease of the company's premises for £300,000. It was commercial misjudgment not to obtain a formal valuation of the lease, but an understandable one, given the explosion of commercial property prices in Wimbledon at that time.
3. The breakdown of the relationship between the two brothers, rather than incompetence, explained their failure to deal with the company's worsening situation.

4. The nature of the business made it difficult to say whether a bad period of trading was any more than a seasonal downturn. The true picture was blurred by a change in management, which in itself could be evidence that the directors had a genuine belief that the business was still viable.

5. The company had an unusual degree of accountancy experience, via the Thomson family, and their mute presence may have explained why professional advice was not sought earlier.

6. Neither G nor I prolonged the life of the company with any view to personal advantage.

Michael Hart QC:

'These factors mitigate, though they do not excuse, the deficiencies in the conduct of WVR to which I have referred. I have to decide in each case whether Ian's and Graham's acts and omissions were in 1988 and 1989 such as to demonstrate their unfitness now to be concerned in the management of a company. The Act requires me to consider whether the unfitness then displayed makes them unfit now to be so concerned: see *Re Bath Glass Ltd* [1988] 4 BCC 130 at p132 per Peter Gibson J. The law rightly exacts high standards of those who claim the privilege of trading with limited liability. Those standards are particularly appropriate where, as here, the adventure was fraught with risk from the outset. In my judgment the lapses from those standards in the case of both Ian and Graham demonstrated a failure to appreciate their responsibilities, and I have found that this failure did in the event damage trade creditors of the business. To that extent they may be said to have been shown to have been unfit to be concerned in the management of a company. It is not, however, every past impropriety which should lead to a conclusion that the director responsible is unfit. Having regard to what seem to me to have been the peculiar combination of family and commercial circumstances in which they found themselves in relation to WVR, I find myself left with a significant measure of doubt as to whether the lapses properly attributable to either of them were sufficiently serious as to compel a finding that either is now unfit to be concerned in the management of a company. That doubt is sufficiently strong to make me conclude that the correct course is to resolve it in their favour.

I turn now to the position of Mrs Woods. This has given me some difficulty. Mrs Woods played no role whatsoever as a director of WVR following the Diga takeover. The Thomsons appeared to her, as indeed they were, to be experienced in the relevant catering skills and to have available to them within their family all relevant accountancy and business skills. They were men of some personal worth. Her agreement with them was that they would be wholly responsible for the running of the business, she retaining a directorship simply as a means of being able to protect her own position as the unlimited guarantor of the company overdraft. In those circumstances, she neither asserted nor accepted any wider responsibility. In taking that attitude, she seems to me wholly to have misconceived her duties as the director of a limited liability company. She seems to have been completely unaware of the wider responsibilities owed by her to the company and its creditors. This attitude (or lack of one) in relation to WVR certainly points in the direction of her being unfit to be concerned in the management of a company. I do not, however, think that the mere fact that she had this attitude drives me inexorably to the conclusion that she is so unfit. I must measure her actual responsibility in relation to the allegations which I have found proved. Given the division of responsibilities on the board, while she must bear some responsibility for not having ascertained the state of the audit of the 1988 accounts, I have no doubt that Ian would have advised her after February 1989 that this matter was well in hand. Equally I have no doubt that until August 1989, the noises she had heard from Ian about the business were on the whole reassuring. I should add that her ability to take a more active interest was in any case compromised at the material time by her own domestic pressures: she had an adolescent daughter and a husband with Parkinson's disease to care for. She alone of the directors has in the event suffered financially, having found herself at the end of the day liable to the bank in the sum of some £140,000. I would also add that the allegations made against her appear to have been made and maintained by Mr Rose in the wholly mistaken belief that she was occupied full-time at the restaurant as 'a meeter and greeter'. In all the circumstances, while her failure to appreciate that she had duties as a director beyond those that she owed to herself was regrettable, and while I accept the argument that, had she appreciated the fact, events might have taken a different course, I do not find her misconduct in relation to WVR to have been so serious as to justify my finding her to be unfit to be concerned in the management of a company.'

Re Working Project Ltd; Re Fosterdown Ltd; Re Davies Flooring (Southern) Ltd [1995] BCC 197 Chancery Division (Carnworth J)

Whether disqualification proceedings were possible after the companies had gone into liquidation

Facts

All three companies had gone into liquidation and disqualification proceedings had been commenced in the County Court against various directors under the unfitness ground in s6 CDDA 1986. The questions that Carnworth J had to decide was whether the court had lost jurisdiction to disqualify when the winding up of a company had been concluded. If it did, the second question was when was winding up concluded for this purpose.

Held

1. Disqualification proceedings already commenced in the County Court did not have to be aborted simply because the liquidator had completed his task.
2. The right to commence disqualification proceedings in the County Court ended when the winding up had been concluded
3. In relation to Fosterdown, proceedings were commenced only after the liquidator had lodged his final return, but before dissolution. The proceedings were allowed to continue because the winding up process does not end until dissolution of the company.

Carnworth J:

'It would be patently absurd if disqualification proceedings, validly commenced in the county court, were at risk of being aborted at any time (even in the middle of the hearing, or after judgment has been reserved), simply because the liquidator has completed his work. No one has suggested any sensible legislative purpose for such a rule. There is no reason why the continuing jurisdiction of the county court in the disqualification proceedings should depend on the speed with which the liquidator is able to progress the winding up. The disadvantages of such a rule (in terms of cost, uncertainty and delay) are obvious.

The only substantial argument in favour of that approach is that it accords with a literal reading of s6. Under subsection (1) it is the "court" which must make the disqualification order. On a strict reading of subs 3(a) and (b), the county court remains "the court" as defined only so long as the company "is being wound up". Accordingly, it is said, once the winding up has been completed, the county court ceases to have jurisdiction to make the disqualification order – whatever stage the proceedings have then reached.

It is, however, permissible to modify a literal reading, where it produces absurdity, and a reasonable alternative is available (see Cross, *Statutory Interpretation* (7th edn. 1990), p47). This is such a case. Where, as here, a section defines a particular court for the purposes of proceedings under that section, the correct inference, in my view, will normally be that the definition is directed to the *commencement* of proceedings. In the absence of express provision, Parliament can be assumed to have intended proceedings properly commenced in a particular tribunal to be carried to a conclusion in that tribunal. In subs 6(3), therefore, the words "for the purpose of the commencement of proceedings" should be regarded as implicit. On this view, provided the respective county courts had jurisdiction at the time of the commencement of proceedings, they were, and are, empowered to carry them to conclusion; and I so hold. It follows that the order made against Mr Hollington's client was validly made.'

His Lordship then considered, and rejected, another submission by counsel for the Secretary of State for Trade and Industry and the Official Receiver and continued:

'The other main question only arises in the case of *Fosterdown*, where the disqualification proceedings were commenced after the registration of the liquidator's final return, but before dissolution. At which point was the "winding up" complete – or, more precisely, at which point did the company cease to be a company "being wound up"?

It seems to me that the winding up is complete when the company is finally dissolved, and not before. The expression "winding up" naturally refers to the whole statutory process designed to secure the completion of the company's affairs, the distribution of its assets, and its final quietus. That process does not end until dissolution.'

Commentary

This is an important judgement on the disqualification jurisdiction of the County Court. If the court had held that jurisdiction to disqualify was lost when the liquidator had completed his task, this would have the unintentional effect of sabotaging a significant number of disqualification cases. Where the liquidation of a company is complete, by the dissolution of the company, then the right to commence proceedings in the County Court is lost. Here the solution is to commence proceedings in the High Court.

15.8 Minority protection

Fayed v *United Kingdom* (Case No 28/1993/423/502) (1994) The Times 11 November European Court of Human Rights

Inspectors' reports did not violate article 6(1) of the European Convention on Human Rights

Facts

In March 1985 the Fayed brothers, acting through their company, House of Fraser Holdings plc, acquired ownership of House of Fraser plc, one of the largest groups of department stores in Europe, which included the famous Harrods store. In April 1987 two inspectors were appointed by the Secretary of State for Trade and Industry, to investigate the affairs of the Fayeds' company and, in particular, the take-over of House of Fraser plc.

The inspectors concluded that the brothers had dishonestly represented their origin, wealth, business interests and resources to the Secretary of State, the press, the board and shareholders of House of Fraser plc, the Office of Fair Trading and their own advisors. During the investigation it was also stated that they had knowingly submitted false evidence to the inspectors.

No criminal charges were brought as it was felt that there was insufficient evidence. The Secretary of State did not bring director disqualification proceedings as he judged it not to be in the public interest. The report was published by the inspectors and the contents were widely reported in the media.

The Fayeds wanted to challenge the inspectors' findings. The domestic remedies of defamation and judicial review were inappropriate. A defamation action would have been met by the defence of privilege and judicial review would not have allowed them to argue that the inspectors' findings were simply erroneous. They therefore complained that there had been a breach of article 6(1) of the European Convention on Human Rights. Article 6(1) provides:

> 'In the determination of his civil rights [eg honour and reputation] and obligations ... everyone is entitled to a fair and public hearing ... by an independent and impartial tribunal ...'

They therefore alleged that the inspectors had determined their civil rights to honour and reputation and that there was no effective domestic remedy to challenge their findings.

Held

There was no violation of article 6(1).

1. The functions of the inspectors were essentially investigative, rather than judicial. The requirement of a judicial procedure in article 6(1) did not therefore apply to investigations by inspectors.
2. The right of access to a civil court in article 6(1) was not absolute and could be subject to implied limitations, but the national authority had to be pursuing a legitimate aim and respect the principle of proportionality. The system of investigations under the Companies Act 1985 and the freedom to report the results by the inspectors were both considered to be in the pursuit of a legitimate aim. The inspectors' freedom to report was matched by considerable safeguards to ensure a fair procedure. Judicial review was available to the Fayeds in this respect, and the reports showed that they were made aware of what information

was required of them. They were also given ample opportunity to reply and furnish evidence in support.

3. The court accepted that a risk of uncompensated damage to reputation was inevitable, if the inspectors were to be given the necessary freedom to report without fear.

4. The court concluded that, in the exercise of their responsibility of regulating the affairs of public companies, the national authority had not exceeded its margin of appreciation in limiting the Fayeds' access to the courts under article 6(1). Further, a reasonable relationship of proportionality did exist between the freedom accorded to inspectors and the legitimate aim pursued in the public interest.

Macro (Ipswich) Ltd and Another, Re [1994] BCC 781 Chancery Division (Arden J)

Unfairly prejudicial conduct – mismanagement

Facts

Mr Thompson (T) was the sole director and majority shareholder of two companies. The business of the companies was that of landlords of residential property and garages. In Companies Act 1985 s459 proceedings, the petitioners alleged various failures of management by T and they sought relief requiring T to purchase their shares.

The petitioners claimed that management by T was inadequate in that T:

1. Failed to attend to the companies' affairs while abroad during the winter period.
2. Between the mid-1930s to 1987 wasted money on building repairs and committed the companies to poor lettings.
3. From 1970 to 1988 received commissions from builders which he failed to account to the companies.
4. From 1970 to 1988 allowed employees to charge 'key money' for granting lettings of company properties.
5. Currently left the property management to an inexperienced person.

Held

There was unfairly prejudicial conduct. The mismanagement by T was serious enough to justify intervention by the court. T was ordered to purchase the petitioners' shares, but the judge declined to appoint an additional director as it was felt that this would make matters worse, rather than resolve the disputes between the parties.

Arden J:

'With respect to alleged mismanagement, the court does not interfere in questions of commercial judgment, such as would arise here if (for example) it were alleged that the companies should invest in commercial properties rather than residential properties. However, in cases where what is shown is mismanagement, rather than a difference of opinion on the desirability of particular commercial decisions, and the mismanagement is sufficiently serious to justify the intervention by the court, a remedy is available under s459.

... In view of Mr Thompson's control and personality, there has since the 1969 reconstruction been no realistic possibility of the appointment of alternative property managers. However, this is not a case where what happened was merely that quality of management turned out to be poor (cf *Re Elgindata Ltd* at pp994–1000). This is a case where there were specific acts of mismanagement by Thompsons, which Mr Thompson failed to prevent or rectify. Moreover, several of the acts of mismanagement which the plaintiffs have identified were repeated over many years, as for example in relation to the failure to inspect repairs. In my judgment, viewed overall, those acts (and Mr Thompson's failures to prevent or rectify them) are sufficiently significant and serious to justify intervention by the court under s461.'

Commentary

This decision is a significant extension of conduct which may fall within s459, but it should not come as too much of a surprise. The possibility of serious mismanagement, as opposed to poor management, amounting to unfair prejudicial conduct had been alluded to before in the mismanagement cases of s459. It was probably only a matter of time before such conduct was found to be sufficiently serious.

Supreme Travels Ltd v *Little Olympian Each-Ways Ltd and Others* [1994] BCC 947 Chancery Division (Lindsay J)

Whether the court could add a non-member as a respondent to a s459 action

Facts

ST Ltd was a preference shareholder in LOEW Ltd and presented a petition under s459 Companies Act 1985. The unfairly prejudicial conduct consisted of allegations that the directors of LOEW Ltd had sold the company's business and goodwill to another company, which they controlled, for a grossly inadequate consideration. The company was thereafter a mere shell and it ceased to trade.

In this action, the petitioners were now seeking to add another company, Owners Abroad Group plc (OAG), as additional respondents, even though it had never been a shareholder, director or an alleged wrongdoer in LOEW Ltd, whose affairs were said to have been conducted in a manner unfairly prejudicial to the interests of the petitioner. By adding OAG as a respondent, it would, along with the other respondents, be obliged to purchase the petitioners' shares, if this relief was eventually granted by the court.

Held

1. Relief could be sought against a non-member of the company.

2. A non-member would not be added, however, when the likelihood of relief sought being ordered against the non-member was so remote as to amount to an abuse of process. This was such a case, as no court would order OAG to purchase the petitioners' shares.

3. The court therefore refused to add OAG as an additional respondent.

Lindsay J (after reviewing the statutory provisions and authorities for guidance his Lordship continued):

> 'That concludes a look at the authorities cited to me. Whilst I would be very willing to follow a pattern that emerged from the earlier cases at first instance, I do not regard any clear pattern as having yet emerged, and I have certainly found nothing conclusive that suggests that the words of s459 and s461 should not be given their full effect. From the existing authorities cited it can be seen that in an appropriate case relief can be sought against a non-member other than the company itself, or against a person not involved in the acts complained of (at least if that person would be affected by the relief sought) and that a person against whom no relief is in terms sought cannot necessarily escape being a respondent, whilst, on other facts, it can be right to strike out a petition, even as against those whose acts are complained of, so long as no relief is sought against such a person.
>
> This summary suggests to me that in point of jurisdiction the wide language of s459 and s461 is not to be cut down. Nonetheless, cases may arise where, notwithstanding that the claim cannot be clearly said to be outside that wide jurisdiction, the likelihood of the court's discretion being exercised so as to lead to relief against, or relief having any material effect upon, a given respondent can be seen to be so remote that the case can fairly be described as "perfectly hopeless", to use Hoffmann J's phrase, and hence that it would be abusive to require that respondent to remain as such or to be added as such. Is this such a case?'

After considering counsels' arguments for both sides, his Lordship felt:

> 'Although the court *could*, if it chose, make a buy-out order against OAG of the kind which the petitioner seeks, it is on the case put in the amended petition, even if wholly true, plain and obvious, in my judgment, that no court *would* make such an order. Had OAG been a respondent from the start it could, in my view, have successfully moved to have the buy-out provisions and its role as a respondent struck out. It not yet being a respondent, it would be an abuse of process were it to be required, against its will, to be a respondent obliged to resist relief which would in practice never be granted.'

Tottenham Hotspur plc, Re [1994] 1 BCLC 655 Chancery Division (Sir Donald Nicholls V-C)

Chief executive dismissed – remained as a director – whether unfairly prejudicial conduct

Facts

In June 1991, the football manager Terry Venables (V) and the entrepreneur Alan Sugar (S) held a 50/50 interest in Tottenham Hotspur plc (Tottenham). It was agreed that V should become the chief executive and that S would be the company's chairman. Later, in December 1991, as a result of a rights issue, both S and V acquired more shares, but due to S's deeper financial pocket, he was able to take up a further £3.85m shares, compared to V's £800,000. S's stake in the company now amounted to 48 per cent and V's to 23 per cent. S held his shares in Tottenham through his privately owned company Amshold Ltd, and V held his shares via Edennote plc, which he owned and controlled.

As a result of disagreements between them, S and V were unable to work together as chairman and chief executive. At a board meeting, it was resolved that V's service contract be terminated and as a result he ceased to be the chief executive.

Companies Act s459 proceedings were commenced by Edennote plc in which it argued that it had a legitimate expectation that V would participate in the management of the company on the basis of shared control existing in June 1991, notwithstanding the later change in the shareholdings of S and V as a result of the rights issue. Edennote plc sought an order that Amshold sell its shares to it and that Tottenham be restrained from acting on the board resolution to remove V and from ending V's service contract.

Held

Edennote did not have a legitimate expectation that V would participate in the management of the company. There was nothing to suggest that V's rights were regulated by anything other than the company's constitution and that the board had the normal right to hire and fire.

Sir Donald Nicholls V-C:

'But nothing was disclosed which would suggest to anybody that Mr Venables's rights in relation to his appointment as chief executive were regulated by anything other than the company's constitution and the formal legal documents. There was nothing to suggest that the board of directors did not have the normal right to 'hire and fire' the company's chief executive, or that there was an agreement or understanding that, if Mr Sugar and Mr Venables should fall out, they were nevertheless bound to continue to support each other indefinitely or even, as proposed in the draft second shareholders' agreement, which was never signed, that for five years Mr Sugar would exercise certain voting rights as Mr Venables might direct.

The case that, in those circumstances, Mr Venables and Edennote or other members nevertheless had an expectation which the court should now recognise and give effect to in the running of this public company is not an easy one.

I appreciate that Tottenham is a very special type of company. Its shareholders were attracted, not by commercial considerations, but by the wish to become more closely linked with and involved in the affairs of the club they support, often passionately. They are football enthusiasts. Even so, with the background of formal documents and published information, Mr Venables's case that he or his company Edennote has been unfairly prejudiced as a shareholder by the recent actions of Mr Sugar is fraught with difficulty.

This being so, 1 do not think it would be right or sensible for me to make an order having the effect of overriding the majority decision of the board and restoring to Mr Venables all or some of his functions as chief executive until the trial. To do so would, in all probability, merely be postponing the date on which *all* concerned must face up to the

fact, that for better or worse, Mr Venables's appointment has been determined and face up
to the consequences of that fact. By all concerned, I mean the directors of Tottenham, its
shareholders, its staff, including above all its players, its season-ticket holders and
thousands of supporters, as well as Mr Sugar and Mr Venables themselves. Whether Mr
Venables's dismissal was in the best interests of Tottenham is not a matter for the court to
decide. That is a matter for the Tottenham board to whom this decision is entrusted
under the company's constitution, although it is a matter on which the shareholders can
express their views to the board. I will not, therefore, make any order regulating the affairs
of Tottenham pending the trial.'

15.9 Liquidation

Arrows Ltd (No 4), Re [1994] BCC 641 House of Lords (Lords Keith,
Jauncey, Browne-Wilkinson, Lloyd and Nolan)

Insolvency – whether liquidators should supply transcripts of private examination
under s236 Insolvency Act 1986 to the Serious Fraud Office

Facts

N was a director and principal shareholder in the company when it went into
liquidation. He was examined by the liquidators under s236 Insolvency Act 1986 and
the Serious Fraud Office (SFO), under s2(3) of the Criminal Justice Act 1987, asked
the liquidators to hand over the transcripts of the examination. The SFO wanted to
consider them in order that they might be used in criminal proceedings against N.
The trial judge ordered that they should not be handed over, unless the SFO give
an undertaking that they would not be used in evidence in criminal proceedings.
This decision was reversed by the Court of Appeal and N now appealed to the
House of Lords.

Held

N's appeal was dismissed.

1. A judge at first instance, in the companies court, does have a discretion to refuse
   to permit the liquidators to hand over the transcripts to the SFO, subject to the
   SFO giving an undertaking not to use them in later criminal proceedings.
2. The judge, however, failed to exercise this discretion properly. It is for the judge
   in the criminal proceedings to decide whether the admission of the transcripts
   would prejudice a fair criminal trial. The trial judge will have all the
   circumstances of the case known to him, which the judge in the companies court
   will not have.

Lord Nolan:

'I have had the advantage of reading in draft the speech prepared by Lord Browne-
Wilkinson. I agree with it in every respect and wish to add only a few words of my own.
    It is hard to believe that Parliament, when authorising the director under s2(3) of the

Criminal Justice Act 1987 to require the production of "documents" meant that he should have a free hand to obtain the records of admissions made by the defendant to other authorities and to use them as part of the prosecution case. It seems anomalous in the extreme that the director should thus be allowed to obtain and use evidence in the form of admissions made by the defendant to others when by s2(8) Parliament has expressly prohibited, save within narrow limits, the use in evidence of admissions made in response to a requirement under s2(2) from the director himself. Yet that is the result which is produced by the language of s2(3).

For the reasons given by Lord Browne-Wilkinson, I can see no ground in principle to support the distinction thus drawn between admissions obtained by way of s2(2) and evidence of admissions obtained by way of s2(3). There may, in fact, be a stronger case for affording some protection to the defendant in respect of the latter. A defendant responding to inquiries under s236 of the Insolvency Act 1986 may well have been less cautious in his answers than if he were being subjected to a s2(2) inquiry by the director.

The director fully accepts, and to some extent relies upon, the overriding power of the criminal court, under s78 of the Police and Criminal Evidence Act 1984, to exclude the documentary evidence obtained under s2(3) if it would be unfair to admit it. The full terms of s78(1) are that the court may refuse to allow the evidence.

> "... if it appears to the court that, having regard to all the circumstances, including the circumstances in which the evidence was obtained, the admission of the evidence would have such an adverse effect on the fairness of the proceedings that the court ought not to admit it."

It seems strange that evidence of admissions by the defendant may be excluded on these grounds, even though it was obtained in strict compliance with an express statutory power. Yet that, as I understand the speech of Lord Mustill in *R* v *Director of the Serious Fraud Office, ex parte Smith* [1993] AC 1 at p43F–G, is undoubtedly the law in relation to answers obtained from the defendant under s2(2), and is, as I have said, accepted by the director, rightly in my view, as applicable to evidence obtained by way of s2(3). It follows that s78 is the one remaining solid bulwark against the possibility of excessive or unfair use by the director of his powers under s2.

The type of fraud which led to the passing of the Criminal Justice Act 1987 is an exceptionally pernicious form of crime, and those who commit it tend to be as devious as they are wicked. It is not in the least surprising or regrettable that Parliament should have entrusted the SFO with the power to call upon a suspected person to come into the open, and to disclose information which may incriminate him. It would be highly regrettable if the power has, in fact, been created in terms which go significantly wider than was intended. But that is a matter which only Parliament can debate and, if necessary, resolve.'

Re Barn Crown Ltd [1995] 1 WLR 147 Chancery Division (Judge Rich QC sitting as a High Court Judge)

Whether third party cheques paid into a company's bank account constituted a disposition of company property contrary to s127 IA 1986

Facts

After the commencement of the company's winding up, its bank collected third party cheques, amounting to £37,000 odd pounds, and credited the company's account with this amount. The liquidator applied for an order that the bank pay over to him this sum of money as it constituted a disposition of company property and was therefore void under s127 IA 1986.

Held

The application was dismissed. There was no disposition of the company's property.

Judge Rich QC:

> 'In collecting payment upon a cheque the bank credits the customer's account with the amount of the cheque. If the account is already in credit, no disposition of the property of the customer takes place in favour of the bank. The amount standing to the credit of a customer's account is increased in return for the surrender of the cheque, which becomes a voucher for payment. It is the drawer of the cheque whose property is disposed of. All that happens between the customer and the banker is an adjustment of entries in the statement recording the accounts between them.'

Commentary

If the company's bank account was overdrawn in this case, then there would have been a disposition of property within s127 IA 1986. There would also be a similar disposition of property each time money was paid out of the account.

Cranley Mansions Ltd, Re [1994] 1 WLR 1610 Chancery Division (Ferris J)

Insolvency – creditor was not bound by a voluntary arrangement

Facts

The company was insolvent and a meeting was called to consider a proposed voluntary arrangement. Mrs Saigol (S), a creditor of the company, attended the meeting and she claimed the company owed her a contingent debt worth £900,000. This was entirely dependent on the outcome of litigation against the company. The chairman of the meeting (Mr Goldstein) put a minimum value on the debt of £1, in order that S could vote at the meeting. The chairman purported to do this under rule 1.17(3) of the Insolvency Rules 1986. The rule provides:

> 'A creditor shall not vote in respect of a debt for an unliquidated amount, or any debt whose value is not ascertained, except where the chairman agrees to put upon the debt an estimated value for the purpose of entitlement to vote.'

The figure of £1 was arrived at without any agreement with the creditor and was therefore a unilateral decision by the chairman. At the meeting, the proposals for the voluntary arrangement were approved by the relevant majority of the other creditors. However, if the debt had been given a value in excess of £1,722, S could have prevented the approval.

S appealed against the chairman's decision to give her debt a minimum value of £1.

Held

The appeal would be allowed. S was not bound by the voluntary arrangement as the chairman had no right to unilaterally ascribe a minimum value of £1 to her debt. The chairman had not 'agreed' within the meaning of rule 1.17(3) of the Insolvency Rules 1986 to put an estimated minimum value on her debt for the purpose of ascertaining the extent of her voting rights. This was a material irregularity.

Ferris J:

'Both Miss Stokes [counsel for the company] and Mr Green [counsel for Mr Goldstein] pointed out that unless the chairman is entitled to put a value upon the claim of a creditor which is unliquidated or unascertained without regard to the wishes of that creditor, the utility of the statutory provisions in respect of corporate voluntary arrangements (and, indeed, individual voluntary arrangements and other matters to be decided at meetings governed by rules as to voting equivalent to rule 1.17) would be greatly reduced. If a creditor is not entitled to vote in respect of such a claim without a value being put upon the claim under rule 1.17(3) or its equivalent (which is a matter to be considered in a moment) a disaffected creditor could stultify proposals for a voluntary arrangement by the simple expedient of failing to concur in a value being put on his claim. The arrangement might then be approved by the requisite majorities of those entitled to vote on it, but it would not be binding on the disaffected creditor. In most, if not all, cases there will be no point in having an arrangement which is not binding upon all creditors.

I see the force of this submission which causes me some anxiety because my decision is likely to affect many other cases. Nevertheless I cannot escape the fact that the relevant words of rule 1.17(3) are "where the chairman agrees to put upon the debt an estimated minimum value", not "where the chairman puts upon the debt an estimated minimum value". Moreover I think it would be perverse to say that the requirement imported by the word "agrees" can be satisfied by an agreement between the chairman and someone other than the creditor, such as the company, as was suggested in argument. In my judgment "agrees" requires some element of bilateral concurrence between the chairman and the creditor in question. If the creditor puts forward an estimated minimum value without prejudice to a contention that his real claim is much larger and if the chairman accepts this, the words of the rule would, in my view, clearly be satisfied notwithstanding that there is nothing in the nature of a contract between the chairman and the creditor. The same would be the case if the chairman took the initiative in suggesting a value and the creditor concurred in this suggestion for the purpose of rule 1.17(3), although not for the purpose of limiting the claim. The matter would be more difficult if the chairman put forward a value for the purpose of rule 1.17(3) and the creditor rejected this for all purposes but nevertheless insisted upon voting. The outcome would, in my view, then depend upon an evaluation of precisely what was said and done.

The present case has some similarities with the third type of case suggested above. On the evidence I take the view that what was said and done was not sufficient to satisfy what the word "agrees" requires. It seems to me that Mrs Saigol claimed to vote in respect of £900,000 but Mr Goldstein treated her as voting only in respect of £1, the latter figure being attributable not to any bilateral consensus between Mrs Saigol and Mr Goldstein but to a unilateral determination made by Mr Goldstein alone. Moreover the evidence does not, in my judgment, justify any inference that it was made clear to Mrs Saigol or her representative that if she voted at all she would be concurring in Mr Goldstein's determination.

I conclude, therefore, that there was an irregularity at or in relation to the meeting of creditors, in that Mrs Saigol's vote was admitted in respect of £1, whereas she was precluded from voting by the opening words of rule 1.17(3), the exception to the general prohibition not being applicable because no "estimated minimum value" had been put upon her debt in accordance with the requirements of the latter part of the paragraph.'

Commentary

Re Cranley Mansions Ltd was distinguished in the case of *Re a Debtor No 162 of 1993* [1994] BCC 994. In the latter case, which did not involve a corporate voluntary arrangement but an individual one, Knox J held that what the Insolvency Rules 1986 require is the chairman's agreement to put a minimum value on a debt, and not an agreement *upon* the minimum value.

Sherborne Associates Ltd, Re [1995] BCC 40 Bristol District Registry (Mercantile List) (His Honour Judge Jack QC, sitting as an additional High Court judge)

Section 214 Insolvency Act 1986 – Wrongful trading – refusal to find non-executive directors liable

Facts

This case was an application by the liquidator of the company for an order that its three non-executive directors, S, I and E, make a contribution to the assets of the company pursuant to s214 IA 1986. The company's business was that of an advertising agency and it was formed in January 1987 with a paid up share capital of £36,000. By early December 1988 the three directors had resigned, and the company was put into liquidation in February 1989 with debts of £178,788.

Board meetings during 1987 illustrated the financial position of the company. At the first board meeting in February, a business plan suggested a required turnover of £450,000 for year ending December 1987. In addition an overdraft of £50,000 was agreed with the bank. At the meeting in March, S stated a turnover of £500,000 was now required to break even and in April the first reference to delaying payments to creditors was made.

At the July meeting, the board was informed that a loss of £27,636 was incurred on first five months trading which S thought 'was a creditable performance'. A turnover of £565,000 was now required to break even. Further losses were considered at the September meeting at which S gave the company until Christmas 'to put things right'. Debtors were now at £25,000 while creditors stood at £45,000.

By the end of September, the company's assets exceeded its liabilities. October, November and December saw further losses and the turnover at the year end was £350,000, a long way short of the forecast.

Two board meetings were held on 22 and 30 January 1988. It was on these dates that the liquidator claimed the directors ought to have concluded that there was no prospect of avoiding liquidation. At the first meeting, S closely examined the three appointed executive directors about their new business prospects and each gave optimistic figures. He also proposed that the company cease trading at the end of February. [The judge found that S did not really mean this and only said it to put pressure on the non-executive directors to drum up new business].The purpose of the second meeting was to decide if the company should cease trading. The net indebtedness was now £78,000. The board went on to approve revised sales forecasts given by the three executive directors, amounting to £1m. Weekly management meetings were agreed to be held with S acting as chief executive. Sherborne continued to trade. The liquidator claimed that these forecasts were wholly unrealistic and that they should not have been accepted.

The company's financial decline continued, despite the recruitment of new people. The figures for the first three months of 1988 showed a loss of £24,859 against a forecast of £7,045. S has a heart attack in may 1988. Despite an encouraging sign in April the results for the first six months of 1988 all showed a loss. The bank then declined to support Sherborne further, although further support was in fact provided by another bank, based on an increase in the company's share capital and the giving of guarantees.

After yet further losses were incurred, at a board meeting in December 1988, I and S resigned and E followed shortly afterwards.

Held
The claim for wrongful trading failed.

1. A wrongful trading claim under s214 IA 1986 survived the death of a director. The claim could therefore be pursued against the personal representatives of S. after his death in 1992.
2. The liquidators claim that I, S and E ought to have realised that there was no reasonable prospect of avoiding liquidation on the two selected dates of 22 and 30 January 1988 failed. Furthermore, it was not open for the liquidator, or the court, to make such a finding based on alternative selected dates which were not specifically pleaded by the liquidator.
3. S was entitled to conclude, in January 1988, that there was a prospect that the company could achieve a turnaround and make a profit. It was 'a reasonable and not a fanciful prospect'.

His Honour Judge Jack QC:

'The outcome is that I am not satisfied that in January 1988 Mr Squire ought to have concluded that there was no reasonable prospect that Sherborne would avoid going into insolvent liquidation. I am not satisfied that he was not entitled to conclude that there was a prospect for the company achieving the turnaround into profit, which was a reasonable rather than a fanciful prospect. It did not need to make the forecast profit of £55,600 to survive, something better than even would probably have done.

The liquidator's case against Sir Charles Irving and Mr Ellwood must also fail. They were in no better position than Mr Squire to conclude whether the company had reasonable prospects of success and indeed were in a rather worse position. The case having failed against him, the central figure, it must fail also against them. Had I concluded that the case against Mr Squire succeeded, I would have had to consider the difficult question of the extent to which, in such circumstances, they were entitled to say that they looked to and relied on Mr Squire. I do accept that these two non-executive directors were entitled to place reliance on the highly experienced chairman who had far the greater involvement with the company and the figures. In particular it was he who had the discussions with the executive directors between the two January board meetings. In my view, where in circumstances such as here, one director seeks to rely on another, the other director's view or conclusion is a matter to be taken into account with the other matters which the director should be taking into account as required by s214(4). I would here have had to conduct a balancing exercise between the facts which I am presuming for this purpose pointed one way and the conclusion by Mr Squire of the opposite. This is an exercise which can only be done on the basis of actual findings.

I was referred to three decisions on s214 which I have not so far mentioned. They are: *Re Produce Marketing Consortium Ltd* (1989) 5 BCC 569, *Re Purpoint Ltd* [1991] BCC 121 and *Re DKC Contractors Ltd* [1990] BCC 903. In each the liquidator was successful. I will not prolong this judgment by summarising the facts in those cases. It is enough to say that there were in each features which made the conduct of the directors plainly irresponsible as well as other matters which can be used to distinguish them from the present case.'

Commentary

This is a disappointing decision on wrongful trading. All three directors, in contrast to some of the earlier cases on wrongful trading, were experienced businessmen, albeit in different fields. The company had never made a profit and none of the sales forecasts were ever achieved. The judgment itself analyses in detail, whether or not a claim for wrongful trading can survive the death of a director and there is an in-depth analysis of the authorities. The existing case law on wrongful trading, however, is dismissed in a single, final, paragraph of the judgment and is distinguished on the basis that in those cases the directors were 'plainly irresponsible'.

15.10 Accounts

Galoo Ltd v *Bright Grahame Murray* [1994] 1 WLR 1360 Court of Appeal (Glidewell, Evans and Waite LJJ)

Liability of auditor

Facts

Gamine Ltd owned all the shares in Galoo Ltd. The defendants (BGM) were the companies' auditors. In 1987 Hillsdown Holdings plc purchased 51 per cent of the shares in Gamine. Between March 1987 and January 1993, Hillsdown made loans worth over £30m to Galoo and Gamine. In May 1991 a further 44.3 per cent of Gamine's shares were purchased by Hillsdown. The above transactions were carried out on the basis of the audited accounts of Galoo and Gamine, which were prepared by the defendants, BGM.

The plaintiffs, Galoo, Gamine and Hillsdown, claimed that the audited accounts of Galoo and Gamine were inaccurate and this was caused by the negligence of BGM, who failed to detect a fraud, whereby items were included in the accounts which, in fact, never existed. Actions were commenced for breach of contract and negligence in relation to Galoo and Gamine, and for negligence only in relation to Hillsdown.

These were interlocutory proceedings in which the court had to decide whether there was a reasonable cause of action. In other words, were the plaintiffs' claims bound to fail?

The claims in contract and tort relevant to Galoo and Gamine were:

1. that they incurred loss by accepting loans from Hillsdown of over £30m;
2. that by relying on the audit, they continued to trade and incur losses which they would not otherwise have done. If they had been alerted to fraud they would have put the company into liquidation. Instead they incurred further trading losses of £25m and paid a dividend of £500,000.

The claims in tort relevant to Hillsdown were that they had suffered loss:

3. by their original share purchase in Gamine;
4. by making loans to Gamine;
5. by the purchase of a further 44.3 per cent of Gamine's shares.

The judge at first instance struck out claims (1) and (2). He also struck out claims (4) and (5), but decided that claim (3) did disclose a reasonable cause of action.

The plaintiffs appealed and the defendants cross-appealed.

Held

The appeals and cross-appeal were dismissed.

1. Acceptance of a loan cannot, of itself, be described as a loss causing damage. If anything, it is a benefit to the borrower. Therefore claim (1) was dismissed.
2. Breach of duty by BGM allowed Galoo and Gamine the opportunity to incur trading losses, but it did not *cause* those trading losses in the sense in which the word 'cause' is used in law. Claim (2) was also dismissed.
3. As it was not alleged that the defendants knew or intended that Hillsdown would rely on their accounts for the purpose of making loans and further share purchases in Gamine, claims (4) and (5) disclosed no cause of action.
4. Claim (3) did disclose a reasonable cause of action. In addition to audit purposes, the accounts were prepared for purpose of fixing the share price of the original 51 per cent purchase in Gamine by Hillsdown. The defendants knew that the share purchase agreement contained provisions to calculate the share price by reference to their audited accounts.

The following extract relates to claim (3).

Evans LJ:

'It is tempting to distinguish between the *Caparo* case [1990] 2 AC 605 and the *Morgan Crucible* case [1991] Ch 295 on the basis that in the latter, though not the former case, the identity of a particular purchaser of shares in the company was known to the defendants when they represented that the company's accounts which they had prepared were fair and true. This excludes individual members of the body of existing shareholders to whom the statutory accounts are published (the *Caparo* case), whilst including an identified take-over bidder, as in the *Morgan Crucible* case. But there could be intervening situations, for example, where an existing shareholder is known to be a potential purchaser of more shares, with a view to acquiring the whole or a majority of the shares. The identification test would not provide the answer in such a case. No duty of care would be owed to such a person, in my judgment, on those facts alone, because the third of the four propositions listed by Lord Oliver in the *Caparo* case [1990] 2 AC 605, 638D, already quoted by Glidewell LJ, as it was by Slade LJ in the *Morgan Crucible* case [1991] Ch 295, 318, would not be satisfied: "(3) it is known either actually or inferentially, that the advice so communicated is likely to be acted upon by the advisee for that purpose without independent inquiry", and, vitally, it could not be said that the auditors in such a case "intended that they should act upon it, for that purpose": per Slade LJ in the *Morgan Crucible* case [1991] Ch 295, 320A.

If it is right to confine the duty of care, meaning, to restrict the class of persons who can recover damages if the adviser/representor is negligent, to cases where the defendant is shown not merely to have known that the individual plaintiff would or might rely upon the representation but to have intended that it should be relied upon, by him and for the particular purpose and without intermediate examination, then the resulting analysis comes close to the "voluntary assumption of responsibility" which has been referred to in many of the authorities but which was discounted as a test of liability in *Smith* v *Eric S Bush* [1990] 1 AC 831, 862, per Lord Griffiths:

"... I do not think that voluntary assumption of responsibility is a helpful or realistic test for liability. It is true that reference is made in a number of the speeches in *Hedley Byrne* [1964] AC 465 to the assumption of responsibility as a test of liability but it must be remembered that those speeches were made in the context of a case in which the central issue was whether a duty of care could arise when there had been an express disclaimer of responsibility for the accuracy of the advice ... The phrase 'assumption of responsibility' can only have any real meaning if it is understood as referring to the circumstances in which the law will deem the maker of the statement to have assumed responsibility to the person who acts upon the advice."

Lord Devlin referred in *Hedley Byrne & Co Ltd* v *Heller & Partners Ltd* [1964] AC 465, 530 to "a relationship equivalent to contract" and it is clear from Lord Griffiths's speech in *Smith's* case [1990] 1 AC 831, 862 that the contractual analogy cannot serve as a definition of the cases where the duty of care may arise. But if the statement is made to an identifiable person and the maker not only knows that it will or is likely to be acted upon but also intended that it should be acted upon for a particular purpose, then these may well exemplify "circumstances in which the law will deem the maker of the statement to have assumed responsibility" to the person who acts upon it: per Lord Griffiths, at p862E. The "indeterminate class" of persons referred to by Cardozo CJ in *Ultramares Corporation* v *Touche* (1931) 174 NE 441, 444 is thus reduced to an inter-personal relationship where liability may be imposed, and it would seem unreasonable and even unjust to do so, in my view, if the defendant could not be said to have assumed responsibility towards the plaintiff, not necessarily as an individual, in the circumstances of the case. It is sufficient for present purposes to note that the relationship by definition must be "voluntary" in the sense that no consideration proceeds from the plaintiff for the defendant's advice.'

Commentary

The effect of this case is that, in addition to the issue of proximity between the auditors and those relying on their statements, it is also necessary to consider causation. In particular, the question to be asked is: did the auditors cause the loss or did they merely allow the opportunity for such losses to occur?

Index

HLT Publications

HLT books are specially planned and written to help you in every stage of your studies. Each of the wide range of textbooks is brought up-to-date annually, and the companion volumes of our Law Series are all designed to work together.

You can buy HLT books from your local bookshop, or in case of difficulty, order direct using this form,

The Law Series covers the following modules:

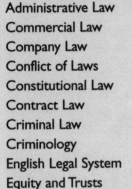

Administrative Law	**Evidence**
Commercial Law	**Family Law**
Company Law	**Jurisprudence**
Conflict of Laws	**Land Law**
Constitutional Law	**Law of International Trade**
Contract Law	**Legal Skills and System**
Criminal Law	**Public International Law**
Criminology	**Revenue Law**
English Legal System	**Succession**
Equity and Trusts	**Tort**
European Union Law	

The HLT Law Series:
A comprehensive range of books for your law course, and the legal aspects of business and commercial studies.

Each module is covered by a comprehensive six-part set of books

● Textbook
● Casebook
● Revision Workbook
● Suggested Solutions, for:
 ● 1985-90
 ● 1991-94
 ● 1995

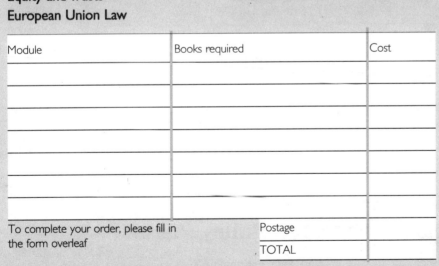

Module	Books required	Cost
To complete your order, please fill in the form overleaf	Postage	
	TOTAL	

Prices (including postage and packing in the UK):
Textbooks £19.00; Casebooks £19.00; Revision Workbooks £10.00; Suggested Solutions (1985-90) £9.00, Suggested Solutions (1991-94) £6.00, Suggested Solutions (1995) £3.00.

For Europe, add 15% postage and packing (£20 maximum). For the rest of the world, add 40% for airmail (£35 maximum).

ORDERING

By telephone to 01892 724371, with your credit card to hand

By fax to 01892 724206 (giving your credit card details).

By post to:

HLT Publications,
The Gatehouse, Ruck Lane, Horsmonden, Tonbridge, Kent TN12 8EA

When ordering by post, please enclose full payment by cheque or banker's draft, or complete the credit card details below.

We aim to dispatch your books within 3 working days of receiving your order.

Name

Address

Postcode

Telephone

Total value of order, including postage: **£**

I enclose a cheque/banker's draft for the above sum, or

charge my ☐ Access/Mastercard ☐ Visa ☐ American Express

Card number

☐☐☐☐ ☐☐☐☐ ☐☐☐☐ ☐☐☐☐

Expiry date

☐☐☐☐

Signature

Date

Publications from **The Old Bailey Press**

Cracknell's Statutes

A full understanding of statute law is vital for any student, and this series presents the original wording of legislation, together with any amendments and substitutions and the sources of these changes.

Cracknell's Companions

Recognised as invaluable study aids since their introduction in 1961, this series summarises all the most important court decisions and acts, and features a glossary of Latin words, as well as full indexing.

Please telephone our Order Hotline on 01892 724371, or write to our order department, for full details of these series.